THE FORTUNES OF
MITCHELL KENNERLEY,
BOOKMAN

Also by Matthew J. Bruccoli

The Composition of *Tender Is the Night*
As Ever, Scott Fitz—(*editor, with Jennifer Atkinson*)
F. Scott Fitzgerald: A Descriptive Bibliography
Supplement to F. Scott Fitzgerald: A Descriptive Bibliography
Apparatus for a Definitive Edition of *The Great Gatsby*
The Romantic Egoists (*editor, with Scottie Fitzgerald Smith and Joan P. Kerr*)
"The Last of the Novelists": F. Scott Fitzgerald and *The Last Tycoon*
Correspondence of F. Scott Fitzgerald (*editor, with Margaret Duggan*)
Some Sort of Epic Grandeur: The Life of F. Scott Fitzgerald
Scott and Ernest: The Authority of Failure and the Authority of Success
Ross Macdonald/Kenneth Millar: A Descriptive Bibliography
Ross Macdonald
Raymond Chandler: A Descriptive Bibliography
Ring Lardner: A Descriptive Bibliography (*with Richard Layman*)
The O'Hara Concern: A Biography of John O'Hara
John O'Hara: A Descriptive Bibliography
Selected Letters of John O'Hara (*editor*)
Just Representations: A James Gould Cozzens Reader (*editor*)
James Gould Cozzens, A Time of War (*editor*)
James Gould Cozzens: A Descriptive Bibliography
James Gould Cozzens: A Life Apart
Nelson Algren: A Descriptive Bibliography

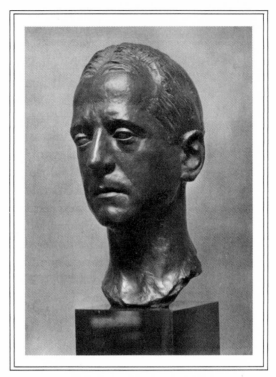

Mitchell Kennerley by Jo Davidson

THE FORTUNES OF MITCHELL KENNERLEY, BOOKMAN

by
Matthew J. Bruccoli

HARCOURT BRACE JOVANOVICH, PUBLISHERS

San Diego   New York   London

HBJ

Requests for permission to make copies of any
part of the work should be mailed to: Permissions,
Harcourt Brace Jovanovich, Publishers, Orlando, Florida 32887.

Library of Congress Cataloging-in-Publication Data
Bruccoli, Matthew Joseph, 1931–
The fortunes of Mitchell Kennerley, bookman.
Bibliography: p.
Includes index.
1. Kennerley, Mitchell, 1878–1950.   2. Publishers
and publishing—United States—Biography.   3. Antiquarian
booksellers—United States—Biography.   4. Anderson
Galleries, Inc.—History.   5. Book auctions—United
States—History—20th century.   I. Title.
Z473.K45B78   1986   070.5'092'4 [B]   86-3105
ISBN 0-15-132671-1

Designed by G. B. D. Smith

Printed in the United States of America

First edition

A B C D E

For Jean *and* Morley Kennerley

This relation will not be wholly without its use . . . if those, who, in confidence of superior capabilities or attainments, disregard the common maxims of life, shall be reminded, that nothing will supply the want of prudence; and that negligence and irregularity, long continued, will make knowledge useless, wit ridiculous, and genius contemptible.

—SAMUEL JOHNSON

The dead keep their secrets, and in a little while we shall be as wise as they—and as taciturn.

—ALEXANDER SMITH

When this world makes having money so important, so essential to well-being, it is hardly reasonable to blame a man for anything he may have done to try to get himself a supply.

—JAMES GOULD COZZENS

Contents

xi

INTRODUCTION

MITCHELL KENNERLEY pursued money, women, and books.

This biography might have been titled "The Quest for Kennerley." My quest appropriately commenced in a bookshop. Twenty-five years ago I found stacks of old book-auction catalogues in the basement of Peter Keisogloff's Cleveland store, and he gave me all of them that I wanted. The best of these catalogues had been issued by the Anderson Galleries in New York and bore the imprimatur MITCHELL KENNERLEY, PRESIDENT on their covers. I was impressed by the circumstance that the same name also appeared as the publisher of important books; but I was occupied with other projects and failed to follow up on Kennerley—thereby diminishing the present work because many key sources were then alive. For the next twenty years Kennerley kept reappearing in my reading: rarely more than a paragraph, but always in connection with books and often implying something improper. Many of these comments have proved untrue or inaccurate. In 1972 I interviewed Jean and Morley Kennerley for my biography of John O'Hara—ignorant of their connection with Mitchell Kennerley. When I admired a bust in their London flat, Morley identified it as his father and seemed rather surprised that I knew who Mitchell Kennerley was. That was another signal I ignored. Other books intervened, but in 1982 I obtained the Kennerleys' permission to attempt this work. They were patiently encouraging. Shortly before his death in 1985 Morley approved my working draft, and Jean has maintained her generous aid.

It is often asserted that notable figures would have succeeded in any time or place, but such tributes are unverifiable. Timing is always crucial to extraordinary careers. This book examines Mitchell Kennerley in the context of the world of books in the early decades of this century. Kennerley operated in two overlapping fields: as a publisher from 1902 until about 1924 and as head of the Anderson Galleries during 1915–1929. The latter activity coincided with the golden era of American book collecting. Golden eras require golden men; Kennerley's world was populated with legendary bookmen. Literary treasures fell like rain upon the auction rooms, and Kennerley was the rainmaker.

Fitzgerald wrote of Gatsby: "If personality is an unbroken string of successful gestures, then there was something gorgeous about him. . . ." Until Kennerley's string broke, he promoted a series of coups through the force of his personality, which combined cool egotism, arrogance, audacity, ruthlessness, recklessness, and charm. Yet personality is destructive when it becomes a substitute for character. It was said that Kennerley knew everybody, but he was an enigma to those who knew him. Jo Davidson commented that he "was a hundred men to a hundred men"[1]: generous friend, implacable enemy, con man, rake, bon vivant, patron of literature. Christopher Morley described him as "incalculably and mercilessly himself."[2] There was a self-destructive component in Kennerley: a compulsion to place himself at risk. Like many men who rise through daring, he needed to test fortune.

PART I

ENGLAND AND AMERICA, 1878–1901

CHAPTER ONE

<hr/>

*The Five Towns—London and John Lane—
New York—Bliss Carman, Thomas Bird
Mosher, and William Marion Reedy—
Money—The Smart Set—Helen Morley*

A SEVENTY-ONE-YEAR-OLD MAN hanged himself in room 1828 of the
Shelton Hotel in Manhattan on 22 February 1950. Mitchell Kennerley,
"former publisher and president of the Anderson Galleries," rated
thirteen column inches in *The New York Times*.[1] The obituary noted
that under his direction the Anderson Galleries auctioned a Gutenberg
Bible for $106,000 in 1926 and that Lord Leverhulme's art collection
brought $1,248,493 in 1927. The summary of Kennerley's publishing
activities mentioned his proprietorship of *The Reader* and *The Forum*
magazines and his 1913 trial on the charge of sending an objectionable
book, *Hagar Revelly*, through the mails. *The Times* did not indicate
that the Mitchell Kennerley imprint had appeared on more than 400
books, including works by Van Wyck Brooks, Edward Carpenter,
Frank Harris, Joseph Hergesheimer, D. H. Lawrence, Vachel Lindsay,
Walter Lippmann, John Masefield, Edna St. Vincent Millay, Edgar
Saltus, Upton Sinclair, H. G. Wells, and Oscar Wilde.

The life of Mitchell Kennerley is a success story, and it is a failure
story. Magazine publisher at twenty-three and head of his own publishing house at twenty-eight, in his forties he was among the most

prominent figures in the book world. No one else was as actively engaged in so many aspects of literature and antiquarian books. In his sixties he was an obscure has-been living on loans.

Mitchell Kennerley's triumphs were fostered by the ebullience of the American Twenties, but his history began in Victoria's England. He was born in Burslem, Staffordshire, 14 August 1878. Disraeli was the Prime Minister. Tennyson, Browning, Meredith, Carlyle, Morris, Swinburne, Arnold, and Ruskin were alive. In that year Hardy published *The Return of the Native*; Gilbert & Sullivan produced *H. M. S. Pinafore*; and Oscar Wilde came to London. In New York vice-suppressor Anthony Comstock—who would subsequently act against Kennerley—was prosecuting an abortionist.

Burslem was one of Arnold Bennett's "Five Towns," now consolidated into Stoke-on-Trent. There were actually six towns, with a population of 130,000, in an area of roughly seven miles by five miles: Burslem (Bennett's Bursley), Tunstall, Hanley, Stoke, Longton, and Fenton. The business of the Five Towns was pottery, and Burslem ("The Mother of the Potteries") was the home of Wedgwood. It was a grim setting of smoking chimneys, slag heaps, and clay pits. Bennett wrote, "The towns are mean and ugly in appearance—sombre, shape-less, hard-featured, uncouth; and the vaporous poison of their ovens and chimneys has soiled and shrivelled the surrounding greenness of Nature till there is no country lane within miles but what presents a gaunt travesty of rural charms."[2] The dominant virtues of the citizens were hard work, thrift, honesty, and self-denial—which, except for work, would not be blatant in Mitchell Kennerley.

Mitchell's mother was Anne Hawley Wood Kennerley (1843–1935), a former milliner and the daughter of a potter's turner. His father, William Snelson Kennerley (1847–1890), a tailor's son, was a solicitor's clerk. Mitchell was the fourth of five children: William Wood (1870), Gertrude Annie (1873), Helen Maude (1877), and Leonard (1885). The Kennerleys were comfortably middle class, residing at 11 Rushton Road in the Cobridge section of Burslem, where the Bennetts also lived on Waterloo Road. The two families were on close terms despite the social distance resulting from the circumstance that Enoch Bennett was a solicitor. The gap was narrowed by the senior Kennerley's political activities; he was Secretary of the Conservative Association of Burslem, Conservative Registration Agent, and elected Borough Auditor, as well as treasurer of the Burslem Cricket Club.

Mitchell was not one of Bennett's jumped-up Bursley poor boys, like Denry of *The Card*. Nonetheless, he was the product of a rigorously class-structured society in which it was obligatory to know your place. He attended the Middle School in Newcastle-under-Lyme until he was twelve, walking three miles each way. After his father died of heart disease in 1890, the family moved to London where the eldest son, William, was in the Science & Art Department of the Board of Education. Mrs. Kennerley lived with the younger children on Mimosa Street in Fulham, and Mitchell entered Chelsea Polytechnic. The earliest London photo of him shows the wide-eyed stare that he retained. Mitchell's schooling terminated before he was fifteen, when he became a messenger at the Civil Service Commission in Cannon Row near Whitehall. By this time he had been encouraged in book-collecting by Bennett, who was eleven years older than Mitchell and had commenced his London journalistic career. While Mitchell was still in Burslem he received a copy of Andrew Lang's *Books and Bookmen,* inscribed "To Mitchell Kennerley on hearing that he was becoming a booklover, from Arnold Bennett."[3] William Kennerley married Bennett's sister Tertia and acted as his informal editor; *The Old Wives Tale* (1908) is dedicated to him. A group of men who met weekly for literary talk in London included Bennett, William Kennerley, Frederic Chapman of the Bodley Head publishing house, bookseller Charles Young, and George Sturt (who became a respected writer as George Bourne). Young Mitchell was allowed to sit in on some of their gatherings.

His messenger rounds afforded Mitchell opportunities to browse in bookshops. He regularly visited Robert A. Cross's antiquarian shop at 5 Agar Street, off the Strand, and soon accepted a job there. The best training for a bookman is the opportunity to handle books; at Cross's Mitchell developed his retentive book memory, for which he became celebrated. One of the Cross customers was publisher John Lane, for whom Chapman worked as office manager and reader. This connection led to Mitchell's employment as Lane's junior clerk or office boy in 1894 at age sixteen: "There were only four members of the staff when

I went to work there and we all did a little—or I should say a great deal—of everything. My desk was nearest the door and I waited on all visitors from the list boys who came to pick up books to the authors and artists who came to see Mr. Lane."[4]

Lane had recently split with his partner Elkin Mathews and set up his bookshop and publishing office at the sign of the Bodley Head at the Albany on Vigo Street in the West End. He was regarded as the principal publisher of the new aesthetic movement, with a list that was strong in modern poetry and belles lettres. The Bodley Head authors included Oscar Wilde, Richard Le Gallienne, Arnold Bennett, John Davidson, Kenneth Grahame, Arthur Symons, Francis Thompson, William Watson, and Henry Harland. Lane's volumes physically and textually proclaimed the message of art for art's sake, with illustrations or designs by Aubrey Beardsley, Walter Crane, and Charles Ricketts. Beardsley's title page for Wilde's *Salome* featured a hermaphroditic horned figure with breasts and a penis. The *Yellow Book* magazine, launched by Lane in 1894—the year Mitchell entered his employ—is permanently linked with Beardsley's erotic black-and-white drawings. Lane enjoyed a reputation as a proponent of book craft; but Kennerley later insisted that "Lane knew next to nothing about making a book and Frederic Chapman his manager and Roland Clarke his bookkeeper and I his youth of all work knew less. . . . All his early publications were planned and printed by that great printer Walter Blaikie, of T & A Constable. . . ."[5] Whoever his teachers were, Mitchell developed a lasting appreciation for typography and paper that influenced his own publications.

John Lane was a "personal publisher" in that his list reflected his taste and interests, but the business was a commercial success. Despite his sometimes controversial publications, Lane was a respectable figure. The Bodley Head was never regarded as a sleazy operation. Under Lane, Mitchell formed his ideas about publishing as an expression of the publisher's personality. He came of bibliographical age and served his apprenticeship at the literary center of the Decadent Nineties or the Yellow Nineties or the Mauve Decade or the Romantic Nineties in London. Perched on his high stool he encountered the parade of celebrated figures who came to the Bodley Head. When he read the current magazines at the library on St. Martin's Lane, he encountered George Bernard Shaw doing the same thing.

Anne Hawley Wood Kennerley
(Courtesy of Kathleen Humphreys)

William Snelson Kennerley
(Courtesy of Kathleen Humphreys)

Mitchell Kennerley, c. 1890
(Courtesy of Kathleen Humphreys)

Edward Hutton, who became an authority on Italian art and lit-erature, has described Mitchell during the Bodley Head period: "He was a good looking, distinguished young man, rather thin + pale + willowy, perhaps rather 'interesting' than distinguished. He had a [mass] of beautiful dark hair which he wore rather long and he wore a 'Liberty' silk tie, green or terra-cotta in a full fluffy bow or passed through a ring in a knot. He was very intelligent, interested in the literary movement. . . . He collected modern first editions, the Mosher pirated edition of English authors and also in a small way Kelmscott Press books. . . . He was friendly + very efficient and absolutely right in Lane's office."[6]

Kennerley later enjoyed explaining that if the impecunious artists and writers who came to the Bodley Head were kept waiting, they would try to borrow small sums from him. He became adept at rushing them into Lane's office, and Lane was so impressed by his efficiency that he decided to put Mitchell in charge of the newly established American branch. When Lane sailed from Liverpool for New York on the *Etruria* in 1896 he took Mitchell Kennerley with him. It seems unlikely, but Kennerley always insisted that he was running the New York operation at eighteen. Even if an older man named J. Jefferson Jones was actually the office manager, the fact that Lane regarded it worthwhile to bring the boy to America testifies to Mitchell's promise as well as his ability to impress those worth impressing.

There are two versions of Kennerley's first experience on New York soil. One is that he found American money on the pier. The other is that he picked up a cigar-store coupon and thought it was American currency. Either version serves to presage his life in America. For Kennerley the streets of New York would be paved with other people's money.

Mitchell Kennerley landed in the America of the Gay Nineties, which succeeded the Gilded Age. In 1896 William Jennings Bryan delivered his "Cross of Gold Speech"; the trade edition of Stephen Crane's *Maggie a Girl of the Streets* was published, along with Charles Sheldon's enormously popular religious book *In His Steps* and the first Frank Meriwell title. The best-selling novel of the year was Sienkie-wicz's *Quo Vadis*. The popular songs were "Sweet Rosie O'Grady," "Kentucky Babe," and "A Hot Time in the Old Town."

John Lane

*The Bodley Head catalogue,
drawing by Edmund H. New*

Whatever the extent of Kennerley's actual authority, Lane was a good place to learn the American publishing business. The New York branch issued its own list, combining English imports with new titles. The initial Lane catalogue from 140 Fifth Avenue included titles by Robert Louis Stevenson, Max Beerbohm, Alice Meynell, and John Davidson. Richard Le Gallienne's *The Quest for the Golden Girl* was the first book published by Lane in America, and Kennerley sat over Will Bradley while he drew the cover design. Kennerley's earliest publishing coup came in 1897 when he paid what was regarded as the recklessly high price of $1,000 for the printing plates and rights to Kenneth Grahame's *The Golden Age*. The New York office also distributed the *International Studio,* which was actually the English *Studio* art magazine with an American supplement. The *International Studio* became a source of difficulty because Lane thought that Kennerley was spending too much on it.

Although major American publishers were flourishing in 1896, the field was open to smaller literary imprints which attempted to be commercial operations—and usually failed. Three such houses were Stone & Kimball (1893–1897), Small & Maynard (1897–1926), and Copeland & Day (1893–1899) which produced attractive books aimed at a literary readership. Many other short-lived imprints appeared because it required little capital to launch a list. There was an American printing revival in progress, with such designers and typographers as Will Bradley, Frederic W. Goudy, and Thomas Cleland at the start of their careers. Kennerley seems to have had an affinity with printers; during his first years in America he shared digs at various times with Bradley, Cleland, and Ingalls Kimball, founder of the Cheltenham Press.

In his early New York months, Kennerley formed lasting friendships with three older men—Bliss Carman, William Marion Reedy, and Thomas Bird Mosher. One of the elements of his success was his ability to attract the attention and affection of first-rate men—as well as women.

The Canadian poet Bliss Carman (1861–1929) is now best known for *Songs of Vagabondia* (1894), written with Richard Hovey. Carman's fifty volumes of verse were inevitably uneven, but his best work celebrated his kinship with nature. Kennerley and Carman almost immediately became close friends after the poet visited the Lane office. In the fall of 1897 Kennerley moved from his Brooklyn lodgings to join Carman at Miss Kelly's boarding house on Fifty-seventh Street. After a short time, they took an apartment at 10 East Sixteenth Street— three rooms and a bath for $40 a month—where they lived for a year. Carman, who was not regularly employed, wrote at the apartment while Kennerley was at work. Le Gallienne was in America and was a regular visitor, as were Hovey and poet Michael Monahan. Hovey later addressed a poem to Kennerley, "The Dramatist. To MK."[7] When Le Gallienne, Kennerley, and Carman went out together, they were followed by urchins attracted by their long hair and bohemian clothes. Among the interests shared by the roommates were women. Kennerley later wrote, ". . . if we were out on a spree, that is having dinner together, with a bottle of wine, and afterwards walked the city street, he was open to an occasional adventure with whoever passed by."[8] A souvenir of these nights on the town is preserved in Kennerley's copy of *More Songs from Vagabondia* (1896) in which Carman wrote in a 16-line parody of Tennyson's "Crossing the Bar":

> *Sunset and good cigar,*
>   *And a great thirst on me;*
> *And may my friends be loafing at the bar*
>   *When I go in to see.*[9]

During the day Carman often received visits from Mary Perry King, the wife of a doctor. "On rare occasions they had intimate relations at 10 E. 16 which they always advised me of by leaving a bunch of violets—Mary Perry's favorite flower—on the pillow of my bed."[10] When Carman moved away—though not because of any falling out with Kennerley—the poet commemorated the apartment in "The Book of Pierrot," a verse sequence addressed to Mrs. King. "The Last Room" opens:

> *There, close the door!*
> *I shall not need these lodgings any more.*
> *Now that I go, dismantled wall and floor*
> *Reproach me and deplore.*[11]

William Marion Reedy (1862–1920) was the editor-publisher of *The Mirror,* a St. Louis political and literary weekly which became *Reedy's Mirror.* A large man with large appetites for alcohol and words, Reedy was regarded as one of the best critics of his time and became an advocate for what was called "the new poetry." Despite the limited circulation of his journal, he enjoyed a national reputation. When Reedy died in 1920 Kennerley wrote a tribute for *The Mirror:*

THE FREE LANCE

BILLY REEDY was the greatest human being I have ever known—a man like Shakespeare. He had a genius for understanding everybody. "To understand all is to forgive all," said Shakespeare, and so it was with Billy. No one was more unworldly—and yet he knew more about the world than anyone else. He never said a word about his own writing but was tireless in praising others. Yet in the pages of the MIRROR I believe there is the finest writing that has been done in America. He could say what he liked as he liked, in perfect freedom, as no other American has ever done. His style was himself, a childlike simplicity.

Wherever we went during our twenty years of friendship and love— and we journeyed to many places and talked with many people—his understanding never faltered. He was always gay and generous and saw the virtue in everyone.

No braver spirit has lived in our time.[12]

Thomas Bird Mosher (1852–1923) has been unfortunately tagged "the pirate of Portland." In actuality this Maine man was a respected publisher of belles-lettres who took advantage of the absence of international copyright to reprint the work of English authors without permission—and often without payment. Reedy called him "the resurrectionist," referring to Mosher's custom of salvaging choice bits of literature. Christopher Morley defended Mosher against the charge of literary malfeasance: "If it be piracy to take home a ragged waif of literature found lonely by the highway, to clothe her in the best you have and find her rich and generous friends—if this be piracy, then let any other publisher who has never ploitered a little in the Public Domain cast the first Stone and Kimball."[13] Kennerley shared Mosher's attitude toward literary loose fish. Commencing in 1891 Mosher produced several series of classic and contemporary writings in elegant

formats, with such titles as "The Brocade Series," "The Lyric Gar-
land," and "The Venetian Series." He also edited and published *The
Bibelot,* a monthly "reprint of poetry and prose for book lovers chosen
in part from scarce editions and sources not generally known." Mosher's success was based on his ability to sell—mostly by mail—rather
precious volumes at reasonable prices; Kennerley would later emulate
certain aspects of the Mosher imprint. When Mosher died in 1923,
Kennerley wrote to the *New York Evening Telegram* crediting his
friend with altering American literary taste:

> It may be said without fear of contradiction that Mr. Mosher made
> popular in America such authors as Walter Pater, Andrew Lang, Arthur
> Symons, Maurice Hewlett and a host of others many years before they
> would otherwise have become known.
>
> During his lifetime he published several hundred volumes, and while
> he had the advantage of selecting already published material there is no
> doubt that he did more for the cause of pure literature in America than
> any other publisher America ever had.[14]

Mosher and Kennerley shared an interest in Aimee Lenalie, the
New York correspondent and French translator for *The Mirror.* Kennerley wrote Mosher reports on the progress of his relationship with
her: "She had a lovely rose with her which she was playing with +
I could have cried when she went away without giving it me. . . ."[15]
But he concurrently pursued other women and picked up $5 prostitutes
in cabarets—one of whom he claimed to be "desperately in love with."[16]
Along with his romantic pose, Kennerley enjoyed phrasemaking and
sent Mosher his Wildeian epigrams:

> Seriousness is only the victim's name for unhappiness.
>
> A woman should be petitioned humbly—and then her consent taken
> for granted.
>
> Marriage is a mistake at the best of times—and is generally committed
> at the worst.
>
> It is only dreams that really happen—and realities bore me.
>
> Comedy is a tragedy with a sense of humour: tragedy is comedy
> without a sense of humour.
>
> I'm so fond of ghosts—most real men + women bore me. I'm getting

into a habit of caring only for the unrealities of life . . . for the dreams of things that do not happen.[17]

Able to win the friendship of men, Kennerley was also attractive and attracted to many women—some of whom advanced his career. He would become known as a compulsive womanizer, and it was said that he ruined himself over women. His 1896 photo shows a handsome face with a head of wavy hair. He was under five feet nine inches and slim, with narrow shoulders that gave his head an outsize appearance, and had a military swagger. His gaze was described as "piercing." After he outgrew his bohemian phase, he was impeccably turned out, usually in dark suits. A pipe was frequently between his teeth. He spoke with a British accent, which was neither Midlands nor upper-class; and his literary conversation was regarded as brilliant.

One of the free-lance artists who sold drawings to the Lane office was the teen-aged Tom Cleland—who as T. M. Cleland became a distinguished illustrator and designer. According to Cleland's later account, Kennerley bought silverware at Gorham's on credit established for him by Mrs. King and pawned it; he was arrested, jumped bail, and returned to England.[18] This report is unverified and probably distorted, but Kennerley was clearly in money trouble by 1898.* In February 1898 he wrote to John Lane blandly explaining away a debt to Mrs. King that she had referred to Lane: "I will also write giving her my account of her loan and the various dates of the different amounts and ask her to kindly verify it. . . . I will then send her a check for interest to date on some even date."[20] That is, he was promising to pay the interest on the debt when he could, but made no commitment about the principal.

Perhaps as a consequence of Kennerley's financial irregularities, H. Hunter Robinson was sent from London to take over the New York office early in 1899, though Kennerley remained on the staff. On 12

---

* On 24 July 1897 the University Press of Cambridge, Massachusetts, threatened suit against John Lane for £250. Although the letter to Lane mentions that "we shall await with interest Mr. Kennerley's arrival,"[19] there is no indication that Kennerley was personally involved in any wrongdoing.

August 1899 Kennerley wrote to Robinson—who was departing for London that day—about a financial tangle involving Le Gallienne. In addition to promising to arrange restitution, Kennerley faintly threatened to expose Lane's business practices:

> Firstly:—I will get a loan on my Life Insurance policy arranged by Monday—how much I do not know. . . .
>
> To sum up the Le Gallienne matter as it stands at this minute. I enclose a letter to my brother—an order for £100. a sum of money lent on mortgage by my father and which is practically mine though I should not have touched it, except for this. This amount you could get immediately.
>
> Beyond this—the loan on policy. If this amount is large enough I will explain the circumstances to Thompson, give him the money and have him cable and write Lane. If it is not large enough to pay all I will pay part of it and get him to cable amount and my brother can pay balance whatever it may be.
>
> Do you think this is all right? I do not think that Lane realizes for one minute how much harm it would have done him to have made the matter public. You have saved him this and if he can be made to realize the exact position he will owe you thanks. I will collect together all Le Gallienne's letters acknowledging debt and give them you to show him if you would care to. LeG. has been known to break contracts:—that he is already in Lane's debt would all be in my favour. If the thing had come to a trail there are things about Lanes business that would have come out that he would rather die than have told—Lastly—I owe you a lot of thanks (and $45!) for realizing my side of the case as you have done. Had it not been for hard luck it would all have been settled long ago.
>
> . . . .
>
> I am taking some morphine to make me sleep as my headache has come back. Can you not cable Lane
>
> BRINGING SETTLEMENT
>
> I hope this is all clear.[21]

Kennerley returned to England shortly afterward and dispatched letters to Lane promising checks for $800 or explaining the delay in delivering them. The matter was settled, and—surprisingly—Lane later did business with Kennerley. In 1920 Lane advised Guy Eglington, whom he had sent to New York as editor of *The International Studio*:

What you say about Kennerley's "flair", I fully recognise. He used to come to the Bodley Head as a collector for a bookseller. I spotted him then, but unfortunately I took him to America too soon. He got a swelled head, which so many of my importations seem to have suffered from at that time. He made it so difficult for me; I could not get any letters, and he grossly neglected the business, inasmuch as he failed to carry out a copyright of one of Locke's novels; so I arrived one morning without any notice, and he could not be found. Of course, I had to get rid of him there and then, and I found he had been lending money to Le Gallienne and taking money himself, all of which has not even now been repaid. It is an old story and a long story, and I do not wish to go into it, at any rate in this letter. You can come by no harm in knowing him, and I quite admit that he is a most interesting personality, but he lacks character, and that in business is fatal; but he is one of the most interesting men known to me. I have no doubt he will be of assistance to you, but I feel it is my duty to put you on your guard.[22]

Before he was twenty-one, Kennerley had perfected the system of juggling debts and borrowing to repay borrowings. That he was able to survive this early crisis, which might have destroyed his career, testifies to his persuasiveness, insouciance, and gall.

While Kennerley was scrambling to evade prosecution in 1899, he managed to become a published poet—apparently his first appearance in print. In April The Brothers of the Book, a press operated by Laurence Conger Woodworth in Gouveneur, New York, privately printed Kennerley's *Two Verses: Modern Love*. This four-leaf pamphlet—with the title appropriated from George Meredith—consisted of eight lines:

Thank God I do not love thee, sweet,
For if I did my heart would break,
While now it does not even ache
At this my kneeling at thy feet.

I look into your eyes and smile,
I kiss your lips, my heart is glad,
My brain is calm, while it were mad
If I did love you, dear, the while.

The two stanzas are Kennerley's entire published poetical works. One hundred copies were printed on handmade paper and an undetermined number on machine-made paper. In later years the poet allegedly destroyed every copy he could find.

Kennerley returned to America in the fall of 1899 and was hired as business manager of a new magazine, *The Smart Set,* at $100 a week, which was a good salary. This magazine was the pre-Mencken & Nathan *Smart Set* published by Col. William D'Alton Mann, owner of the scandal-mongering *Town Topics.* Despite Mann's unsavory reputation, *The Smart Set* was conceived as a respectable monthly with an emphasis on light fiction and social satire. It resembled a cross between a literary journal and a college magazine; there was considerable verse, both serious and humorous, and jokes were inserted to fill out the pages. As the title was intended to indicate, the original plan was to solicit contributions from society people; since they either wouldn't or couldn't write, *The Smart Set* turned to professionals. Because the editor, Arthur Grissom, was hospitalized when the magazine was being set up, Kennerley organized the staff and solicited material. He claimed responsibility for the first six issues.[23] Kennerley persuaded Mann to offer prizes of $1,000 for a prose satire and $500 for a verse satire—which were widely advertised. The prose contest was won by H. C. Chatfield-Taylor and Reginald de Koven for "The Idle Born"; the pseudonymous Momus, Jr., won the verse prize for "The Charge of the Four Hundred." The first issue of March 1900 included work by Theodosia Garrison, Edgar Saltus, Sewell Ford, Bliss Carman, Charles Frederic Nirdlinger, and Charles Vale—all of whom later published books with the Mitchell Kennerley imprint.

In 1901 Kennerley was in Boston and Cambridge as advertising manager of *The Smart Set.* The reasons for his move are unknown; it seems unlikely that the advertising for a New York magazine would have been handled in Massachusetts. Cleland was in Boston operating the Cornhill Press, doing jobs printing and publishing a few collector's items. Kennerley and Cleland were sharing an attic on Beacon Hill at The Hermitage, 1 Willow Street, when their landlady told them to dress their best because a rich lady from Cleveland was coming to dinner. They tossed a coin for their one good tie, and Kennerley won.[24]

Helen Rockwell Morley was considered "culture-mad"; an Anglo-

Mitchell Kennerley, New York, 1896 (Courtesy of
Morley and Jean Kennerley)

THE SMART SET

A MAGAZINE OF CLEVERNESS

Vol. 1	MARCH, 1900	No. 1

CONTENTS

YEARLY SUBSCRIPTION $3.00   SINGLE COPIES 25 CENTS
The entire contents of this magazine are protected by copyright, and must not be reprinted.
Entered at New York Post-Office as second-class mail matter.
Issued Monthly by Ess Ess Publishing Company, 1135 Broadway, New York.

phile, she had traveled extensively. Although she was unmarried at thirty-four—ten years older than Kennerley—Helen was an attractive woman. Her father, Jesse Healy Morley, president of the Cleveland Light and Coke Company, was described by the press as "a five times millionaire" with business interests in mining and manufacturing. He was reported to have refused to do business with John D. Rockefeller, whom he considered a sharper.

Although Cleland claimed that Helen was treated as a joke between them, Kennerley married her in Cleveland on 10 December 1901. The wedding arrangements indicate that the bride's family was less than delighted by the match. The engagement was announced in a one-sentence note in the *Cleveland Plain Dealer* on 1 December. The wedding ten days later rated seven column inches: "Yesterday at 12 o'clock noon Miss Helen Rockwell Morley, daughter of Mr. and Mrs. J. H. Morley of No. 728 Prospect Street, was very quietly married to Mr. Mitchell Kennerly of New York. Only the relatives and the closest friends of the family were present."[25] The bride was unattended, and there were no groomsmen. Despite appearances, it was not a marriage of necessity—apart from the groom's financial requirements. The recent death of Helen's brother precluded an elaborate wedding reception. The newlyweds departed immediately after the wedding breakfast for New York where they set up housekeeping in a nine-room apartment at 391 West End Avenue. His lavender carriage was regarded as one of the sportier rigs on the New York streets. Kennerley loathed Cleveland and thereafter avoided it.

PART II

PUBLISHER,
1902–1914

CHAPTER TWO

The Reader—*Mitchell Kennerley,*
Publisher—The Forum—*Frank Harris*—
Upton Sinclair—*Frederic W. Goudy and*
Kennerley Old Style

AT TWENTY-FOUR KENNERLEY launched his own magazine, *The Reader,*
with offices in the Herald Building at 10 West Twenty-third Street.
He was the publisher and general manager; the editorial staff included
Herbert Copeland of the defunct Copeland & Day imprint, critic
William Wallace Whitelock, and Francis Bellamy, author of "The
Pledge of Allegiance"—as well as Aimee Lenalie, Kennerley's erst-
while inamorata. Copeland—whom Kennerley described as "a charming, dissipated, ineffectual person"—was supposed to act as editor, but
he left after several months of sporadic work.[1] The source of Kenner-
ley's backing is unknown, but the obvious explanation is that it was
Morley money.

The first issue appeared in November 1902. A 25 cent monthly with
emphasis on literary criticism, *The Reader* was generously illustrated
with photographs of authors. There were few well-known contributors, but again they included writers who would join Kennerley's
literary stable. The November issue published W. B. Yeats's "Spinning
Song," Carman's rendering of Sappho's lyrics (suggested by Kennerley),
"The Pastime of Book-Collecting" by Temple Scott, and the first in

"The Literary Guillotine" series anonymously contributed by White-lock. (When these articles were published by Lane in 1903 the book was dedicated to Mitchell Kennerley.) A review signed M. K. treated volumes of verse published by Mosher:

> The four volumes here brought together bear strenuous witness to the happy faculty of selection and presentation which never seem to desert their editor and publisher, Mr. Thomas B. Mosher. Again Mr. Mosher is to be congratulated upon issuing thoroughly charming editions of volumes which will make intimate appeal to the hearts of all true book lovers.
>
> "The Poems of Ernest Dowson" is to us one of the most fascinating of all Mr. Mosher's publications. Ernest Dowson is dead now, and there is nothing more to be heard of him than is contained in this book; or to be said of him than is so admirably said by Mr. Arthur Symons in the personal study of his friend and his work included in the volume. In this respect the book is gratifyingly complete, in singular contrast to the curious, wayward life of Dowson himself, with its startling contrasts and lamentable failures. But in one thing at least—his poetry—Dowson did not fail. His poem "Cynara" will live for ever in anthologies, while the rest of his work will always have interest and fascination for those who care for poetry.
>
> A delightful specimen of book-making is "Fragilia Labilia," by John Addington Symonds, a reprint of one of twenty-five copies privately published for the author in 1884. Symonds's verse was too much the recreation of a prose-writer, and too conscious of its inspiration ever to be popular, but it has interest and charm far above the verse of the day. Here is a characteristic verse:
>
>> *Come not to stir again*
>> *The old sad dream of pain,*
>> *To smile and weep:*
>> *Your melancholy eyes,*
>> *Your soft remembered sighs,*
>> *Oh, let them sleep.*
>
> In issuing a second volume of the poems of Swinburne, Mr. Mosher should soon dispose of his limited edition of the two noble volumes containing the three series of "Poems and Ballads."
>
> A complete reprint of the 1870 edition of Rossetti's "Poems" in a

satisfactory and beautiful volume, uniform with the volumes of Swin-burne, is equally welcome.[2]

At this time Kennerley was planning another magazine to be called *The Guide,* which never appeared.

The Kennerleys' first child, Jesse Healy Morley Kennerley—who would be known as Morley—was born in October 1902. Helen's father died in June 1903. His last will and testament executed in February 1903 was designed to prevent Kennerley from inheriting the Morley fortune[3]—probably an indication that he had become suspicious of his son-in-law's financial probity. Morley left his estate in trust for fifteen years, with Helen Kennerley receiving the same share of the income as her brother Charles and Morley's grandson Frederick H. Morley, Jr. After the trust terminated, one-third of the principal would go to Jesse Healy Morley's widow, with the remaining two-thirds divided as follows: a third to Charles, a third to Frederick, and a third in a *lifetime trust* to Helen. In the event of Helen's death her share would go to her children; if she died without issue, it would be divided between Morley's son and grandson. There was no way Kennerley would ever get his hands on the principal. Still his wife would draw the income from 22 percent of a multimillion-dollar estate. The 1906 probate accounting for the estate shows that Kennerley had repaid $1,612.50 and Helen $5,498.98 on notes held by Jesse Healy Morley.

Helen's inheritance was no doubt responsible for a change in the Kennerleys' style of living. In 1903 they rented a summer home in Mamaroneck, which Helen bought in November—paying $16,000 for the house and 27 acres. The staff of the large house included a coach-man, gardener, nursemaid, cook, Helen's personal maid, and other servants. Mamaroneck—about 20 miles from the city in Westchester County—became their main residence. Kennerley enjoyed the life of a country gentleman and kept horses. There were many weekend vis-itors from the literary world, and Carman often came out to ride. Helen continued to travel, with and without her husband. In 1904 they went to England and brought his mother to America for a five-year stay. During a Paris visit Kennerley bought the sixth known copy of Samuel de Champlain's *Des Sauvages* (1603) on a bookstall for the equivalent of 4 cents; this narrative of Champlain's first expedition to

Canada, which describes the selection of the site for Quebec, brought $2,900 when Kennerley put it up at auction in 1907.[4]

The Kennerleys' second child, Mitchell, Jr., was born in February 1906; and Helen suffered a miscarriage in 1908. The domestic life of the Kennerleys was marred by sexual problems. Helen apparently believed that sexual intercourse should be reserved for procreation. It is exceedingly improbable that Kennerley would have remained faithful to any woman, but Helen's sexual economy provided a rationalization for his infidelities—if one was required. Their incompatibility was mitigated by Helen's conviction that her husband was a genius.

The Reader was sold to Bobbs-Merrill of Indianapolis in 1904, and Kennerley began organizing his own publishing house. It did not require much capital to launch an imprint. A small list of titles could be published for $3,000, and American publishers could obtain part of the edition of an English book on deferred payment. Kennerley has been called the first modern publisher in America; yet his publishing style was more English than American, drawing heavily on English authors and English taste.

Kennerley's cousin Arthur Hooley performed most of the editorial functions, from reading manuscripts to working with the authors. A shy man with a speech impediment, Hooley published his own work as Charles Vale. Before coming to America, he had collaborated with Bennett on two plays. He was closely associated with Kennerley's ventures for more than twenty years; but in the early years of their connection he had reservations about his flamboyant cousin, writing to William Wood Kennerley: "I find myself interested in his pose, but indifferent to his personality, + quite unimpressed by his ability. Yet the latter is very real, in many ways. . . . Probably the 'trade' element, which in its cruder aspects distresses me, has got on my nerves a little, at present."[5] The cable address for the office at 116 East Twenty-eighth Street was PEKARIS; there were those who thought that PECCAVI (I have sinned) would have been more appropriate. One of the tenants in the building was Frederic W. Goudy, proprietor of the Village Press, who was struggling to make a living as a type designer. Kennerley was able to offer him a few assignments for title pages and book jackets. Goudy became America's greatest typographer, and Kennerley's name would become permanently linked with his.

RIGHT: *Mitchell Kennerley, Jr., Helen Morley Kennerley, and Morley Kennerley (Photo by Arnold Genthe; International Museum of Photography at George Eastman House)*

BELOW: *At Mamaroneck in 1903: (sitting) maid and nurse; (standing) Mrs. Jesse Healy Morley, Mitchell Kennerley, coachman, maid, gardener; (on rock) Mrs. Morley's companion, Morley Kennerley, Helen Morley Kennerley (courtesy of Morley and Jean Kennerley)*

LEFT: *Bliss Carman and Mitchell Kennerley at Mamaroneck (Courtesy of Morley and Jean Kennerley)*

BELOW: *Mitchell and Morley Kennerley in lavender carriage, New York City (Courtesy of Morley and Jean Kennerley)*

The literary market Kennerley invaded was dominated by romantic fiction. The best-selling novelists of 1906 were the American Winston Churchill, Owen Wister, Robert W. Chambers, Meredith Nicholson, George Barr McCutcheon, Margaret Deland, and Rex Beach—along with Upton Sinclair, Edith Wharton, and Ellen Glasgow. The first Mitchell Kennerley list for spring 1906 consisted of three books: a new edition of Edgar Saltus's *Imperial Purple* (1892), a history of the Caesars; *Modern Love,* a poetry anthology; and Kenneth Brown's *Sirocco,* a novel dealing with the rescue of an English girl from a desert harem.[6] These books represent a mixture of the literary and the commercial that would characterize the Kennerley imprint. At that time most novels had a list price of $1.50; the bookstores bought at 40 percent discount, and many retailers sold novels for $1.35. Kennerley offered *Sirocco* to the trade for 81 cents in lots of five copies.[7]

The volume most representative of the twenty-seven-year-old publisher's taste was *Modern Love,* which Kennerley probably edited. (Mosher's first book had been an unauthorized edition of Meredith's *Modern Love.*) This collection of verse by such Nineties poets as Housman, Dowson, Wilde, Yeats, Davidson, and Henley imitates the books published by Mosher. Kennerley's own "Modern Love" verses were included as an unattributed epigraph. There were 1,000 copies on Van Gelder handmade paper bound in boards at $1 and fifty numbered copies on Japan vellum* in half leather at $3.

Edgar Saltus was a wealthy and elaborately educated New Yorker whose work combined scholarship with sensationalism. "It is the shudder that tells," he announced. Kennerley admired his lush style, but Wilde observed that "passion struggles with grammar on every page." Kennerley enjoyed telling the anecdote that Cecil Rhodes had instructed a bookseller to supply him with all the books about ancient Rome but canceled the order after reading *Imperial Purple* because it told him everything.[8] The contract for the Saltus work reveals Kennerley's caution or his disinclination to corrupt authors with money. The first printing of *Imperial Purple* was 1,000 royalty-exempt copies; if it sold out, Kennerley had the option of paying 15 percent royalty

---

* A smooth paper resembling vellum (parchment) originally handmade in Japan.

on subsequent printings or giving the plates to Saltus.[9] *Imperial Purple* required multiple printings; and Saltus published five more books with Kennerley—three of which were new works.* The connection terminated in 1909 when "Saltus chose to quarrel with me for no reason at all."[10]

From the start Kennerley's books were printed in readable type on good quality paper. The sedate bindings were goldstamped on dark cloth. Title pages bore the MK monogram which was usually blindstamped on the back cover. Kennerley claimed to have been the first publisher to provide a list of all the author's other books on a separate preliminary page (now known as the card page or ad page).

In the summer of 1906 Kennerley had two more titles for sale: an import of Robert Sherard's *The Life of Oscar Wilde* ("with a full and detailed account of Wilde's death, gathered from the lips of the man who was holding him in his arms when he died") and a new edition of Saltus's *Mary Magdalen* (1891). Four more books were advertised as "in preparation": Sewell Ford's humorous *Shorty McCabe*; the first edition of Saltus's *Historia Amoris: A History of Love, Ancient and Modern*; Swinburne's *Anactoria and Other Lyrical Poems* (1,000 trade copies and 50 numbered copies); and an import of Alexander Smith's *Dreamthorp: A Book of Essays Written in the Country*—one of Kennerley's favorite books. The imports were sheets of English books supplied to Kennerley with his title page and binding, although in some cases the unbound sheets were delivered for binding in America.

Before the end of 1906 Kennerley also brought out Saltus's essays, *The Pomps of Satan,* and Victoria Cross's *Six Women.* Vivian Cory Griffin, an English writer who used the pseudonym Victoria Cross, became a dependable seller for Kennerley, and he published a dozen of her books. His 1907 ad for *Life's Shop Window* and *Anna Lombard* proclaimed her " 'The Great English Novelist' "[11] without attribution

---

* *The Amazing Emperor Heliogabalus* by J. Stuart Hay of Oxford University was withdrawn from sale in 1911 when it was discovered to incorporate 60-odd unacknowledged passages from three of Saltus's works published by Kennerley—*Imperial Purple, Historia Amoris,* and *The Pomps of Satan* (" 'Taken' from Edgar Saltus," *New York Times Review of Books* [23 July 1911], 454).

for the boast. The former went through at least thirteen printings by 1908, and the latter title supposedly sold 81,000 copies. It is likely that Kennerley acted as the American distributor—rather than publisher— for several of the Victoria Cross volumes. Copies of *To-Morrow?* and *Paula* have been noted with Kennerley's label pasted on the title page of the Walter Scott Publishing Co. English editions.

Cross's *The Eternal Fires* (1910) was described as "putrescently purient" by *Reedy's Mirror,* which provided a synopsis detailing the novel's absurdities. Irene, the heroine, is impregnated by Apollo who promises to smite with lightning any man who kisses her. After bearing the god's child, Irene is sought by several would-be lovers, but Apollo's warning keeps her chaste. She agrees to take a platonic cruise with millionaire Haynes, who nonetheless attempts to possess her. Haynes is struck dead; the yacht ignites; Irene's body is burned, but "the Soul and her God rose ever upward, winging their flight to the Milky Way, to the eternal plains of Light."[12]

At the same time that he was pushing Victoria Cross, Kennerley commenced The Little Classics series (also known as The Little Omar Classics)—dainty volumes of verse, including *The Rubaiyat, The Song of Songs,* and Vernon Lee's *Sister Benvenuta and the Christ Child.* "Exquisitely printed on antique wove paper" and bound in cloth, they sold for 40 cents each or $2 for boxed sets of five volumes. All were imports from English publisher Grant Richards, who provided bound copies at three pence-half penny each (about 8 cents). Thus Kennerley's gross on 1,000 copies was $240—less shipping, overhead, and distribution costs.

Richards (1872–1948) and Kennerley did considerable business together between 1906 and 1911, taking each other's bound books or printing plates. Kennerley's usual order was for only 200 or 300 copies. Six books appeared with their joint imprint. They also copyrighted books for each other, printing a few copies for deposit in order to protect their rights in the titles. Like Kennerley, Richards was undercapitalized; Kennerley's expedient of ignoring matters that he did not want to deal with placed a strain on the relationship. In 1907 Richards wrote him, "Will you forgive my pointing out that other publishers with whom we do business do answer letters?"[13]

An imported 1907 title was Frank Richardson's *2385 Mayfair.* Ken-

*Mark Twain with Mitchell
Kennerley and Mitchell
Kennerley, Jr., aboard ocean
liner, summer 1907 (Courtesy of
Morley and Jean Kennerley)*

*First Kennerley ad in Publishers'
Weekly (12 May 1906)*

nerley hoped that this English novelist would provide another Victoria Cross bonanza and advertised him as " 'the wittiest man in London.' "[14] The three Richardson books published in 1907 sold moderately well. Although there was a financial panic that year, Kennerley released some twenty-one titles during 1907. (The totals for the volumes Kennerley published in a given year are approximate because his books sometimes appeared in the year preceding or the year following the dates on the title pages; contrary to trade practice, he rarely identified the reprintings of his books.) His list could not support a strong sales and promotional effort. In the early years there were only two traveling salesmen for the entire country—one of whom, Laurens Maynard (formerly of Small, Maynard) covered the South, Pacific Coast, Northwest, and the larger cities in the East and West. Kennerley relied on reviews and word of mouth, believing that books find their own readers. His sales strategy seems to have been formed by the conditions of English publishing: a small territory with an identifiable book-buying class and influential critical periodicals. Even when Kennerley had a strong property, he was unable to push it aggressively. Despite his chronic liquidity problems, he boasted that he had never published a book at the author's expense.

During 1907 Kennerley set up headquarters as The Little Book-Shop Around the Corner at 2 East Twenty-ninth Street, taking the name from The Little Church Around the Corner, which was opposite. The neighborhood was a center for bookshops and art dealers; the American Art Association, the leading auction gallery, had a building facing Madison Square. It was customary for the principal publishers to operate retail stores. Brentano's, Dutton, Putnam, Scribner, and Dodd, Mead had shops selling the books of all publishers. Kennerley's plan was to imitate the Bodley Head by selling only his own books; but his backlist was small, and he enlarged the stock to include imported volumes of fine printing and became the New York agent for Thomas Bird Mosher. The Little Book-Shop Around the Corner was the first of its kind in America. The manager was Montrose J. Moses, the author of *Children's Books and Reading,* a 1907 Kennerley volume. The publishing office was on the same premises; Carman, Le Gallienne, and Saltus were frequent visitors, along with diplomats Brand Whitlock, Robert Underwood Johnson, and Myron T. Herrick. English authors gravitated there on visits to America. Goudy was a regular, and the shop became a hangout for other typographers, such as Bruce Rogers and Everett Currier. Temple Scott, a Kennerley author, recommended a young Englishman named Laurence Gomme to succeed Moses as shop manager.[15] The place resembled an incubator for publishers. Both Gomme and Scott (born Isaac Henry Solomon Isaacs) would briefly have their own imprints.

At the end of its second year of operation the imprint did not show promise of becoming notable or innovative. Kennerley could not yet afford to gamble on unknown American writers, but English books could be had on deferred payment. The years 1908 and 1909 were devoted to list-building, with more than sixty new titles. Kennerley began a respected line of literary criticism with Moses's *Henrik Ibsen,* John C. Bailey's *The Claims of French Poetry,* and J. A. Hammerton's *George Meredith in Anecdote and Criticism* (co-published with Grant Richards). In 1908 Kennerley republished Robert Hichens's *The Green Carnation,* an 1894 *roman à clef* about Oscar Wilde—adding a key to the characters. The printing plates cost him $25, and the book sold several thousand copies.

On the 1909 list was Van Wyck Brooks's first commercially pub-lished book, *The Wine of the Puritans,* which inaugurated his inter-pretation of American culture. Kennerley was alerted to Brooks by Dan Rider, who served as Kennerley's London agent and scout. Rider's bookshop in St. Martin's Court off Charing Cross Road was a gathering place for writers—especially Americans in London.[16] Brooks had put up half the money for the Sisley London edition of *The Wine of the Puritans,* which had not sold. Kennerley was able to acquire 200 sets of unbound sheets for nine pence each—an investment of less than $40. He decided to publish it in America despite Hooley's cautious report:

> The little book has value, though it is neither complete nor incon-troversial. But it would be good enough to publish, if you cared to spend time and money upon a production which could not appeal to a wide circle. For the style, if not the matter, would militate against popularity: it is not cheap enough, and obvious enough. But, on the other hand, there is no question of brilliancy. The book is thoughtful and pertinent,

but it is above the heads of the ordinary reading public, and not quite big enough to make an important impression on the reflective and discerning. Yet it has interested me, though it presents no new discoveries. The impersonal treatment, the absence of fidgety cleverness, of straining after effect, deserve some recognition. But it would probably be wiser not to accept the book.[17]

Brooks published two more books with Kennerley, *John Addington Symonds: A Biographical Study* (1914) and *The World of H. G. Wells* (1915). In 1916 he was threatening legal action for unpaid royalties. Kennerley's contracts were not munificent. He usually tried to exempt the first 500 copies from royalties and rarely offered an advance. That the sums involved were so small indicates the Peter-to-Paul nature of the business. On a $1 book, the royalty on 500 copies amounted to $50.

When Brooks published his autobiography in 1954 he was able to take a generous position on his first American publisher:

> . . . but when years later Mitchell Kennerley took his own life in New York I wondered that there had been so few to praise him. What did it matter in the end that he sometimes played a double game? He made little or nothing out of his exasperated authors, and who else would have printed them, who else would have looked at their first little books, which Kennerley delightedly acclaimed and so charmingly published? Like John Lane in England . . . he backed books often at a loss, with a feeling for talents that no one but he distinguished; and he should be remembered as the friend of a whole generation of writers whom, in surprising numbers, he first brought out.[18]

In a foreword to Gomme's unpublished memoir of Kennerley, Brooks wrote: "I think of him as one of the bright notes in the springtime of the century at a time when all things literary seemed to be beginning."[19]

The 1909 list also included John Davidson's *Fleet Street and Other Poems*—co-published with Grant Richards—perhaps the only modern book with a suicide note as a foreword. Davidson jumped into the sea from the Penzance cliffs in March 1909.

> The time has come to make an end. There are several motives. I find my pension is not enough; I have therefore still to turn aside and attempt

things for which people will pay. My health also counts. Asthma and other annoyances I have tolerated for years; but I cannot put up with cancer.

A surprise success of the year was Theodosia Garrison's book of verse, *The Joy o' Life*, which sold 10,000 copies.

Kennerley's account of A. S. M. Hutchinson's *Once Aboard the Lugger* (1909) provides a view of the way business was done when publishing was still partly a game:

> I remember receiving the English proofs from an agent one Saturday in the old days of simultaneous publication to secure copyright with the offer of American rights for fifty pounds if I could copyright within 14 days as English publication would not be postponed to give the agent more time. . . . I read it over the weekend and bought the rights and sent paperbound, complete printed copies to Washington within the prescribed time and duly published the book.* It did quite well and sold two or three modest editions. F. P. A. [Franklin P. Adams] became an enthusiastic admirer and boosted it in his column.[20]

Kennerley later disposed of the plates and rights to the A. L. Burt publishing house for $3,000. He missed out on Hutchison's next novel, *If Winter Comes*, a best seller.

In his search for American material Kennerley found John G. Neihardt, a Nebraska poet and novelist who wrote about the early West. Kennerley hailed him as "the biggest poet in American poetry since Whitman."[21] Neihardt's first Kennerley title was *Man-Song* (1909), a book of lyrics. When he was in the money Kennerley was willing to assist his authors. Neihardt wrote him in 1909: "The brotherhood that shines through your offer of a loan can help me more than the hundred dollars could. . . . You are one of those who have seen the vision—all the intricate world working at once—the joy and the pain,

---

* Between 1891 and 1909 an English author could obtain American copyright protection by depositing two copies of his book at the Library of Congress, but only if those copies were printed from type set in the United States. In 1909 the law required that the copies be set, printed, and bound in the United States.

and the deep, singing pity of it."[22] Four more Neihardt titles appeared with Kennerley's imprint—*A Bundle of Myrrh* (1911), *The Dawn-Builder* (1911), *The Stranger at the Gate* (1912), and *Life's Lure* (1914)—but his verse epics of the West were published after Neihardt and Kennerley parted.

The most notable of Kennerley's 1909 publications were Frank Harris's *The Bomb* and *The Man Shakespeare and his Tragic Life Story*. Harris (1855–1931) was a brilliant and notorious figure in the London literary scene, but he is now mainly remembered for his pornographic *My Life and Loves*. Born in Ireland, he attended the University of Kansas and returned to England where he became the editor or proprietor of important newspapers and magazines—including *The Saturday Review* and *Vanity Fair*—and went to prison for contempt of court in a libel case. Harris was a friend of Shaw and Wilde, who remarked that "Frank has been invited to all the best houses in London—once!" Kennerley had published Frederic Carrel's *John Johns*, a *roman à clef* about Harris, in 1908.

Kennerley and Harris were curiously alike. Both were promoters and womanizers; both were unreliable with money; and both had a built-in self-destruct mechanism—a compulsion to push their luck. Kennerley's assessment of Harris has the ring of autobiography: "Harris was a fascinating person, absolutely honest about everything except money. You could not buy his praise. You were 'unstable' if you failed to back his desires and plans. He was a magnificent host—with your money."[23] During the summer of 1909 Kennerley and Harris met in London and together they hatched big plans. Harris wrote him: "We should make your office the centre of literary America, the place where the American Academy will be founded, as well as the first American journal devoted to books."[24] Kennerley proposed to pay Harris £400 a year for "all your book rights here on account of royalties."[25]

The Bomb was a novel based on the Chicago Haymarket riot. Kennerley wrote in his copy: "This was the first book by Frank Harris which I published. I read an English review and sent to London for a copy. I was enthusiastic and wrote Harris I would publish it and asked him to write a foreward which I would copyright as it was too late to copyright the book. The lettering on the titlepage + cover was drawn by Frederic W. Goudy."[26] *The Bomb* attracted considerable attention in America, and Emma Goldman proclaimed it "the Bible of Anarchism."

In offering his Shakespeare study to Kennerley, Harris announced: "I prove the old views of him to be all wrong: He was a snob + a lecher + a self-conscious artist—an extravagant kindly fellow whose unhappy love for a maid of honor Mary Fitton brought him nearly to madness. It will cause a sensation. In one of his prefaces George Bernard Shaw says I know more about Shakespeare than any man."[27] Kennerley's account of the publication of this book is:

> Harris showed me the first chapters of "The Man Shakespeare" and told me no English publisher would encourage him to go on with it. I was thrilled by these early chapters and gave him an advance and a contract to publish in America. He completed the work and it was greeted by Arnold Bennett, Francis Hackett, Temple Scott, Middleton Murry and many others as the finest interpretation of Shakespeare ever written.[28]

The Man Shakespeare was a psychological reconstruction from the autobiographical evidence Harris found in Shakespeare's works. Although scholars dismissed it, the book sold surprisingly well. Arnold Bennett wrote, "It has destroyed nearly all previous Shakespearian criticism, and it will be the parent of nearly all the Shakespearian criticism of the future."[29] Kennerley's promotional pamphlet proclaimed: "A most astonishing and fascinating book: the finest product of the synthetic criticism, finer because far truer than Carlyle's 'Cromwell' or Renan's 'Life of Jesus.' Mr. Harris has not been afraid to paint in the shadows. As biography, this book must rank with Boswell's 'Life of Johnson'; as art, it must rank above it."[30] In 1912 Kennerley announced in *Publishers' Weekly* that 100 copies had been distributed at the request of J. P. Morgan, who instructed him: "I am of the opinion that the contents of this book are of such value to students of English literature that I would ask you to send copies to the libraries and colleges where you consider it will be of service, forwarding bill for same to me."[31]

Grant Richards in *1909*. Pencil
drawing by Henry Lamb

Front cover for promotional
booklet published by Kennerley
(Bruccoli Collection)

FRANK HARRIS

THE MAN OF TO·DAY
AND TO·MORROW

This is a copy of the first
edition of "The Man Shakespeare"
from which the English edition
was published a year later. I
met Harris in London on my
first visit after publishing
an American edition of "The
Bomb" which I bought from
his English publisher John
Long. Harris showed me
the first chapters of "The
Man Shakespeare" and told
me no English publisher
would encourage him to
go on with it. I was
thrilled by these early
chapters and gave him
an advance and a contract
to publish in America. He
completed the work and it
was greeted by Arnold Bennett,
Francis Hackett, Temple Scott,
Middleton Murry and
many others as the finest
interpretation of Shakespeare
ever written.

Kennerley's note on The Man
Shakespeare (Bruccoli Collection)

When Kennerley delayed payment, Harris complained to Bennett: ". . . Kennerley leaves me in the dark: he won't write—d—n him! I'm afraid he's as unstable as water—that handsome face—I ought to have mistrusted fine signboards at my age. . . . Besides you warned me!"[32] Kennerley did advance Harris £1,100 during 1910–1913 and published *Montes the Matador* (1910), *The Women of Shakespeare* (1912), *Unpath'd Waters* (1913), *Great Days* (1914), and *Contemporary Portraits* (1915). *The Women of Shakespeare* was not a critical study, but an attempt to determine the influence of women on him: "The immortal significance of Shakespeare's life, the history of his soul, is the story of his love for the imperious gypsy-wanton Mary Fitton. Till he met her he knew little of life and less of women: through her he came to knowledge of both and to much self-knowledge. There is nothing in all literature more enthralling, nothing more instructive, than the flower-like growth of Shakespeare's soul in the 'maddening-fever' of passion."[33] Among the characters Harris was able to trace to Mary Fitton's inspiration were Rosaline, Julia, Juliet, Portia, Beatrice, and Rosalind.

At the end of 1912 Kennerley arranged for Harris to give a series of lectures in New York on such topics as "Shakespeare as Friend and Lover," "Shakespeare's Teachings and the Modern Spirit," "The Fiction of Today," "Christianity vs. Individualism and Nietzsche," "The Artist and the Millionaire," "The Rhythm of Things and the Future of Man," and "England and America in Religion and Practice." Engraved invitations were sent to prominent people, and, according to Kennerley, the lectures were enthusiastically received. Harris spent a Christmas at Mamaroneck and played Santa Claus for the Kennerley children. When Harris returned to England, Kennerley saw him off. On board the ship before sailing Harris discovered that one of his gloves was lost and insisted on going back to look for it on the pier. Kennerley settled the matter by throwing the remaining glove overboard.

Kennerley's financial dealings with Harris were complicated, with Kennerley deferring payments or offering payment in the form of notes due him. Long before "cash flow" became a catchphrase, Kennerley was a virtuoso at juggling accounts payable and accounts receivable. One of the complicated Kennerley-Harris transactions involved Harris's *Oscar Wilde: His Life and Confessions*. Kennerley had it set in type in 1912 and agreed to hold the plates until Harris released the book for publication. It is not entirely clear why publication was delayed, but the possibility of suppression was certainly involved. In 1915 Kennerley received $250 from Harris on account and agreed to manufacture the book for him at cost: $1,500 for 1,000 copies.[34] The work appeared in New York in 1916 as "Printed and Published by the Author." Kennerley's copy is inscribed to "the only publisher who has even shown a touch of genius, or sympathy with any manifestation of it, from his friend, the author, Frank Harris. 3 Washington Square. N. In this year of Dis-grace, 1916."[35]

The publication of *Oscar Wilde: His Life and Confessions* is shrouded in unverifiable anecdotes. One version is that Kennerley compelled Harris to sign a contract with Albert Boni—stipulating that 1,000 royalty-free copies be supplied to Dan Rider for English distribution in payment of Harris's debts to Rider—by threatening to attach Harris's future earnings to satisfy his $45,000 debt to Kennerley.[36] It is highly improbable that Harris could have gotten this much money from Kennerley, who didn't have it. The Wilde volumes were duly printed, but shortly before publication Boni asked Harris about the account of Walter Pater kissing Wilde's shoes in homage. Harris replied, "No, Boni, of course it isn't true. But it will sell books." Boni immediately went to the bindery and had the title page bearing his name removed from every copy.[37]

In 1910 Kennerley's title pages began inconsistently appearing with New York and London locations, but the only London office was Rider's bookshop. The thirty-five-odd books published by Kennerley that year included Le Gallienne's *Orestes*, the *Later Poems* of Father John Bannister Tabb, and two volumes by Mrs. Belloc Lowndes—*Studies in Wives* and *The Uttermost Farthing*. Another Englishman, E. Temple Thurston, provided two novels, *The Greatest Wish in the World* and *Sally Bishop*. The latter work dealt with a fallen woman, and Thurston's wife divorced him because he insisted on the necessity of conducting personal research into the subject.

The Critical Biographies Series commenced in 1910 with Arthur Ransome's *Edgar Allan Poe*. Lord Alfred Douglas threatened a libel action against Ransome's *Oscar Wilde* (1912), and the book was withdrawn by its London publisher. Nine volumes appeared before this series terminated in 1913. Kennerley eventually published sixty-eight volumes of literary criticism—roughly 15 percent of his output. The self-proclaimed English all-around genius Allen Upward—poet, dramatist, novelist, lawyer, pedagogue, journalist, adventurer, anthropologist, philologist, and philosopher—was represented by two books in 1910. *Lord Alistair's Rebellion* is a novel about the victimization of genius by society. At the end Alistair announces: " 'I am your Christ. . . . I have inherited the evil strain, and by so doing I have saved you from it; I have carried it off from you, like a drainpipe.' " Hooley's report advised Kennerley: "The book has vitality and originality, and is therefore worth handling. The prospects of popularity are extremely small: yet a clever book always has possibilities—if only of disaster."[38] The risk of disaster did not intimidate Kennerley. He was receptive to controversial books and eccentric authors, ready to publish any book that interested him—if the author did not require a substantial advance. In *The New Word* Upward examined the meaning of "idealist" in the context of the Nobel Prize for "work of an idealist tendency"— thus demonstrating that he was a leading candidate for the award. Ezra Pound agreed, but Sweden withheld its bounty nonetheless. The 26 May 1910 issue of Reedy's *Mirror* referred to Kennerley as a publisher "whose specialty seems to be books of all kinds of daring" and reviewed six of his titles: *Sally Bishop, The New Word,* the anonymously published sonnet sequence *Thysia,* Victoria Cross's *The Eternal Fires,* Sewell Ford's *Just Horses,* and Mrs. W. K. Clifford's *Plays.*

Michael Monahan, the author of five Kennerley volumes, had been publishing *The Papyrus* since 1903. More a hobby than a commercial venture, this "Magazine of Individuality" was largely written by Monahan, although it printed or reprinted short pieces by American and European writers. The monthly sold for 10 cents a copy and had a small circulation. By 1910 *The Papyrus* had fallen on hard times, and Monahan announced that "a kind fortune has drafted Mr. Mitchell Kennerley to run the business end of the publication. . . . Mr. Kennerley and I have taken no pledge NOT TO SUCCEED or to REFUSE THE MONEY! I mention this, lest any people, Friends of the Idea, should feel backward, under the new order, in acting upon their generous impulses."[39]

Kennerley served as publisher-of-record into 1912, when Monahan resumed responsibility.

A much more serious 1910 undertaking was Kennerley's assumption of control over *The Forum*, a respected but unprosperous monthly. His return to the magazine field was a sensible move, for it was customary for book publishers to have their own journals—as did Scribners, Harper, Putnam, Lippincott, and others. A house-controlled magazine—but not a house organ—could promote the publisher's books in advertising and in reviews. More usefully still, it provided a talent pool for authors; new writers could be introduced in the magazine, and books could be given prepublication visibility through serialization.

The Forum had been founded in 1886 by Isaac L. Rice, corporation lawyer, manufacturer, and reformer. Under its first editor, Lorettus Sutton Metcalf, it became a prominent journal of political and social opinion. Although articles about literature were permitted, fiction and verse were excluded. In 1907 editor Frederick Taber Cooper introduced fiction and poetry. When Kennerley became the publisher he enlarged the space devoted to literature and art. He acquired control of *The Forum* without investing any money. (The stockholders in 1915 were Isaac L. Rice, Nathan Bijur, Isaac Bijur, M. S. Wallach, Oswald Ottendoefer [deceased], P. J. Goodhart, Lehman Brothers, Louis Windmuller Estate, and A. Bijur.) There was no masthead, but Arthur Hooley was listed as the editor in the statement of ownership and management. *The Forum* sold for 25 cents.

The first issue under Kennerley, July 1910, carried his name on the front cover as publisher. It continued the serialization of George Meredith's *Celt and Saxon* and H. G. Wells's *The New Machiavelli*—which had both commenced before Kennerley's involvement. The lineup of contributors under the Kennerley-Hooley regime was impressive despite the pay scale of 1¢ per word with a $50 maximum for a story or article: Frank Harris, Bliss Carman, H. Granville Barker, Arthur Davidson Ficke, Witter Bynner, Vachel Lindsay, Maurice Maeterlinck, Maurice Hewlett, Leo Tolstoy (the first authorized translations of "Three Days in the Village" and "A Dream"), Ezra Pound, Richard Le Gallienne, Jack London, Van Wyck Brooks, Edgar Saltus, John Reed, W. B. Yeats, Edward Carpenter, Robert Frost, John G. Neihardt,

John Drinkwater, Lady Gregory, Walter Lippmann, James G. Huneker, D. H. Lawrence, Joseph Hergesheimer, Zoë Akins, Rabindranath Tagore, Conrad Richter, Lord Dunsany, H. L. Mencken, Sherwood Anderson, and Edna St. Vincent Millay. A score of them were or would become Kennerley authors. *The Forum* was the principal advertising medium for Kennerley books, and they were frequently mentioned in the critical notices. The most controversial work in *The Forum* was Bynner's May 1913 "Tiger," a verse drama about an upper-class man visiting a brothel to break in a girl who has been abducted into white slavery; she is his daughter. "Tiger" was defended as a moral lesson, and it was denounced as salacious. Reedy wrote in *The Mirror*: "There wouldn't be white slaves if pure girls' fathers and brothers did not demand for their lust's appeasement the virgin daughters of other fathers."[40] Kennerley published *Tiger* as a 60-cent volume in 1913. Bynner inscribed a copy for him:

> *For Mitchell Kennerley (who dared*
> *To [grab] the beast while others stared)*
> *Let this inscription be a token*
> *Of the time the Tiger was house-broken!*[41]

The Forum had a strong Celtic strain, publishing material by and about the writers of the Irish Renaissance, as well as articles on what was called The Irish Question. After the outbreak of the Great War the magazine printed articles proposing peace plans. When it became clear that the war would not be over by Christmas, *The Forum* attracted favorable attention by printing The Sermon on the Mount in the January 1915 issue. *The Forum* proclaimed itself "The Leading American Review and Magazine"; but it lost money, and Kennerley gave it up in 1916.

The 1911 list of some fifty books included three novels by Leonard Merrick—*Conrad in Quest of his Youth*, *The Man Who Understood Women*, and *The Position of Peggy*. Kennerley wrote a long article for the *New York Times Review of Books* tracing the vicissitudes of Merrick's career:

> No one could talk of his books now to Merrick . . . without realizing
> the intense and unaffected gratitude transfiguring the man for the Amer-

ican Nation's welcome of the work which the Britishers had ignored. He speaks glowingly of the generosity of W. D. Howells, who was the first to call attention to the novels in New York. . . . He has been writing his soul out in the English language for English-speaking men and women—producing, against crushing odds, novels which the public of his own country have allowed to fall dead year by year for half a lifetime—and, before it was too late, it has been America that has placed him in the front rank of successful living novelists.[42]

Seven books by Merrick appeared with the Kennerley imprint between 1911 and 1914. William Dean Howells declared of *The Actor-Manager* in 1912 that "I can recall no English novel in which the study of temperament and character is carried further or deeper. . . ."[43] Merrick apparently sold well, but he is now forgotten. His books were taken over by Dutton in 1918.

Love's Coming of Age: A Series of Papers on the Relations of the Sexes was the first of six books by Edward Carpenter (1844–1929) published by Kennerley between 1911 and 1917. An English disciple of Walt Whitman, Carpenter advocated simplicity of life (he took up sandal-making) and brotherly affection. He is now regarded as a "pioneer socialist and gay liberator"; but his scholarly sexual studies generated no controversy and escaped censorship. Carpenter's subsequent Kennerley titles included *The Intermediate Sex: A Study of Some Transitional Types of Men and Women* (1912) and *Intermediate Types Among Primitive Folk: A Study in Social Evolution* (1914).

Two books by Upton Sinclair appeared on the Kennerley list for 1911, *The Fasting Cure* and *Love's Pilgrimage*. Sinclair was famous as a reformer for *The Jungle* (1906), the novel that prompted pure food legislation; he was also known as an eccentric because of his theories about diet, sex, and marriage—which he put into practice. *The Fasting Cure*, which advocated systematic self-starvation, appeared with frontispiece of the author Before and After. The book went into a second printing, but Kennerley declined Sinclair's offer to rewrite it as a novel.

Love's Pilgrimage was submitted as the first of three projected novels openly dealing with Sinclair's marriage and divorce. Thyrsis (Sinclair) marries Corydon (Meta Fuller Sinclair) with the intention that they live together as brother-and-sister "soul comrades." In the words of Kennerley's reader, "At last guided by a hint from a doctor that Corydon may be suffering from this utterly unnatural life, Thyrsis yields to his own passion, stimulated by constant proximity. In a powerful scene, the consummation of the marriage is described, in detail. A period of love-madness follows."[44] The report warned about the possibility of censorship problems but insisted that the novel was in no way impure.

Sinclair provided a "Scenario" for the rest of the trilogy:

> The novel when completed will embody the author's ideas upon love, sex and marriage. These ideas, while not conventional, are in no sense those of "free-love." They are, in brief, that economic necessity determines marriage custom, for the protection of the mother and the child. Economic conditions are changing, and customs are changing with them. The end to be sought is the perfect child, and the perfect rearing of the child; and laws and conventions must leave room for experiment, here as everywhere else in life.
>
> There will be no didacticism in any part of the book. Whatever ideas it has to set forth will be embodied in the narrative. The external story will be as follows:
>
> Corydon and Thyrsis are traced through four years more of poverty and degradation, during which their health is wrecked and their hopes blasted. Passion dies between them. Thrysis continues to write—'The Higher Cannibalism', a social satire; 'The Genius', a drama portraying a young violinist in the meshes of commercialism. (This play is staged, and is ridiculed by Broadway, but makes a great impression in England and Germany); and finally, 'Social Art, an Essay in the Economic Interpretation of Literature'—a work of revolutionary criticism which causes an international sensation.
>
> But success comes too late to Corydon and Thyrsis; they are dead to joy. Thyrsis becomes a social lion; studies the mammonism of the ruling classes, and sets it forth in a terrific book of satire, "The Exploiters". There his power is ended, his vision is dead; while Corydon is a nervous wreck, on the verge of suicide. She has several sentimental love-adventures, and Thyrsis finally brings her to realise that the only hope is to get a divorce from him, and meet some man who can give her the personal love and daily companionship she needs.
>
> They separate, and the result is an immediate recuperation of Thyrsis'

THE FORUM

THE LEADING AMERICAN REVIEW AND MAGAZINE

Announcement in The Forum

THE FORUM is now issuing its fiftieth volume. It is an appropriate time to invite the attention and criticism of the public.

The Forum makes no appeal to ignorance, or prejudice, or prurience, or incompetence. It is not read by imperfectly educated and imperfectly developed men and women. It *is* read by the thinking, earnest people of the nation; by those who believe in the future of their country, but do *not* believe in waiting with folded hands for progress to overcome the inertia of the sluggish or the crude antagonism of the reactionaries. It is read by those who believe in ideals, but not in ranting; by those who have passed beyond the narrow limits of provincialism in politics, literature, art, and the knowledge of life.

There has been no question as to the place of The Forum in American letters and its value to American life. Addressing perhaps the most intelligent public in the world, and throughout the world, it has opened its pages to the free discussion of all vital topics, while maintaining the only attitude that should now be possible:—To seek, and to speak, the truth; to attack ignorance and prevent the crimes and follies that spring from ignorance; and to attack especially that deadly prudery which, in the name of so-called morality, will tolerate daily the most loathsome practices in every village, town and city in the country, but will *not* tolerate—much less encourage—any sincere effort to bring home to the conscience of humanity a clear realization of the corruption of "civilization" and of the necessity for action,—now, and here.

Steadily, month by month, year by year, The Forum has built up, under its new direction, a position of exceptional influence and interest. Without prejudice or bias, it has led the way in all vital movements,—or strengthened those who were already leading the way,—so that public opinion, now accustomed to truer and saner standards of thought, would be amazed if confronted with the conditions of even a few years ago.

The Forum has published, and will continue to publish, the best work that could be secured, whether the author were world-famous or entirely obscure. More and more, it will develop the policy of diversity of interest, so that it will appeal, not only to the expert, but to every intelligent reader. It will touch every side of experience, and it will print the best essays and articles, the best short stories and plays, and the most significant poetry produced in the country to-day.

After the fullest reflection and comparison, the editors of The Forum claim, deliberately, that no review or magazine in the world has the interest, the influence and the inspiration of The Forum.

Frontispiece for The Fasting Cure *(Courtesy of Lilly Library, Indiana University)*

Mr. Sinclair's expression, as shown in the upper photograph, used to be called "spiritual." Systematic fasting has evolved the athletic figure pictured below.

powers. Corydon meets a young poet with whom she has a remarkable love experience, whereby her whole being is made-over.

The story will be prophetic in its outlook. The characters are left in every way victorious—physically, mentally and morally; they retain all their intimacy and their intellectual and spiritual oneness. In the course of their life they become familiar with many movements—Christian Science, Socialism, Physical Culture, etc., and they study and absorb what is most vital in current literature. The book will be in this way a sort of guide to modern ideas.

The book is obviously, in certain aspects, autobiographical. As to what extent this is the case, the author has nothing to say, nor are his publishers to refer to it—except, of course, to the extent of quoting from published reviews. . . . . It may be well to add that the portion of the book here submitted contains about all that will be open to criticism as to propriety.[45]

Love's Pilgrimage does not attack Sinclair's adulterous wife. Instead, it makes a feminist case for the emotional and intellectual needs of women. The dedication page reads: "To those who throughout the world are fighting for the emancipation of woman I dedicate this woman's book."

Kennerley's letter of acceptance provides an example of his willingness to gamble on the books that appealed to him:

During the last three days I have read the book myself, and consider it a most remarkable and splendid piece of work. My inclination is to publish it, and I should suggest no expurgation whatever on the ground of "legal" morality. It would not interest me to have the opinion of any lawyer on this subject. I think there are two or three trifling sentences that strike a false note, and as they are so rare, I should like to see them deleted. Also, I should like to see you edit the letters to a considerable extent. There is some splendid work in them, but I think that at least half of them could be cut out without interfering with the thought of the story.

I should not, however, care to publish the present manuscript as the first volume of a trilogy, as you suggest in your latest word, but should prefer to bring out the book as a complete work. Do you care to complete the manuscript, and then to let me see it as a whole? "The Song of Songs" by Sudermann, contains over two hundred thousand words, and "It Never Can Happen Again" by William de Morgan, considerably over three hundred thousand, so there would be nothing too extraordinary in publishing a novel containing two hundred and fifty thousand, as you suggest would be the length of your completed novel. I imagine that upon reflection you will see that this is the finer way to issue the book, and from a business point of view, I think it would be the most profitable.

I wish I could see you, and that we could talk the book over. Is there any chance of your being in New York within the next few weeks? I must say at once that I should not care to undertake the publication of the book if you are in the opinion that it is likely to have a large sale. It may have a large sale, but I am most emphatically of the opinion that it is too sincere and tragic to sell more than a few thousand copies. It is not a book that there would be any advantage in booming in a sensational manner, and, in fact, I should not care to publish it if this was necessary.[46]

Despite Kennerley's words of caution, he probably sensed a success de scandal, for he paid Sinclair an advance of $1,250.* The 600-page novel started off selling a thousand copies a week; but when the details of the Sinclairs' divorce and Meta's affair with poet Harry Kemp (who became a Kennerley author) hit the newspapers, sales stopped. Kennerley told Sinclair, "If people can read about you for two cents, they are not going to pay a dollar and a half to do it."[47] In 1912 Kennerley published his final book by Sinclair, *Plays of Protest*, but declined a novel about venereal disease.

Kennerley occasionally took over a book from another publisher and advertised it as his own publication. Two such important titles were the Irish Cuala Press limited editions of William Butler Yeats's *Synge and the Ireland of his Time* (1911) and *The Green Helmet* (1910). The

---

* Kennerley distributed special advance copies of *Love's Pilgrimage* to start word-of-mouth publicity: "This edition is for private circulation only and it is requested that you do not let it out of your possession until actual publication has taken place." Kennerley also distributed an eight-page pamphlet, *Four Letters about Love's Pilgrimage*—consisting of letters to Sinclair from Robert Herrick, Eden Phillpotts, Frederik Van Eeden (who pronounced it "very nearly one of the great books of the world"), and Sinclair's reply to Herrick.

latter was distributed in America with a label stipulating "THIS BOOK IS NOW PUBLISHED BY MITCHELL KENNERLEY."

The most typographically distinguished volume bearing Kennerley's imprint appeared in 1911. The limited edition of H. G. Wells's *The Door in the Wall and Other Stories* was proposed by Alvin Langdon Coburn as a vehicle for his photographs. Kennerley commissioned Goudy to design the book, and sample pages were printed in Caslon type by Norman T. A. Munder. Kennerley's 1924 account follows:

> The specimen pages set by Mr. Munder were excellently done, but a certain feeling of 'openness' in their appearance bothered Mr. Goudy. (He did not then realize that it was the wide fitting of the Caslon that prevented the solid, even effect he was so intent upon securing.) Mr. Goudy explained to me the kind of page he would like. He wanted an appearance in the whole page of more solidity and compactness, but he wanted to secure it without putting any more color in the individual letters than was already in the Caslon shown on the specimens from Mr. Munder. Mr. Goudy knew of no type that seemed to possess exactly this character—those available were either too formal or refined or too free and undignified for use in a book of this sort.
>
> No other solution of our difficulty being at hand, Mr. Goudy suggested the making of a new face which might have its first use in this book and which afterwards might be offered to other printers for their work.* We agreed upon this course of action, and the drawings were begun for the letter now known as 'Kennerley Old Style.'
>
> Mr. Goudy always had been attracted by the type imported by Bishop Fell for use at the Clarendon Press (Oxford) and from it he took his inspiration for the new letter. As the drawing progressed he soon drew away from the pattern letters in his endeavor to modify the old form and give to it a new expression of beauty and usefulness. The drawings were about one inch high and were completed before February 18, 1911.

_____

* Christopher Morley claimed that the Kennerley type face was originally designed for the Kuppenheimer clothing company, which declined it ("The Bowling Green," *Saturday Review of Literature*, 17 [5 March 1938], 14, 18). But Goudy stated that the Kuppenheimer designs became his Village type (*A Village Press Collection Given to Vassar* [Poughkeepsie, 1932]).

By March 25th the type had been cut and cast in the sixteen-point size, and Mrs. Goudy began setting trial pages for the book.

It was here that an interesting fact was disclosed. Mr. Munder's trial pages in Caslon were thirty-eight ems wide and averaged about fourteen words to the line. The new pages set in Kennerley were only thirty-six ems wide (two ems narrower) but the lines contained the same number of words as the longer Caslon lines, and frequently we gained a word or

> Now that I have the clue to it, the thing seems written visibly in his face. I have a photograph in which the look of detachment has been caught and intensified. It reminds me of what a woman once said of

> Now that I have the clue to it, the thing seems written visibly in his face. I have a photograph in which that look of detachment has been caught and intensified. It reminds me of what a woman once said of him—a

syllable without unduly close spacing. The new face was flexible. Its close-fitting quality made it possible to space words closely without loss of legibility. We had devoutly wished for this result but could not be certain of it until the type actually had been cut.

Up to this time the new face had not been named. Mr. Goudy insisted, since the type had its first use in a book of my publishing, and since it was in conference with me that the idea of it was first conceived, that it be named 'Kennerley'—and 'Kennerley' it was. I consented, for I felt certain that I should never be called upon to apologize for any of the misdeeds of my typographic namesake.

Thus was completed our book, 'The Door in the Wall,' and thus came into being a new letter that has gained more friends all over the world in its short lifetime than has any other similar creation of any age. Following its popularity as a foundry type, Kennerley lately has been adapted to use on the Monotype machine, which will mutiply, of course, its influence for good in the realm of modern printing.

. . . .

The making of Kennerley type, as often is the case with creations that are truly great, came about in a most natural and casual way. As the work progressed, inspiration gained impetus—but Mr. Goudy himself did not dream when he had completed his task how fine a thing he had given to the world. Kennerley was the result of an unpremeditated attempt on the part of its designer to correct an effect of looseness in the pages of a book, which effect had been sensed but at the time neither analyzed nor called by name. Eventually it was revealed that the unclassified idea behind Kennerley was both artistic and scientific. As demonstrated in the completed face, it gave us proof that the proper close-fitting of the letters in the words of a page would bring to the page an effect of solidity without blackness, and would correct the openness that detracts from the whole picture, however readable may be the type itself.

It is a big thing to create a type face that may live through centuries. Artists paint pictures, and we look and are pleased; write poems, and we read our way to ecstasy; compose music, and in the listening we are inspired; but a really beautiful type face, that combines simplicity with practicability, that conforms to the untranslatable spirit of its own age, becomes much more a part of the daily life of every one of us than any picture, or poem, or musical composition.[48]

Kennerley Old Style was acclaimed as one of the great original faces produced in America. B. H. Newdigate wrote, "Since the first Caslon began casting type about the year 1724, no such excellent type has been put within the reach of English printers."[49] Goudy, who retained the rights to Kennerley, leased it to the Lanston Monotype Machine Co. and to the Caslon type foundry in England. He later designed Kennerley Italic, Kennerley Bold, Kennerley Bold Italic, and Kennerley Open Caps. Its wide acceptance conferred a sort of immortality on Mitchell Kennerley. The face continues to be widely used, but there is the occasional type catalogue that lists it as "Kennerly." Three days after completing Kennerley Old Style, Goudy designed an entirely new face for the title page and story titles of *The Door in the Wall*, inspired by the lettering in the Roman Forum and accordingly named Forum Title.

As with many of the events in Kennerley's career, it is impossible to be dogmatic about when Kennerley Old Style was actually first used in a book. *The Door in the Wall* is usually credited with this distinction, but it seems clear that Kennerley type was used to print 1911 books that appeared before the Wells volume. Kennerley stated that the first use of the type was in the four-page prospectus printed for *The Door in the Wall*.*

---

* Melbert Cary's *A Bibliography of the Village Press* (New York: The Press of the Woolly Whale, 1938, p. 88) stipulates that Kennerley type was used by Goudy in a 1907 article for *Graphic Arts*, but this journal did not commence publication until

Frederic W. Goudy (Photograph by Clarence H. White)

THE DOOR
IN THE WALL
And Other Stories

BY

H·G·WELLS

ILLUSTRATED
WITH PHOTOGRAVURES FROM
PHOTOGRAPHS BY

ALVIN LANGDON COBURN

NEW YORK & LONDON
MITCHELL KENNERLEY
MCMXI

The Door in the Wall
*(11" by 14½"); the
monogram is in red.*

Six hundred copies of *The Door in the Wall* were printed in November 1911; but publication was delayed by the spoilage of Coburn's
photogravures, which were to be inserted in the books. When the
crate arrived from England, it was discovered that a nail had acciden-
tally been driven through the photogravures. Only three hundred copies were published with all ten illustrations. The remaining copies
were sold with a label explaining the circumstances. Sixty copies of
the Kennerley edition were issued in England in 1915 with Grant
Richards's title page; these numbered copies were signed by both Wells
and Coburn.

The Door in the Wall is a large-format book (11 inches by 14½
inches) on French handmade Glaslan paper. The copies were not numbered, and the colophon does not identify the type face. The book was
executed in the conservative taste that characterized Kennerley's publications. The only use of color is on the title page, where the MK
device is in red. The binding is goldstamped plum-colored boards with
a cloth shelfback and printed label. Copies sold for $7.50—a bargain
even then. (Perfect copies are worth up to $1,000 now.) Wells was
supposed to receive two shillings or 50 cents per copy, but he and
Kennerley quarreled over the royalty. The lavish projects of Kennerley
and other publishers of the time were possible because material and
labor were so cheap. At a guess *The Door in the Wall* cost about $1,000
to produce.

The pressure of Kennerley's activities produced a form of neuras-
thenia, requiring visits to William Muldoon's health camp in 1910 and

---

1911. Cary lists three other 1911 books set in Kennerley: *Verses by Henry Gorlet
McVickar* (privately printed in June), Bliss Carman's *Address to the Graduating Class
MCMXI of the Unitrinian School of Personal Harmonizing Founded by Mary Perry
King* (privately printed in October), and Michael Monahan's *Heinrich Heine* (published by Kennerley). There is a strong probability that *Heinrich Heine* was in fact
the first book published by Mitchell Kennerley from Kennerley Old Style and Forum
types, although it was preceded by the Wells prospectus. The Monahan volume was
copyrighted on 3 November 1911; the Wells on 11 December 1911.

Walter Pater's Conclusion to his book The Renaissance, privately printed for Ken-
nerley by Goudy in 1910, is incorrectly described as printed from Kennerley type in
The Village Press: A Retrospective Exhibition (New York: American Institute of Graphic
Arts, 1933, p. 16).

1911. He was subject to bouts of depression all of his life. Kennerley's inability to maintain his juggling act became especially evident in his deteriorating relationship with Grant Richards, who wrote him for-bearingly: "I think that you treated me very badly when you were in London, but everything has to be forgiven to people of moods and temperaments."[50] Four years of pleading letters were required before Richards received his copies of *The Door in the Wall*; Kennerley dis-regarded Richards's requests for royalty statements; and some of his checks bounced in London. During this period when he neglected his publishing business Kennerley declined Richards's offer of the Amer-ican rights to James Joyce's *Dubliners*.

CHAPTER THREE

D. H. Lawrence—Vachel Lindsay—
Hagar Revelly—The Lyric Year—
Joseph Hergesheimer—Alfred A. Knopf

WHILE KENNERLEY was flourishing—if not prospering—as a publisher, there were significant developments in the rare-book auction field. In 1911 the dominant position of the American Art Association was challenged when the upstart Anderson Galleries secured the library of Robert Hoe. Up to that time, it was believed that major private libraries could be auctioned only in London because American dealers and collectors were insufficiently sophisticated to pay top prices for great books and manuscripts. The Hoe sale made New York a serious contender for the position of rare book center of the world. When Hoe's library was sold at the Anderson Galleries in 1911–1912, it was the richest American book auction to that time, realizing $1,932,056.60. The principal bidder was dealer George D. Smith, representing railroad tycoon Henry E. Huntington, who was commencing his intensive effort to create the Huntington Library. In three years Kennerley's career would be intertwined with the endeavors of Smith and Huntington.

Kennerley was directly involved in another series of Anderson sales in 1912 when the contents of Emilie Grigsby's residence were auctioned. Miss Grigsby was the ward (the term carried an innuendo) of traction magnate Charles T. Yerkes—the model for Theodore Dreiser's Frank Cowperwood—and served as his hostess in New York and England while he was financing the London underground system. She was acclaimed as the most beautiful woman in the world; she collected art and traveled with $800,000 in jewelry; she occupied a building at the corner of Park Avenue and Sixty-seventh Street which the press described as "a house of mystery." She was the convent-educated daughter of a Cincinnati madame. King Edward VII gave her a foot-stool; Pope Leo XIII gave her an indulgence and a lock of his hair; George Meredith and Henry James admired her; Rupert Brooke spent his last night in England at her home. It was alleged that World War I was prolonged because the British generals who weekended at her country home delayed returning to the front.[1]

When Emilie Grigsby was sitting for sculptor Jo Davidson in 1910 Kennerley accompanied her to the Manhattan studio. After Yerkes's death, she decided to move to England and put the contents of her New York residence up at auction. Kennerley was helpful in securing the Grigsby sale for the Anderson Galleries and was hired to promote it. The sale ran for two weeks in 1912 and was an unexpected social and financial success as curiosity about the house of mystery attracted bidders from high and low society. The art and furniture brought $193,067. Her 6,000-volume library realized $13,187—rather more than it was worth because some highly proper personages felt compelled to buy the volumes they had inscribed to her.[2]

While Kennerley was listening to the money songs emanating from the auction galleries, he began to achieve recognition as an innovative literary publisher in 1912. Reviewing Merrick's *The Actor-Manager* in the new *Smart Set*, H. L. Mencken complained about William Dean Howells's hyperbolic introduction: "But, here, of course, I make no charges against Mr. Kennerley, a publisher alert and courageous, who deserves all the help he can get from reviewers."[3]

The most successful 1912 endeavor in terms of exposure for the Kennerley imprint was *The Lyric Year*. Kennerley announced a poetry competition in which three prizes totaling $1,000 would be paid and 100 of the submissions would be published in a volume. The editor was Ferdinand Earle, a wealthy artist and poet, who put up the prize money. His *Sonnets* had been co-published by Kennerley and Elkin

Mathews in 1910. Known in the newspapers as "Soul Mate Earle," he figured in four messy divorces and was later declared insane by the Paris courts after kidnapping his son.[4]

Earle claimed that he examined 10,000 submissions by 2,000 poets before selecting the 100 poems for *The Lyric Year*. The poets published included William Rose Benet, Witter Bynner, Donn Byrne, Bliss Carman, Madison Cawein, John Erskine, Arthur Davidson Ficke, Harry Kemp, Joyce Kilmer, Richard Le Gallienne, Vachel Lindsay, Edwin Markham, Sara Teasdale, Ridgeley Torrence, Louis Untermeyer, John Hall Wheelock, and Willard Huntington Wright. Earle proposed to give first prize to Edna St. Vincent Millay's "Renascence"; but he was outvoted by the other two judges, William Stanley Braithwaite (a Negro who was poetry editor of the *Boston Transcript*) and Edward J. Wheeler (editor of *Current Opinion* and president of the Poetry Society of America). The $500 first prize was awarded to Orrick Johns's "Second Avenue"; the two second prizes of $250 each went to Thomas Augustin Daly's "To a Thrush" and George Sterling's "An Ode for the Centenary of the Birth of Robert Browning." Although Millay came in fourth, the twenty-year-old poet—who had not yet entered Vassar—was launched by her first appearance in a book.

"Renascence" is a 214-line quasi-mystical meditation on God, death, and nature—opening:

> *All I could see from where I stood*
> *Was three long mountains and a wood;*
> *I turned and looked the other way,*
> *And saw three islands in a bay.*

The poet's spiritual development is traced as her death wish is overcome by the reviving power of nature—hence the title, which means rebirth. The poem concludes with a declaration of the inspired soul's power to transcend the limitations of life:

> *The soul can split the sky in two,*
> *And let the face of God shine through.*
> *But East and West will pinch the heart*
> *That cannot keep them pushed apart;*

> *And he whose soul is flat—the sky*
> *Will cave in on him by and by.*

"Renascence" was praised as a profound lyrical achievement; but the iambic tetrameter couplets sound jingly, and the childlike, playful tone is inconsistent with the intended high seriousness of the theme.

Kennerley's ad copy for *The Lyric Year* boasted that "For the first time in the history of American letters, complete expression is given to the whole of the living poetry of the country."[5] It garnered attention for all involved. The $2 book required a second printing* and was called the most important verse anthology published in America; but—inevitably—the judges' qualifications and selections were challenged. Writing in *The Forum* as Charles Vale, Hooley hailed the volume as a literary event and printed a long excerpt from "Renascence." He concluded in a burst of metaphors: "There have been some suspicions that the soul of America was becoming flat, but the sky will not cave in while there are such poets to uphold it, with the stars shining, as *The Lyric Year* reveals."[6] Nonetheless, the volume was not really a salvo in the battle for modern poetry. *The Lyric Year* was freighted with flowery diction along with the free verse. Kennerley announced in August 1912 that annual volumes of *The Lyric Year* would follow, but none appeared.

Kennerley paid Millay $25 in April 1913 for two *Forum* poems and requested a meeting at which he expressed interest in publishing a volume of her verse; she declined because she did not think there were enough strong poems for a book. He invited her to Mamaroneck and gave her a copy of Harris's *The Man Shakespeare*. Millay reported to her family: "He's not old at all, as I thought he would be, about thirty-five or under, & he's a dear, and I'll bet she's a dear, and there are two kiddies."[7]

In the summer of 1912 Kennerley announced that he would henceforth publish a new volume of poetry every month, offering a discount

---

* The second printing was not so identified, but several of the poems were emended between the first and second printings. The printings can be differentiated by the alteration of "careful" to "polite" at page 25, line 11.

to subscribers. These volumes were never developed into a series, and no further announcements were made for the monthly project. But Kennerley issued verse regularly and claimed that he brought out more books of poetry and drama than any other publisher of his time.

During 1912 Kennerley published his first volume by D. H. Lawrence, a novel *The Trespasser*, importing Duckworth's English sheets with his own title page. This account of an affair between an unhappily married musician and his pupil ends in his suicide. Hooley was not impressed: "A clever book, which suggests that the author is worth taking up, without special regard to any individual work."[8] The year's other titles included three by Leonard Merrick along with *Baby's Teeth to the Twelfth Year, The Laws of American Divorce, The Road Map of the Stars* (a fold-out chart of the constellations), *Defense de la Poesie Française a l'usage des Lecteurs Anglais*, and Frank Swinnerton's critical study of George Gissing. Kennerley also developed an interest in photography as art; *Old Chinatown*, a book of Arnold Genthe's photographs, appeared with text by Will Irwin. Genthe became one of Kennerley's close friends, as did photographer Alfred Stieglitz.

As the result of the combination of literary quality and a well-publicized court case, Kennerley became a celebrated publishing figure in 1913. His list for that year had more than fifty titles—including D. H. Lawrence's *Sons and Lovers*, the only novel Kennerley published that has achieved classic status. *Sons and Lovers* was originally published by Duckworth in London; and Kennerley informed Lawrence's English agent Edward Garnett: "I have just finished reading 'Sons and Lovers', and think it is the biggest novel I have read in years. If Mr. Lawrence can keep this up he will surpass all other modern novelists. I do not suppose it will sell to begin with, though sometimes a good book does sell."[9] Kennerley brought out a new American edition at $1.35. An excerpt, "Derelict," was published in *The Forum* for September 1913, and Kennerley advertised the novel more energetically than was his custom. One ad was a statement signed by Kennerley: "I do not ask you to buy it, but I do tell you that 'Sons and Lovers,' by D. H. Lawrence, is one of the great novels of the age."[10] Another ad reproduced a telegram from Jack London: "NO BOOK LIKE IT SPLENDID SAD TREMENDOUS TRUE IT SWEEPS ONE OFF HIS FEET WITH THE POWERFUL HUMAN IMPACT OF IT IN IT ARE THE HEART AND HURT OF

LIFE ALL THAT IS SORDID ALL THAT IS NOBLE ALL BLENT TOGETHER IN THE FLUX OF CONTRADICTORINESS THAT IS SWEET FIRM FRAIL PALPI-TANT HUMAN MAIL ME HIS OTHER BOOKS AND SEND BILL."[11]

Kennerley imported the Duckworth edition of Lawrence's *Love Poems and Others* in 1913, paying 1 pence each for books with the Kennerley title page—about $25 for 100 copies. He informed Duckworth: "As you will readily understand this transaction will prove a loss to me, and I am only taking the books out of courtesy to the author."[12] In 1914 Kennerley followed *Sons and Lovers* with Lawrence's play *The Widowing of Mrs. Holroyd*. Kennerley's edition was the first edition; he printed 1,000 sets of sheets and sold 500 to Duckworth. Lawrence rewrote the play in proof and acknowledged that Kennerley "nobly forbore with me."[13]

When Kennerley acquired American rights to *Sons and Lovers*, he took an option on Lawrence's next two novels for advances of £25 each against 10 percent royalty. Lawrence submitted *The Rainbow* in 1914, but publication was prevented by the writer's wrath at Ken-nerley's failure to make promised payments. Kennerley paid Lawrence $72 in royalties on 600 copies of *The Trespasser* and the £25 advance for *Sons and Lovers*, but made no further remittances. Lawrence asked poet Amy Lowell to intercede: "My agent writes me that he also fails utterly to arouse any echo of response from that gentleman in New York. Tell him about the £25 cheque promised, and the £10 non-valid cheque that came and returned to him, bad penny that it was. Tell him how the hollow of his silence gets bigger and bigger, till he becomes almost a myth."[14] That such a small sum was at issue reinforces the point that Kennerley's publishing operation was never remunerative. Witter Bynner, another author who did not receive royalties, expressed the proper philosophy, acknowledging that Kennerley "spoke near and far of his faith in us and sent uncounted copies of our work to helpful persons in many directions, all the while as troubled by his book-keeping as we were and as wishful as we were that he might, finan-cially, be doing better by us."[15] Kennerley regarded himself as a pub-lisher, not a bookkeeper.

In 1913 Kennerley launched The Modern Drama Series, announcing that "Every country having produced modern plays of genuine merit will be represented." Twelve volumes appeared between 1913 and

1915: Hjalmar Bergstrom, *Two Plays*; Henry Becque, *Three Plays*; Hen-rik Ibsen, *Peer Gynt*; Giuseppe Giacosa, *Three Plays*; Lawrence, *The Widowing of Mrs. Holroyd*; Zoë Akins, *Papa*; Arthur Davison Ficke, *Mr. Faust*; George Bronson-Howard, *The Red Light of Mars*; Leonid Andreyev, *Two Plays*; Lord Dunsany, *Five Plays*; Arthur Schnitzler, *Three Plays*; and Edith Ellis, *Mary Jane's Pa*. Some of these volumes represented the first English-language translations of the plays. The Modern Drama Series was edited by Edwin Bjorkman, whose 1913 critical study *Voices of Tomorrow* bore this dedication page:

> *Dear M. K.:*
> *What makes me dedicate this book to you is neither the faith you showed in my work when others viewed it with complete indifference, nor your generous and faithful friendship, often more mindful of my interests than of your own, but the fact that you seem to me one of those foresighted few who have come to realize that "success in business" is a meaningless term unless used as a symbolical equivalent for "service rendered."*

Kennerley endeavored to boost the series by writing "The Day of the Published Play" for the *New York Times*. After noting that the first book of modern plays he remembered was *Three Plays* by Robert Louis Stevenson and W. E. Henley—given to him by Arnold Bennett in 1892—Kennerley made a bad prediction:

> . . . today the serious literary artist is writing plays with a view solely to publication. In fact, with the notable exception of Bernard Shaw, the best plays written today are being published before they are pro-duced, and more often than not they are not produced at all. . . . There are just as many people looking today for the great American play as for the great American novel, and when it comes it will come in book form. Let us hope that it will come soon![16]

Nonetheless, Kennerley cut himself in on a share of the stage rights of the plays he published. He explained in his cover letter to the contract for Zoë Akins's *Papa* that publication would make her play more attractive to producers. "Of course, if we are both wrong, and a production is not secured, I shall lose money on the book, but I am quite prepared to put all my energies into an effort to secure an offer

Edna St. Vincent Millay

D. H. Lawrence, c. *1915*

Emilie Grigsby by Jo Davidson
(Photo by Steven Tucker; courtesy
of Vassar College Art Gallery)

for you from one of the managers."[17] The Modern Drama Series was disposed of to Little, Brown in 1916.

Hooley's only novel, *John Ward, M. D.*, appeared under his Charles Vale pseudonym in 1913. Kennerley gave it full-page ads in *The Forum* quoting reviews, for he remained convinced that critical notices were crucial to a book's reputation—if not to its sales. The novel went into a second printing but has been forgotten. What was then classified as a "problem novel" (a work of fiction dealing with social questions), its subjects were eugenics and clairvoyance. Dr. Ward has a herditary streak of wild passion, "a taint in the blood"—as well as second sight. When he discovers that Lady Winters, the woman he loves, is also corrupt, he renounces happiness: "There must be no new life, no little form with the taint of devils." In attempting to deal with sexual corruption inoffensively, the novel occasionally becomes puzzling. The psychic element suggests that Hooley may have encouraged Kennerley to publish several works on spiritualism.

An enduring 1913 publication was Vachel Lindsay's first book, *General William Booth Enters Into Heaven and Other Poems*—which, with Millay's *Renascence*, became one of Kennerley's two most important verse volumes. When Kennerley heard about the book from Witter Bynner, he wrote to Lindsay accepting it sight unseen. "Whatever may be in the book I should want to publish it."[18] The title poem launched Lindsay's fame and was a key work in the "New Poetry" movement—verse drawing on American material and employing the sounds of American speech. "Perhaps the most remarkable poem of the decade," declared the *Review of Reviews*; and in *Harper's* William Dean Howells called it "a fine brave poem."[19] "General William Booth Enters Into Heaven" was intended to be sung to the hymn tune for "The Blood of the Lamb" and carried instrumental directions:

> [*Bass drum beaten loudly.*]
> *Booth led boldly with his big bass drum—*
> *(Are you washed in the blood of the Lamb?)*
> *The Saints smiled gravely and they said:*
>   *"He's come."*
> *(Are you washed in the blood of the lamb?)*

Lindsay—who was chronically poor—sent Christopher Morley to plead for his money. Kennerley replied: "Of course I won't pay Lindsay any royalties! He has such disgusting table manners."[20] With the help of a lawyer, Lindsay eventually collected half of his royalties from Kennerley.[21] After one more book with Kennerley, *Adventures While Preaching the Gospel of Beauty* (1914)—which Kennerley described as "the most truly American book I have ever read"[22] and serialized in *The Forum*—Lindsay moved to Macmillan with his most famous work, *The Congo.*

Christopher Morley (1890–1957) was then beginning his career as all-around man of letters: journalist, critic, essayist, poet, novelist, editor, and literary talker. Their friendship lasted for the rest of Kennerley's life—perhaps because Morley never published a book with him. At a lunch Kennerley made one of the sweeping pronouncements he was given to: "No red-headed man ever wrote a good poem." William Rose Benet, who was present, objected, "I would not go that far." Kennerley replied, "I know. That is why I got there first"[23]—followed by the throaty bark which was his laugh. In attempting to analyze Kennerley's character after his death, Morley wrote: "Incredible, enchanting, and remorseless man! Innumerable anecdotes recur to me, of his wit, his malice, his law-unto-himself. . . . he had to dominate or destroy. . . . his astonishing genius as connoisseur and litmus-paper sensitivity to artistic moods, his peremptory & instantaneous reactions—sometimes so disturbing to us of slower minds!"[24] Michael Arlen inscribed a copy of *The Green Hat*: "To Mitchell Kennerley Irony and courtesy—I'd like to be able to write with those qualities."[25]

Kennerley took satisfaction in publishing the first books of young authors. When George P. Brett, head of the Macmillan Company, sent a message that he would be glad to publish the third book by any author whose first two books Kennerley had published, Kennerley replied that he could not return the compliment.[26] The 1913 list included first books by Max Eastman and Walter Lippmann. Kennerley agreed to publish Eastman's *Child of the Amazons and Other Poems* in 1912, correctly predicting that it would not sell the first 500 royalty-exempt copies. The author's letters "begging, beseeching, demanding" publication were ignored; the book did not appear until June 1913. Nonetheless, when Kennerley read Eastman's article "Understanding

Germany" in *Harper's Weekly* he asked him to write a book with that title in 1916. Eastman replied that he didn't know enough about Germany but would like to collect his pieces about the war and world federation. Kennerley agreed to take this volume provided that the title be *Understanding Germany* and that it include a long chapter opposing America's entrance into the war. Uncharacteristically, Kennerley gave him a $600 advance. Eastman later described *Understanding Germany* as "by a man who had never been in Germany, never studied its institutions, never read its history—and moreover wasn't writing about it!"[27]

In *A Preface to Politics*, written at Kennerley's urging, the twenty-three-year-old Lippmann applied Freud to political theory: "The measure of our self consciousness will more or less determine whether we are to be the victims or masters of change." It was serialized in three issues of *The Forum* and published in cloth ($1.50) and paper covers (50¢). *A Preface to Politics* was widely reviewed, and Lippmann became recognized as the spokesman for his generation of radicals. Kennerley advertised it as "The Book That Has Made Politics Interesting!" and prepared two mail-order pieces with excerpts from reviews. Lippmann's second book with Kennerley, *Drift and Mastery: An Attempt to Diagnose the Current Unrest*, followed in 1914, and was praised by Theodore Roosevelt: "No man who wishes seriously to study our present social, industrial and political life can afford not to read it through and through and to ponder and digest it."[28]

Although he was high-handed with his authors, Kennerley regarded it as an act of betrayal for a writer to leave his imprint. In 1916 Lippmann reported to Van Wyck Brooks, who was planning to sue Kennerley for back royalties:

> I never had the least trouble with him on my first two books. His statements came promptly and so did the cheques. He always answered my letters and I really had no cause whatever for complaint. When I left him and took the third book to Holt Kennerley was infuriated and for a year I could get no statement out of him. . . . then a strange thing happened, about ten days ago I received a very cordial letter from Kennerley with a statement covering a whole year but no cheque [the amount due was $384.45]. . . .
>
> I do not believe that you will get very far through the Author's League. I understand that there are any number of complaints filed

against Kennerley and that no action has been successful. In fact I do not believe that there is any author on record who has not been badly treated by Kennerley.[29]

Kennerley maintained his close connections with the London literary scene and in 1913–1914 published five volumes by Richard Middleton, an English poet and story writer who had committed suicide in 1911 at twenty-nine in despair over his poverty. Middleton's best-known work was *The Ghost Ship*, for which Arthur Machen provided the introduction.

In the spring of 1913 Kennerley brought out *Hagar Revelly*, a novel by Daniel Carson Goodman, a physician and "social hygienist," whose *Unclothed* (1912) had also been published by Kennerley. The history of two sisters compelled to support themselves in New York, *Hagar Revelly* contrasts the vain Hagar with the high-principled Thatah. Hagar resists the seductions of her employer, Greenfield; but it is a near thing:

> And she, utterly helpless in his grasp, intoxicated by the cataclysmic enormity of her first real entrance into the secrets of sexual passion, clung to him, returning throb for throb, pulsation for pulsation; while through the light fabric of her thin skirts she could feel the warmth of his body penetrate into her own.[30]*

She subsequently becomes pregnant by another man ("The next instant they were struggling desperately in each other's arms, and a moment later he had won her.") who abandons her. Thatah raises Hagar's child and ultimately wins the good man Hagar wants to marry. Thus virtue is rewarded and selfishness is punished. Goodman's prose is earnestly moralizing, as in the conclusion:

> Dare we further dog-ear the pages of Hagar's life?
> Is it within our province to analyze and dissect the comedy of fate and circumstance—to approach life with lens and forceps, as though it were a magnified Proteus, and, when it suits our fancy, to pinch off an

---

* This passage was rewritten when the novel was reprinted by Macaulay in 1914.

inquisitive pseudopodia from the protozoan bulk, to hold aloft for the appreciation of fellow students?

Who shall take the divine prerogative in dispensing rewards to those spent in travail—to those who must needs traverse the labyrinth of life's doldrums? In the idea of the parable, the good are rewarded—the bad made to suffer. But is justice so dispensed? Can reward dripping hot from the pen always finish the story? . . .

We live on hopes, expectations—hanging speculatively in mid-air over the abyss . . . tight-rope walkers on the road to destiny. Only with our eyes far ahead are we able to keep to the present task. Dare we, then, revert our gaze to a faltering fellow-traveller?

Experience teaches more than meditation. The abyss gaped deep and shadow filled. Had not Hagar peered into its depths?

In addition to expounding his views on sexual morality, Goodman discoursed on the economic plight of female shop clerks.

Hagar Revelly can be described as a tepid version of Dreiser's *Sister Carrie*. It attracted no particular attention upon publication. Reedy declared in his *Mirror*: "Coming as it does at mid-stroke of six o'clock, the publisher should dispose of about 978,562 copies in no time—provided the department stores will handle such a document *ex parte* against themselves. In its kind, as art, it is the best yet."[31] In August Kennerley ran an ad in *Publishers' Weekly* quoting a letter from muck-raker Ida M. Tarbell: "You have found out a secret more difficult than why girls go wrong, and that is why thousands upon thousands of girls go right in spite of hardship and work and sacrifices of every kind. I don't remember ever to have seen in any literature a more truthful presentation of the real reasons why some girls go wrong and others do not than you have worked out in 'Hagar Revelly.' "[32] Kennerley advertised the novel energetically, and by August his ads claimed that it was in its third printing.

On 23 September 1913 Anthony Comstock, Secretary of the Society for the Suppression of Vice, arrived at 2 East Twenty-ninth Street with a policeman and a federal marshal. Earlier in the year Comstock had threatened to suppress "September Morn"—thereby selling hundreds of thousands of prints of the shivering naked damsel. William Cleary, the bookshop clerk, was arrested on a Magistrate's warrant for selling an immoral book. Acting in his capacity as a Post Office inspector,

Comstock arrested Kennerley on a federal complaint charging that he "did unlawfully, willfully, and knowingly deposit or cause to be deposited in the mails of the United States for the purpose of mailing and delivering a certain book entitled 'Hagar Revelly.' "[33] All the copies of *Hagar Revelly* in the shop were confiscated as well as the 2,000 copies at the bindery. Cleary's bail was set at $500 and Kennerley's at $1,500. In similar cases publishers had paid the fine and withdrawn the book. *Hagar Revelly* was the first American novel defended in court by its publisher. After putting up bail, Kennerley announced to reporters:

> It is absurd. The book has been praised on all sides by competent critics as a strong piece of fiction and one deserving of praise. I published "Hagar Revelly" in January, 1913, at the time of the height of the discussion relating to low wages paid in department stores and its effect on the morality of the girls employed.
>
> The book is the life history of two girls, sisters, one Hagar Revelly and the other Thatah Revelly, and it portrays Thatah as a girl of high character and Hagar as a girl of unmoral nature. If a young girl read this book from beginning to end and was asked its effect upon her, she would undoubtedly reply that the book had brought her to tears, and to an awful sense of the danger of life to an unthinking girl who had to make her own way. The fact that the girl of right instincts, with knowledge of the world but without money, can go straight is the shining thread that runs throughout the book.
>
> 'Hagar Revelly' can only offend those who have not passed beyond the narrow limits of provincialism in politics, literature, art, and knowledge of life. I have received no complaint regarding the book from any source whatever, but have received letters from all over the country commending its publication. Mr. Comstock's action was a complete surprise to me and the only way in which I can explain the action is by his own confession that he has not read the book through.
>
> We will demand that the book be read throughout from cover to cover by the jury. This may entail some hardship upon the jury, for the story is a long one, but we are determined that the work shall not be judged by a half dozen carefully culled paragraphs.[34]

Interviewed by the press, Goodman—who was never charged—declared that "The picture of the whole book is to teach young girls that vice, though glittering, ends in misery and unhappiness. . . ."[35]

Reedy's Mirror editorialized in October under the heading "Immorality's Fons et Origo":

> For publishing Dr. Daniel Carson Goodman's novel, "Hagar Revelly," Mr. Mitchell Kennerley has been arrested at the instance of Anthony Comstock. The book is not immoral. It surely will not lead any girl or boy astray. Indeed, if they read it, they will be better able to avoid the attractions of vice. They will see plainly *Hagar's* miserable finish, as the loose wife of a characterless husband. But why argue about the subject? The prosecution of Mr. Kennerley will boom the book. The Comstockians afflict us to oscitancy. If they were people who could think, they would see that there's more insidious incitement to immorality in one volume of pragmatism than there could be in a hundred "Hagar Revellys." Teach people that that is truth which is useful and they will apply the philosophy on a solely hedonistic, sensual and selfish level of action. Bad philosophy is the great generator of bad morals. "Hagar Revelly" is a demonstration against pragmatism, the survival of the fittest and all that. If we are going to strike at immorality, the jails will be bulging with modern, practical philosophers. Beside them, the most salacious novelists are the veriest innocents.[36]

A Federal Grand Jury indicted Kennerley, and on 2 December Judge Learned Hand of the U.S. District Court dismissed a demurrer to the indictment, on the ground that a jury was required to pass on the moral character of a book; under the Hicklin rule a judge could decide only that a book is so clearly innocent that it should not be brought to a jury, which Hand declined to do.* But Judge Hand's opinion went on to question the Hicklin rule, thereby preparing the way for the *Hagar Revelly* trial to become a test case in the law of obscenity:

> . . . I hope it is not improper for me to say that the rule as laid down, however consonant it may be with mid-Victorian morals, does not seem to me to answer to the understanding and morality of the present time,

---

* In 1868 Lord Chief Justice Cockburn ruled in the *Queen* v. *Hicklin* and *The Confessional Unmasked*: "I think the test of obscenity is this, whether the tendency of the matter charged as obscenity is to deprave and corrupt those whose minds are open to such immoral influences, and into whose hands a publication of this sort may fall." The Hicklin rule therefore tested obscene publications in terms of not the general reader, but the abnormal reader.

as conveyed by the words, "obscene, lewd, or lascivious." I question whether in the end men will regard that as obscene which is honestly relevant to the adequate expression of innocent ideas, and whether they will not believe that truth and beauty are too precious to society at large to be mutilated in the interests of those most likely to pervert them to base uses. Indeed, it seems hardly likely that we are even to-day so lukewarm in our interest in letters or serious discussion as to be content to reduce our treatment of sex to the standard of a child's library in the supposed interest of a salacious few, or that shame will for long prevent us from adequate portrayal of some of the most serious and beautiful sides of human nature.

. . . To put thought in leash to the average conscience of the time is perhaps tolerable, but to fetter it by the necessities of the lowest and least capable seems a fatal policy.[37]

Cleary was fined $50 in December. In pronouncing sentence Judge Moss of the Court of Special Sessions stated: "You are only the clerk, and if we had the publisher of the book we would not have dealt so leniently with him. This book is obscene and filthy."[38]

Kennerley's trial opened on 5 February 1914 at the Criminal Branch of the U.S. District Court before Judge Thomas. Assistant U.S. District Attorney John N. Boyle prosecuted; Kennerley was defended by John Quinn and John L. Lockwood. Quinn, who was in charge of the courtroom trial, was a brilliant lawyer as well as a prominent collector of books and modern art. On the opening day Judge Thomas refused to hear the testimony of the literary experts Quinn and Kennerley had assembled: Norman Hapgood (editor of *Harper's Weekly*), Prof. Jeremiah Jenks of New York University, J. B. Kerfoot (literary editor of *Life*), and Leonard Abbott (literary critic for *Current Opinion*). Thomas ruled that the hypothetical questions prepared for these witnesses by Quinn dealt with facts, of which the jurors were to be the judges. Quinn was then denied permission to submit to the jury for purposes of comparison passages from Milton, Shakespeare, Dryden, and Scott.[39]

When the trial resumed on the second day, the courtroom was crowded with literary figures and suffragettes, including Mrs. Ines Milholland Boissevain, Edwin Bjorkman, George Cram Cooke, Susan Glaspell, B. W. Huebsch, and Francis Hackett. Most had copies of *Hagar Revelly* and turned the pages as Quinn and Boyle read passages to the jury. The jurors had been provided with the novel and were urged to read it by both the prosecution and defense. In addition to arguing that *Hagar Revelly* was a novel of moral purpose, Quinn attacked Comstock: "The man who brought this charge possessed a filthy mind. Honi soit qui mal y pense." In summation Quinn reminded the jury that the felony charged against Kennerley was punishable by a long prison term and a heavy fine. The District Attorney argued that the novel possessed no literary merit, that it was boring and had been written only to make money; he claimed that in engaging in the commercial enterprise of publication Kennerley was "either unmoral or unconsciously immoral."[40]

The trial closed on the third day, 9 February. In charging the jurors Judge Thomas reaffirmed the validity of the Hicklin rule and invited them to bring in a guilty verdict: "So you will see from this rule that it is not a question for you to determine whether this book would tend to corrupt the morals of any one of you or of the Court or of counsel. . . . but of determining whether or not it might be injurious to the morals of any person. If it would then it is obscene under the statute."[41] After deliberating for five and one-half hours the jury brought in the unexpected verdict of not guilty. Helen Kennerley rushed forward to congratulate her husband, and Kennerley was surrounded by his literary friends. Later he made a statement for the press:

> I am delighted with the verdict, but I am not surprised. At no time have I felt I was on trial, but rather my lawyers were on trial. I feel that Mr. Quinn and Mr. Lockwood, my attorneys, have handled my case magnificently, and I am very grateful to them.[42]

He added that he planned to resume sale of *Hagar Revelly*.

After the verdict the *New York Evening Post* editorialized that Kennerley's case was undoubtedly aided by his reputation as a courageous publisher of works "with considerable merit but of little promise as best-seller."[43] It is dubious that the members of the jury would have been so well informed. B. W. Huebsch, a small publisher of advanced literature—who had unsuccessfully attempted to have the Booksellers' League of New York pass a resolution protesting the proceedings against Kennerley[44]—wrote a letter to *Publishers' Weekly* calling attention to the significance of the trial:

> Mr. Kennerley was prosecuted for publishing and mailing a book in which freedom of expression went no further than in a hundred novels of the past decade. Nobody seriously denied that it possessed both literary merit and social significance. It would have been a simple matter for Mr. Kennerley to plead guilty (following precedents in the cases of booksellers) and pay a fine, but to his credit he chose the difficult, hazardous, and expensive alternative of standing trial. His acquittal by a jury is a vindication of a free press and a triumph for democracy. Specifically the case concerned Mr. Kennerley alone, but actually he fought for a principle and thus made every American publisher his debtor.[45]

Huebsch had published his first list in 1906—the same year that Kennerley began. Although Huebsch took over D. H. Lawrence after Kennerley lost him, the two publishers remained on good terms. Huebsch won what Kennerley squandered; his imprint enjoyed literary distinction, authorial loyalty, and solvency.

Despite his statement to the press, Kennerley made no effort to capitalize on the publicity afforded *Hagar Revelly*. In 1914 Kennerley sold *Hagar Revelly* to the Macaulay Company, a publisher of inexpensive reprints, which bowdlerized the text. There were at least half a dozen titles originally published by Kennerley on the Macaulay list, suggesting that he sold the plates for ready money. Goodman subsequently sued Kennerley for $20,575, claiming that more than 100,000 copies of *Hagar Revelly* had been sold, for which he had received only $372 in royalties (corresponding to sales of 2,755 copies).[46] The outcome is unknown, but Goodman's sales figure is unlikely. Goodman left the practice of medicine for screenwriting and became a movie executive. In October 1914 Quinn was trying to collect his $1,000 fee. Kennerley promised to send $500 in November with a note for the balance.[47]

In August 1913—before the *Hagar Revelly* trial—Kennerley leased the six-story building at 32 West Fifty-eighth Street for fifteen years at an aggregate rent of $200,000 and began renovating it into the Mitchell Kennerley Building. The basement and first floor were to be his new publishing premises; the upper floors were rented as apartments or offices. Alfred A. Knopf, eighteen months out of Columbia University, who was employed as Kennerley's general factotum in 1914 at $25 per week, has described the ambience at the Mitchell Kennerley Building.[48] The receptionist was a former mistress Kennerley hadn't been able to get rid of; and Walter Lippmann asked Knopf, "Who's that woman who's always in heat?" The waiting room was sometimes occupied by creditors, whom Kennerley would take to lunch—but not pay. There was a procession of women into Kennerley's office, and an upstairs apartment was utilized as a love nest. One of the employees was Braxton Grigsby, Emilie's "broken-down brother," and Kennerley had her nude photo on his desk.[49] Miss Grigsby may have subsequently sued to recover money from Kennerley.[50] Although the Little Book-Shop Around the Corner had been sold in 1912 to Laurence Gomme and Donald Vaughan, Kennerley still planned to combine publishing with a literary salon. In the fall of 1914 he started a series of informal Sunday afternoon gatherings in his Fifty-eighth Street office, at which the press and others were invited to meet authors. The series opened with a reading by Vachel Lindsay, followed by an afternoon with Frank Harris lecturing on David Graham Phillips.[51]

One of the callers at Fifty-eighth Street was Belle da Costa Greene, director of the Pierpont Morgan Library and one of the most respected figures in the rare-book world. A formidable scholar, she had become Morgan's librarian at twenty-two in 1905. Described as the "outrageous" or the "exotic" Belle Greene, she was the veteran of many affairs, numbering Bernard Berenson among her lovers. Her background was obscure; but her dark complexion prompted speculation that she was part Negro, about which she freely joked. Since Kennerley's receptionist resented her, Miss Greene usually waited in a cab for him. Kennerley would announce his departure by saying that he was going to the Biltmore Baths. By 1914 Kennerley had begun quietly to deal in rare books, selling a Walt Whitman collection to the Morgan Library for $600.[52]

Alfred Knopf's duties included going on the road to sell books, but he was frustrated by Kennerley's apparent indifference to sales. Kennerley didn't promote *Sons and Lovers* as hard as Knopf thought it deserved and countermanded Knopf's plans to "sell the guts out of

Hagar Revelly"[53] after it was cleared in court. Knopf believed that John Quinn advised Kennerley not to push it. After Knopf had experienced his own censorship problems, he decided that Kennerley had been right in declining to take advantage of the trial publicity: ". . . if a book of no importance in an artistic or literary sense . . . was attacked, you couldn't continue to sell it except as a dirty book, willy-nilly."[54]

In Knopf's view Kennerley "had no real competition in really good books, in distinguished books, especially by younger people"; but he wasted his opportunities by alienating promising authors over royalties while treating undeserving authors "with the utmost generosity."[55] When Harris hosted a large and expensive lunch at the St. Regis Hotel, he handed the bill to Kennerley, who accepted it without demur. Knopf's final assessment was that Kennerley was "a damn bad publisher" and had "no influence at all on the writers of the day."[56] Nonetheless, Knopf acknowledged that he learned valuable lessons about book production during his apprenticeship with Kennerley: "I became associated with a man who had a very fine sense of typography and of sound conservative book-making."[57]

Kennerley passed up the chance to publish Theodore Dreiser in 1914. *The Titan*—the second volume of the Cowperwood trilogy, based on Charles Yerkes—had been written under a contract from Harper; but Harper halted production after announcing the novel, anticipating censorship. Knopf, who was about to start working for Kennerley, obtained a set of the proofs from Dreiser and hoped to persuade Kennerley to take over publication. Knopf informed Dreiser that "MK was personally rather close to Yerkes—so he's interested—See?"[58] Whether or not Kennerley was actually Yerkes's friend, the problem was that Bernice Fleming, Cowperwood's mistress in *The Titan*, was obviously drawn from Emilie Grigsby. Dreiser complained to H. L. Mencken: "Mitchell Kennerley tells Knopf that I have handled Emily Grigsby in a cheap, slanderous & sensational way, rehashing old fables. In justice to her he could not publish it."[59] Mencken replied, "The impertinence of the fellow makes me laugh. He was scared stiff by the 'Hagar Revelly' affair."[60] *The Titan* was published by John Lane in New York and London, although Kennerley attempted to dissuade Lane: "I presume that by now you have made inquiry of Chapman, and learned from him that the friend to whom I referred is Miss Grigsby. I am sure that in England 'The Titan' is a libel on her, and I should not at all be surprised to see her start action against the publisher."[61] She wisely kept quiet. Knopf also touted W. H. Hudson's *Green Mansions*, which Kennerley declined to publish but allowed him to import "a few sheets" of Hudson's *Adventures Among Birds* in 1915. *Green Mansions* became Knopf's first success when he set up his own publishing house.

Kennerley published some sixty titles in 1914, his largest list. The catalogue elicited a paean from Bliss Carman:

> Many thanks for your poem! The vulgar world call it a catalogue; but Pan recognizes it as the Young Shepherd's Calendar, a record of ambition, produced with heart's blood and burning.
>
> You have done a lot of things for which you will get neither pennies nor thanks (hardly)—nothing but the commendation of your own best self and a few who care for you and for good things in books. You have tried to make publishing something more than a bare commercial enterprise. If the result seems very small and the returns in kind very meagre, don't lament! The artist gets very little beside the affection and loyalty of his friends. You always have that. And for the rest, let us hope that the really paying books will come in in sufficient numbers to make up for all these luxuries you have allowed yourself—Such as Daughters of Dawn and Earth Deities.
>
> The said Daughters and Deities are certainly appreciative of your gift of a little life in this vast world of books.[62]

Daughters of Dawn (1913) and *Earth's Deities* (1914) were verse drama collaborations by Carman and Mary Perry King espousing François Delsarte's Unitrinianism—a philosophy of education based on the rhythms of music, dance, and poetry. These publications, which could not have been commercially promising, were expressions of Kennerley's affection for Carman.

The most important first novel on the 1914 list was Joseph Hergesheimer's *The Lay Anthony*. Hergesheimer had been unsuccessfully writing for fourteen years when his work was accepted by *The Forum*. Kennerley expressed interest in seeing a novel by Hergesheimer, who submitted *The Lay Anthony*. The letter of acceptance sounded the

Adventures while Preaching
The Gospel of Beauty
by
NICHOLAS VACHEL LINDSAY

In the summer of 1912 Mr. Lindsay walked from his home town, Springfield, through Missouri and Kansas, up and down Colorado and into New Mexico. His rules were "to have nothing to do with cities, railroad money, baggage or fellow-tramps. Such wages as I made I sent home, starting out broke again, spending just enough for one day's recuperation out of each pile. . . I always walked penniless. My baggage was practically nil."

For his board and lodging, when he didn't help harvest, he offered "Rhymes to Be Traded For Bread" with the Gospel of Beauty that it contained.

And this new book is simply Mr. Lindsay's story of that extraordinary walk with an account of the various adventures that befell him and with a number of charming poems interspersed.

MITCHELL KENNERLEY 🟡 PUBLISHER NEW YORK

Dust jacket, Adventures while Preaching the Gospel of Beauty

Belle da Costa Greene

familiar warnings. It is customary for a publisher to advise a fledgling novelist not to expect wealth and fame; nonetheless, Kennerley's claim that he was willing to lose money on books was truthful.

> I have read "The Lay Anthony" and congratulate you upon an un-usual achievement. I wish that we could talk over the question of its publication, as I am afraid that my proposal to you may sound somewhat crude in writing. First of all, I should like to publish your book, but it is extremely likely that it would have a very small sale, and it is almost certain that the book will be a financial loss to me.
>
> I am quite willing that this should be so, but I do not want there to be any chance of your being disappointed. Your book may "catch on", but the chances are against it. I will do all I can for it, and will at least promise you a large number of reviews, and I am quite sure that the majority of them will be favorable. But reviews do not sell many copies of a book. The large public is utterly undiscriminating, and buys only books which are popular, or supposed to be popular.[63]

Kennerley hedged his bet by exempting the first thousand copies from royalty payment.*

The Lay Anthony recounts Tony Ball's attempts to live up to his fraudulent reputation as a voluptuary and then to live it down. Mencken—who became a strong Hergesheimer supporter—pro-nounced judgment: "In brief, the book is botched in the writing; the author's planning is far ahead of his execution. But let us at least remember him as one who made a creditable attempt. Novels with genuine ideas in them are not so common that we can afford to sniff at them."[65] The ads for *The Lay Anthony* featured a signed statement by Kennerley:

> Instead of trying to describe this book, I prefer to tell you why I am publishing it.
>
> Chiefly because I believe that "The Lay Anthony" is a fine piece of work. To me it has in some measure the great qualities of Meredith's

---

* The contract for *The Lay Anthony* stipulated no royalties on the first 1,000 copies, 10 percent of list price on the next twenty copies, and 15 percent thereafter. It is virtually certain that "twenty copies" was an error for "twenty thousand copies."[64]

"Richard Feverel." My first reader's report was in part as follows: "I announce to you a great book; a book beautiful, noble, thrilling. It has held my feebleness awake all night and left me tingling so I can scarce write steadily . . . . could anyone, any normal person, read it coldly? No, it has the grip, the thrill." And from my second reader: "A truly remarkable book . . . . a romance of young love handled with distinction and grace." This man thought it too good to sell. Then I read "The Lay Anthony"; and knew that it must be published. A fourth reader, as enthusiastic as any of the others, is convinced that the book *will* sell: he feels that readers will be quick to take advantage of an exciting story, well told, that happens in addition to have two perfectly stunning heroines as well as to possess many of the qualities of great literature.[66]

The Lay Anthony was not a strong seller; but Kennerley published Hergesheimer's second novel, *Mountain Blood* (1915), and accepted "God's Cabaret"—which never appeared under that title—before the customary royalty disputes terminated their relationship.

Frank H. Simonds's *The Great War: The First Phase* (1914) was announced as the first American history of World War I. According to Kennerley, he commissioned the book after reading Simonds's *New York Evening Sun* editorials on the assassination at Sarajevo. It was followed by *The Great War: The Second Phase* in 1915. Doubleday, Page then signed Simonds for an illustrated history of the war. Kennerley brought suit against the publisher; and Doubleday, Page settled for $4,000—before the judge decided in their favor.

The Kennerley imprint became identified with Walt Whitman in 1914, partly as a result of Kennerley's connection with Whitman disciple Horace Traubel. The *Complete Leaves of Grass* was published in four formats from a 60-cent paperbound "Popular Edition" to a $2.50 "India Paper Edition" in leather; the *Complete Prose* was published in a "Library Edition" and a "Popular Edition." That year Kennerley also published Basil de Selincourt's *Walt Whitman: A Critical Study*. His most ambitious Whitman project was Traubel's *With Walt Whitman in Camden*. Traubel had written out his conversations with Whitman commencing in 1888 and preserved documents relating to Whitman. Kennerley took over the first two volumes of *With Walt Whitman in Camden*—published by Small, Maynard in 1906 and by Appleton in 1908—and published the third volume in 1914 at $3. He announced that the work would be completed in eight volumes; but no further volumes appeared because Kennerley ran out of money. In 1915 he asked Traubel to arrange a loan from one of Whitman's wealthy admirers:

> I never tried to borrow from a Bank and have therefore no credit for that purpose at any New York Bank today. I usually borrow from a relative when I am in need but all their money is in Saving Banks subject to ninety days call. . . . I want to borrow anywhere from one to five thousand dollars for four months and will gladly pay 8% per annum. My business is worth $80,000 net and I am insured for $15,000.[67]

Still looking for a dependable money-maker, Kennerley published three books by English novelist John Trevena (Ernest George Henham) in 1914: *Granite*, *Sleeping Waters*, and *Wintering Hay*. Samuel Butler was represented by three imports, including his influential *Note-Books*. *Forum Stories* edited by Charles Vale, a collection of sixteen stories reprinted from *The Forum*, was an attempt "to do for the American short story what 'The Lyric Year' did for American verse."[68] The volume made no impact because the writers were unimportant—except for John Reed, whose fame depends on his activities in the Russian Revolution.

The first of the four Kennerley volumes "written down by" spiritualist Elsa Barker appeared in 1914, *Letters from a Living Dead Man*. Identified in the book as X, the correspondent from beyond the grave was subsequently revealed as Judge David P. Hatch, who died in 1912. Kennerley claimed that this book required four printings. The epistolary spirit communicated two more books to Barker: *War Letters from the Living Dead Man* (1915)—in which the Judge declared, "When I tell you the story of this war as seen from 'the other side' you will know more than all the chancelleries of the Nations"—and *Last Letters from the Living Dead Man* (1919).

In March 1915 the Mitchell Kennerley Publishing Company was incorporated with a capital of $135,000. The incorporators were Arthur Hooley, A. Jocelyn, H. McGrath, and Kennerley; Jocelyn and McGrath have not been identified. The 1915 list was reduced to forty titles. Confessional works that generated attention—but not large sales—

were Donald Lowrie's *My Life Out of Prison* (sequel to *My Life in Prison*, 1912) and Robert Steele's *One Man*. Steele's memoir in novel form was recommended by Mencken, who titled it and performed some editorial work. The dust jacket carried Mencken's declaration that "I have never read a more remarkable story" along with his long flap blurb. Steele was the pseudonym of R. A. Lindsay who related his life of theft, drink, and venery. Mencken reviewed it in *The Smart Set* as "one of the most absorbing human documents ever published in America. . . . autobiography almost unbelievably cruel and betraying, autobiography that is as devoid of artistic sophistication as an operation for gall-stone."[69] The force of the work, Mencken asserted, derived from the circumstance that the author "is simply too stupid, too ingenuous, too moral to lie. He is the very reverse of the artist; he is a born and incurable Puritan—and in his alleged novel he draws the most faithful and merciless picture of an American Puritan that has ever got on paper."[70] Mencken's case for *One Man* was based on what the author inadvertently revealed, for the writing is sentimental and burdened with appeals to God's mercy. The book sold about 5,000 copies (of which the first thousand carried no royalty) before Kennerley let it go out of print; but Mencken clung to his conviction as late as 1919: "To this day I marvel that so dramatic, so penetrating and so curiously moving a story should have failed so overwhelmingly. . . ."[71] Lindsay published nothing else.

It was customary for publishers to develop multiple series—often inexpensive lines that drew upon their backlists. Kennerley had the respected Modern Drama Series; and in 1915 he launched the Railroad Novels, consisting of three titles: John Selborne's *The Thousand Secrets*, Winifred Graham's *Can a Man Be True?* and a resuscitated 1911 novel, W. Holt White's *The Man Who Dreamed Right*. The Railroad Novels promptly expired. Another stillborn project of 1915 was Kennerley's attempt to publish *The Giant's Thumb*, a volume of verse by diabolist Aleister Crowley ("The Great Beast"). It is not known what prevented publication; but given Crowley's reputation for depravity, fear of suppression may have been involved. The volume survives only in a single set of page proofs printed in London.[72]

During 1915 John Quinn and Ezra Pound were discussing a new literary journal to be financed by Quinn. Pound's assessment of Ken-

nerley as a possible publisher for the project was that *The Forum* was
too old-fashioned:

> Now about Kennerley. He has got a bad name (very likely undeservedly)
> for not paying his bills. He paid me in two cases, in a third he held up
> the stuff for two or three years and then paid, so I have no personal
> grumble, save that he is stuck, dead, in the nineties and that he likes
> to keep people waiting two hours in his shop for the sake of making
> himself seem important WHICH HE AINT, NOT IN THE LEAST.[73]

After some fourteen months with Kennerley, Knopf decided to go
into publishing on his own: "I learned how not to publish by working
for Kennerley. . . . I think that if Mitchell had been honest, I never
would have become a publisher."[74] This remark is disingenuous. Knopf
was ambitious and had strong literary enthusiasms that he was eager
to back. His role as Kennerley's underling did not satisfy him. The
elegantly tailored Knopf was described as resembling a prince from a
Persian miniature; two princes in one office may have been too many.
The formal break was made in a letter on 21 May 1915:

> Dear Mr. Knopf:
> I am writing you this letter to prevent any possible misunderstanding.
> When you told me some weeks ago that you had decided to become
> a publisher, specializing in Russian literature, I felt that you had made
> a wise and fortunate decision; and in spite of my regret at losing the
> value of your services I was very glad for your sake. I realized that on
> the small capital at my command I was unable to run the kind of business
> that would satisfy your ambitions or be able to pay you a salary justified
> by your ability.
> Out of regard for the splendid service which you have rendered me,
> and my personal feeling toward you, I was quite willing that you should
> use my time and offices during the early stages of your preparations.
> Now I am coming to the real point of this letter, and it is one which
> has caused me more concern and disappointment than I like to confess
> to. Some weeks ago when looking on your desk for a proof I came across
> a letter from Mr. Hergesheimer. I consider that all letters addressed to
> this office by anyone with whom we have business relations belongs to
> me, even if for the sake of momentary convenience it is addressed per-
> sonally to an individual. I read Mr. Hergesheimer's letter and was

Mitchell Kennerley and Bliss Carman (Photo by John Drinkwater; courtesy of Vassar College Library)

Alfred A. Knopf

shocked to find that you were negotiating with him for the publication by you of a book by him. I did not speak to you about it at the time for two reasons: one a selfish one that I had more important matters on my mind at the time, and the other that I did not wish to act hastily. During the last two weeks I have given very careful consideration to the question, and cannot bring myself to see in your negotiations with Mr. Hergesheimer other than a betrayal of confidence which makes it impossible for you to remain with me any longer. I am therefore going to ask you to resign your position with me to take effect immediately upon receipt of this letter.

I am quite willing to believe that in your negotiations with Mr. Hergesheimer you had no feeling of impropriety. The one thing I have always given and demanded has been absolute loyalty between an employer and employee. I have never been happy over using the printed cards which you brought to us from Doubleday, Page & Company, and you will remember at the time that I pointed this out to you.

I shall not show this letter to anyone, and I want you to believe that it is written without any ill feeling on my part. I shall watch your career with great interest, and if there is anything I can do for you at any time I shall only be pleased to do it. You have been of great service to me, and that is all that I shall care to remember.

Before leaving tomorrow will you please place on file in the office, or if necessary destroy, all letters - including personal ones - that may have come to you in connection with your association with my business. I should not like any letters addressed to me to go out of my possession, similar, for instance, to Mr. Edson's letter to Doubleday, Page & Company.

Yours faithfully,
Mitchell Kennerley.[75]

Knopf had twelve weeks' back pay coming to him. His publication of Hergesheimer's *The Three Black Pennys* in 1917 was their first joint success.* Speculation about what might have been achieved by a Kennerley & Knopf partnership is intriguing. Within three years Knopf was beating Kennerley at his own publishing game.

---

* In 1917 Knopf negotiated with Kennerley for Hergesheimer to purchase the printing plates of *The Lay Anthony* and *Mountain Blood* for $250. Hergesheimer also offered to accept the bound copies and sheets for both titles in lieu of the $70 royalties owed him.[76]

PART III

THE ANDERSON GALLERIES, 1915–1929

CHAPTER FOUR

The Anderson Galleries—George D. Smith—
Henry E. Huntington—Jap Herron—
Edna St. Vincent Millay—Spectra

MITCHELL KENNERLEY was named president of the Anderson Galleries in 1915, when he was thirty-seven. Although books continued to appear with his imprint, publishing became an avocation rather than his main occupation. Kennerley had no experience in the auction business—apart from his role in the 1912 Grigsby sale—but he enjoyed a wide reputation as a bibliophile. Moreover, he was regarded as an able promoter and a man who knew everybody in the book world. These attributes recommended him to the owners of the Anderson Galleries, which was challenging the supremacy of the American Art Association. It was rumored that Belle Greene's influence as a buyer for the Morgan Library was a factor in Kennerley's appointment.

Although the rationale for auctions is simple—the highest bidder gets the item—in practice there are many opportunities for chicanery. The most common form of fraud is "picking bids off the chandelier," when the auctioneer calls out phantom bids to drive up the price.*

---

* This practice led to an investigation of the principal New York and London auction houses in 1985 when it was discovered that paintings were being announced as sold at high prices when in fact they had not been sold. The galleries involved claimed that they were protecting the market.

One auctioneer of the Twenties remarked that he needed only three bidders: a live one and two posts. It is difficult to prevent the running up of prices because of three auction practices. The common custom of bidding by prearranged signal makes it impossible to verify the bidding. One dealer will be raising as long as his glasses are on top of his head; another will bid by winking. Usually the auctioneer closes the bidding with an identification of the buyer, but bidders who prefer anonymity are accommodated. The second practice involves the way in which mail bids are executed. In addition to taking bids in the sale room, the auctioneer exercises bids for absent bidders—so that he may or may not be acting on actual bids when no one is bidding in the room. Successful absentee bids are described as "sold to order." The third bidding complication results from reserves placed by the consign-or—the lowest price that will be accepted. When such an item fails to make its reserve, it is "bought in"—in effect sold to the consignor. (Until recently there was no indication in the catalogue that a reserve had been placed on a particular lot. Now the existence of a reserve is indicated by a dot or some other mark, but the reserve figure is not stipulated.) Reserves were less common in the Kennerley era than in the highly speculative art market of the eighties. Yet despite the pos-sibilities for duplicity, the book sales at the Anderson Galleries and the American Art Association were regarded as honest. Frederick A. Chapman, the head auctioneer—or crier—at the Anderson Galleries, was considered a pillar of rectitude. There was, however, an under-standing that certain antique sales at both houses were faked by dealers trying to drive up the value of their stock. Furnishings—especially oriental rugs—had a way of returning to their roosts after being sold at auction.

In the early years of the twentieth century the New York auction scene was dominated by the American Art Association under the leadership of Thomas E. Kirby ("The Million-Dollar Voice"); for art properties the American Art rivaled the London auction houses. Be-ginning in 1885 Kirby built a reputation for integrity in what was then regarded as a shifty business of rigged sales and auctioneer-dealer col-lusion. He banished the ring system—which flourished in English auc-tions—from operation at the American Art. Under the ring, a cadre of dealers agreed not to bid against each other; one member of the ring would bid on an item, getting it low. The public auction would be followed by a private sale—called "the knock-out"—among the ring members to reallocate the properties and divide the proceeds. When a property worth £1,000 was put up at public auction, a member of the ring might buy it for £100. In the knock-out, it could bring £500. The £400 difference went into a pool to be divided by the ring. The knock-out buyer—who might not be the dealer who originally bought it at the auction—would still be in a position to make a substantial profit. If an outsider attempted to buy a property the ring was interested in, the ring would bid it up at the auction, and the loss—if any— would be absorbed by the pool. The important London and New York auctions of the nineteenth century were run for dealers. Private collectors were not encouraged to bid, and the catalogues were not overly informative. Consequently, private owners were wary about consigning their property for auction. Kirby changed all that at the American Art Association. He insisted on conducting "unrestricted public sales" and welcomed private bidders. The lavish American Art catalogues were intended to attract collectors. Even so, an unrestricted public auction could be confusing to outsiders.

The auction houses normally took a 10 percent commission from the consignor. There was no charge to the buyer. (Both buyers and sellers pay commissions now.) But the 10 percent fee was negotiable and could be shaved for a major collection. Advertising and cataloguing might be extra charges, and elaborate art catalogues cost thousands to produce. It was possible for an unwary consignor to be charged an actual commission of 30 percent.

Until 1911 the main American action was in art (including furniture and rugs), and the American Art dominated the field. The American Art sold libraries, but Kirby had no enthusiasm for books. The big spenders were art collectors, not bibliophiles. There were smaller auction houses in New York, Boston, and Philadelphia; but the chief competition came from the Anderson Galleries, which customarily got the American Art leavings. The Anderson Galleries was started as the Anderson Auction Co. in 1900 by John Anderson, Jr., who three years later combined it with Bangs & Co.—the oldest continuing book auctioneer in America. Anderson sold out to Major Emory S. Turner in 1907, and in 1911 William K. Bixby became a part owner. Bixby, the retired head of the American Car and Foundry Company of St. Louis, owned one of the most valuable collections of literary and historical manuscripts in America. The sale of the Henry W. Poor Library in 1908 and the Robert Hoe library in 1911–1912 initiated the Anderson Galleries's decades as the leading book auction establishment.

Hoe was appropriately a manufacturer of printing presses. He lived across from J. P. Morgan at Madison Avenue and Thirty-sixth Street; although he was a small millionaire compared to his neighbor, Hoe had 16,000 books—including two copies of the Gutenberg Bible. He wanted his library to be put up for auction after his death for the pleasure of other bibliophiles: "If the great collections of the past had not been sold where would I have found my books?" Arthur Swann, the Anderson's book expert, compiled an eight-volume catalogue of some 1,700 pages. The seventy-nine sessions totaled $1,932,056.60, making the Hoe library the most valuable sold to that time. (This record stood in America until the Thomas W. Streeter sale of 1966–1969, which brought $3,104,982.50.*) If inflation is factored in, the Hoe total was worth ten to twelve millions in today's money. The Hoe average was a then-impressive $132 per lot. Thereafter the Anderson catalogues carried the slogan "Where the Hoe Library was sold."

The heroes of the Hoe sale—apart from the late collector—were George D. Smith (1870–1920) and Henry E. Huntington (1850–1927). Smith, a poor boy who prospered mightily, has been called the greatest book dealer who ever lived. (The only other contender for that distinction is Dr. A. S. W. Rosenbach, a younger man who was trounced by Smith at the Hoe sale.) It was said that the only thing Smith ever read was the racing form; but he never forgot a book title—or a price. Smith had already broken the London ring by outbidding everyone else. In so doing, he helped to move the center of the rare-book market from London to New York. Books follow money, and the big money was in America. By driving up prices, Smith convinced collectors that books were as valuable as old masters—and less susceptible to faking. A "Rembrandt" might be

---

* The Britwell Court Library of S. R. Christie-Miller was sold in London from 1910–1927 and realized £604,500 or over $3,000,000.

by anyone, but a Shakespeare *First Folio* was the real thing. Smith did not restrict himself to bidding for clients; he also spent lavishly for stock and did not care what he paid for a book he wanted. Smith preached a sermon to the tycoons: "When the rulers of kingdoms to-day have crumbled into the dust and their names forgotten of the people, the memory of a maker of a great collection will be a household word in the mouths of thousands. This is the royal road to fame!"[1]

Smith's greatest disciple was Henry E. Huntington, the hardware clerk who had become a railroad and traction magnate as manager of the Southern Pacific for his uncle, Collis P. Huntington, and developer of the Pacific Electric interurban system. He consolidated his fortune with that of his uncle by marrying Collis's widow, Arabella, in 1913; but he didn't need the extra fifty million dollars. In his early sixties Huntington began forming the greatest private library in the world, which he would present to the public. In fifteen years he spent more than fifteen million dollars on books for his library and art gallery, which was built in San Marino, California. Huntington knew what he wanted and was in a hurry. Whenever possible, he bought entire collections by private treaty. Operating with Huntington's bankroll, Smith could not be outbid. On the rare occasions when "the old man," as Smith referred to him, lost his nerve, Smith might buy the book for himself. At the Hoe sale Smith spent a million dollars for Huntington—half the total. Smith and Huntington paid $50,000 for Hoe's Gutenberg Bible printed on vellum, setting the record price for a book. It had cost Hoe $25,000.*

Record prices are set by brave bidders and slightly less courageous underbidders. In the first decade of the twentieth century a new breed of book collectors began to transform a gentleman's avocation into a fierce competition. Inevitably there were the nouveaux riches trying to buy culture or respectability; but the library builders were motivated by love of books as well as by love of the game.

---

* Popularly known as the first printed book, the Gutenberg Bible was more accurately the first book printed from movable type in the western world. Some authorities contend that because the Bible is such a magnificent printing achievement it could not have been Johann Gutenberg's first effort at Mainz in 1454–1456. In any case, it wasn't truly a rare book. At the time of the Hoe sale forty-six copies on vellum and paper were known—of which Hoe had one of each.

George D. Smith
(Photo by Arnold Genthe)

Henry E. Huntington

The uninitiated have difficulty in comprehending the rationale for rare-book prices. They can accept that a famous painting is valuable because it is unique. But what makes a printed book worth $10,000 or even $100? Antiquity and rarity are not the determining factors. Most old books are worthless; most scarce books are worthless. A book is valuable because it is a monument of literature or history or print-ing—and because at least two collectors want it. The monetary worth of a book is usually based on the combination of cultural significance and sentiment: it represents the first appearance in print of words that have endured.

There are many reasons for making a volume collectible—some of which have little to do with the text. Books are collected for their bindings and illustrations or as specimens of fine printing (press books) or as exemplars of early printing. When an author has achieved a certain status among collectors, everything he wrote becomes desider-ata; fugitive publications or juvenilia may bring higher prices than masterpieces. The element of competition is always involved in any field of collecting. The true bibliophile enjoys the challenge of forming a library of difficult books on the basis of a plan.

After a book has become established as a collector's item, factors such as rarity, condition, and provenance (its ownership pedigree) affect its price. Association value (an inscription or annotations by the author, for example) will multiply its worth manyfold. Scholars un-derstand the sound textual reasons for preserving the original texts of masterpieces. In the early centuries of printing, copies of a book from the first edition would vary as the result of corrections made during the course of printing.* Therefore a copy of the first edition of these

---

* As popularly applied, the term *first edition* is misleading. It actually means the first printing of the first edition. In the period of stereotyping there may be many reprintings from the first-edition printing plates. But for the fifteenth century through the early nineteenth century, the first printing was normally the only printing of the first edition.

The *first edition* includes all the copies printed from a single setting of type. The *first printing* consists of the copies printed from a single setting of type at one time (without removing the type from the press). The terms *first issue* and *first state* have been much abused by booksellers and cataloguers; they properly refer to variant copies within one printing.

books not only preserves the work as it first appeared in print but also provides evidence for establishing the accurate or definitive text. The case for the value of manuscripts is clearer, for—apart from their uniqueness and strong sentimental appeal—they permit the literary scholar to reconstruct the process of creation and the historian to witness history. Nonetheless, it is doubtful that most collectors—then as now—really comprehend the textual significance of their activities. They preserve and cherish books for reasons of pleasure and pride of ownership. To be sure, there have always been speculators and ig-norant accumulators along with the book lovers. There are worse things to do with money.

Book collecting is not strictly an endeavor for the affluent. A fat bank account is required in the auction rooms and specialist shops; but bibliographical knowledge is as important as cash. Rare books are where you find them. Many collectors of modest means have assembled distinguished libraries by scouting for unrecognized rarities—or sleep-ers. The best collectors know their books.

In 1915 Major Turner sold his controlling interest in the Anderson to John B. Stetson, Jr., the bibliophile son of the hat manufacturer. Wil-liam K. Bixby retained his investment. It was rumored that George D. Smith owned a piece of the Anderson. (It was also alleged that Ken-nerley was secretly involved in Smith's business.) Kennerley may have acquired a small holding of Anderson stock at the time of his appoint-ment as president in 1915, but he was an employee. The Anderson Galleries moved to the former Hyde mansion at Madison Avenue and Fortieth Street in 1915, and Kennerley transferred his publishing op-eration to that address.

Recognizing that he could not challenge the American Art in the art field, Kennerley elected to build on the fame of the Hoe sale and make the Anderson Galleries the leading American book-auction house. His duties as president required him to find consignments and organize the sales. Kennerley was not an auctioneer and did not preside over the sales. Indeed, he made a fastidious point of refusing to enter the sale room while an auction was in progress.

The New York auction season ran from September to late May. Both the American Art and the Anderson suspended sales during the summer months when the action shifted to London. The smaller American houses—The Walpole Galleries, Charles F. Heartman, and Scott & O'Shaughnessy in New York; Stan V. Henkels and Samuel T. Freeman in Philadelphia; and Libbie in Boston—operated through the summer.

Since sales were scheduled months in advance, it is impossible to identify the first consignment Kennerley brought to the Anderson. There were thirty-nine sales of books, autographs, and manuscripts during 1915–1916, his first season as president. The earliest book sale that bore Kennerley's mark was the March 1916 sale of the Huntington duplicates with additional material from Bixby and E. Dwight Church.[2] Since Huntington purchased entire libraries, he was accumulating duplicate copies that would have been the stars of other collections. Huntington was an auctioneer's dream come true because he bought and sold at auction; moreover, he applied the proceeds of his sales against future purchases.

Headlined as the "Biggest Rare Book Auction Since the Hoe Sale," the Huntington-Bixby-Church sale of 1,141 lots sold in five sessions for $63,009.50. Of the total, $43,515 was realized by Bixby's consignment, which included superb manuscripts: Charles Reade's *The Cloister and the Hearth* ($2,260), sixteen volumes of Revolutionary War orderly books ($2,100), Poe's review of Simms's *The Wigwam and the Cabin* ($1,200), and Irving's *Tales of a Traveller* ($1,950). Smith was the leading buyer; the best of the Bixby and Church items therefore went to Huntington.

Other important 1915–1916 Anderson sales were the John Edgar Burton Lincolniana and Civil War material,[3] and the John Boyd Thacher autograph collection.[4] The Edwin Coggeshall collection of Dickens and Thackeray—the largest sold in America—brought the season's top figure of $93,935.80 for 1,237 lots.[5]

There was a flow of major book collections to the auction rooms because only a few collectors—notably Huntington, Morgan, and Henry C. Folger—were assembling permanent libraries destined to form public institutions. Collectors who were not determined to preserve their libraries developed a strong curiosity to find out what their books were "really worth"—often pleading a space problem in mitigation. The tax laws did not then encourage institutional gifts, and heirs had little compunction about disposing of Father's books. Moreover, the auction catalogue provided a suitable memorial to the collector—thereby making auction sale more appealing to the widows and children of bibliophiles.

Kennerley understood that the Anderson catalogues could serve the double purpose of attracting consignments and encouraging bids. The catalogue front cover that he inherited had cuts of Gutenberg, Faustus, and a renaissance printing shop—conveying an impression of antiquity and scholarship. The back cover usually carried an extract from the will of Edmond de Goncourt:

> My wish is that my Drawings, my Prints, my Books—in a word, these things of art which have been the joy of my life—shall not be consigned to the cold tomb of a museum, and subjected to the stupid glance of the careless passer-by; but I require that they shall all be dispersed under the hammer of the Auctioneer, so that the pleasure which the acquiring of each one of them has given me shall be given again, in each case, to some inheritor of my own tastes.

Under Kennerley the Anderson descriptions gradually became fuller, and facsimiles of the major items became obligatory features of the Anderson Galleries's catalogues. Arthur Hooley, Kennerley's versatile man of letters, compiled many of the literary catalogues and took pains to make them readable. Although most of the big bidding was by dealers, Kennerley recognized the importance of the catalogues in stimulating the interest of the collectors who acted through dealers. The Anderson catalogues not only provided bibliographical descriptions but also explained the importance of the items to the tycoons—some of whom were self-educated. During the twenties the auction catalogues competed with the *Wall Street Journal* for the attention of "the boys," as the collectors were called.

Depending on the value of the items, book descriptions could be quite elaborate. (Dealers would have preferred that the catalogues be as uninformative as possible because they wanted to buy cheap.) The Anderson maintained a reference library and staff of cataloguers whose work required considerable research. Christopher Morley wrote in praise of book catalogues:

Why, I often wonder, should anyone worry about not being able to go to college, or subscribe to correspondence courses, when he may have gratis whole carloads of auctioneers' and booksellers' catalogues? The rudiments of literature and history, for example, which I was sent to college to study, I was too green to grasp; but I have picked up an honest smattering since, mostly by suggestions in catalogues. As Melville said of the whaling ships, so I can truly say of the Anderson Galleries and the American Art Association, they have been "my Yale College and my Harvard." . . . Unknown benefactors, the stockholders of those gallant athenea, those dioscuri of culture, have spent a great deal to keep me supplied with catalogues, the textbooks of my illumination.[6]

The elements of a full description included the bibliographical citation, a note on condition, and, when appropriate, the provenance and a comment on the rarity of the item. The more valuable entries carried a statement on the significance of the work. The degree of hard sell varied with the anticipated worth of the item. For books that were expected to break four figures the description might occupy a full page. No estimated prices were provided then; but they are now supplied in catalogues for the benefit of amateurs. Bidders at the Anderson were expected to know what the material was worth.*

Arthur Swann, the man responsible for the Hoe catalogues, had transferred to the American Art. There was intense rivalry between the book departments of the two houses, and Kennerley nurtured a permanent enmity toward Swann. Both houses had spies. Although some bookmen regarded the American Art catalogues as the more scholarly, the Anderson became more attractive to bibliophiles and dealers simply because it obtained most of the major sales. Kennerley created a club-like ambience at the Anderson. It was a place to hear some of the best book talk in town or find companions for a convivial meal. Kennerley was often available late at night and through the

---

* One of the benefits of the cataloguing process for the consignor was that hidden treasures might be identified by the cataloguers—especially in cases where the collector was dead. For example, in 1923 when the library of the late William H. Winters was put up at the Anderson, the cataloguers discovered in a bundle of clippings the first book printed in San Francisco. This law volume was the only copy ever sold at auction and was acquired for Huntington at $3,150.

weekends. The sales—especially the evening sessions—were social occasions preceded or followed by food and drink.

While providing a resort for collectors, the Anderson was nonetheless dealer-oriented. The gallery provided the service of executing bids for collectors, but they were urged to act through dealers who charged a 10 percent commission on successful bids only. Privates could, of course, bid for themselves; but it was better for a collector to act through a dealer—especially for important books—in order to reduce competition. Dealers bought for stock as well as on commission, but a dealer who accepted a bid could not compete against his customer. Bids placed with dealers were limit bids; that is, the dealer would not go beyond the top figure set by the collector. Buy-at-any-price instructions were discouraged by dealers because they made for bad feelings. Kennerley established a liberal policy on deferred payments to enable dealers to buy for stock. The important dealers were granted terms of 2–4–6 or 3–6–9. Thus they could pay for their purchases in installments over six months or nine months—allowing them time to sell the material. Since the auction house was required to settle with consignors in thirty days, Kennerley had a chronic cash-flow problem. Private bidders were expected to pay for auction purchases immediately, but certain wealthy collectors were slow payers.

As president of the Anderson Galleries, Kennerley continued to operate his publishing house with his left hand. He admitted to Grant Richards in March 1916: "For the last year or two I have been hopelessly driven, and since July twelfth last, when I took over the management of the Anderson Galleries, I have paid almost no attention to my publishing business. I have now arranged to bring the publishing business down to Fortieth Street, and with a competent man in charge am taking this opportunity of putting everything in order."[7] Although he withdrew from The Forum at the end of 1916, he published seventeen books that year—including the Spectra hoax.[8] Irritated by such new poetic schools as the Imagists and the Vorticists, Witter Bynner invented the spoof school of "Spectrism" while attending a ballet performance of The Spectre of the Rose. He invited Arthur Davison Ficke to participate, and they concocted a batch of Spectrist poems with the reputed help of ten bottles of scotch. Bynner wrote as Emanuel Morgan and Ficke as Anne Knish.

OPUS 15

Despair comes when all comedy
  Is tame
And there is left no tragedy
  In any name,
When the round and wounded breathing
  Of love upon the breast
Is not so glad a sheathing
  As an old brown vest.

Asparagus is feathery and tall,
And the hose lies rotting by the garden-wall.

—EMANUEL MORGAN

OPUS 195

Her soul was freckled
Like the bald head
Of a jaundiced Jewish banker.
Her fair and featurous face
Writhed like
An albino boa-constrictor.
She thought she resembled the Mona Lisa.
This demonstrates the futility of thinking.

—ANNE KNISH

Bynner and Ficke, who had both been published by Kennerley, sent him their collection of Spectrist poems; and he surprised them by offering to publish it as a book. They let him in on the gag, but he stuck to his offer. The volume appeared in the fall of 1916 with a cover drawn by Ficke and a solemn introduction by Anne Knish:

An explanation of the term "Spectric" will indicate something of the nature of the technique which it describes. "Spectric" has, in this con- nection, three separate but closely related meanings. In the first place, it speaks, to the mind, of that process of diffraction by which are dis- articulated the several colored and other rays of which light is composed. It indicates our feeling that the theme of a poem is to be regarded as a prism, upon which the colorless white light of infinite existence falls and is broken up into glowing, beautiful, and intelligible hues. In its second sense, the term Spectric relates to the reflex vibrations of physical sight, and suggests the luminous appearance which is seen after exposure of the eye to intense light, and, by analogy, the after-colors of the poet's initial vision. In its third sense, Spectric connotes the overtones, adumbrations, or spectres which for the poet haunt all objects both of the seen and the unseen world,—those shadowy projections, sometimes grotesque, which, hovering around the real, give to the real its full ideal significance and its poetic worth. These spectres are the manifold spell and true essence of objects,—like the magic that would inevitably encircle a mirror from the hand of Helen of Troy.

Biographies were invented for the authors. Both were said to be Pittsburgh residents. Morgan was described as a painter who had returned from twenty years in Paris; Budapest-born Knish was identified as the author of a volume of poems in Russian.

Kennerley published 660 copies of *Spectra*, announcing it with an article by Knish and Morgan in *The Forum*.[9] The poems were praised by Edgar Lee Masters, John Gould Fletcher, Eunice Tietjiens, and in *Reedy's Mirror*. Bynner wrote a deadpan review of the volume for *The New Republic*: "It may be that the spectrists are offering us a means toward the creation or understanding of the essential magic of poetry. Their attempt, at any rate, goes deeper than the attempts of any of the other latter-day schools in that it cuts under mere technique."[10]

New Spectrist poems were accepted by *Poetry*, *Reedy's Mirror*, *The Little Review*, and *Others*. Thomas Raymond, the bibliophilic candidate for mayor of Newark, New Jersey, campaigned by reading from *Spectra*; he was elected. Despite the invisibility of Knish and Morgan, the hoax flourished until April 1918, when Bynner admitted the imposture. The inevitable result of the disclosure was for critics to retaliate by insisting that the *Spectra* poems were better than anything else by Bynner and Ficke. Kennerley maintained silence.

In 1916 Kennerley published J. S. Machar's *Magdalen* as "The First Volume of 'The Slavic Translations' "; one other title, *In the War: Memoirs of V. Veresaev*, appeared in this series. Publishing and auctioneering did not fill Kennerley's plate. He sponsored the 1916 Forum Exhibition at the Anderson, announced as the largest showing of "the more modern paintings" ever held. Some two hundred paintings by seventeen artists were included: Ben Benn, Thomas Hart Benton, Oscar Bluemner, Andrew Dasberg, Arthur G. Dove, Marsden Hartley, S. Macdonald-Wright, John Marin, Alfred Maurer, Henry L. McFee, George F. Of, Man Ray, Morgan Russell, Charles Sheeler, A. Walkowitz, and William and Marguerite Zorach. Willard Huntington Wright (later the author of the popular S. S. Van Dine mystery novels), a member of the selection committee along with Alfred Stieglitz, wrote a report of the show for one of the last *Forum* issues published by Kennerley.[11] The exhibit catalogue was separately published under the Anderson Galleries's imprint.[12] As photographer, publisher, and gallery proprietor, Stieglitz was proclaiming the doctrines of modern art; and the Anderson became his base of operation in 1921. He later acknowledged Kennerley's support: "The Forum Show in the old Anderson Galleries in 1916 was your doing + has become historic. I also know that you have followed the whole development of modern thought in every phase + fought for it."[13]

The Kennerleys' residence in 1916 was at 22 West Seventy-third Street. Helen Kennerley's brother made a revealing diary entry that year: "Mitchell has given Helen's allowance into her hands. . . ."[14] The inference is that up to then he was receiving her trust-fund income. Helen and Mitchell frequently quarreled. She had been spoiled as a rich man's daughter and expected to get her own way. Her tactic in domestic disputes was to claim she was the unselfish one and that what she wanted to do was best for all concerned: other people were behaving selfishly. Their older son, Morley, recalled that his mother "was never completely happy if everything was organized and going smoothly . . . and was bound to suggest something else and change plans."[15] Helen was possessive about the children, insisting on making the decisions about their rearing. Kennerley was an aloof and increasingly absent father. When Morley's Cleveland grandmother gave him Liberty Bonds, his father took them for safekeeping; the bonds were never seen again. Morley later commented that his father had a "communal outlook on money."[16]

During the 1916–1917 season, Anderson held forty-two book sales as against eleven at the American Art. In November the Anderson presented the first of the five sales of the Young library. Minneapolis bibliophile Carleton Young, F.R.G.S., LL.D., LH.D., had devoted his

life to assembling inscribed books by American and European authors.*
The Paris *Figaro* styled him "Le Roi de Livres." Young employed a
staff to dispatch volumes to their authors for signing; and he traveled
Europe purchasing inscribed books of deceased authors and persuading
living figures to write in their books for him. The first batch of books
Young sent to Tolstoy for signing in Russia was lost; the second was
confiscated; the third was hand-delivered to Tolstoy (who sweetened
them with the original draft of his letter to the Czar protesting the
Kishinef massacre) and smuggled out of Russia.

Young decided to dispose of his collection, explaining in a letter
printed in the Anderson catalogue that he had offered to present the
"gems" to the Library of Congress but "insurmountable obstacles arose."

> The collection was increasing with great rapidity; it became the largest
> of the kind in the world, requiring not only my own attention but that
> of a librarian and eight assistants, including cataloguers and translators;
> my correspondence reached 5,000 letters a year, and I endeavored to
> reply personally to each letter; the result was that my health became
> impaired and my physician advised me to abandon the work.[17]

The first four catalogues were devoted to inscribed books, and the fifth
listed uninscribed volumes. Subsequent sales in 1919 were restricted
to letters and manuscripts.

The star lot in the first Young sale consisted of 24 signed Tolstoys,
which brought $1,325. One of the volumes included Tolstoy's holo-
graph admonition against gathering worldly treasures: "You believe
that your well-being consists in riches and honours, we believe in
something else. Our belief shows us that our advantage is not in
violence but submissiveness; not in wealth but in giving everything
away, and we, like plants in the light, cannot help striving in the
direction where we see our advantage."[18] The total for the 4,683 lots
in the first five Young sales was only $33,210.25; there were many

---

* A *signed copy* is one in which the author has written his name. An *inscribed copy*
(or *presentation copy*) is one in which the author has written a comment or sentiment
for the recipient. The *dedication copy* is the copy inscribed to the dedicatee. The terms
inscription and *dedication* are frequently confused. There is normally only one dedication copy.

bargains, and most of the books went for under $10. Twenty-seven dollars bought the inscribed copy of Hardy's *Well-Beloved*: "The interest aimed at in this novel being of an ideal or subjective kind, external events have been used as ancillary to that aim merely."[19]

In November 1916 came the first of the Herschel V. Jones sales at the Anderson. The publisher of the *Minneapolis Journal*, Jones derived more pleasure from acquiring books than from keeping them. The money from his sales always went into more books. With the exception of Huntington, Jones bought and sold more great books than any other collector of his time. His November sale included the eighteenth- and nineteenth-century English books he had decided to dispose of so that he could concentrate on the English Renaissance and incunabula.* The catalogue explained that "in order to make the sale truly representative of himself as a collector he has added a large number of very rare and valuable books, manuscripts, autograph letters, original drawings, and fine bindings that will appeal strongly to the mature collectors."[20] These appealing items included two Books of Hours as well as manuscripts by William Harrison Ainsworth, Robert Louis Stevenson, Lord Byron, and Mark Twain. The 608 lots realized only about $20,000—of which Smith spent $3,298, mostly for Huntington.

November also brought the start of the Frederic R. Halsey print sale.[21] The first nine sessions up to April 1917 realized $377,244.25. Later Halsey sales brought the total to $438,371. There were more than 10,000 items, and François Janinet's "L'Aveu Difficile" set the American record for a print at $11,000.

The 1916–1917 season was notable for three auctions of Huntington duplicates. The three-session sale of his French books in November brought $39,916.25.[22] (A noteworthy aspect of book auctions at the time is that cheap items sold alongside expensive ones; raises of 25¢ or 50¢ were not unusual.) The French books were followed in January 1917 by Americana† duplicates from the E. D. Church and Britwell Court libraries, which Smith had purchased en bloc for Huntington.

* *Incunabula* (from the Latin for cradle) or *incunables* are books printed in the fifteenth century—the first century of European printing. They are also known as Fifteeners.
† Americana consists of works about the discovery and history of North America—not American literature.

The catalogue justifiably proclaimed itself "The Most Remarkable Library of Rarities on the History of the American Continent Ever Offered in this Country or Europe."[23] The 308 items brought $107,664.50—an impressive average of $349.56—and the highest total since the Hoe sale.

The third Huntington sale of the season followed in February-March 1917 when there was another Huntington-Bixby assemblage.[24] Again Bixby's manuscripts outshone Huntington's material; Bixby was stripping his shelves, whereas Huntington was culling his acquisitions from the McKee, Poor, Chamberlain, Church, Arnold, Hoe, and Halsey collections. Huntington's take amounted to $11,953.60 of the $52,126.05 total; at the same time he was one of the largest buyers of the Bixby consignment through Smith. Smith's purchases from the Bixby lots included the Orderly Book account of Benedict Arnold's treachery and Major André's trial ($1,052), an "Elephant Folio" of Audubon's *Birds of America* ($3,500), Jefferson's household account book ($1,025), two James Whitcomb Riley manuscripts and fifty-eight of his letters ($1,055), thirty-four drawings by William Makepeace Thackeray ($1,150), and the manuscripts of Henry David Thoreau's "A Yankee in Canada" ($725) and "Sir Walter Raleigh" ($750).

Since Bixby was an investor in the Anderson as well as a consignor, his dealings with Kennerley became complicated. In January 1917 Reedy reported to Mosher on Kennerley's recent trip to St. Louis:

> I know no more about Kennerley's status with the Anderson galleries than you do. He told me just about what he appears to have told you.
>
> I am worried about the matter because I recommended Mitchell to Mr. Bixby and fear that I may possibly have gotten Mr. Bixby in bad. Mitchell doesn't appear to pay any attention to any business except the entertainment of beautiful women. I am in doubt whether I should approach Mr. Bixby on the subject or not. I fear that Mitchell's neglect of financial matters is hurting Bixby, because rumor has come to me from New York that Bixby is broke. This isn't so. Mitchell blew in here and stayed for three-quarters of an hour and left on the next train with thirty thousand dollars. This was eight months ago + I think the simple fact of the matter is that the dancing ladies get all the coin. I know that some writers out here complain that they have received checks from Kennerley which have been returned to them marked "no funds."

You can see what a delicate matter it is for me to go to Bixby, being a friend of Kennerley's. On the other hand, I am a friend of Bixby's and would like to save him from any bad consequences, considering that I had a hand in getting him connected up with Mitchell—although in fact it was with Stetson that Mitchell made his first connections. If there is anything I can do to help you get your money, of course I am willing to do it. I have about half made up my mind to see Mr. Bixby, because while I like Mitchell I am now firmly convinced that he hasn't any of the qualifications of a business man, and he may cost Bixby a great deal of money. So far as Stetson is concerned, I think that Mitchell hypnotized him as well as Bixby. I think that Stetson and Bixby both put up a lot of money to carry over the galleries on Mitchell's representation that he could secure the sale of the Morgan pictures. This is all I know about it.

What I write you is of course strictly in confidence. I want to help you and I don't want to hurt Kennerley or Bixby. I am rather muddled but I think I'll see Bixby in a day or two. Meanwhile I hope that you will be able to get some money out of Mitchell. But if you can't get it through John Quinn I don't know any way you can get it outside of a suit at law.[25]

At this time Quinn wrote on behalf of Michael Monahan, who was trying to survive by selling copies of his books published by Kennerley, asking him to supply Monahan with books:

He says that he has not had a statement from you in nearly two years. He feels that to shut off the books now at this critical time is to do him a deadly injury and to quite spoil the chances of a mutual adjustment.

. . . .

I don't want to intervene in this matter in a legal way or professionally for various reasons. I refused Mosher's request that I take his case against you, and have not had a line since I wrote to him. But I think Monahan's case stands on a different basis. I hope you will discontinue the embargo and let Monahan hear from you as to what you will do.[26]

Apart from Kennerley's "dancing ladies," the gallery's financial problems can be attributed to the circumstance that—despite the high totals for the Huntington sales—there was not yet big money in auctioning books. A $100,000 book auction was regarded as remarkable; but 10 percent of that is $10,000—against which there were heavy overhead costs. A dealer's profit on a single book transaction might be as much as the auction house's total commission on an entire library. The large profits were still in art, not books; and American Art dominated the art market.

Endeavors which require handling other people's money can be demoralizing. Auctioneers own nothing, yet they sell treasures; they deal in large sums but earn only commissions. Some auctioneers develop the feeling that the properties and money they handle are really theirs. As Kennerley dealt with millionaires he came to regard himself as one of them. He spent money that he didn't have, although what he spent it on—apart from women—remains a mystery. He was open-handed with money, if he had it. When Isadora Duncan—reputedly one of Kennerley's lovers—sailed for Europe in 1917 there was no money to pay for the passage of her companion, Mary Desti. Kennerley went to see Duncan off and provided the necessary funds.[27]

Kennerley lived well, but his entertainment and travel were charged to the Anderson. Perhaps his expense account ate into the profits. Given his opportunities to acquire books, it is surprising that he did not assemble a valuable personal library. He owned some fine books and manuscripts, most of which found their way into the auction room discretely buried in various sales. At least once Kennerley tried to prosper by real estate investment. In 1917 he bought on mortgage a 9,000-square-foot plot near Carnegie Hall—144–146 West Fifty-seventh Street and 139–141 West Fifty-sixth—on which there were three four-story buildings.[28] He does not appear to have held on to this property.

There may never have been a time when Kennerley was actually affluent, even after he became the principal stockholder in the gallery. The Anderson accounting is now unrecoverable, but it is clear that Kennerley regarded revenue as profits. There would always be more money after the next sale.

The list of books published by Kennerley in 1917 fell to twenty, but one of them was the most famous American volume to appear with his imprint.* Edna St. Vincent Millay's first book, *Renascence and*

---

* Since copies of *Renascence* were deposited at the Library of Congress on 21 December 1917, the book was really a 1918 publication.

Other Poems, which included twenty-three poems, was not an immediate success. The first edition of 750 copies (perhaps 900) was a $1.50 volume on AGM Glaslan handmade paper. It was a close imitation of the design for William Watson's *Lachrymae Musarum* (London: Macmillan, 1892), which Kennerley regarded as "one of the most perfect pieces of bookmaking of the 19th Century";[29] and the spine lettering was drawn by Goudy. There was a simultaneously published collector's printing signed by Millay and limited to fifteen numbered copies (actually seventeen) on Japan vellum at $10. Kennerley's copy was #17, inscribed "To Mitchell, With a little yellow rose, Edna."[30] Most of these signed copies were given away by Kennerley, who would see it become a $750 book. Kennerley was generous with review copies, as was his custom. *Pearson's Magazine*, edited by Frank Harris, pronounced *Renascence* "the greatest poem written in America since 'When Lilacs Last in the Dooryard Bloom'd.' "[31] Kennerley's ad was headlined "A BOOK OF REAL POETRY!":

> Miss Millay's poems have a remarkable freshness, sincerity and power. They do not depend upon curious and involved artifice, upon waywardness of method or metre, upon the presence of what should be absent. They do not present uncouthness, or mere triteness, as strength. They are not facile outpourings of one form of shallowness, nor the curt trivialities of another. They deal, as poetry should deal, primarily with emotion; with the sense of tears and of laughter, in mortal things; with beauty and passion; with having and losing.[32]

Kennerley did not function as a line editor. Arthur Hooley worked closely with Millay, who valued his advice on revising her poems. The Kennerleys were attentive to Millay when she took up residence in New York. One night in September 1917 they took her to dinner at the Plaza and the theater. At the end of the evening Millay became sick from the gasoline fumes on Fifth Avenue and fainted. Kennerley got her into a cab and held her hand while she vomited. The Kennerleys brought her to their apartment where Helen tended to Millay and put her to bed.[33]

A Christmas Day letter from Millay to Kennerley—probably dating from 1917—expresses her gratitude to him and develops an assessment of his character:

SPECTRA

New Poems

EMANUEL MORGAN
ANNE KNISH

THIS IS NUMBER 17 OF FIFTEEN
COPIES PRINTED ON JAPAN VELLUM

For Mitchell

With a little yellow rose,

Edna.

RENASCENCE

AND OTHER POEMS

BY

EDNA ST. VINCENT MILLAY

❡ Miss Millay's poems have a remarkable freshness, sincerity, and power. They do not depend upon curious and involved artifice, upon waywardness of method and metre, upon the presence of what should be absent, or the absence of what should be present. They do not avoid rhythm and music as dangerous intrusions in modern poetry. They do not present uncouthness, or mere triteness, as strength. They are not the facile outpourings of one form of shallowness, nor the curt trivialities of another. They deal, as poetry should deal, primarily with emotion; with the sense of tears and of laughter, in mortal things; with beauty and passion; with having and losing.

MITCHELL KENNERLEY PUBLISHER NEW YORK

TOP LEFT: *Front cover,* Spectra

ABOVE: *Dust jacket,* Renascence
(*Courtesy of Lilly Library,*
Indiana University)

LEFT: Renascence (*Courtesy of*
Vassar College Library)

Dear Mitchell Kennerley,—

I have not infrequently thought that you are one of the best men in the world. Today I am quite sure of it,—although it may be that many people who know nothing about it know better.——You have been just now so ever especially good to me, in turning yourself into a Santa Claus for the indulgence of my vanity and my vice and my deathless childhood that I have a hurt in my heart to do something to please you. I want this letter to make you know just how much my friend I feel you to be,—my friend at all sorts of times, when I'm a little girl and when I'm a big girl and when I'm not sure just what it is that I am.

I don't believe anybody else ever felt quite the same towards you or about you as I do.

I mean so much what I say that my handwriting is cramped.

It seems to me that this is the first letter I've written you for a long time when I've used the inside as well as the outside of the sheet. It is a long letter, you see.——It really is. I have been a long time writing it; which is not usual with me. And before I began it I sat for some time thinking it, wondering what I should say, and what I should not say, and what I should on no account forget to say.

I suppose you are a very busy man,—Your desk's always cluttered.— Yet you are never too busy to think of other people. You are not like anybody else I ever knew.

I wonder whether more people love you or hate you. You could probably be quite perfectly hateable. But I don't know anyone who does hate you. And I do know people, beside myself, who love you very much.

Is this letter funny?—Does it make you laugh?—Or do you understand it?—If you do understand it, then, out of the-hurt-that-I-have-in-my-heart-to-please-you, I have at least given you something nice to think about.

—Edna St. Vincent Millay[34]

Given the amorous readiness of both parties, there were inevitable rumors that they became lovers. Indeed, Millay's letter can be read as an invitation to commence an affair. Despite Kennerley's reputation as a lothario, he was discreet about his liaisons.

The Millay cult had not yet blossomed, and *Renascence* did not sell in 1917. Kennerley disposed of copies by advertising "TEN BOOKS OF POEMS FOR $5 WITH A FREE COPY OF 'RENASCENCE' BY EDNA ST. VIN-CENT MILLAY."[35] It may not have gratified the poet to see her book being given away; but her publisher's conviction that Millay "is the greatest lyrical poet America has produced"[36] made him stick with her work. A second edition of *Renascence* was produced in 1919; there were four more Kennerley printings in the twenties.*

When Kennerley delayed publication of *Second April*, Millay complained to Witter Bynner in 1920: "I write Mitchell all the time, and he won't answer my letters; and every time I call up the office they tell me he is out, and I know dam well he is so near the telephone all the time that I hear his breathing. . . . This is one big reason why I wish you were in town. You are both [Bynner and Ficke] so much bigger than he is, it would be a great comfort to me, somehow, even if you should think it advisable not to beat him up."[37] Kennerley's stalling cost him *A Few Figs from Thistles*, Millay's most popular collection, which was brought out by another publisher in 1920; but he published two new Millay volumes in 1921—*Second April* with 44 poems and *Aria da Capo*, a verse play on the absurdity of war.† *Second April* required three printings in its first year; but by then Kennerley was no longer actively publishing and had difficulty distributing his books, as shown by his ad in *Publishers' Weekly*: "Possibly your bookseller will tell you that there is no such person as Edna St. Vincent Millay, and that there are no such books as 'Second April' and 'Renascence,' in which case they will be sent post-paid on receipt of price by the publisher."[39] Later in the twenties Millay's celebrity as the exemplar of passionate living and female liberation boosted her sales; but she was then being published by Harper.

In 1922 Millay instructed an editor who wanted to reprint her poems: "As to the possible reaction of Mr. Mitchell Kennerley,—we should worry. I hardly believe that Mr. Kennerley is anxious to become

---

* The second edition retained the 1917 title-page date; but it was printed from reset type on MBM watermarked paper. This edition was reprinted in 1921 (twice) and 1924 (twice).

† Kennerley had instructed the printer to use up a supply of Dutch handmade paper left over from *Spectra* for *Aria da Capo*. "I expected about a 1000 copies and was shocked when informed that the total was only 400 which was not enough to fill advance orders + review copies. I ordered another edition of a thousand copies on domestic paper."[38]

involved in a law-suit with me, in which he would, I should think, cut a rather ridiculous and unpopular figure, since from one year to the next I receive from him not one penny of royalties on any of the three books of mine which he has published."[40]

During the year that gave birth to *Renascence* Kennerley published one of his most curious volumes, *Jap Herron: A Novel Written from the Ouija Board.* There was no author's name on the title page, but the frontispiece was a portrait of Mark Twain. The introduction by Emily Grant Hutchings of St. Louis detailed how the novel had been dictated to her by the spirit of Samuel Langhorne Clemens. At that time there was considerable interest in the ouija-board compositions of the seventeenth-century spirit Patience Worth who also communicated through Hutchings. Reedy wrote respectfully of Worth's work and published her verse in *The Mirror.* When Hutchings brought him the novel dictated by Mark Twain, Reedy steered it to Kennerley.

Jap Herron is the sentimental story of a noble country newspaper editor, the runaway boy he adopts, and their efforts to improve their town—the men who uncorrupted Bloomtown. It includes ample satirical material about small-town life and some sharp observations on human behavior:

> The father of the little Herrons was a kingfisher. He spent his hours of toil on the river bank and his hours of ease in Mike's place. One Friday, good luck peered through the dingy windows of the little shanty where the Herrons starved, froze or sweltered. It was Friday, as I remarked before. Mary was washing, against difficulties. It had rained for a week. The clothes had to dry before Mary could cash her labor, and it fretted Jacky Herron sorely. His credit had lost caste with Mike, and Mike had the grip on the town. He had the only thirst parlor in Happy Hollow. So Jacky smashed the only remaining window, broke the family cup, and set forth defiantly in the rain. And in the fog and slashing rain he lost his footing, and fell into the river. As it was Friday, Mary had hopefully declared that luck would change—and it did![41]

At best, it is a readable imitation of Mark Twain.

Reedy agreed to write an introduction for Kennerley's edition but developed reservations about becoming identified "with any spook business" after he learned that Hutchings's collaborator was the daugh-

ter of a country newspaper editor and therefore knew about the material in *Jap Herron*.[42] Reedy provided "My Acquaintance with Jap
Herron," but requested Kennerley not to print it. After admitting that
Jap Herron "is more like Mark Twain might do it, than like the work
of anyone else," Reedy stated that he did not believe in the possibility
of spirit communication. "Of 'Jap Herron,' as of the Patience Worth
works, I have but to say that they are the only writings of so called
spirit origin that I have ever seen, that are not beneath contempt but
are of a charm and power to make it seem plausible that people who
pass out of life do not pass into a neutral condition of ridiculous
triviality of interest and performance not to say imbecility."[43] Since
this statement was clearly not an endorsement, Kennerley omitted it
from the book.

Jap Herron attracted no praise upon publication. The *New York
Times* reviewer commented, "If this is the best that 'Mark Twain' can
do by reaching across the barrier, the army of admirers that his works
have won for him will all hope that he will hereafter respect that
boundary."[44] In June 1918 Harper & Brothers—which had publishing
rights to Mark Twain's work—sought an injunction to restrain further
publication of *Jap Herron*, demanding an accounting of the proceeds
from its sale and the destruction of all unsold copies. Claiming that
Jap Herron was an attempt to deceive book buyers, Harper cited the
circumstances that it had declined the novel before it was submitted
to Kennerley and that Hutchings had been forbidden the use of Mark
Twain's name or portrait. Apart from infringement on the exclusive
use of "Mark Twain"—which was a registered trade mark—Harper
claimed that *Jap Herron* was of such slight literary merit as to damage
Twain's reputation. James N. Rosenberg, who was retained to defend
Kennerley, declared: "We will put the issue up to the Supreme Court.
We will have a final ruling on immortality."[45] Rosenberg was a Kennerley author, as well as a painter and successful lawyer. Reedy's
statement to the press did not strengthen Kennerley's case: "Parts of
it are good, as typical of Mark Twain as I can remember from my early
readings, but other parts are sloppy—awfully sloppy and sweet and
sentimental; usual best-seller stuff!"[46] The case never came to trial.
Kennerley recalled in 1940: "Without publicity and advertising very
few copies of the book were sold. The remaining copies were eventually
destroyed."[47]

One of the benefits of continuing to publish books while running the Anderson was that the Mitchell Kennerley imprint could be utilized to oblige bookmen. One man worth obliging was Abraham Simon Wolfe Rosenbach, Ph.D., who was on his way to becoming the most famous bookdealer who ever lived. George D. Smith dominated the scene in 1917, but Dr. Rosenbach was a contender. He combined salesmanship with scholarship. Smith knew what books were worth, but Dr. Rosenbach knew prices and literature. He had written his dissertation on the Spanish influence on English Renaissance literature, and he was able to convey his love of books to wealthy collectors. Moreover, Dr. Rosenbach had an almost mystical belief in the value of great books—and priced them accordingly. His catalogues bore this biblical proverb: "It is naught, it is naught, saith the buyer; but when he is gone his way then he boastest." Kennerley and Rosenbach needed each other, and they shared the same pleasures: books, women, and the table. Dr. Rosenbach consumed a bottle of whiskey a day; although Kennerley was a drinker, he was not in the Doctor's class. Reports about Kennerley's alcohol consumption are contradictory, but he was not an alcoholic.

Dr. R—as he was identified in the salesroom—became the biggest and certainly the most celebrated buyer at the Anderson. In 1917 Kennerley published Dr. Rosenbach's *The Unpublishable Memoirs*, a collection of loosely linked stories about an unprincipled bibliophile. The book did not sell, but it gained wide exposure in the rare-book world from the complimentary copies distributed by author and publisher. Dr. R's only work of fiction, it was nicely calculated to stimulate interest in book collecting and to enhance the author's reputation as a book raconteur.

With his publishing business suffering from neglect, Kennerley hired his former employees Laurence Gomme and Laurens Maynard in 1917 to run it for him, instructing Gomme:

> I have completely neglected my publishing business because I have been very much occupied with the Anderson work and because I have not felt like giving my odd moments to those whom I have had in charge. Now that you have come to work for me I am going to do all I can to help the publishing business toward a success or I am going to give it up entirely. . . . While I intend you should have complete charge of the

THE FORTUNES OF MITCHELL KENNERLEY, BOOKMAN

business I want to keep in complete touch with all that goes on, and wish all duplicate letters, bills, etc. brought to me each night.[48]

When Maynard died in October, Kennerley made the funeral arrangements, prompting Carman's observation that "He is very kind in emergencies."[49] Gomme put the company records in order and hired salesmen; but "Kennerley again lost interest in the business and after Gomme prepared some of the Authors' Royalty accounts, he and Gomme parted company."[50]

CHAPTER FIVE

*A New Location—The Jones, Forman, and
Huntington Sales—The Death of Smith
and the Ascendancy of A. S. W. Rosenbach—
The Disputed Renoirs—The Portrait of
Mr. W. H.—Horace Fish—Alfred Stieglitz*

THE 1917–1918 ANDERSON SEASON opened late, in December, because of the move to a new location. On the corner of Park Avenue and Fifty-ninth Street at 489 Park stood the impressive building of the Arion Society, a Germanophile organization. War fever compelled the Arions to terminate their Gemütlichkeit; and Kennerley secured a long-term lease on the building, which occupied a 125-foot by 90-foot plot, for the bargain rent of $28,000 a year. (He later rented the street-level corner to a bank for $25,000 a year.) When the American Art Association erected an elegant building at Madison and Fifty-seventh in 1923, the poles of the American auction world were three blocks apart.

The Arion building was renovated to provide a gathering place for the trade and to attract visitors to the exhibitions. The main auction room on the first floor, which accommodated 300, presented a club-like atmosphere with dark oak paneling and red upholstery. There was also a smaller sales room. Major sales were black-tie events held in the evening when the bidders were well-fed and primed with alcohol. Kennerley hosted presale dinners for the big spenders. At important occasions the sale room was lavishly decorated with flowers—a Kennerley trademark. His desk had fresh flowers daily; and Kennerley was amused when one of his detractors remarked that he never trusted a man who kept flowers on his desk. The new Anderson location was convenient to the Plaza Hotel at Fifth Avenue and Fifty-ninth, where Kennerley maintained a suite after he became estranged from Helen.

The second and third floors had offices and exhibition rooms. No admission was charged for these presale exhibits, which attracted large turnouts. The fourth-floor attic was later converted into a glass-roofed art gallery where space was rented for exhibits of painting, photography, and sculpture. It was Kennerley's plan to make the Anderson a center of interest for the arts, and rooms were rented for recitals and lectures. Space was also let to art and jewelry dealers. Kennerley offered Stieglitz a rent-free room as headquarters for his magazine *Camera Work*.[1] Willard Huntington Wright, the first director of art exhibits, was succeeded by Walter Grant, an energetic promoter. An exhibition of Sir William Orpen's war paintings for the benefit of blinded soldiers was the first art show at the new location.

In addition to its auction business the Anderson appraised and catalogued private libraries. These services provided a conduit for material to the sales room. An auction house lives from sale to sale, and Kennerley was engaged in a bitter competition with the American Art for prime consignments.*

Kennerley held court in his second-floor office. Christopher Morley evoked this room and its lord in his autobiographical *John Mistletoe*:

> Now that it exists no longer, it cannot be unseemly to say that Mistletoe found Mitchell Kennerley's carefully guarded sanctum in the former Anderson Galleries building the most interesting chamber in New York. The first port of call for visiting collectors and connoisseurs of all the arts, an attentive listener heard there the shrewdest backstage talk about books and life. There is a delicious spice of boyish mischief

---

* In 1915 Kennerley hired his friend Francis Bellamy to write an advertising brochure for Anderson. It was subsequently taken over by Arthur Hooley but was never printed. The typescript for "The Anderson Galleries What They Are & What They Do: A Century of Auctioneering" is at the Clements Library, University of Michigan.

in the great financiers who are the top-rank collectors, and the boy learned to carry many assorted secrecies without flinching. It was always his intention to attempt a catalogue raisonné of the books on the shelves of that room. . . . Such a catalogue, done with the proper inside information, would imply the richest part of a history of our own times.

Such a history would have to record that Kennerley, probably more than any other editor, was first to remark and put between covers (either in *The Forum* or in books) much of the finest stuff of our day. . . . Kennerley was unquestionably the first Modern publisher in this country, in the particular sense in which the word is used nowadays. In matters of literary sensitiveness few others have ever caught up with him.

· ·

At one end of that hospitable room, behind a tall barrier of filing cases, was a little basin with running water where hands might be laved. From that sheltered corner occasionally arose the gratifying clatter of oscillated ice, as M. K. mingled some specially aromatic cocktail, or withdrew from his low rows of pigeon-holes a crusted bottle of sherry from the officers' mess of the frigate *Constitution* (the irony here is used to please his visitors), or rum from the India Docks, or a bottle of *fine* that had been in Napoleon's own cellar at the Palais des Tuilleries, or some of Francis Joseph's 18th century Tokay. Those filing cases contained every conceivable precaution of civilized emergency, from ingenious corkscrews and pipe reamers and fly swatters to spare shirts and clean napkins and shaving cream. Once by some chance Mistletoe found himself on the way to an evening dress engagement but had forgotten to bring black socks. Time was pressing, haberdashers in that part of town were closed. In an inspiration of despair he directed the taxi to the Anderson Galleries. Yes, M. K. was there as usual. "Have you got any black socks?" he cried anxiously. M. K. went calmly to the famous filing cases and drew out a sheaf of beautiful silk hosiery. They fitted perfectly.

One never knew whom he might meet in that magic place. Once J. M. was in the hidden washstand corner, cleansing his hands. He heard someone enter the room, and a voice which he knew instantly was unlike any other in the world. Deep, vibrant, with far-away bells of loneliness and passion; melancholy and humorous at once, and a noble spacious timbre like someone speaking in a cathedral—what forgotten rumors of childhood did it recall, when he had been told about that voice? There had never been more than one—but surely it couldn't be. . . .

He came out from behind the partition. It was. Mitchell said "I want you to meet Mrs. Patrick Campbell."

Sometimes, instead of going out for lunch, two little shiny buckets of chicken salad and sandwiches would be sent over from the Plaza. Over a glass of the *Constitution* sherry a narrative mood might come upon the host, and Mistletoe sat entranced by unexpurgated memoirs of the Nineties. Not to have known that room would have been to miss the finest flavor of publishing aesthetics.[2]

Morley, who was competent to judge, was impressed by Kennerley's knowledge of literature. "I don't think anyone knew as much as he about the great yrs of the fin-de-siècle in which he grew up; always there were on his desk odd vols of poetry or essays, with neat little cardboard marker-slips in them, something he wanted to tell me about."[3] One of Kennerley's trademarks was that he wore white socks because a friend had developed blood poisoning from colored socks. Morley described Kennerley's ankles as "twinkling" down the Anderson halls.

Kennerley did not become an American citizen until September 1919. Although he was overage for the draft (thirty-nine in 1917), his English friends held it against him that he took no part in the war. His participation was restricted to publishing war-related books, including two political studies by George D. Herron in 1917, *The Menace of Peace* and *Woodrow Wilson and the World's Peace*. Herron, a former Congregational minister with socialist and pacifist convictions, became an ardent supporter of Wilson and a passionate foe of Germany. After his wife had divorced him for domestic irregularity, he married into the Rand fortune and helped organize the Rand School of Social Sciences. Kennerley ran a full-page ad in *Publishers' Weekly* offering purchasers of either Herron work a free copy of the same book.[4] A return coupon was printed on the dust jackets. The publisher also tried to encourage bookshop orders by paying half the shipping charges. It was assumed that the Rand money was behind this generosity. Kennerley published two subsequent volumes by Herron, *Germanism and the American Crusade* (1918) and *The Greater Way* (1919). In 1918 Kennerley brought out a sixty-page anti-Hun propaganda piece, *Hate with a Will to Victory*, by playwright J. Hartley Manners, offering to fill orders for 100 copies at the cost of manufacture.

RIGHT: *William Marion Reedy*

BELOW: *489 Park Avenue. The figure on the front steps has been identified as Mitchell Kennerley. (Rare Books and Manuscripts Division. The New York Public Library. Astor, Lenox and Tilden Foundations)*

Mitchell Kennerley in his office at the Anderson Galleries
(Courtesy of Morley and Jean Kennerley)

Christopher Morley and
Mitchell Kennerley (Photo by
Arnold Genthe; courtesy of
Morley and Jean Kennerley)

Appropriately, the first Anderson sale at the Fifty-ninth Street location was another collection of Huntington's surplusage on 10 December 1917.[5] The 493 items of English literature brought $46,212.25. (Three days earlier the books and prints of Diamond Jim Brady brought $28,051.50 for 613 lots at the American Art.) Dr. Rosenbach paid the top price of $3,450 for Shelley's corrected copy of *A Refutation of Deism* (1814). Not yet powerful enough to dominate sales in the manner of Smith, Dr. R tried to buy the most expensive book—preferably an association item that would make good newspaper copy.

The next day 330 lots of Huntington Americana totaled $106,026.50.[6] The star item, Sir Martin Frobisher's *A True Reporte of the Laste Voyage Into the West and Northwest Regions* (1577), went to Smith for $4,750. Champlain's *Des Sauvages*—the copy Kennerley had once bought for four cents—brought $3,600; it had been acquired by Huntington when he purchased the E. D. Church Library. The $152,238.75 total for the two December Huntington sales was modest compared to what art was bringing at the American Art. Kennerley was not ready to compete in that market; but he was determined to dominate the book and manuscript field.

There were two more Huntington sales that season. In February 1918, 1,035 lots of English literature brought $88,028.60.[7] The star item—headlined in the catalogue as THE GREATEST MILTON VOLUME EVER OFFERED / THE DEDICATION COPY OF "COMUS"!—brought $9,200 from Smith, who sold it to Herschel Jones. Despite the headline boast, it was John Milton's collaborator, Henry Lawes, who inscribed the copy to "Iohn Lord Viscount Bracly, Son and heire apparent to the Earle of Bridgewater, &c," who had taken a role in the first performance. Nonetheless, it was a great copy of a great book with an impeccable pedigree, having been acquired when Smith purchased the Bridgewater Library for Huntington.* Bookmen were puzzled by Huntington's decision to dispose of it.

The fourth Huntington sale of the season came in April 1918 when 598 additional items of English literature realized $94,289.80.[8] The

---

* Kennerley privately printed W. N. C. Carlton's *Notes on the Bridgewater House Library* as a 1918 Christmas keepsake.

excitement was provided by a glorious run of Shakespeare quartos,*
all of which were bought by Smith:

Life of Cambises, King of Percia (first edition, 1585—formerly attributed to Shakespeare) $1,550

The Lamentable Tragedy of Locrine (first edition, 1595—formerly attributed to Shakespeare) $7,600

Love's Labor Lost (first edition, 1598) $2,700

Henry IV, Part 1 (second edition, 1599) $1,900

*The True Tragedie of Richard Duke of Yorke and the death of good
King Henrie the Sixt* (second edition, 1600—the source for Shakespeare's *Henry VI, Part 3*) $2,050

A Midsummer Night's Dream (second edition, 1600) $2,350

Much Ado About Nothing (first edition, 1600) $10,000

Henry V (first edition, 1600) $5,000

The Merchant of Venice (first edition, 1600) $3,200

The Merchant of Venice (second edition, 1600) $3,450

The Merry Wives of Windsor (first edition, 1602) $2,350

King Lear (second edition, 1608) $2,800

Hamlet (third edition, 1611) $1,550

*The First and second Part of the troublesome Raigne of Iohn King of
England* (third edition, 1622—the source for Shakespeare's *King
John*) $2,650

*The Lamentable and True Tragedy of Master Arden of Faversham in
Kent* (third edition, 1633—formerly attributed to Shakespeare)
$1,550

The season's climax came when the Winston H. Hagen collection
of English literature was sold in seven sessions during May 1918.[9] In

---

* The quartos were the small-format editions of the individual plays printed
before the 1623 edition of the collected plays known as the Shakespeare *First
Folio*. (A quarto was produced by folding a standard sheet twice to make four leaves
or eight pages.) The quartos were originally sold unbound for pennies; regarded as
ephemeral, few were preserved. Apart from their rarity, the quartos have great textual
value.

the introduction to the catalogue, Beverly Chew, one of the most respected bibliophiles of his time, stated: "Never before have any such collections of the works of Donne, Dryden, Gray, Milton, Pope and others been offered to the bids of the public." He cited a volume of four poems by John Skelton—which brought $9,700—as the greatest rarity in the sale. Chew's preamble concluded with a formulation of what would become a familiar credo during the next decade. When Hagen had been advised to spend less on books, he had replied, "No, my books are worth more than your bonds." The sale total justified Hagen's faith: $145,425.25 for 1,466 lots. The highspots were the Kilmarnock edition of Burns's *Poems Chiefly in the Scottish Dialect* ($2,750), Gray's *Elegy Wrote in a Country Church Yard* ($4,350), Milton's *Lycidas* ($3,500), Pope's *The Dunciad* ($2,025), Shakespeare's *Second and Third Folios* ($2,950 and $5,900), the 1640 Shakespeare *Poems* ($5,010), and Wyatt & Surrey's *Songs and Sonnets*, known as *Tottel's Miscellany* ($4,125). Some of these prices would look like bargains before the end of the Twenties.

In 1918 Kennerley was elected to the Grolier Club of New York, a group of distinguished bibliophiles; he had been proposed by Chew, who described him as a "gentleman of pleasant address."[10] Only eight books were published by Kennerley in 1918—as against forty for Knopf— none of literary distinction. The most important volume was *The Alphabet: Fifteen Interpretative Designs Drawn and Arranged with Explanatory Text and Illustrations by Frederic W. Goudy.* The Master's treatise on type design, it was set in Kennerley and Forum by Bertha M. Goudy and printed by William Edwin Rudge, with twenty-seven full-page plates. The 1,000 large-format copies were reasonably priced at $6. A second edition was published by Kennerley in 1922.

Kennerley's most curious 1918 publishing effort involved Gerald Stanley Lee's *The Air-Line to Liberty*, which advocated that the Great War be replaced with an advertising war. The Allies and Germany would bombard each other with propaganda dropped from planes. Lee—a prolific reform writer and editor of the magazine *Mount Tom* in Northampton, Massachusetts—believed that he had a divinely appointed mission. Before publication he wired Kennerley: . . . YOU AND I ARE TWO LITTLE BOYS MAKING HISTORY HARRY AND BELIEVE ME I HAVE HEARD FIFTY CITIES CALLING I KNOW THAT I KNOW THE

CREATOR HAS STATIONED AT LEAST ONE MAN IN EVERY CITY WHO IS NOT A FOOL AND WHO WILL PAY A THOUSAND DOLLARS DOWN NOT TO KEEP ON LISTENING TO THE GROANS OF TWENTY NATIONS MAKE THE PRESSES GROAN. . . . YOU AND I TOGETHER ARE MAKING A WAGER ON THERE BEING A GOD.[11] Kennerley placed a full-page ad in *Publishers' Weekly* offering to provide stores with copies to be given away at the end of thirty days: "If a bookseller cannot sell a book, it isn't worth the cost of carriage back to the publisher."[12]

The auction business was regarded as depressed during the war years because of the excess profits tax and the interruption of the New York–London trade. With peace came the inception of Kennerley's glorious epoch at Anderson. There were forty-one book sales during the 1918–1919 season—including two Huntington sales (English literature, $17,840.95 for 636 lots;[13] Americana, $17,610.35 for 241 lots)[14] and three more sales of Young's inscriptions and manuscripts ($15,671).[15]

The chief event of the season—one of the milestone book auctions—was the Herschel V. Jones library sold in three parts on 2 December 1918, 29–30 January and 4–5 March 1919.[16] He had become interested in Americana and was selling his literature to acquire capital and shelf space for his new darlings. Jones's introduction to the first catalogue closed with a warning against imposing import restrictions on rare books: "These men [the dealers] have secured for America by their painstaking work the literature of the past centuries. It is the plain duty of this Nation to leave the way open and free to the incoming of such treasures, that they may be forever at hand for the benefit of the students in schools and colleges."

Although there was concern before the opening session that the 11 November Armistice would depress prices because of an anticipated influx of books from Europe, the Twenties bull market in books began in December 1918 at the Jones sale. The library ranged from incunabula to Eugene Field but was particularly rich in the Elizabethans, the blue chips of bibliomania. The total for the three Jones sessions was $391,854.60, with an average price for the 1,727 lots of $277—as against the 1911 Hoe average of $132. Nevertheless, this library was not, as has been erroneously reported, the most valuable per volume auctioned in America to that time; two Huntington Americana sales in 1917 had higher averages.

The top bid was Smith's $14,250 for the Bridgewater *Comus* (which he had bought for $9,200 in the February 1918 Huntington sale), setting the record price for Milton. Twenty-eight Shakespeares brought $84,783, an average of $3,029. It was predicted that the star item would be the 1609 quarto of Shakespeare's *Sonnets*, the first copy to be auctioned in America and one of the two in private hands. A price in excess of $20,000 was expected; but auctioneer Chapman announced before the bidding that the authenticity of the title and dedication leaves had been questioned.* Even so, it brought $10,500 from Smith bidding for Henry C. Folger. (After the sale comparison of this copy with the William A. White copy revealed that the questioned leaves were facsimiles in both.) *Gammer Gurton's Needle* (1575), one of five known copies of the earliest published English university play, brought $10,000 from dealer Max Harzof in forty-five seconds of bidding; it had sold in July in London for £700 ($3,500). The Jones sale established William Blake as a major desideratum: *America. A Prophecy* (1793, one of two copies in America colored by Blake; $3,600) and *Europe: A Prophecy* (1794, one of two copies in America colored by Blake; $4,600). Neither of these volumes had ever before appeared at an American auction. Smith dominated the nine sessions, and it was said that he was "the competitor against the field." He spent $264,418.10, acquiring 1,011 items for Folger, Carl Pforzheimer, William Randolph Hearst, Charles W. Clark, John L. Clawson, and for stock—but mostly for Huntington.

Henry C. Folger (1857–1930), president of the Standard Oil Company of New York, was quietly assembling the greatest Shakespeare collection in the world. One of the features of his collecting that baffled his contemporaries was the acquisition of multiple copies of the *Folios*: seventy-nine *First Folios* (1623), fifty-eight *Second Folios* (1632), twenty-four *Third Folios* (1664), and thirty-six *Fourth Folios* (1685). Folger's conviction that collation of these copies would be crucial in establishing

---

* During the eighteenth and nineteenth centuries missing leaves were replaced by hand-lettered facsimiles which were often very difficult to distinguish from the real leaves. In some cases there was doubtless an intention to deceive, but in many cases the insertion of facsimiles was the result of a collector's innocent desire to complete a cherished volume.

the texts of Shakespeare's plays proved correct, although the collector did not live to see his instinct vindicated. Folger tried to buy books secretly because John D. Rockefeller did not approve of his obsession. After it was announced that Folger had paid $100,000 for a Shake-speare volume, Rockefeller told him, "We wouldn't want to think that the president of one of our major companies would be the kind of man foolish enough to pay $100,000 for a book."[17] Unhappily, Folger never saw his books assembled as a library. Since there was no space in his home, the books were locked away in vaults. After his death the Folger Shakespeare Library was built in Washington, D.C., by his bequest. When the building was dedicated, it held some 90,000 books and pamphlets and 4,500 pre-1700 manuscripts.

The Halsey-Van Duzer and the Crawford sales were held in Feb-ruary 1919—between the second and third Jones sales. The collections of Frederic R. Halsey and Henry S. Van Duzer were combined with other properties; the 1,072 lots of mainly English and American lit-erature totaled $158,749.60.[18] Halsey had previously sold his larger collection to Huntington. Smith went to $11,600 for Halsey's *Tam-erlane* (1827)—the record for Poe's first book. Only four copies were known at that time; and the previous record was $2,050, set in 1900.

The 987 lots in the John W. R. Crawford catalogue included 116 Robert Louis Stevenson items, which contributed about $7,600 to the total of $24,637.15.[19] The star was *The Sunbeam Magazine*, hand-written by Stevenson while a schoolboy, which brought $2,600 from Smith. The passion for Stevenson was one of the characteristics of collecting taste in the first decades of the twentieth century. Stevenson had died in 1894 and was a sentimental favorite of both readers and bibliophiles. One of the elements that makes an author appealing to collectors is the existence of privately printed pieces and juvenilia. There was an abundance of this material for Stevenson. The same was true for Rudyard Kipling, the other favorite modern.

Six new titles appeared with the Kennerley imprint in 1919 and only one in 1920—the year in which Knopf published eighty-two titles and Huebsch forty. None of Kennerley's books was of any importance, but one of the 1919 publications elicited a special advertising effort. *The Choice*, a novel by printing executive Maurice Weyl, chronicles the marriage of an intelligent man and a beautiful but stupid woman.

He assumes that he will be able to improve her, but she is implacably uneducable. Kennerley ran a series of six ads in the *New York Times* under the headline "The Adventures of a Novel." Each was signed by him, but there was no publication information—not even the price of the novel. The fifth ad described Kennerley's decision to publish:

> When Maurice Weyl brought me the manuscript of "The Choice" he told me it had been declined by two of the big manufacturing pub- lishers. The manuscript appeared over-bulky and it was with scant enthusiasm that I asked him to leave it with me.
>
> Before I start reading a manuscript (authors please note) I have my boy divide it into sections of fifty pages and put paper-fasteners through each section. After "The Choice" had been treated in this manner I took the first three sections home in my overcoat pocket. One night in bed after reading everything else near by, I took up the first section, and then the second section, and then the third—and then I wanted to get up and dress and go to the office for the rest of the story.
>
> "Here at least," I said to myself, "is a born story-teller."
>
> MITCHELL KENNERLEY[20]

The Choice received some encouraging reviews, and Kennerley pub- lished Weyl's next novel, *The Happy Woman*, in 1920.

The auction business was becoming a cornucopia. In order to keep the money machine operating at the Anderson, there had to be more and bigger sales every year. The success of the Jones sale encouraged other collectors to cash in at what seemed to be the top of the market. There were forty-four Anderson book sales during the 1919–1920 sea- son as against the twenty-two at the American Art. In the fall of 1919 the Anderson catalogues began carrying the line MITCHELL KENNERLEY, PRESIDENT on the covers. By this time he had acquired 120 of the 3,500 shares of the Anderson stock. After Kennerley rented the corner of the Anderson building to the Pacific Bank for $25,000 per year, he required $75,000 to renovate the top floor into exhibit rooms. He tried to borrow $100,000 from the Pacific Bank on the security of *their* lease. This ingenious plan fell through, but he was able to borrow $75,000, which Huntington guaranteed; the loan was repaid in 1921.[21]

Charles F. Heartman, the outspoken proprietor of a small auction house specializing in Americana, provided a roll call of the dealers who were active in the twenties. His comments convey an impression of the colorful personalities who made the game exciting:

> Whitman "I revolutionize the game" Bennett; Barnett J. "What difference does it make?" Beyer (Somewhere on the pinnacle he stubbed his toe); Alfred J. "Give it to me" Bowden; Ernest E. "Only I know how to sell books" Dawson; R. H. "Gentleman" Dodd; James F. "the one and only" Drake; Edward E. "Poker-face" Eberstadt; P. K. "Enough said" Foley; pathetic Robert E. Fridenberg; Alfred E. Goldsmith (who could have been among the biggest); Chas. E. "Yankee" Goodspeed; George "No enemy" Grasberger; Byrne Hackett, (who never settled down to brass tacks); Lathrop C. "Pre-occupied" Harper (If anybody should tell him about the troubles of the book business he will say "But you should have to worry over real estate"); Elmer V. Heise, (who never misses an auction sale); suave George E. Hellman; Walter M. "Sensitive and sentimental" Hill; Merle "High-spot" (I wish I had never done it) Johnson; "Jew" (no disrespect) Dr. Rosenbach; Joseph F. "Grand old man" Sabin; slightly effeminate, charitable Percy J. Sabin; Alvin J. "Kike" Scheuer, (who notwithstanding his large purchases and prompt payments was disliked by everybody); Charles "Dandy" Sessler; the greatest of all of them, the never-equalled "Bulldog" George D. "Try to take it away from me" Smith; Bill "Cincinnati" Smith; Oscar "Afraid" Wegelin; Edgard E. "Harvard" Wells (too much of an idealist); Doctor Gabriel "Rutgers" Wells (Two souls, but always cash to buy with). . . .[22]

The eleventh and twelfth Huntington duplicate sales of English literature, French drama, and Americana in January and March 1920 realized only $18,968.75.[23] The highest total of the season came from the three sales of Henry F. De Puy's Americana between November 1919 and April 1920, in which 2,641 lots brought $160,338.35.[24] Considered at that time the richest collection of Americana to be auctioned, it was particularly strong in early books relating to New York. The forty-two Jesuit Relations* were bought by Smith for Huntington at $19,000; Smith also paid $5,600 for John Florio's translation of Jacques Cartier's *A shorte and briefe narration of the two navigations and dis-*

---

* Reports by the Jesuit missionary-explorers in the New World.

coveries to the North-west parts called Newe Fraunce (London, 1580).

Another rich sale was the February assemblage of consignments from Roland R. Conklin, Mary E. Plummer, Henry H. Peck, and others, which brought $138,416.55 for 1,070 lots.[25] The top bid was Smith's $2,000 for *The Laws and Acts of the General Assembly of New Jersey* (Perth Amboy: William Bradford, 1723)—the first book printed in New Jersey. On 6 February there were two anonymous "nugget sales" (small collections of choice items) which realized high averages. William Augustus White's 100 volumes of mainly English literature brought $21,645.50.[26] Alfred T. White's 70 items of historical Americana totaled $53,804.50 ($768.64 per volume).[27] Smith bid $6,750 for the *A Platform of Church Discipline* (1649); known as the *Cambridge Platform*, it was the earliest book from the press of Samuel Green in Cambridge, Massachusetts.

The most important literary sale of the season was the collection of H. Buxton Forman in March and April 1920, which stimulated competition for nineteenth-century English literature.[28] The qualifications for a major auction were present: association books and manuscripts from the library of a distinguished English scholar-collector. In point of fact, they were no longer Forman's property. He had been persuaded to sell his collection en bloc to John B. Stetson, Jr.—an Anderson stockholder—under the assumption that it would be kept together; but Stetson put it up for auction.

When the catalogues appeared, Forman's son charged that the collection had been silently supplemented with other books—some of which were Kennerley's property. Auction regulars remarked that at an Anderson sale you never knew whether you were actually buying from Kennerley. He acquired rarities—Stevenson and Wilde, for example—which disappeared from his shelves as he included them in auctions. There was never a sale of books identified as Kennerley's property, which would have been regarded as a violation of ethics; auction houses were not supposed to own the material they sold, but this rule was laxly interpreted. It was also considered improper for auction houses to broker private sales, yet Kennerley offered whole collections to Huntington and others on a commission basis. It is unclear whether he was acting privately or on behalf of the Anderson in these transactions.

THE GREATEST MILTON VOLUME EVER OFFERED
THE DEDICATION COPY OF "COMUS"!

92000 595. [MILTON (JOHN).] [Comus] A Maske Praesented At Ludlow Castle, 1634: On Michaelmasse night, before the Right Honorable, Iohn Earle of Bridgewater, Vicount Brackly, Lord Praesident of Wales, And one of His Maiesties most honorable Privie Counsell. Small 4to, full calf, WITH THE BRIDGEWATER CREST IMPRESSED ON SIDES.

London: Printed for Hvmphrey Robinson, 1637

THE EXCESSIVELY RARE FIRST EDITION. Dedicated by H. Lawes to "Iohn Lord Vicount Bracly, Son and heire apparent to the EARLE OF BRIDGEWATER," etc. In the Dedication, Lawes says that it was "not openly acknowledg'd by the Author," and that the publication of the piece was occasioned by the trouble which he had in making transcripts from the original MS. to give away to friends.

The present copy is an exceptionally crisp and perfect copy, and extremely interesting by the fact of having some contemporary corrections made in ink on the margins, or between the lines, one change occurring on page 27, where "reproachfull" is deleted, and "contemptu[ous]" written on the margin.

This is beyond question one of the most valuable volumes ever offered for sale. The excessive rarity of "Comus" is apparent, and known to all collectors and scholars, but it is really epoch-making when the dedication copy in superb condition of one of the masterpieces of all time is offered at public auction. "Comus" was dedicated to the Earl of Bridgewater, the young Lord Brackly, who took the part of the "Elder Brother" when it was first acted before his father on Michaelmas night, 1634. This volume therefore was probably the DEDICATION COPY and has been, as far as can be traced, in the Bridgewater Library since it was first published. About the year 1800 it was rebound and the Bridgewater Crest impressed upon its sides. The Bridgewater Library has been preserved intact from early in the 17th Century until its purchase by Mr. Huntington last year, and this, the famous Bridgewater "Comus," has always been mentioned among the first of its treasures. (See frontispiece.)

14000 596. MILTON (JOHN). The Reason of Church-government Urg'd against Prelaty. In two Books. *Rule and woodcut vignette on title.* Small 4to, full dark blue levant morocco, Jansen style, gilt edges, by Rivière.

London: Printed by E. G. for Iohn Rothwell, 1641

FIRST EDITION. Exceedingly Rare. Sigs. Title; A-H5 in fours. The Halsey copy.

31000 597. MILTON (JOHN). Areopagitica; a Speech of Mr. John Milton For the Liberty of Vnlicenc'd Printing, To the Parliament of England. Small 4to, full green levant morocco, gilt back, gilt panelled sides, gilt edges, by The Club Bindery (corner of title margin repaired).

London: Printed in the Yeare, 1644

Description of Comus; English Literature from the Library of Henry E. Huntington (*4–6 February 1918*)

Front cover of Forman Catalogue (Courtesy of the Pennsylvania State University Library)

George D. Smith died shortly before the opening of the Forman sale, having suffered a stroke during an argument with a purveyor of suspect Washingtoniana. There was concern that the book market had also incurred a stroke. Who else would be able to dominate auctions and push prices steadily higher?

Kennerley wrote in tribute to Smith:

George D. Smith was the greatest book dealer the world has ever known. There have been rare book dealers in England for centuries who have sold great books and helped to form great libraries, but George D. Smith was essentially a product of the time, and was the first man to deal in great books in a great way. He was not satisfied with selling single volumes, but dealt in great collections. No library was too large for him to consider purchasing, nor, for that matter, was any single book beneath his attention. At the sight or the mention of a book his eyes lit up with interest and enthusiasm. He lived books eighteen hours a day for the last thirty-seven years.

There is not a great collector of books of the last forty years who has not dealt with George D. Smith. Since the Hoe sale nine years ago he had bought and sold a greater volume of books than all the other dealers in rare books in the world put together, and he has bought for Henry E. Huntington what is now the greatest private library in the world, ranking second only to the British museum, and in some respects surpassing it. He has done what can never be done again. Untold millions could not now purchase such a collection.

There are many collectors in America who today will look on their shelves and be grateful that they took George D. Smith's advice when he said to them about some rare volume, "Buy it. You will never see another copy. Ten years from now it will be worth twice—three times— what you can buy it for today." George D. Smith lived long enough to see his prophecies fulfilled many times over. At the sale of every great collection he saw books which he had sold for a few hundred dollars bring as many thousand. When everyone said that he had paid a big price for a book, his invariable reply was "I got it cheap." When the Bridgewater copy of Milton's "Comus" was sold in one of the sales of Mr. Huntington's duplicates, people lifted their hands, but six months later the same copy was sold in the Jones sale for $14,250, but when it was knocked down to him, Mr. Smith's remark was "The next time it will be $20,000."

First, last and always George D. Smith preached the value of rare books and he raised their prices accordingly, so that within the last few years they have come to take rank in the public mind with pictures and rare art objects. His passion for books was irresistible and contagious and many of the great collectors of today owe it to him that they collected books. Perhaps Mr. Smith's most outstanding characteristic was an extraordinary and unfailing memory. When a book came up for sale he recognized at once the copy, the prices at which it had been sold in previous sales and the history of every collector who owned it. He has left behind in his well-known store on Forty-Fifth Street a stock of books that would in themselves constitute a great library, and it is hoped that the name of George D. Smith will not be allowed to die out of the active business life of New York. He is one of the rare few whose names will forever remain a tradition in the history of his times.[29]

The Forman sales provided forty-four-year-old Dr. Rosenbach with the opportunity to declare himself Smith's rightful successor. The best items were segregated in the first catalogue of 1,000 items, which brought $150,685—an impressive figure for nineteenth-century liter-ature then. The twenty-seven Keats and 143 Shelley entries were particularly strong. Dr. R spent almost half of the total: he bought twenty-five Shelleys for $30,274, including the annotated copy of *Queen Mab* at $6,000 which he resold to composer Jerome Kern. But Dr. R was the underbidder on the star item, the twenty-seven-page manu-script (2½ inches by 4 inches) of Shelley's *Julian and Maddalo*, which went to Chicago dealer Ernest Dressel North for $16,500.

A photo of the Forman sale taken when the Shelley lots were offered presents an un-gala impression. The room is not crowded, and the occasion is not dressy. Dr. R is in the last row at the left next to the pillar. At his side is A. Edward Newton, his fellow-Philadelphian who wrote a series of popular books about books—including *The Amenities of Book Collecting* (1918)—that did much to spread the bibliophile gospel. Frederick Chapman is in the rostrum; young Anthony Bade, who would succeed him as the chief Anderson auctioneer, stands facing the room at the lowest desk.

Forman's copy of Keats's *Lamia, Isabella, The Eve of St. Agnes and Other Poems* inscribed by Keats to his fiancée Fanny Brawne went to Dr. R at $4,050. For $800 he acquired a short letter from the dying Keats to Fanny: "I dare not think of you or write much to you." When other Keats love letters were sold in 1885 Oscar Wilde had written a sonnet lamenting that the precious relics had been exposed to "the brawlers of the auction mart." After the Forman sale Christopher Morley wrote a sonnet commemorating the Rosenbach purchase. Morley presented manuscripts of his poem to Kennerley and Rosenbach; both claimed to own the original, but it is clear that they both had fair copies (not the first draft). Kennerley produced a facsimile of his copy as a Christmas keepsake in 1927.[30]

Dr. R regarded Poe material as the most valuable in American literature and bought the thirty-eight-page manuscript of "The Spectacles" for stock at $9,100; it was the most expensive American item in the Forman sale. The Forman Library—for which Stetson had paid $80,000—brought $178,739.80; the profit was divided between Stetson and the Anderson.

A week after the opening Forman sale the great library of Walter T. Wallace was sold at the American Art. Although $300,000 was predicted, the 1,560 lots brought only $153,766.50.[31] The failure was blamed on the death of Smith and the flood of major sales that spring; Kennerley said that the American Art didn't know how to hold a proper book auction.

Rosenbach's ascendancy was encouraged by Kennerley, who needed a dealer to support the market and make headline purchases. Rosenbach received special terms from the Anderson. He was permitted to extend his payments over twelve months, whereas other dealers had to settle in six or nine months. For a time they were boon companions, but the Doctor never trusted Kennerley. Rosenbach remarked to his assistant, John Fleming, that Kennerley was the only man in the rare book trade he feared because he never knew when Kennerley would do something reckless that would place them both at risk.[32]

Between the first and second Forman sales Stetson disposed of his Oscar Wilde collection at the Anderson in April 1920.[33] The finest Wilde collection ever sold at auction, the 473 lots brought $46,686. The top item, twenty-five letters to Lord Alfred Douglas—whose relationship with Wilde led to Wilde's imprisonment—went to Dr. R for $7,900. The underbidder was Gabriel Wells, who spent much of his career in that role. Dr. R also picked up Wilde's manuscripts for "The True Value of Criticism" ($2,150) and "The Decay of Lying"

($1,525). The revised typescript for *The Importance of Being Earnest* brought $500 from Dr. R; in 1981 it made $99,000 at Christie's—the record price for a modern literary manuscript.

This season stimulated the growing interest in native Americana—material relating to the exploration and settlement of North America, as distinguished from earlier European accounts of the New World. In addition to the De Puy collection, there were two sales of early California material[34] and the first part of Dr. Frank P. O'Brien's "remarkable collection of the books and pamphlets published by Beadle and Adams dealing with the character, condition, exploits, stories, biography and history of the pioneers."[35] Prices were still reasonable for this material. The two Californiana sales totaled only $11,908.75 for 666 lots; and the 322 O'Brien lots brought $3,198.30, which was regarded as extraordinary. Americana was energetically pursued by Dr. R. One of his strengths was that, unlike most dealers, he did not specialize: his interests embraced all of literature and history.

The 1919–1920 season brought the dissolution of George D. Smith's empire. Although his business continued to operate, there was no one to direct it with his daring. Smith left a gross estate of $1,676,000 with a net value of about 20 percent; but he was heavily in debt for unsold books purchased on long-term notes.* Moreover, he had been devoted to the sport of kings and had maintained a racing stable. It was not unusual for him to bet $5,000 on a race. Kennerley was an administrator for the estate, which was in need of ready money to pay debts and provide for Smith's widow and posthumously born child.

In May 1920 the first of a series of disposal sales from Smith's magnificent stock was held at the Anderson.[37] The headnote explained: "All the books and manuscripts described in this catalogue were purchased by Mr. Smith in London and Paris in December, 1919, and January, 1920, and at the time of his death were in the Customs or

---

* When Smith bought the Bixby collection for Huntington in 1918, he gave Bixby a note for $500,000 and posted as security $623,000 in Safety Insulated Wire & Cable Company bonds. There was no market for these bonds when the note came due in 1923. With difficulty Kennerley persuaded Huntington to purchase the bonds from Smith's estate for $398,720.[36]

In an Auction Room
(Letter of John Keats to Fanny Brawne,
Anderson Galleries, March 15, 1920

How about this lot? said the auctioneer;
One hundred, may I say, just for a start?
Between the plum-red curtains, drawn apart,
A written sheet was held .... And strange to hear
(Dealer, would I were steadfast as thou art)
The cold quick bids. (Against you in the rear!)
The crimson salon, in a glow more clear
Burned bloodlike purple as the poet's heart.

Song. That outgrew the singer! Bitter Love
That broke the proud hot heart it held in thrall—
Poor script, where still those tragic passions move—.
Eight hundred bid: fair warning: the last call:
The soul of Adonais, like a star .....
Sold for eight hundred dollars — Doctor R!

For Mitchell Kennerley
November 11, 1920 — Christopher Morley

FROM MITCHELL KENNERLEY, CHRISTMAS 1927
AND HELEN KENNERLEY

TOP: *Anderson Galleries at the H. Buxton Forman sale, 15–17 March 1920 (Courtesy of The Rosenbach Museum and Library)*

LEFT: *Christopher Morley poem (Courtesy of Morley and Jean Kennerley)*

on the Ocean. They have all been delivered direct from Customs to the Anderson Galleries, and have never before been offered for sale in America." Many of these books were from the great Newdigate Library in Warwickshire. The 1,000 items realized only $47,419.25.

All of the Smith sales would be disappointing. A book or manuscript has no firm value; it is worth what someone is willing to pay. There are great variations in the prices the same item can be sold for by different dealers. Smith's salesmanship, reputation, and influence over collectors had made it possible for him to get top prices. The great G. D. S. could have sold his stock for a fortune, but the dealers were bargain-hunting; and collectors were reluctant to bid high on a dealer's stock.

The Anderson did not yield the art field to the American Art. During the 1919–1920 season there were thirty-five sales of paintings and antiques at the Anderson as against fifty-three at the American Art. A February 1920 Anderson sale included thirty-six signed Renoir sketches, which fetched $7,140.[38] Another sale of ninety-six pastels, mostly signed by Renoir, was held in April.[39] C. Lewis Hind prepared a statement for the second catalogue defending the first group against charges by Renoir's son that they were fakes. (For a time Hind lived in an apartment at the Anderson Galleries; Kennerley regarded him as the best conversationalist he knew and said that Carman and Hind were the two men whose friendship he most valued.) Hind authenticated both groups of Renoirs, but concluded with a fudging statement:

> . . . I am desired by Mr. Mitchell Kennerley to say that these 96 Renoirs will be sold entirely on their merits, as delightful, delicate, and dainty works of art. You are invited to decide whether you will buy through your eyes or through your ears. You can bid for them as by Renoir, or as by somebody else, some amazing Unknown who ought to be Renoir, but may not be. To dogmatize on the matter of their authenticity is ridiculous. That could only be done by someone who was in the Master's atelier when he made these spring-time pastels. I do not dogmatize. I but reiterate my opinion that they are by Renoir, and place before you this statement of all the facts known to me about the Renoir sale.

The ninety-six pastels brought $3,078 after Chapman announced from the rostrum that the drawings had been the property of the late Baroness von Zimmerman: "It is proposed to announce a meeting at the galleries when the full and complete authenticity of the drawings and paintings and the motives for the unsupported attack will be explained."[40] There was no report of such a meeting.

On 26 May 1920 Lucien Mignon, a former student in Renoir's atelier, wrote to Kennerley claiming the sketches in both sales as his own work which he had sold to an unnamed American dealer in October 1919. When Mignon's claim was published, Kennerley stated:

> I never heard of Lucien Mignon, and I doubt the story of the forgeries. Pierre Renoir is a boy about 18 years old, and it appears that he will believe anything dealers tell him. I have known these Renoirs for the past nine years. They were the property of Baroness von Zimmerman, who died two years ago in California, and she bought them from Renoir's model. I prefer not to say anything further until I learn more about this man Mignon and communicate with Paris. We are still searching for further information in Paris about the history of the paintings.[41]

Kennerley's secretary subsequently revealed that the disputed Renoirs had been brought to the Anderson by C. V. Miller of the Louis IV Antique Company on Fifth Avenue.[42] Miller was unavailable for a statement. There was no further newspaper coverage. Kennerley's papers at the New York Public Library include his canceled personal refund checks to some of the Renoir purchasers; it is therefore likely that he was the actual owner of the sketches at the time of the sale.

Kennerley was always attracted to bookshops. Despite the moribund state of his publishing house he undertook a new venture in the fall of 1920, setting up the Neighborhood Bookshop. Laurence Gomme was hired to manage this business at Park Avenue and Fifty-sixth Street, which sold new books and a selection of antiquarian volumes from Smith's stock. Kennerley envisioned a chain and later added a second shop at Madison Avenue and Seventy-third Street. Although the Neighborhood Bookshop made money, Kennerley sold out in 1922, explaining to Gomme: "I have decided that I have got about all the fun that is coming to me out of your shop. . . ."[43]

Kennerley issued a sanguine statement to launch the 1920–1921 season: "I believe that in every respect that we are going to have the most astonishing season on record. The number of book collectors has increased several times in the last few years due perhaps to the leadership of Henry E. Huntington, the courage of George D. Smith, and the ability and enterprise of the increasing number of rare book dealers."[44] Nonetheless, the new season seemed dull after the excitements of 1919–1920, although there were thirty-nine Anderson book sales. Most of the interest was generated by the six Smith disposals,[45] which totaled $200,434.55 for 2,447 items—a wretched average of $81.91. Among the treasures in Part VI were Burns's manuscript for "The Bonnie Moor-Hen" ($400), the second quarto of *Love's Labour's Lost* ($700), Shelley's seven-page letter to his publisher defending *Laon and Cythna* ($845), and the only known copy of John Taylor's 1631 *Complaint of Christmas* ($785). Charles Heartman asserted that Smith's treasures had been looted; "some priceless Americana were slaughtered, in many cases for less than ten cents on the dollar."[46]

Three notable private collections were sold in 1920–1921. E. W. Coggeshall's association books numbered only seventy-eight lots but brought $17,726.[47] After disposing of his Dickens and Thackeray at the Anderson in 1916, Coggeshall started a new collection and reacquired some of the books he had sold. The Herman Le Roy Edgar collection of Americana was the richest sale of the season, bringing an "astonishing" $128,668.75 for 696 lots (an average of $184.86).[48] It included twenty Indian treaties, the largest group of Jesuit Relations ever auctioned (forty-seven, totaling $11,000), and a run of books on witchcraft and sorcery. Edgar's star item was George Beste's *A True Discourse of the late Voyages of discoveries, for the finding of a passage to Cathaya. . . .* (1578) at $4,600. The most important literary sale of the season was John L. Clawson's later English literature of 534 lots for $71,500.75.[49] He retained his superb collection of early English literature, but the trade expected to see it go on the block. After a collector disposes of part of his library, he becomes susceptible to selling the rest. It is also the case that he often starts all over again.

In addition to the three Edgar sales, Americana was represented by Part II of the O'Brien sale[50] and the William Loring Andrews collection.[51] Andrews's copy (one of three known) of the 1731 William

Bradford map of New York City fetched $6,500—the record price for a printed item relating to New York. The buyer was Cortlandt F. Bishop, who would presently acquire both the American Art Association and the Anderson Galleries.

Nineteen twenty-one, Kennerley's last year as an active publisher, was highlighted by Millay's *Second April* and *Aria da Capo*. Although occasional books appeared with his imprint through the Twenties, they were mainly published for his own pleasure. In June 1921 the *New York Times* announced that Kennerley would publish the lost manuscript of Oscar Wilde's *The Portrait of Mr. W. H.*,[52] a work of fiction that identified W. H.—the dedicatee and "onlie begetter" of Shakespeare's sonnets—as a boy actor named Will Hughes. Wilde had first advanced this theory in an 1880 essay and enlarged it into a 28,000-word book for John Lane and Elkin Mathews in 1893. Publication was delayed, and the manuscript disappeared at the time of Wilde's arrest. The Will Hughes theory—based on puns in the sonnets ("A man in hew all Hews in his controlling")—was not original with Wilde, having been advanced in the eighteenth century. However, Wilde's conviction for pederasty combined with his insinuation of Shakespeare's homosexuality had made the manuscript unpublishable in England. Kennerley sought Hooley's judgment, who reported that there were no grounds for censorship: "I certainly cannot conceive that anyone, not in himself hopelessly tainted, could impute even an adumbration of evil to a book written in such a vein, and such a spirit."[53]

At the time that he announced the forthcoming publication Kennerley declined to provide the provenance for the manuscript; but on 20 June the *New York Post* printed an interview in which he explained that *The Portrait of Mr. W. H.* had been in the hands of one of Wilde's literary friends at the time of his arrest. The friend had retained the manuscript; it was discovered by his sister after his death and sent to Kennerley for authentication. "But it was like having a million-dollar bank note—it couldn't be cashed. Although one may possess a man's writings, one cannot legally publish them without permission of the author, or, if he be dead, from the executor."[54] Kennerley revealed less than he knew. The manuscript had been in the possession of Frederic Chapman, Lane's office manager. Before the discovery was announced, Kennerley sold the manuscript for Chapman's sister to Dr. Rosenbach for $3,000.[55] The Doctor was unable to dispose of it at $5,500 and kept it in his own collection.[56]

After difficulties, Kennerley obtained the American copyright from the Wilde estate with the provision that no edition was to be published in England until thirty days after the appearance of the American edition. The prospectus for *The Portrait of Mr. W. H.* offered the 1,000 numbered copies at a prepublication price of $10. "No more than ten copies will be sold to any single subscriber. . . . The price of any copies that remain unsold . . . will be advanced to fifteen dollars." The volume was printed in Kennerley type on handmade paper, with a facsimile of the final manuscript page. No controversy ensued. In 1927 Kennerley was involved in the discovery of another lost Wilde manuscript, *The Duchess of Padua.*

Alongside the promoter in Kennerley there was always the word lover, even when his devotion seemed misguided. In 1921 he became the publisher of Horace Fish with *The Great Way: A Story of the Joyful, the Sorrowful, the Glorious*—a novel Kennerley announced "will establish Horace Fish as a stylist, as no American has succeeded in establishing himself, since Hawthorne."[57] He later wrote a memo on his involvement with this self-destructive author:

> In 1918 I received by express the manuscript of a novel "The Great Way" by Horace Fish. I read it and was fascinated by its color and vivacity but it was very uneven and overwritten in parts and I returned it to the author. But I didn't forget it!
>
> A few months later my friend Helen Freeman was looking for a play and I thought of "The Great Way." I told her about the manuscript and said it would make a grand play and I wrote the author asking him to send the MSS to me again. This time he brought it and I told him what I thought of it in detail and suggested that Miss Freeman should read the manuscript and afterwards talk it over with him, which was done. Fish came to admire Miss Freeman and she helped him with advice and encouragement to revise "The Great Way" so that I agreed to publish it, which I did in 1921. Miss Freeman helped considerably in rewriting the book and it is dedicated to her.
>
> I did everything I could to make the book a success: sent letters and books to innumerable friends and acquaintances and advertised it gen-erously in the newspapers. . . . The book sold pretty well but just wouldn't become a best seller.

. . . .

There was no doubt in my mind that Horace Fish was a genius—but a most unpleasant one! He was a nervous wreck, and physically unpleasant, from dissipation. He smoked and drank constantly and was unreliable in every respect. He did not seem to know—or care—whether he was drunk or sober, clean or dirty.

He had an appealing way with him and a lot of stray men and women worshipped at his shrine of genius and debauchery.[58]

The Great Way is set in Spain, as are all of Fish's published novels, and follows the career of a girl of the streets who becomes an opera star. Many of the reviews were extremely laudatory, hailing Fish as a brilliant new literary star. Frank Harris wrote in *Pearson's Magazine*: "I would rather have written this book than any I have read in the last ten or twelve years."[59]

Kennerley published Fish's 1922 volume of connected stories, *Terassa of Spain*; and in 1924 he co-published with Huebsch *The Saint's Theatre: A Novel* and *The Wrists on the Door*—a promotional booklet for Fish's work that included a 1919 story Kennerley described as "the most powerful American short story of our times."[60] In *The Wrists on the Door* a childless man is rebuked by the spirit of the son he never had for denying him life. Kennerley provided Fish an allowance while he was writing a long novel entitled "Alchemy." When the work was submitted, the readers' reports by Hooley, Temple Scott, and Christopher Morley were unfavorable. Morley commented: "Mark you, there *is* a strength in it, but ruined and beslavered with words and all the suetty clap-trap of melodrama and coincidence. . . . Even for a reading-audience of governesses and slaveys, I don't feel sure of it."[61] The novel remained unpublished at Fish's death in 1928.

Horace Fish may well be the only forgotten Kennerley novelist who merits reconsideration. Despite stylistic excesses and contrived plotting, he effectively conveyed the local color of Spain: his portrayals of Spanish character are still interesting—if not entirely convincing. The reviews of his books clearly attest that Fish's contemporaries detected evidence of genius in his fiction.

The 1921 publication that provided Kennerley the most satisfaction was *Walt Whitman in Mickle Street* by Elizabeth Leavitt Kelley, the

THE PORTRAIT
OF MR W. H.
AS WRITTEN BY
OSCAR WILDE

SOME TIME AFTER THE PUB-
LICATION OF HIS ESSAY,
OF THE SAME TITLE, AND
NOW FIRST PRINTED FROM
THE ORIGINAL ENLARGED
MANUSCRIPT WHICH FOR
TWENTY-SIX YEARS HAS
BEEN LOST TO THE WORLD

PUBLISHED 1921 BY
MITCHELL KENNERLEY
489 PARK AVENUE
NEW YORK

LEFT: *Title page of* The Portrait of Mr. W. H. *(Bruccoli Collection)*

BELOW: *Advertising card for* The Great Way *(Bruccoli Collection)*

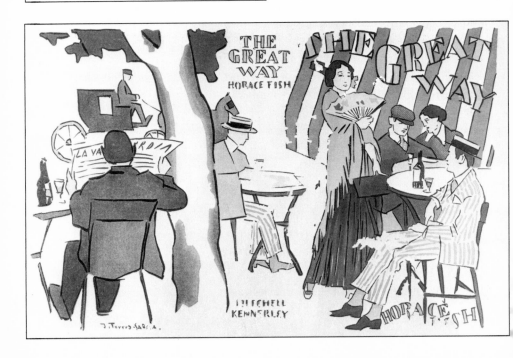

nurse who cared for him during his final illness. The publisher told Stieglitz that it was "the best trade edition I ever made and one of the best trade editions ever made."[62] This chaste volume is bound in brown cloth with gilded top edge and a printed paper label on the spine; Kennerley's name or monogram does not appear on the binding. Surprisingly, the text was not set in Kennerley type. The dust jacket reproduces Marsden Hartley's painting of Whitman's house; and the jacket spine identifies the volume as a "LIMITED EDITION" with the price of $2.50—although no limitation is specified in the book.

Only four Kennerley titles appeared in 1922, including a large-format edition of Goudy's *Elements of Lettering* at the bargain price of $5. At this stage Kennerley was disposing of his backlist to raise cash and to disburden himself of the warehousing problem. In May and June he ran ads in *Publishers' Weekly* headlined "40 BOOKS FOR $10":

> Send me ten dollars and I will send you, prepaid, forty different books of a published value of at least fifty dollars, selected from the thousand titles I have published during the last twenty years. If you are not delighted, return the books and I will refund the money.[63]

(There were two exaggerations: He had not published a thousand titles, and he had not been a publisher for 20 years.)

Kennerley's endeavors to make the Anderson Galleries a cultural center were abetted by his friendship with Alfred Stieglitz. As the leading photographer and promoter of modern art, Stieglitz mounted a series of influential exhibits at the Anderson, commencing with a 1921 retrospective of his own work—proposed by Kennerley, who wrote him: "I feel very confident that there will be a number of sales as it will be something new to the New Yorker to buy photographs— not to mention such photographs."[64] This show was followed by six Stieglitz-produced exhibits between 1921 and 1925, featuring the work of Stieglitz, Marsden Hartley, Georgia O'Keeffe, Charles Demuth, Arthur Dove, John Marin, and Paul Strand.[65] The 1922 exhibit-sale of 117 paintings by Hartley and seventy-five by James N. Rosenberg netted Hartley $4,913, on which Kennerley refused to take a commission.[66] The 1922 auction of forty living American artists was a monetary failure,[67] but it attracted attention to the Anderson. Kennerley wrote to Stieglitz in 1924: " . . . you and Georgia O'Keefe will be welcome here at any time by everyone of us without any thought of making any money out of commissions. . . . We shall all receive you just as gladly if no pictures or photographs are for sale."[68]

In 1925 Stieglitz rented Room 303 at the Anderson for $1,800 a year, naming it The Intimate Gallery, where sixteen exhibits of American painters were mounted over the next four years.[69] One of Stieglitz's announcements explained his purpose:

> The Intimate Gallery is a Direct Point of Contact between Public and Artist. It is the Artist's Room. It is a Room with but One Standard. Alfred Stieglitz has volunteered his services and is its guardian Spirit.
> The Intimate Gallery is not a Business nor is it a "Social" Function. The Intimate Gallery compares with no one nor with anything.[70]

Stieglitz wrote to Kennerley in 1923: "She [Georgia O'Keeffe, his wife] is as wonderful as ever—about as *White* as white can be—And I have a passion for Whiteness in all its forms—That's why you mean so much to me—You have a whiteness few can see for so few have whiteness—"[71] Kennerley later informed him that "I think of you always and it is one of the chief comforts of my life. It helps me to forgive myself."[72]

The Stieglitz exhibits were supplemented by a wide range of shows organized by Walter Grant, the Anderson art director. These included work by Augustus John, Gari Melchers, and Jerome Blum (with a catalogue introduction by Theodore Dreiser), as well as exhibits by George Luks's students, The Louis Comfort Tiffany Foundation, and the New Society of Artists—which drew 1,200 to its opening. A surprise success was the 1921 show of the work of the fourteen-year-old Pamela Bianco. The 1925 Brown and Bigelow calendar art competition attracted 2,000 entries. Also in 1925 the Anderson mounted an exhibition of all the production stages for Joseph Pennell's *The Adventures of an Illustrator*; Robert Underwood Johnson gave the address at the opening, which was attended by Nicholas Murray Butler, Owen Wister, Cass Gilbert, Walter Damrosch, Henry Van Dyke, and Elihu Root. The 1929 showing of Jo Davidson's five-ton statue of Senator Robert M. La Follette required the Anderson floor to be reinforced, and Park Avenue was closed off while the work was being moved.

In November 1922 Kennerley privately exhibited six fifteenth-century French tapestries depicting "The Hunt for the Unicorn" from the La Rochefoucauld family's castle at Verteuil. Admission was restricted to "about ten of the most important men in New York," and the offering price was $1,200,000. After a short time the tapestries were removed without explanation. It was announced in February 1923 that John D. Rockefeller, Jr., had purchased them for $1,100,000 from Edouard Larcade, Vice President of the Syndical Chambers of Curios and Fine Arts in Paris. There were conflicting reports as to whether Larcade was the actual owner or the agent for the La Rochefoucaulds. The French press was indignant, claiming that the family had pledged not to remove the tapestries from France. It was disclosed that the tapestries had been transferred from New York to London for the sale, enabling Larcade to save $377,000 in taxes. After the purchase Rockefeller brought them back to America duty-free as antiquities. Anderson's cut on the transaction was not revealed.[73]

The otherwise dull 1921–1922 season was noteworthy for the Charles Dickens collections that came to the auction block. The American Art sold Frederick Corder's Dickens in January 1922,[74] but the Anderson handled two major Dickens collections and a Thackeray collection during February. On the first of the month Dr. R. T. Jupp's Dickens collection brought $32,508.75 for 491 lots.[75] This auction was regarded as the most enthusiastic since the Forman sale; much of the buying was by collectors, not dealers. The top price was $3,500 for *The Pickwick Papers* in parts.* The manuscript describing the creation of *Pickwick* brought $2,200. On the sixth of January Henry S. Van Duzer's Thackerays totaled $32,848.50 for 350 lots,[76] with Belle Greene taking *The Exquisites* for the Morgan at $2,350; *Vanity Fair* in parts made $2,100. The next week William G. Wilkins's Dickens collection of 575 lots brought $9,667.[77]

---

* Dickens's novels—and those of other popular writers of the period—were issued serially in separate paper-covered installments before book publication. Since these pamphlets were read to pieces or stripped of their covers for binding, complete sets in good condition are rare.

Americana was represented by *The West Its History & Romance*,[78] featuring thirty-nine volumes of documents relating to Fort Sutter; Dr. R took them for the reasonable price of $8,450. The third part of Dr. O'Brien's western Americana brought $10,292.85 for 672 lots in March 1922,[79] but Kennerley privately sold O'Brien's 2,100 additional Beadle Dime Novels to Huntington. Kennerley informed the press that Huntington had selected *California Joe; or the Angel of the Wilderness* and *Old Grizzly Adams the Bear Tamer* to read on the train trip to California.[80]

Whatever problems other people had with Kennerley, he maintained a good, but formal, business relationship with Huntington; they were never on a first-name basis. In response to Kennerley's 1922 request for a letter of introduction he could use with European consignors, Huntington wrote: "My dealings with Mr. Kennerley, both personally and in a business way, have always been most pleasant. I am sure that anyone having undertaken business connections of whatsoever nature will appreciate, as I have, the careful consideration of the business man, and the courteous treatment of the gentleman, which Mr. Kennerley will certainly give."[81]

The most valuable sale of the season came in May when Theodore N. Vail's 1,358 lots fetched $120,819.75.[82] Vail was president of AT&T; it was said that "Bell created the telephone and Vail created the telephone business." The *Cambridge Platform* brought $5,700—$1,050 down from 1920. Vail's four Shakespeare *Folios* were sold individually for $17,250 to Gabriel Wells, who paid the top price of $9,500 for the *First Folio* with facsimile title page. Many of the Twenties bull-market prices would be bargains now. In 1985 the four *Folios* were auctioned at Sotheby's in New York for $708,400; the repaired copy of the *First Folio* made $638,000.

The 1922–1923 season started with the four parts of the Henry Cady Sturges collection (American literature, $19,243; English literature, $15,285.75; Americana, $9,028.35; and autographs, $5,828).[83] American literature still lagged behind English literature. Most of Sturges's 1,958 lots of American books went for under $10; one volume reached four figures when Dr. R went to $1,625 for William Cullen Bryant's *The Embargo* (1808). The only known copy in the original boards of Phyllis Wheatley's *Poems* (1773)—the first collection of verse by an American black—was worth $27.50. Washington's 1788 letter to Jonathan Trumbull expressing his reluctance to accept the presidency fetched $1575: "May Heaven assist me in forming a judgment: for at present, I see nothing but clouds and darkness before me."

A sale of books from the collections of Dr. Thomas A. Emmet, James S. Hardy, Mrs. Julie Le Gallienne, and S. H. Taylor totaled $40,653.50 for 485 lots;[84] it included Emmet's complete set of autographs for the Signers in an extra-illustrated volume of John Sanderson's *Biography of the Signers of the Declaration of Independence* at $19,750—which would soon seem a giveaway price. A collection of 1,157 lots of *A Great Collection of Original Source Material Relating To The Early West And The Far West* (described as having "more items of extraordinary rarity and importance—some hitherto unknown—and more examples of early and excessively rare Western imprints than any other collection that has ever been publicly dispersed") brought $42,952.45 for 1,157 lots.[85] The thirteenth Huntington duplicate sale, 1,014 lots of *Literature of the West*, realized only $20,924.50. If the bottom of the Huntington barrel was being reached, it had been a marvelous barrel.[86]

The most important sale of the season was held in January 1923 for *The Later Library of Herschel V. Jones.*[87] The catalogue included the collector's letter to Kennerley:

> After the disposal, four years ago, of my library of English Literature, I proceeded to collect one hundred rare Elizabethan books, with accompanying minor, but important volumes, for the sole purpose of giving me comfort in the time of bereavement over the loss of my friends.
>
> Instead of their proving a comfort, I find myself miserable in being compelled to face the impossibility of collecting another English Library.
>
> I shall be happier with none than with the few. Therefore, I am sending them to you for disposal.

Jones had not retired from the field; his interest had shifted to Americana. Moreover, he enjoyed the auction-room competition for his books; since he usually turned a profit, the spectacle was doubly enjoyable.

The 212 Jones items totaled $137,865.50 (an average of $650 as against the impressive average of $277 in the 1918–1919 Jones sale). Dr. Rosenbach bought 80 percent of the items, spending $127,535—of which $42,000 was for Clawson. The star item was Christopher Marlowe and Thomas Nash's *The Tragedie of Dido Queene of Carthage*

(1594); boasting the Yardley-Henderson-Reed-Steevens-Roxburghe-Brydges-Heber-Kemble-Devonshire-Huntington pedigree, it was catalogued as "The most important play with the exception of Shakespeare's own, that has ever been offered for sale." There were three known copies, of which the other two were institutionalized. Dr. R took it at $12,900 for Folger. Other major rarities included Cicero's *Tullye of Old Age*, printed by William Caxton, England's first printer, in 1481 ($9,850); Robert Green's *Morando* ($3,200); John Lyly's *Comedie of Alexander, Campaspe and Diogenes* ($4,350) and *Sapho and Phaon* ($3,450); Anthony Munday's *Fidele and Fortunio* ($3,400); Shakespeare's 1640 *Poems* ($4,800); and the first copy of Edmund Spenser's *Amoretti and Epithalamion* to be auctioned in America ($8,600).

While the auction business was booming, Kennerley's own finances were a muddle of borrowings to repay borrowings. His financial dealings with lawyer-author-artist James N. Rosenberg during the period of Anderson's rising fortunes present a record of his jugglings of relatively small sums.[88] 2 October 1919: Kennerley sends Rosenberg 120 shares of Anderson stock and assigns $10,000 of life insurance policies (against which there were small loans) to Rosenberg. 29 September 1920: Kennerley sells Rosenberg shares of Anderson stock in return for $543.52 and cancellation of a $500 debt. 29 September 1920: Kennerley sends Rosenberg $10,000 of life insurance policies as security for $4,000 loan. 8 March 1921: Kennerley borrows 120 shares of Anderson stock from Rosenberg and gives him note for $5,217.50; Kennerley to use stock for loan collateral. 7 March 1924: Kennerley declines purchase of 120 shares; will repay Rosenberg $3,737.03 in "a few days." 26 March 1924: Kennerley sends Rosenberg $737.03 and note for $3,000. Kennerley has $60,000 worth of Anderson stock; will borrow against stock to pay Rosenberg $3,000 "in a few days." 28 January 1927: Kennerley sends Rosenberg 250 shares of Anderson stock (worth $25,000) as collateral for $12,500 bank loan; Kennerley claims to own over 90 percent of $350,000 Anderson capital stock. 28 February 1927: Kennerley repays $12,500 bank loan guaranteed by Rosenberg. These transactions probably resulted from Kennerley's efforts to gain control of the Anderson Galleries stock. Since the stock never paid dividends, disgruntled investors were ready to sell out to him.

CHAPTER SIX

The John Quinn Sale—the Clawson,
Leverhulme, Arnold, Chew, Adam,
and Goodyear Sales—Button Gwinnett—
The Gutenberg Bible

THE SALE OF JOHN QUINN'S LIBRARY at the Anderson remains the greatest auction of modern literature. The 12,108 lots were sold in thirty-two sessions between November 1923 and March 1924.[1] Quinn collected modern authors in depth at a time when other collectors concentrated on the "high spots" of early literature. Because of his friendship with—and patronage of—contemporary writers, he was able to acquire rich manuscript holdings for Conrad and for Joyce, Synge, Yeats, and other figures of the Irish Renaissance. The five-volume catalogue was the most readable ever produced by the Anderson, and is still used for bibliographical reference. In addition to the manuscript facsimiles and portraits—several of which had been commissioned by Quinn from John B. Yeats—the author lists were preceded by headnotes written by Hooley, which ranged from brief biographies to critical essays. The *New York Herald* stated that the headnotes brought the Quinn catalogues within the boundaries of literature.[2] Since Hooley had known some of the authors, he was able to make personal observations on them:

Bliss Carman—it is not impertinent to be personal with historic figures—is a man of striking appearance, tall, lithe, blue-eyed, and with a royal crown of fair hair scarcely greying. His philosophy of life—beauty, restraint in freedom—shows in his features, as in his works. Walking in country or city, talking in workshop or forum, he presents the ideal picture of a poet, meditative, touched with the spirit of dreams, but alive, human, and with memories of full days and energizing passions.[3]

Conrad is regarded by some admirers as the greatest novelist writing in the world today, not merely in the English language, but in any language. Through all the variety and strangeness of his incidents and settings, there is a continuing unity of method and purpose. The artist is concerned not simply with the weaving of words, the presentation of a phase, a segment of existence: he challenges the whole illusive circle, works out the large problems (to each individual life) of human destiny.[4]

But to discuss the book [Ulysses] here, or give any adequate idea of its scope and symbolism, beauty and squalidity, strength and weakness, is impossible. The outpouring of the stream of consciousness, turbid or clear, placid or seething (it is rarely placid) conveys a remarkable effect, mitigated occasionally by a sense of monotony. But the work is an epic. That anyone should want, or have wanted, to suppress it, only shows the large prevalence of little logic. One does not suppress natural phenomena: they are neither moral nor immoral.[5]

Quinn explained in his foreword that his decision to sell his library was forced on him by the necessity of moving from his large apartment. Although the lack of shelf space is a familiar lament for collectors, it is not convincing in Quinn's case. He was a wealthy man who could well afford ample library quarters. His friends later suggested that he had a premonition of his death from cancer, which came four months after the final session. Quinn described the catalogues as "a record in part of the admirations, the enthusiasms and affections of a lifetime"— a sound definition of a personal library. "I cannot go through or attempt to write about or to tell about what these books and manuscripts, which contain a world of beauty and romance or enshrine the records of friendships and of interests and enthusiasms, have meant to me, for they seem to me to be a part of myself, even though I may smile a little at my own feeling." A man of prodigious energy and quick temper, Quinn attempted to supervise the sale. He provided descriptions for the items and checked proofs of the catalogue, protesting what he regarded as the inadequacy of the printed descriptions.

Part One, comprising A to C of the authorial alphabet, was sold on 12–14 November 1923. The Joseph Conrad items, 1780–2010, were auctioned out of sequence at the second evening session in order to generate publicity. They included the greatest assemblage of Conrad manuscripts ever sold.

#1780.   *Almayer's Folly.* MS. 315 pp. $5,300
#1781.   *Almayer's Folly.* Revised TS, 280 pp. $650*
#1783.   *An Outcast of the Islands.* MS, 516 pp. $4,100
#1788.   *The Nigger of the "Narcissus."* MS, 194 pp. $4,500
#1797.   *Lord Jim.* Incomplete MS, 362 pp. $3,900
#1802.   "Youth." MS, 43 pp. $2,000
#1806.   "The Heart of Darkness." Incomplete MS, 211 pp. $1,500
#1807.   *Typhoon.* MS, 191 pp. $5,100
#1808.   *Typhoon.* Revised TS, 133 pp. $725
#1811.   *Falk.* MS, 247 pp. $3,100
#1812.   "To-Morrow." MS, 81 pp. $1,800
#1821.   *Nostromo.* MS, 763 pp. $4,700
#1836.   "The Inland Sea." MS, 59 pp. $2,000
#1842.   *The Secret Agent.* MS, 637 pp. $3,900
#1855.   "The Secret Sharer." MS, 126 pp. $2,400
#1860.   "A Smile of Fortune." MS, 140 pp. $2,300
#1862.   *Under Western Eyes.* MS, 1351 pp. $6,900
#1868.   "Freya of the Seven Isles." MS, 224 pp. $3,500
#1880.   *Chance.* MS, 1,252 pp. $6,600
#1882.   *Chance.* Revised TS, 645 pp. $775
#1888.   *One Day More.* MS, 60 pp. $1,800
#1890.   "The Inn of the Two Witches." MS, 75 pp. $1,500
#1895.   "Because of the Dollars." MS, 96 pp. $1,200
#1896.   "Because of the Dollars." MS & TS, 62 pp. $750
#1906.   "The Partner." MS, 84 pp. $1,400
#1907.   "The Planter of Malata." MS, 182 pp. $2,450
#1918.   *Victory.* MS, 1,139 pp. $8,100. The record for a living author.

* A revised TS is a typescript with the author's manuscript revisions.

#1919. *Victory.* Revised TS, 636 pp. $850
#1929. *The Shadow-Line.* MS, 235 pp. $2,700
#1931. "Admiralty Paper." MS, 20 pp. $1,750

The 231 Conrad items brought $110,998* (an average of $480.51), of which Dr. R spent $72,000. He took every important manuscript—except for *Under Western Eyes,* which was acquired by Gabriel Wells. Dr. R was mainly buying on his own—not for clients—because he believed in Conrad's enduring stature. After Huntington declined them, some of the best Conrad manuscripts went into Rosenbach's own collection. Jerome Kern acquired seven of the manuscripts during or after the sale. Conrad accounted for almost half the dollar total of the entire library, but Quinn was dissatisfied. The day after the Conrad session, he wrote to the auctioneer, charging that because Chapman had been ignorant of the value of the items he had opened bidding too low and cut off the bids too soon: "You ought to read the catalogues before you sell any more of the items."[6]

Since he had bought the manuscripts from Conrad for about $10,000, Quinn was criticized for making 1,000 percent profit on a friendship.† He responded that he had allowed Conrad to set the prices when the author needed the money. Quinn reacted angrily when Frank N. and Nelson Doubleday, Conrad's American publishers, suggested that he ought to share the proceeds with Conrad. In an abusive letter written—but not sent—to Nelson Doubleday, he denied that he had ever pledged not to dispose of the manuscripts during Conrad's lifetime.[7] Quinn told Kennerley that the Doubledays were largely responsible for his decision to include the manuscripts in the sale because they had slighted him during Conrad's recent American visit.[8]

Conrad made no comment on the sale to Quinn, but he wrote with heavy irony to Frank N. Doubleday after seeing the *London Times* report:

---

* In 1985 the forty-six page MS of Conrad's "The Tale" was offered for sale at $45,000.
† It is considered improper for collectors to sell manuscripts given to them by authors—at least while the authors are alive—but there was no ethical problem involved in Quinn's sale of manuscripts he had purchased from writers. Presentation copies of books are regarded as the recipient's property and are routinely sold when collections are dispersed.

Georgia O'Keeffe Exhibit, Anderson Galleries (Rare Books and Manuscripts Division. New York Public Library. Astor, Lenox and Tilden Foundations)

John Quinn

Alfred Stieglitz, Self-Portrait, 1910 (Private Collection, Philadelphia Museum of Art)

All of you who went must have had a tense sort of evening at that sale. Was the atmosphere vibrating with excitement, or, on the contrary, still with awe? Did any of the bidders faint? Did the auctioneer's head swell visibly? Did Quinn enjoy his triumph lying low like Brer Rabbit, or did he enjoy his glory in public and give graciously his hand to kiss to the multitude of inferior collectors who never, never, never dreamt of such a coup? Well, it is wonderful adventure to happen to a still-living (or at any rate half-alive) author.

The reverberation in the press here was very great indeed; and the result is that lots of people, who never heard of me before, now know my name, and thousands of others, who could not have read through a page of mine without falling into convulsions, are proclaiming me a very great author. And there are a good many also whom nothing will persuade that the whole thing was not a put-up job and that I haven't got my share of the plunder.[9]

The second part, D through H, on 10–12 December 1923 included Lady Gregory (75 items), Lord Dunsany (36), John Davidson (46), Maurice Hewlett (83), Thomas Hardy (69), John Galsworthy (80), and Lafcadio Hearn (71). It brought only $16,181.10 for 2,237 items. The top price was $250 for the forty-seven-page MS of Hearn's "Mimi-Nashi-Hoiche."

The third part, I through M, on 14–16 January 1924 was distinguished by long runs of Henry James (164 items), Rudyard Kipling (149), Andrew Lang (218), John Masefield (117), and George Moore (142). Kipling's Echoes (Lahore, India, 1884) brought $1,170. Quinn had placed reserves on two George Meredith manuscripts: $925 on "Alsace Lorraine, An Ode" and $1,200 on "Napoleon, An Ode." They were bought in for him when they reached only $650 and $750. The 344-page manuscript of Moore's most important novel, Esther Waters, brought $600. Among his own properties that Kennerley anonymously inserted in the Quinn catalogues were the limited and trade copies of Millay's Renascence—which fetched $92 and $37.50.

Most of the interest in the third part was generated by the manuscript of Ulysses. (In 1922 Kennerley was involved in a scheme to smuggle copies of the Paris Ulysses into America with the help of the captain of an ocean liner.)[10] Quinn had paid James Joyce $1,200 for the 1,200 pages and placed a $2,000 reserve on them. When the bidding ended with Dr. R's $1,975, Kennerley let the manuscript go and explained to Quinn that it had reached that figure only because he had persuaded the Doctor to go after it.[11] The manuscript was never resold. One of the reasons why Dr. Rosenbach was referred to by the press as a bibliophile, whereas his competitiors were identified as dealers, was that he really was a collector. Some of his best purchases found their way into his personal library—which is now the Rosenbach Museum & Library in Philadelphia.*

Joyce was outraged by the sale of his manuscript and declined Quinn's offer to share the $478.75 profit (after commission) on *Ulysses* with him. It was believed that Joyce resented the disparity between his prices and Conrad's. Joyce's ire was aggravated when he learned that Quinn had placed a higher reserve on the two Meredith poems than on *Ulysses*: ". . . I consider such a sale now and by a wealthy man (who had made me part owner of the MS before the sale) a grossly stupid act which is an alienation of a valuable property. It is a pity that I was obliged to write such a letter [to Quinn] but what is one to do when a MS of 500,000 words is sold by an admirer who on the same day buys back a few pages of not very meritorious verse by a prose writer for almost the same sum?"[12] At Kennerley's urging, Quinn asked Joyce to write out for Dr. R the final six pages of Molly Bloom's closing soliloquy, which had been added in proof. Joyce countered by asking Quinn to approach Rosenbach about selling *Ulysses* to a group of Joyceans who planned to donate it to the Bibliothèque National.[13] When Dr. R met Joyce in Paris he declined to sell the manuscript but offered to buy the corrected proofs. Joyce's reaction was expressed in a pun on Rosenbach's nickname: "When he receives a reply from me all the rosy brooks will have run dry."[14]

There were other Joyce sleepers. The 164-page manuscript for *Exiles* with a letter from Ezra Pound went for $195; Quinn had paid $250 and placed a $200 reserve on it. The 198-page manuscript of Joyce's

---

* It is safe to predict that the manuscript would now break a million dollars; twenty-seven leaves of a fair-copy manuscript of *Chamber Music* sold for $99,000 ($3,700 per leaf) in the 1986 Gilvarry sale at Christie's. An inscribed copy of the first edition of *Ulysses* reached $38,500; but Quinn's signed copy made $130 in 1924.

translation of Gerhardt Hauptmann's *Before Sunrise* brought $100—
which was Quinn's purchase price as well as his reserve figure. Three
sets of tearsheets for *A Portrait of the Artist as a Young Man*—each
set corrected by Joyce—for which Quinn had paid $100, reached the
reserve of $75. The third part of the sale brought a total of $31,705.85
for 2,325 items. Quinn bitterly complained that his library was being
slaughtered, which was harder to take because the newspaper reports
gave the impression that he was making a fortune on his literary friends.

Part Four, M–S, sold on 11–13 February, was distinguished by more
in-depth author collections. The 242 William Morris items brought
$4,244, with the 270-page manuscript for *The House of the Wolfings*
contributing $475. The highest price among the fifty-five Ezra Pound
items was $52.50 for his first book, *A Lume Spento* (an inscribed copy
sold for $18,000 in 1977); the 19-page revised typescript for *Three
Cantos* brought $5.50; and Pound's very rare second book, *A Quinzaine
for this Yule*, fetched $3.75 (a copy of the second printing made $11,500
in 1984). There were sixty-two Dante Gabriel Rossetti items, among
which the author's revised copy of *Poems* reached only $65. George
Bernard Shaw was represented by ninety-eight items, and the top Shaw
price of $90 was brought by the privately printed acting edition of *The
Shewing Up of Blanco Posnet*. Part four totaled $16,967.70 for 2,201
lots.

The final and largest part of the Quinn collection was sold 17–20
March. It opened with ninety Robert Louis Stevenson items. The
Stevenson market was still bullish, and $1,200 was low for the fifty-
nine-page manuscript of an unrecorded play, *Monmouth*. This play,
thirteen Stevenson letters, and a verse fragment were Kennerley's
property and brought him $4,020. The largest run in the Quinn sale
was 372 items for Algernon Charles Swinburne, which totaled $3,436.85.
Bargains abounded, and the twelve-page manuscript for "Athens"
brought only $35. Two hundred seventy-seven Arthur Symons items—
with considerable manuscript material—provoked no competition. John
Millington Synge was represented by fifty-four items, including the
authorial typescripts for three major plays (Synge wrote directly on
the typewriter): *In the Shadow of the Glen* (22 pages, $310); *The
Playboy of the Western World* (118 pages, $750); and *Deirdre of the
Sorrows* (94 pages, $410). The 117 H. G. Wells items included *The*

4929 ORIGINAL AUTOGRAPH MANUSCRIPT of "Exiles," written on 164 pages, quarto, together with title-pages and page of characters, 169 pages in all. In a crushed blue levant morocco solander case.   *195.*

THE COMPLETE MANUSCRIPT, beautifully written in the author's unusually legible hand. Each of the title-pages is inscribed: *"Exiles: a play in three acts. By James Joyce,"* and at the foot of each of these title-pages Joyce has written: *"Present address: Seefeldstrasse F 3ᵗᴴ, Zurich: Switzerland."*

Laid in with this Manuscript is an A.L.s. from Ezra Pound to Mr. Quinn, written on a wrapper for the Manuscript: *"Dear Mr. Quinn. Here at last are the two remaining acts of Joyce's Play."* The mailing wrappers to Mr. Quinn in Ezra Pound's hand are also laid in.

4930 EXILES. A Play in Three Acts. 12mo, boards, cloth back.   London, 1918   *4⁵*
First Edition.

4931 EXILES. A Play in Three Acts. 12mo, boards, cloth back.
First American Edition.   New York, 1918   *.5ᵈ*

4932 CHAMBER MUSIC. 16mo, cloth, uncut.   London, n.d. [1918]   *9⁵⁰*
First Edition.

4933 CHAMBER MUSIC. 12mo, boards, uncut.   New York, 1918   *1.*
First Authorized American Edition.

4934 EXILES. A Play in Three Acts. 12mo, cloth.   London, [1921]   *..2⁵*
Second Edition.

4935 DUBLINERS. 12mo, cloth.   London, [1922]   *1⁵⁰*
Second Edition.

4936 ORIGINAL AUTOGRAPH MANUSCRIPT OF "ULYSSES," written on over 1200 pages. In four blue morocco slip cases.   *1975.*

THE COMPLETE MANUSCRIPT of this remarkable work, one of the most extraordinary produced in modern times and hailed by critics as epoch-making in modern literature.

The first slip case contains: Part I: Telemachus, Proteus, Nestor. Part II: Calypso, Lotus Eaters, Hades, Eolus, Lestrygonians, Scylla and Charybdis.

The second slip case contains Part II continued, made up of the following: Wandering Rocks, Sirens, Cyclops, Nausikaa, Oxen of the Sun.

The third slip case continues Part II and contains: Penelope, Ithaca, and Part III down to page 618 of the book.

The fourth slip case contains from page 618 to the end of the work.

In a recent review of Ulysses by Mr. T. S. Eliot he refers to Mr. Aldington's attack upon Mr. Joyce as "a libel on humanity" and quotes Thackeray's shameful attack upon Swift, Thackeray having damned Swift for the conclusion of the Voyage to the Houyhnhnms, which Mr. Eliot writes "seems to me one of the greatest triumphs that the human soul has ever achieved." Referring to the form as well as the content of Ulysses, Mr. Eliot writes: "Psychology (such as it is, and whether our reaction to it be comic or serious), ethnology, and The Golden Bough

THE FIRST PAGE OF THE ORIGINAL AUTOGRAPH MANUSCRIPT
OF JAMES JOYCE'S GREAT NOVEL "ULYSSES"
[NUMBER 4936]

Door in the Wall—identified as "the first book to be printed in the now world-known 'Kennerley' type"—at $17.50. Walt Whitman was the most extensively represented American, with 149 items totaling $1,156; the 1855 *Leaves of Grass* was a bargain at $160. There were 180 Oscar Wilde items, of which *The Happy Prince* inscribed to his wife brought the top price of $375.

The last major author in the sale was William Butler Yeats; the 273 items ($7,061.50) were strong in manuscripts, inscriptions, and private printings because of Quinn's close association with Yeats. The forty-two-page manuscript for "J. M. Synge and the Ireland of his Time" brought the top price of $380; and the eighteen-page manuscript of "The Wild Swans at Coole," one of Yeats's major poems, went for $250. Two inscribed copies of *Mosada*, Yeats's first book, brought $260 and $300. (The uninscribed copy at the 1986 Gilvarry sale reached $36,300.) *Nine Poems Chosen from the Works of William Butler Yeats*, privately printed for Quinn by Kennerley in 1914, fetched $12; it is now a thousand-dollar item. The 3,059 lots in Part Five totaled $23,736.20.

The grand total for the 12,108 Quinn lots was $226,351.85. The appalling average of $18.69 becomes even worse if Conrad is factored out: $9.71 per item. Quinn claimed that after the 15 percent commission and reserves were deducted, he ended up with $170,000 for material that had cost him a quarter of a million. It pained him to lose money, but it probably distressed him more to have some of his great possessions go begging. Collectors expect to see their judgment vindicated.

Many items went for a dollar or less. A collector who was willing to forgo dinner could have gone home with valuable books. The $10,000 judiciously spent at the Quinn sale could have returned $100,000— or even a million—in 1986. Nonetheless, books and manuscripts are always risky as a long-term investment: $10,000 cash invested at 5 percent in 1924 and compounded annually would have appreciated to $187,000 by 1985. Some blue-chip Twenties authors—notably Stevenson and Kipling—never increased in value, or even collapsed.

The postmortem conclusion was that the sheer bulk of the collection had been more than the market could absorb; but the real explanation for the debacle was that Quinn was ahead of his time. In 1924 the textual significance of revised typescripts and proofs for moderns was generally unappreciated. The Quinn sale has been credited with changing American collecting tastes. It did not. The moderns were still regarded as untested. John Quinn's monument as a bibliophile was the five-volume catalogue, not the auction itself.

Kennerley tried to retain some of the proceeds. On 15 May 1924 the Anderson owed Quinn a balance of $97,288.88; Kennerley offered him "an absolutely safe investment for $100,000 for five years at 8 percent interest payable monthly," explaining:

> We do not owe a penny in the world and we have a building which I am told by real estate experts we could easily rent at a net profit of $100,000 a year. We can borrow to any amount from three banks on collections when we need to loan our customers money; but I am tired of sticking to the job as closely as I have done and I want to borrow $100,000.00 on the security of our lease so I need not worry about our balances and overdue accounts. For instance, W. R. Hearst very often owes us thirty or forty thousand dollars for several months, and some times some of our trade customers hold us up on payments for a few days or a few weeks, which means I have to be on the job here and go out and borrow from some bank.[15]

Quinn replied that he did not care to tie up his money in a long-term investment. Kennerley's claims that he wanted to free himself from the pressure of the day-to-day operation of the Anderson became increasingly familiar over the next five years. After Quinn's death, Kennerley offered Huntington a group of Morris, Meredith, and Swinburne manuscripts from the sale—including *The House of the Wolfings*: "I have bought this collection for $2,000, and you may have it for $2,200.00."[16]

While the Quinn sale was in progress Kennerley tried to secure the Stephen H. Wakeman collection of American literature, which was particularly strong in the nineteenth-century New England writers. In February 1924 he wrote to the executor of the Wakeman estate offering terms of 10 percent plus expenses or an inclusive 17½ percent commission:

> You could not sell at a better time than the present. Prices of desirable association copies of rare books have never been higher and there have never been more collectors of large means than at present. There is no

doubt that the present high prices of desirable books, which to some people appear fantastic, are, to a great extent, due to the leadership of Mr. H. E. Huntington. One of the chief reasons why I would advise an early sale is that Mr. Huntington is now alive, and while he would not buy many of the important items in the Wakeman collection, as he already has them, he would bid on a large number of the unimportant items. Furthermore, the fact that Mr. Huntington is still alive and actively buying has a great moral effect on other collectors. Furthermore, the book trade was never in a stronger position than it is today under the leadership of Dr. A. S. W. Rosenbach, who is the acknowledged leader of the book trade all the world over. Dr. Rosenbach is a staunch supporter of our sales, and of the books he has bought at auction during the last ten years, I think it may be safely said that ninety per cent have been bought at our sales.[17]

Despite Kennerley's pitch, the Wakeman collection was sold at the American Art in April 1924, bringing $67,586 for 1,280 lots ($52.80 average).[18] Although the total was not substantial the Wakeman sale was influential in stimulating collector interest in American literature.

There were two other important Anderson sales during the 1923–1924 season. In November, following the opening Quinn sessions, the library of Mrs. Phoebe A. D. Boyle brought a surprising $101,548 for 368 items of literature and modern illuminated manuscripts in jeweled bindings; the top price was $5,000 for Thackeray's manuscript lectures on King George I and King George II.[19] The December sale of Western Americana totaled $32,713.30 for 922 lots.[20] Volumes 2 and 3 of the *Deseret News*, the first newspaper in the Rockies, was the top item at $2,015; a volume of original Louisiana Cession Documents (1803–1804) brought $1,275.

At the end of the 1923–1924 season, the Anderson announced total sales for books and manuscripts of $574,888.30 (of which almost half came from Quinn); the American Art announced $667,216.75 for books, manuscripts, and prints. These figures are not comparable, but they indicate that auctioning literary properties was not a bonanza, despite the literary treasures moving through the Anderson.

Quinn was one of the world's leading collectors of modern art, with some 2,500 paintings and 150 sculptures—including Van Gogh, De-rain, Kuhn, Matisse, Rousseau, Brancusi, Picasso, Gris, Seurat, and

Roualt. He left the collection to be sold at the discretion of his ex-ecutors, who did not know much about modern art. Kennerley exerted himself to secure the entire collection for the Anderson. He offered a $250,000 guarantee and proposed to exhibit the paintings for a month to generate interest in a new museum of modern art; and Stieglitz placed himself at Kennerley's service for the endeavor. But Quinn's executors became convinced that a sale of this magnitude would fail in America. The collection was sold piecemeal privately and at several auctions in America and Europe—including a 1927 sale at the Amer-ican Art. The final take was about $400,000.

In 1923–1924 the Anderson had remunerative auctions of furnish-ings: the art and furniture of William G. Rockefeller ($139,659)[21] and the William W. Nolen sales of American antiques and art ($146,343.50).[22] As the Anderson became more active in the art field, Kennerley availed himself of the expertise and contacts of Karl Freund, an Austrian-born dealer, who scouted Europe for furniture and paint-ings. His specialty was to arrange exhibitions of interiors which were then auctioned. Freund's sale in 1924 realized $197,839.[23] The March 1925 sale totaled $217,018.50 for the furnishings from Freund's apart-ment, along with art from Sion House, Twickenham, and the early American furniture of Henry F. De Puy.[24] Freund also mounted art shows at Anderson: "The Horse in Art" (1926) and "Dogs in Art" (1927).

Kennerley implemented his plan to make the Anderson a center for the arts by staging interesting events. The handpress on which William Morris had printed the Kelmscott Press books was brought to America and displayed at the Anderson in March 1924. During the exhibition Frederic and Bertha Goudy printed two keepsakes—one of which, an edition of *Renascence*, was sold as copies came off the press. When Mahonri Young modeled a clay bust of Joseph Pennell at the Anderson, a policeman was called in to manage the crowd.

The 1924 episode of the lost David statue of George Washington demonstrates the difficulty of establishing the truth about many of Kennerley's activities. Although the newspaper reports—which em-anated from Kennerley—are contradictory, the history of the bust is clear up to a point. The French sculptor Pierre Jean David (David d'Angers) executed the marble bust in 1828; it was presented to the

United States by national subscription and placed in the old Congres-sional Library. The charred bust disappeared when the Library burned in 1851. Around 1914—possibly as late as 1920—it was sold as an unidentified work to a New York marble dealer for a "trifling sum." After several years the dealer had it cleaned and recognized the subject. According to one published report, Kennerley bought it for $25, "but had no idea of its value until Jo Davidson, Paul Bartlett and Daniel Chester French, sculptors, saw it."[25] Kennerley's own memo explains that after his attention was called to the bust by Davidson and Bartlett he bought it for $2,584 and sold it to Huntington for $10,000.[26] His correspondence with Huntington reveals that Kennerley claimed to be acting for "the man who owns the Washington bust" and that the actual selling price was $5,000.[27]

Four Kennerley volumes appeared in 1924, two of which were the Horace Fish titles co-published with Huebsch. He again obliged his best customer by publishing a limited edition of Dr. Rosenbach's *An Introduction to Herman Melville's Moby-Dick*. No new volumes with the Kennerley imprint appeared during 1925–1928.

The fall of 1924 brought the start of five record-setting seasons at Anderson. The fondness for records was characteristic of the Twenties ebullience, in and out of the sales rooms. The men who had been preaching book values competed to enforce their sermons. "Auctions speak louder than words," Kennerley quipped. As great collection followed great collection to auction, the law of supply and demand was reversed. Supply stimulated competition because material was being sold that might well never come on the market again. There was a growing emphasis on rare books and manuscripts as investments, and Dr. R bulled the market.* A new breed of dealers, such as Barnet Beyer and Alwin Scheuer, sold books to speculators. Collectors or heirs who were undecided about disposing of libraries were persuaded to cash in at the peak by the results of the headline sales. More to the point, they were persuaded to sell at Anderson. Major sales generated more major sales; high bids inspired higher bids.

---

* In May 1925 at Sotheby's in London Dr. R set the record for an American book: £6,800 (about $34,000) for the only known copy of John Eliot's Algonquin translation of Richard Baxter's *Call to the Unconverted* (Cambridge, Mass., 1664).

The first notable sale of the 1924–1925 season was the William Harris Arnold collection in November,[28] at which 1,130 items of mostly English literature totaled $148,723.50–twice the presale estimate. The prices were attributed to the election of Calvin Coolidge, which promised four more years of prosperity. Arnold was a respected bibliophile who had written books about book-collecting. He also had a keen sense of prices. When he sold two earlier collections in 1901 he had published an accounting of his costs showing substantial profits. The introduction to the 1924 Arnold sale catalogue by R. B. Adam—a distinguished collector whose own books would go on the block during the next season—expressed the bibliophile's credo:

> Let us remember that "Life and Gold have wings", and that we should buy books and letters, while we may.
>
> Association books,—books with a personal interest, such as are many of Arnold's,—are the collector's hope. Does it not arouse your imagination to touch a book that has upon the margins of its pages the pencillings of some immortal author; or to handle a book presented by one of fame to another, such as the one inscribed, "To William Wordsworth, from the Author, in affectionate reverence", or to look upon an autograph letter or a manuscript of one of the "few great voices of Time"?
>
> There is a joy passing belief in the possession of books which bear the stamp of perpetuity—old volumes "dark with tarnished gold", rare quartos, and first editions: but in books with autograph inscriptions, in letters and manuscripts of great writers, whose names shine brightly in "fame's proud Temple", there is a more intimate reflection of the mind than there is in the printed work, and the autograph which cannot be duplicated is to be highly prized.

The star was the 190-page incomplete manuscript of *Kidnapped*, which Dr. R took for Huntington at $10,000—a record Stevenson price. Another record was made when the MS of Stevenson's "Requiem" ("Home is the sailor, home from the sea") fetched $1,500 from Dr. R—the highest price yet for a single page of modern manuscript. (The highest MS price at the Quinn sale was $87.50 per page for Conrad.) Other Stevenson highs at the Arnold sale were $2,000 for the dedication copy of *A Child's Garden of Verses* and $2,000 for the first draft of *Travels with a Donkey*. The most remarkable printed items were six Tennyson "trial firsts" (prepublication copies printed for the author's use) which brought $27,800. When Tennyson's *The Victim* went for $9,000, the joke circulated that it must have had a Shakes-pearian connection; the old-timers weren't accustomed to seeing nine-teenth-century books bringing such prices.

Thirty of Arnold's items reached $1,000 or more—including the MS of Burns's "Queen Mary's Lament" ($2,050), Grant's letter book with communications for Lee's surrender ($2,400), a Keats letter in rhyme ($3,000), the earliest known document written in New York ($3,600), and Washington's copy of *The History of the Rise, Progress, and Es-tablishment of the United States of America* ($4,100). A presentation copy of Hawthorne's *The Scarlet Letter* reached $625; the same copy made $15,400 in 1985.

The most valuable literary sale of the Anderson season was the library of the late Beverly Chew, one of the older generation of col-lectors who had been active in Hoe's time. After disposing of his American literature en bloc to J. Chester Chamberlin in 1900, Chew had devoted himself to two collections of English literature before and after 1800. He sold the earlier part to Huntington in 1912 and then started all over again, buying back some of his books at the Huntington sales. Chew had been a much-admired figure, and his friends competed to honor him by acquiring his books. The pre-1800 material sold in December 1924 brought $145,366.50 for 474 items—an average of $306.68.[29] The star was the *First Folio* with a facsimile title page at $11,700 (the same copy had fetched $8,000 in 1920). Chew's *Fourth Folio* (1685) brought $950; the same copy sold for £5,500 at Sotheby's in 1985. *Paradise Lost* ("probably the finest copy now available") reached $5,600—three times the previous record. Other highs were Blake's *Songs of Innocence and of Experience* with fifty-four colored plates at $5,500 (Chew had paid $1,700), Ben Jonson's *Works* at $3,000 ($600 in the Hoe sale), *Robinson Crusoe* with the two sequels at $5,350, and Gray's *Elegy* at $4,650. Dr. R accounted for $50,170, a rather tame performance for him. The Chew collection of post-1800 English lit-erature, sold in January 1925, was much less interesting;[30] the 857 items totaled $14,507.50. There were few $100 books, and the top bid was Wells's $570 for Keats's 1817 *Poems*.

One of the collectors who consigned material in 1925 was former

Assistant Secretary of the Navy Franklin D. Roosevelt, who had been buying at the Anderson since 1909. Even though his individual pur-chases rarely amounted to more than $5, he occasionally had to be dunned. His Americana was sold with that of John B. Copp and "some additions" in January 1925 to make up 338 undistinguished lots, of which Roosevelt's property brought $859.[31] One hundred fifty-four naval prints and paintings consigned by Roosevelt brought $920.50 in a separate auction.[32] The accounting for these sales reveals what the actual cost of selling at the Anderson could amount to for unimportant material. After the charges for cataloguing and advertising were added to the 10 percent commission, Roosevelt was billed $618.50 on the $1,779.50 total—or 35 percent. Only owners of major collections could insist on an inclusive fee.

The two final anticlimactic Huntington sales consisted of odds and ends. In December 1924 and January 1925, 446 lots of English literature brought $8,248.25[33] and 434 lots of Americana brought $6,469.25.[34] The fifteen sales of Huntington duplicates and surplussage between 1916 and 1925 totaled $593,935. Huntington's sales—as well as his purchases—were a key factor in Kennerley's success at Anderson.

January 1925 brought two interesting auctions of Orientalia. Ken-nerley author Arthur Davison Ficke sold his 362 Japanese prints and 180 Chinese girdle clasps and buckles for about $34,000;[35] and the Alfred E. Hippisley collection of seventeenth- and eighteenth-century Chinese porcelains brought $49,726 for 286 items.[36]

During the 1924–1925 season the Anderson produced 114 auction catalogues, of which thirty-eight sales (71 sessions) of books and man-uscripts totaled $604,049.25. After the Arnold and Chew sales are deducted, the remaining thirty-six literary sales amounted to $295,451.75—a modest average of $8,207 per sale. The American Art reported $807,401.50 for books, manuscripts, and prints. At the close of the season Anderson issued a sanguine summary and forecast:

> The outstanding feature of the season was the comparatively small number of choice manuscripts and books which were offered and the high prices which were bid for them. Every time a rare and desirable book or manuscript appeared a record price was bid. In the opinion of the Anderson Galleries, the demand for choice books and manuscripts

will from now on exceed the supply. Nearly all the desirable ones which have been offered during the last three or four years have been bought by public institutions or by private collectors whose collections will eventually be bequeathed to institutions. There are, of course, a few important private collections in America which will be sold "by way of the auction" when their owners die, but these cannot begin to supply the extraordinary demand there is today in America from the large and increasing number of collectors.[37]

Kennerley became a father for the third time on 29 April 1925 when a son was born to Diana Norman at her residence, 328 West Eighty-sixth Street. The birth certificate identifies Mitchell Kennerley of 489 Park Avenue as the father; Diana Norman's "name before marriage" is given as Diana Roberts; she was thirty and had been born in London. The child was named Richard Kennerley and raised as Kennerley's son. Kennerley may have later married Diana to legitimize Richard; no record of the marriage has been found, but a document for a Mexican divorce was among Kennerley's papers at his death.

Diana Norman was the stage name of Diana Jacobs, who was also known as Diana Roberts. She had been a show girl and appeared in the Ziegfeld Follies. After Diana left the stage she designed dresses and hats; she claimed to have named the "White Shoulders" perfume. Kennerley lived with her intermittently for about ten years at 40 West Seventy-seventh Street. In the Twenties and Thirties she listed herself as Mrs. D. Norman, and in the Forties as Mrs. M. Kennerley. When Jo Davidson's bust of "Mrs. N." was illustrated in the *International Studio*, Karl Freund wrote: "It is like a tale which could not remain untold. At first contemplation one wonders if one had not known it since childhood, so astounding is its esthetic appeal. There is a de-votional humbleness in the modeling of this beautiful head which recalls the monastic dreamers. . . ."[38] Kennerley later presented this bust with others by Davidson to Vassar College.

Kennerley launched the 1925–1926 season with the boast that America had become the center of the rare-book trade:

> Every one knows that it is American competition which has made the high prices of London auctions for many years and from fifty to ninety-five per cent of the books, pictures and furniture and other art

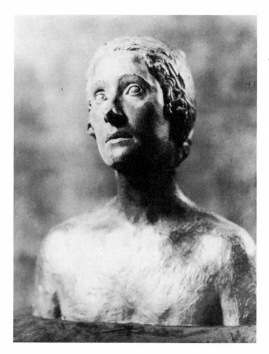

Diana Norman by Jo Davidson
(Courtesy, Vassar College Art Gallery)

Diana Norman (Courtesy of
Michael Kennerley)

objects which are sold by auction in London comes to America shortly afterwards. You cannot go into an important private library in America without finding hundreds of books with the bookplates of Huth, Christie-Miller, and other great English collections that were dispersed in London in recent years. The large proportion of the business done by the English booksellers is with American collectors and with American booksellers. When Quaritch pays a high price for a book at auction in London the chances are one hundred to one that he is bidding for an American client. Naturally, the American bidder would bid more at auction in New York where he could examine the object in which he was interested than he does in London where there is a risk of condition and minor imperfections which necessarily control his bid. Then there are a number of large collectors, dealers, libraries and museums who do not bid in the English market but who are bidders at American auctions.[39]

The season would be the richest yet at the Anderson, with the Manning, Adam, Williams, and Clawson libraries—plus a Gutenberg Bible and the Leverhulme art from England.

The autograph collection of Col. James H. Manning had 1,769 lots which realized $115,527.25 in January and February 1926.[40] The most important group was a complete set of the fifty-six Signers of the Declaration of Independence, which sold individually for the record total of $46,925.50. The previous record, established in 1924, was $26,502. (A set of the Signers made $320,000 at auction in 1984.) The rarest of these autographs is that of Button Gwinnett, who signed little before the Declaration and was killed in a duel shortly afterward. Only nineteen examples of his signature were known at the time. A will witnessed by Gwinnett brought the record bid of $22,500 ($1,607 for each letter of his name) from Dr. R at the Manning sale, possibly the highest price to that date for a single signature;* the same document had sold for $4,600 in 1912. The underbidder, autograph dealer Thomas F. Madigan, predicted that a Gwinnett signature would be worth $50,000 within five years. He was right. A better buy at $1,800 was

---

* The state of Georgia unsuccessfully sued the Manning estate for recovery of this document, claiming that it had been looted during the War Between the States.

Caesar Rodney's 4 July 1776 letter describing his ride to cast the vote that carried the Delaware delegation: "It is determined by the Thirteen United Colonies, with out even one decenting Colony—We have now Got through with the Whole of the declaration, and Ordered it to be printed. . . ."[41] The Manning sale also included manuscripts by Poe, Whitman, Tennyson, Burns, Dickens, and Thackeray.

In February the books of the late Arabella Huntington were sold, described as "The Private Library Removed from 2 East 57th Street."[42] Mrs. Huntington was not a serious collector; she had bought illustrated books and fine bindings to keep her husband company. Nonetheless, the 516 lots realized $50,063.50.

R. B. Adam was one of the big three Buffalo collectors—along with Clawson and Goodyear—who sold at the Anderson. His English literature occupied three sessions on 15–16 February 1926.[43] Adam's introduction to the catalogue explained that he was retaining his Samuel Johnson collection and selling the rest of his library in order "to give what I can spare of what remains to me of my days and nights to the study of the Johnsonian era." He added an encouraging message to other bibliophiles:

> There is no necessity, as many may think, to have a lot of "learned lumber" in one's head, or such a deal of money in one's purse to become a book collector, and to add to the charm and interest in life that book collecting gives. True, the finer editions of the great writers have risen to high prices, and undoubtedly they will continue to advance; but the range of collecting is limitless, and the desire of the collector, once truly begun, is never ending.

A. Edward Newton was host at a dinner for the Adam sale; the catalogue signed by the bibliophiles who attended testifies to the spirit of book-fellowship inspired by R. B. Adam. Stronger testimony is the total, which was $122,188 for 433 lots. As in the Chew sale, the collector's friends competed to honor him, and it was reported that some of the books brought ten times their presale estimates. The star item was *Comus*, which Dr. R took at $11,500. Milton also attracted the second highest price, $10,000 from Byrne Hackett of the Brick Row Bookshop for the Britwell copy of *Paradise Lost*. Other high prices were $4,000 for *The Pickwick Papers* in parts, $4,200 for a 1488 edition of Homer in Greek, $5,900 for Milton's *Lycidas*, $5,300 for Shakespeare's 1640 *Poems*, and $3,900 for Spenser's *The Faerie Queene*.

After the Adam evening session on 15 February 1926 there was a separate sale of one book, the Gutenberg Bible.[44] This perfect copy on paper had been acquired from the Benedictine monastery at Melk, Austria, by London dealer Edward Goldston for £12,000. Unable to sell it privately, Goldston had turned it over to the Anderson. Kennerley transported the two volumes back from England in two suitcases, which he kept in his cabin so as to be able to take them to a lifeboat. An elegant separate catalogue was prepared by Seymour de Ricci. In a signed prefatory note Kennerley wrote: "This is the third time in the last fifteen years [there were two copies in the Hoe sale] that the Anderson Galleries have had the privilege of selling by auction an example of this greatest of all typographical monuments. It is to be feared that the opportunity may not again come before us of securing a worthy and permanent resting place for a book with such unrivalled spiritual, historical and artistic associations." De Ricci puffed:

> The Gutenberg Bible is one of the rarest books in existence. It is four times as scarce as the First Folio of Shakespeare. Some forty-five copies are known, of which more than twenty are imperfect. Only four other copies (and two single volumes) are still in private hands: one of these is imperfect, and two others are practically promised to public libraries. To the best of our knowledge, this and one other copy are the only perfect examples of The Gutenberg Bible which are ever likely to come on the market.
>
> . . . .
>
> For every collector, for every museum, for every cathedral, for every individual or body of individuals with a soul, the sale of the Melk copy of the Gutenberg Bible is the unique opportunity of keeping safe for posterity one of the noblest and most inspiring achievements of the human hand.

Kennerley expected the Gutenberg to bring $75,000; but he tried to cover his bet by soliciting a bid of $100,000 from Huntington, who declined because he already had a vellum copy.[45]

At 10:30 P.M.—after an interval to allow the bidders to fortify themselves following the Adam session—the curtains were opened to reveal the two spotlighted volumes, and the crowd applauded. Anthony Bade was in the rostrum and started the bidding at $50,000 — the price at which Smith had acquired Hoe's vellum copy for Huntington. Belle Greene, who had three Gutenbergs at the Morgan Library, made the honorary opening bid. Gabriel Wells raised to $55,000. Thereafter it was between Dr. Rosenbach and Wells with raises of $500 and $1,000. At $70,000 they passed the record for a printed book set by Smith in London for Shakespeare's *Venus and Adonis and The Passionate Pilgrim* in 1919. Wells dropped out at $83,000. Then W. Evarts Benjamin became the surprise competitor. Benjamin wanted to present the Gutenberg to the Cathedral of St. John the Divine in memory of his wife, a Standard Oil heiress. At 10:35 P.M. Dr. R took it at $106,000 (the highest price for a printed book until he paid $151,000 for the *Bay Psalm Book* in 1947). The Doctor was acting for Edward Harkness of Standard Oil and had been given a limit of $75,000. Harkness paid him $106,000 plus ten percent without protest and gave the volumes to Yale. Rosenbach assured the press that the time would come when a million would seem cheap for the Gutenberg Bible. (In 1978 a Gutenberg sold at auction for $2,200,000.) At forty-eight Kennerley had brought off his greatest book coup. The triumph was sweetened when the best the American Art could do by way of competition was to sell eight Gutenberg leaves in March for $1,750.

February 1926 also included a sentimental sale for Kennerley, the collection of the late Oliver Henry Perkins.[46] Kennerley wrote a recollection of Perkins for the catalogue, reiterating his claim that New York had become the rare-book mecca:

> Oliver Henry Perkins was my first American friend. I met him in 1894 in a little secondhand bookshop off the Strand in London, where he came in to ask if we had a book he wanted. We took to each other at once and I saw him nearly every day when we were in the same city. . . . I believe he bought ninety-nine per cent of his books in London, as did nearly all the collectors of his day. He died in 1912, before the Hoe Sale brought the rare book business to America.

Perkins's collection was strongest in bindings, extra-illustrated volumes, and illuminated manuscripts. There were no major rarities, and the highest price was $950 for a presentation copy of Dickens's *American Notes*; the 887 items totaled $38,500.25.

In most American auction seasons May was a dull month; but May 1926 was a stunner at the Anderson as Kennerley endeavored to scoop up the loose money before the summer London auctions. On 17 May the autograph collection of Dr. George C. F. Williams[47] included two Gwinnett signatures at $19,000 (sold to Dr. R) and $10,500. The set of Signers sold individually for $37,688.50, and Williams's 879 lots totaled $74,112.

Three days later the sale of *The Splendid Elizabethan & Early Stuart Library of Mr. John L. Clawson* began; it proved to be the most valuable—except for Hoe—sold in America to that time.[48] The 926 items totaled $642,687.50—an extraordinary average of $694.05, as against $277 for the 1918–1919 sale of Jones's English Renaissance collection. The Clawson books, acquired between 1914 and 1923, marked the peak of enthusiasm for the English Renaissance. A year before the Clawson sale Kennerley had obtained an option to purchase the collection for $900,000 and unsuccessfully attempted to broker it en bloc. He offered it to William A. Clark, Jr., explaining that Clawson had recently taken a young wife and wanted to buy her a pearl necklace. Kennerley included a list showing that thirty-two of the rarest books had cost Clawson $158,182 of a total expenditure of about $625,000.[49]

Dr. R received special terms allowing him to stretch payments for his Clawson purchases over twenty-four months, with 6 percent interest on the balance after one year. Kennerley explained to Clawson: "you can judge . . . what would happen to the book business if Rosenbach died."[50] Before important sales Kennerley and Dr. R had private meetings to decide which items the Doctor would compete for. These strategy sessions do not indicate that the auctions were rigged in Dr. R's favor. The purpose of the operation was to maintain the market, not secure bargains for the Doctor. Nevertheless, Dr. Rosenbach was probably provided inside information on reserve figures, which gave him an advantage in bidding.

Kennerley provided a hard-sell foreword to the Clawson catalogue:

In this collection there are two hundred and ten books printed before 1600 and seven hundred and sixteen books printed before 1700, many

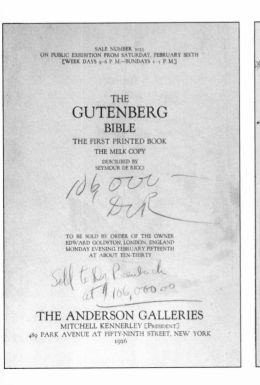

*R. B. Adam catalogue, 15–16 February 1926, signed by the
Boys (Courtesy of Morley and Jean Kennerley)*

of them in superb original condition. The miracle is that they have survived at all. No wonder some of them are unique. The fact that one or more original blank leaves are present or missing in the front or at the end of a book does not make that volume perfect or imperfect, provided no text is missing.* A collector who confined himself to books containing such blank leaves could not form a library. We have not always mentioned when they are present, or absent.

. . . .

It is an opportunity that may never recur on anything like the present scale. The rarest treasures of the book world are steadily passing into permanent institutions, and the chances of obtaining coveted volumes are correspondingly decreasing.

The star item, again, was *Comus*, for which Dr. R paid $21,500 on behalf of RCA president Owen D. Young. (Smith had bought this copy at the Huth sale for £800 and sold it to Clawson for $8,000.)

The Doctor took the quarto *Much Ado About Nothing* for stock at $21,000; it had reached $11,900 in the 1919 Jones sale. There were five other five-figure books:

John Gower, *Confessio Amantis*. $20,000 (Dr. R for stock). Clawson's cost had been $13,000.
William Painter, *The Palace of Pleasure*. $16,000 (Dr. R for Carl Pforzheimer). Cost $7,500.
Troilus and Cressida, first quarto. $11,000 (Dr. R). Cost $9,500.
Othello, first quarto. $10,700 (Dr. R). Cost $6,772.
Spenser, *The Shepherd's Calendar*. $17,700 (Dr. R for Frank Bemis).

The 37 Shakespeares brought $121,250. One hundred fifty-five of the 926 Clawson items brought $1,000 or more. Dr. R spent $447,500, two-thirds of the sale total, of which his bids for financier Carl Pforzheimer amounted to $200,000. Since Rosenbach had sold Clawson many of the books, he was obliged to support their value. After the

_____

* A shaky claim. It ignores the question of whether the blanks were conjugate leaves or inserted binder's leaves. If the missing blanks were originally part of a preliminary or terminal printed gathering, then the books in question were incomplete.

sale he informed the press: "There is one lesson to be learned from this sale, and that is that books of great rarity in the finest possible condition return the handsomest profits to the collector."[51]

In 1940 Kennerley wrote a memo on the Clawson sale disclosing the arithmetic practiced at the Anderson:

> John L. Clawson formed a very great library of Elizabethan books but had no real love of books. He was lured into buying books by George D. Smith and Dr. Rosenbach, who staged parties for him and introduced him to H. E. Huntington, Beverly Chew, H. V. Jones and others. He gloried in the fame his books brought him but after the death of George D. Smith he lost interest and often talked to me of selling. January 1926 I was in Buffalo, Clawson said he would sell if I would guarantee him 650,000. gross which I did.
>
> . . . .
>
> The total of the sale was 642,687$\frac{50}{}$, less 10% inclusive commission $579,000$\frac{77}{}$ against the next amount guaranteed 585,000$\frac{00}{}$ leaving a deficit of 5,795$\frac{23}{}$ which I paid.[52]

Kennerley's personal promissory note for the amount reveals that the Clawson sale—and no doubt others—was his private speculation. He probably turned a profit on the deal. The gross was $57,687.50 more than the guarantee, and it is unlikely that Kennerley paid the Anderson the full seller's commission.

The brilliant 1925–1926 book season was accompanied by Kennerley's first serious challenge to the American Art's domination of the art field. In September 1925 Kennerley acquired the contents of The Hill, the home of British soap tycoon Lord Leverhulme. The collections had already been scheduled for sale in London, but Karl Freund informed Kennerley that the heirs were nervous about the English market. Kennerley sailed for England and was able to cancel the London sale by guaranteeing $1,000,000—which he borrowed from a bank in order to pay the family up front. It was a bold gamble, for the Leverhulme collections were disparaged by experts who challenged the painting attributions and the authenticity of the furniture. Promotion and publicity brought it off.

On his return to America Kennerley announced what the *New York Times* called "the most sensational coup in the London art world of recent times," and he boasted that the catalogue "will be the most complete ever printed for an auction sale."[53] It was understood that Lord Leverhulme had spent £630,000 on his collections and $2,000,000 was expected from the Anderson auction. Kennerley stated that "it was an open secret in the trade in London that the 'knock-out' system, if applied to the Leverhulme collection, would net the dealers who worked in cooperation a half million dollars."[54] He reported to Stieglitz in October: "This week I expect to buy out our largest stockholder outside myself. We shall have a very big year. Two of my people from the Leverhulme house arrived this morning more enthusiastic than when I left them. They talked three millions—if it brings half that I shall be satisfied."[55] The ballyhoo received free aid when the Earl of Mayo asked the British courts to block export of the national treasures.

The Leverhulme collections—which reportedly cost $75,000 to transport from England—were divided by categories into six lavishly illustrated catalogues (2,331 lots) to be sold at twenty sessions in February and March 1926.[56] The first catalogue described 625 pieces of English furniture, tapestries, silver, bronzes, and objects of art. Kennerley's foreword stated, "I believe this is the first time that the executors of an estate in Europe have consigned an important and valuable collection of works of art to be sold by auction in America. This is the reason for the unparalleled publicity given in the press all over the world to this sale."

The *New York Times* account of the opening session on 9 February conveys the excitement that Kennerley had generated:

Sale in a Grand Setting

The sale was held in a large, rectangular room, whose immense length and width made its ceilings appear comparatively low. The whole seemed to have been carved out of a bed of red plush—walls, carpeting, chairs, stage, and light coverings. A few rich tapestries, huge mirrors in gilded frames and other art objects decorated the place.

In one corner of the room near the stage, where the articles were displayed one by one, stood the chief auctioneer, F. A. Chapman, a middle-aged man in a swallow-tail coat, who displayed a remarkable facility in suiting the mood of his audience with what might be called a vocal change of pace. He was brisk, business-like and efficient when he began his auctioneering for each article, asking for such-and-such a bid. He was mildly humorous and good-natured when the first bid was only half what he asked. Then, as the bids came bigger and bigger, he would break into a sort of musical sing-song, increasing the tension of the bidders. At last he would reach the climax and make the sale with an intonation that could be compared to a bishop chanting a litany in a cathedral. Then, having run the gamut of business man, comedian, thespian and priest, he would repeat the process. How he ever held out through 130 repetitions of this is a mystery to the layman.

Articles Brilliantly Displayed

At Mr. Chapman's right was a regulation stage, with red velvet curtains that were drawn and reopened between each brace of sales. Every article offered for sale was displayed on stands covered with red plush, against a cloth of gold background, brilliantly illuminated from above and below.

The audience was quiet and reserved in its bidding, which was sometimes exciting, but always restrained. Bidders caught the eye of the nearest auctioneer by merely lifting a hand or a catalogue—a slight gesture that sometimes meant "raising" the previous bidder as much as $1,000. One dealer made most of his bids by leaning back nonchalantly and pulling the coat of an auctioneer standing near him. The auctioneer appeared to translate these tugs into dollars, according to their strength. A few times, when competition for some articles was unusually keen, excitement and tension showed themselves in loud shouts, sometimes two or three persons yelling the same amount at the same time.[57]

The newspaper headlines proclaimed the success of the first five sessions: "BRITISH BID HIGH TO KEEP PRIZED ART"; "CITY'S ART PRESTIGE ENHANCED BY SALE—Record Prices at Leverhulme Auction Strengthen New York's Bid to Be World Centre"; "ART PRICES SOARING IN LEVERHULME SALE—Some Pieces Sell for Double and Triple the Estimate of English Appraisers."[58]

At the end of Part I the take was $641,810; Kennerley had recovered 64 percent of his guarantee—with six more parts left. The top items were a panel of sixteenth-century tapestry ($15,000), nine Chippendale chairs ($15,000), a suite of seven William and Mary pieces ($12,500), a pair of eighteenth-century satinwood commodes ($11,600), a pair of seventeenth-century Aubusson table covers ($5,000 each), a pair of

Adam satinwood bookcases ($8,000 each), four panels of Aubusson tapestry ($13,800), six panels of Aubusson tapestry ($34,000), and an eighteenth-century satinwood bookcase ($11,500). Among the prominent figures who bid personally or through dealers were Mrs. George F. Baker, Jr., Mrs. Bernard Baruch, Clarence Dillon, Sir Joseph Duveen, Gov. A. T. Fuller, Carl Hamilton, Fritz Kreisler, J. P. Morgan, Condé Nast, Mrs. Potter Palmer, Mrs. Henry Walters, and Mrs. Richard Whitney. Frank Partridge, a leading London dealer, denied that he was bidding on behalf of the royal family, for whom he had acquired pieces before the Leverhulme collection was shipped to America.

Part II comprised 296 paintings sold in three evening sessions, 17–19 February. The star item was $31,000 paid by Governor Fuller of Massachusetts for Millais's *Caller Herring.* Fuller, whose fame rests on his refusal to commute the death sentences for Sacco and Vanzetti, also bought Shee's *The Annesley Children* for $8,500. The number-two painting was Goya's *Portrait of Pepe Illo,* which went to Joan Whitney Payson for $25,000. (She later owned the New York Mets.) Gainsborough's *Portrait of a Young Girl* made $20,000; Hoppner's *Miss Mary Rycroft,* $8,000; Raeburn's *Sir Brooke Boothby,* $6,000. There were paintings that would prove to be extraordinary bargains: ten Reynolds portraits fetched $21,900, and nineteen Constable landscapes fetched $8,025. The total for the paintings was $347,190. If Kennerley's guarantee was based on a million dollars less commission, he had more than made his nut at this point.

Part III, the single session on 20 February devoted to 163 porcelain items, totaled $43,285. A seventeenth-century Chinese vase brought $3,100, and a forty-five-piece Worcester dessert service with Shakespearian scenes fetched $2,000. The art library, Part IV, required two sessions on 22–23 February. There were no great books, and the 398 lots totaled only $16,211.50. The highest price was $3,200 for a group of 5,000 English caricatures in twenty-five volumes, including original art by Rowlandson, Cruikshank, Alken, and Leech. Part V—the second group of furniture, tapestries, and rugs—required four sessions on 24–27 February. The best furniture had been sold in Part I, but the 571 remaining lots totaled $151,309. The high price was $3,100 for a sixteenth-century Flemish tapestry of the life of Joseph.

The Leverhulme extravaganza concluded with Parts VI and VII in a single catalogue of 356 drawings, prints, and watercolors sold in three evening sessions on 2–4 March. Gov. Fuller paid the top price of $3,200 for Rembrandt's pen-and-brush *An Interior by Lamplight*. The $46,687.50 total brought the Leverhulme grand total to $1,248,493—the second highest figure reached at Anderson under Kennerley. His gamble had paid off. Despite the newspaper reports of Anglo-American competition, most of the bidding by English dealers was on behalf of American clients. Kennerley claimed that less than two dozen pieces had been bought on English orders.

With the substantial contribution of the Leverhulme sale, the 1925–1926 Anderson season total reached $4,820,000 for seventy-four art and thirty-one book sales—Kennerley's best season so far. A sense of the activity at the Anderson is provided by the February–March sales list:

1 February.	Manning Autographs
8 February.	Mrs. Huntington's Library
9–13 February.	Leverhulme I
16 February.	Garrett Clocks
17–19 February.	Leverhulme II
15 February.	Adam Library
15 February.	Gutenberg Bible
20 February.	Leverhulme III
22 February.	Leverhulme IV
24–27 February.	Leverhulme V
2 March.	Mrs. Huntington's Rugs
2–5 March.	Leverhulme VI–VII
3 March.	Porcelains
5 March.	English Silver and Sheffield Plate
17 March.	Rothbart Modern Art
18 March.	Adam Art
18 March.	Mrs. Huntington's Furniture
23 March.	Perkins Library
25 March.	Gliss & Aylward Libraries
25 March.	Naval and Marine Collection
26 March.	Khayat Near Eastern Antiques
30 March.	Bodman Paintings

The 1926–1927 season was a letdown after the spectacular events of the preceding months. There were important literary and historical manuscripts scattered among the sales, but the only great collection was the Goodyear autographs.

November 1926 brought four interesting auctions. The Harry Glemby collection of English literature, strong in Stevenson, totaled $98,612 for 607 lots; it featured $6,350 for the 150-page MS of *Catriona*.[59] At the Theodore Sedgewick sale Dr. R paid the "sensational price" of $28,500 for a Gwinnett signature,[60] blandly announcing, "The increase of $6,000 in the price of a Gwinnett autograph simply represents an increase in the value of Gwinnett's signature."[61] Kennerley undoubtedly took private satisfaction in auctioning John Lane's collection of Aubrey Beardsley drawings for $30,875.[62]

The fourth November sale attracted special attention, although the material was not valuable or extensive, because of its consignor: *The Books of a Busted Bibliophile Alias A. Edward Newton*.[63] His books about book-collecting had made him the best-known American bibliophile. Newton was not broke; he was culling his library "in order that I may buy more." The catalogue featured a Newtonesque introduction:

> . . . the more I get the more I shall spend—at Rosy's [Rosenbach], or at Walter's [Hill] or Drake's, or drop into those "Wells of English undefiled" [Edgar Wells and Gabriel Wells]; not to mention "dear Mabel" [Zahn of Sessler's], whose skill in separating a man from his money is unsurpassed.
>
> And, reader, you may hardly credit the statement, but I have a feeling of reluctance at parting with these books, although I have so many left: it is like turning a cold shoulder on a poor relation. Take even that miserable copy of "Dr. Johnson and the Fair Sex": when I took it from its shelf this morning, it seemed to say, "Surely you are not going to part with me! You have told me that you loved me a hundred times." No doubt I have: could I tell her that I had found a fairer copy? Perish the thought.
>
> Something tells me that if some of these outraged volumes get into the hands of unscrupulous lawyers (or is this phrase tautological?), a lot of actions may be started for desertion, or non-support, or something, which it may give me a lot of trouble to defend.

W. H. Craig's *Doctor Johnson and the Fair Sex* (London, 1895) fetched $2. The top price was $875 for a volume of Henry Alken's sporting plates. The total for 194 items was only $9,891, yet it was more than they would have brought had they not been connected with Newton. Just as Newton collected association items, so books from his library became association items. Nine of the books in the sale were the property of Yale's Chauncey Brewster Tinker; they brought $1,113. Prof. Tinker was then on the trail of the James Boswell papers believed to be in the possession of Lady Talbot de Malahide, and Newton relayed Kennerley's advice: "Seduce and then blackmail the lady."[64]

A December 1926 nugget sale consisting of 200 lots from some twenty consignors brought $42,910.[65] The top price was Dr. R's $9,000 for fifty-seven Lord Nelson manuscripts, including the plans for the Battle of Trafalgar; the Doctor also took a Lincoln letter with the phrase "A house divided against itself cannot stand" for $5,000.

In February 1927 Anson Conger Goodyear of Buffalo sold what was regarded as the best privately owned autograph collection in America.[66] The 355 lots of literary and historical manuscripts which he had recently assembled at a cost of $54,674 brought $155,708—a strong average of $438.61. During the auction Goodyear attempted to hush his wife as she squealed with pleasure at the bids. It was another Rosenbach show. His purchases included Lincoln's speech on "Slavery and Secession" ($4,700), two groups of Thackeray letters ($14,500 and $15,000), a Keats letter ($5,500), the six-page preface to *Jane Eyre* ($5,800), and Charles Lamb's seventy-seven-page commonplace book ($6,900).

Rosenbach had been the subject of a *Saturday Evening Post* article in which he had declared:

Rare books are a safe investment . . . the stock can never go down. A market exists in every city of the world. New buyers constantly crop up. The most ordinary, sane and prosaic type of business man will suddenly appear at your door, a searching look in his eye, a suppressed tone of excitement in his voice. Like the Ancient Mariner, he takes hold of you to tell his story—for he has suddenly discovered book collecting. And if it happens to be at the end of a very long day, you feel like the Wedding Guest, figuratively beating your breast the while you listen. He returns again and again, enthralled by this new interest which takes him away from his business. If he is wealthy he already may be surfeited with Luxuries of one sort or another; but here is something akin to the friendship of a charming and secretive woman. He takes no risk in becoming satiated; there is no possibility in being bored; always some new experience or unexpected discovery may be lurking just around the corner of a bookshelf.[67]

He proceeded to back his claim in March 1927 by executing the boldest bid of the year: $51,000 for a Gwinnett letter—$22,500 above his own 1926 Gwinnett record.[68] The only known Gwinnett letter on public affairs, it was found among family papers by John Cecil Clay, a needy artist who had read Rosenbach's magazine article about Gwinnett autographs. Clay had known Kennerley when they were Mamaroneck neighbors and took the letter to him. (Two days after the discovery, the barn in which the letter had been stored burned.) Written 12 July 1776, the letter dealing with the beginning of the American Navy was also signed by John Hancock, Robert Morris, Francis Lewis, George Read, and Arthur Middleton—all signers of the Declaration of Independence. Before the sale it was hyperbolically announced that: "One of the greatest authorities on American historical documents, who carefully examined this latest find, said the letter with its numerous celebrated signers was second only in interest to the Declaration of Independence among historic American papers."[69] The bidding opened at $5,000; there were $5,000 raises to $20,000 and $2,500 raises to $30,000. At $30,000 only Rosenbach and Gabriel Wells were bidding; they exchanged thousand-dollar raises until Dr. R set the world record for a letter at $51,000. It was estimated that the price of the page was twenty-five times that of all the manuscripts sold in America in 1894–1895. The Doctor had bought his fourth Gwinnett at the Anderson in fifteen months; he had previously paid $22,500, $19,500, and $28,500. This made-up sale consisted entirely of autograph material, including Grant's letters about his Mississippi campaign ($1,782.50) and Lord Stirling's oath of allegiance witnessed by Washington at Valley Forge ($450). The last important book sale of the season was the collection of Dr. William C. Braislin, covering the history and development of the West.[70] Printed native Americana was still an undervalued field, and the 1,993 lots totaled only $48,375.

Emboldened by the success of the Leverhulme sale, Kennerley became more active in the art field. During the summer of 1926 he wheeled and dealt in Europe, reporting to Stieglitz from the Paris Ritz: "Morley [his son] and I have just returned from Salzburg + Basle. Confidentially: I have bought the greatest armor collection in the world, that of the Archduke Eugen, F. M. of Austria: —over 3500 pieces. I shall not announce it until it is out of the country. In London I closed sales for The Marquis of Reading—a great + charming person—The Earl of Lytton, Lord Islington and a collection formed by the late Lord Grimthorpe. And other lesser collections. . . . I have never worked so hard on so little sleep."[71]

In November 1926, 824 art pieces collected by the late Nathan Samuel Kaplan, inventor of artificial pearls, brought $138,245; the top item was Gobelin's tapestry "The Court of Apollo" at $5,050.[72] There were six important Anderson art sales during January 1927: Frank Lloyd Wright's Japanese prints, Tom G. Cannon's English porcelain, H. Kevorkian's Eastern art, and the collections of the Marquess of Reading, Lord Grimthorpe, and H. I. H. the Archduke Salvator of Austria.

Kennerley was not the only expert in juggling loans; auctions were a resource for collectors who borrowed against the anticipated worth of their possessions. It is the nature of collectors to be sanguine about appreciated values. Wright's Japanese antique prints were sold "by order of the Bank of Wisconsin."[73] The 346 items realized $36,975. After the sale, Wright's wife, from whom he was legally separated, obtained an attachment of the proceeds, alleging that she was part owner of the collection and that Wright owed her support payments. Kennerley contended that the Anderson took the collection as security for a $25,000 loan to Wright in 1925, and that Wright had subsequently transferred ownership of the collection—subject to the Anderson lien—to the Bank of Wisconsin and Joseph M. Boyd for additional loans of $52,576. The Anderson succeeded in establishing its right to retain the auction proceeds against Wright's debt which had increased to $37,181 with interest.[74]

Cannon, "the renowned expert," sold his collection of eighteenth-century English porcelain in four sessions.[75] The 866 lots, including the largest number of Worcester pieces ever sold in America, brought

$85,470—a satisfying result for the Burslem-born Kennerley. The Ke-vorkian Near and Far Eastern art did much better: $83,910 for 252 lots.[76]

When the *Berengaria* docked in New York on 17 September 1926, the passengers included Secretary of Treasury Andrew W. Mellon, financiers J. S. Bache and Bernard Baruch, and George Arliss (from whom Kennerley obtained another lost Wilde manuscript); but the lead paragraph in the *Times* article was devoted to Kennerley's an-nouncement that he had arranged to auction the art and furnishings of the Marquess of Reading and Lord Grimthorpe.[77] His acquisition efforts in England had been facilitated by the Leverhulme publicity. Kennerley's memo on the Reading sale explains: "I bought the things outright but gave Lord Reading a contingent interest so that I might announce the sale as sold by his order."[78] The contract stipulated a £3,000 nonreturnable advance against the gross proceeds; the com-mission was 15 percent, with additional charges for shipping, cata-loguing, exhibiting, and advertising.[79] The 82 lots sold in January 1927 brought $22,165, and Kennerley reported to Reading that the galleries had been able "to net a small commission of $1,016.75."[80] His Lordship does not appear to have received more than the advance. The following week the contents of Woodlea, Virginia Water, Surrey, home of the late Lord Grimthorpe, were auctioned with the remaining Reading properties and the paintings and sculptures of Archduke Leopold Sal-vator.[81] The 168 lots totaled $58,230, with the top price of $4,000 for Van Dyke's *Descent from the Cross*.

There were subsequent Anderson sales of Grimthorpe and Salvator properties, but titled Europeans brought Kennerley more publicity than revenue. An exception was the March 1927 sale of the Fortress Ho-henwerfen armory, the property of the Archduke Eugen, which showed the development of arms and armor from the fifteenth century. After the deal was made, Kennerley left his son Morley behind to oversee the packing and shipping of the material from the virtually inaccessible castle near Salzburg. The five-session sale brought a comfortable total of $114,148—with the top price of $9,100 for a piece of sixteenth-century horse armor.

At the close of the 1926–1927 season the American Art Association announced a gross of $6,238,025 for eighty-four book and art sales.

The Anderson take was estimated at about half that for ninety-three sales. Each house accused the other of commission cutting, and the profits were slim. The highest manuscript price of the American Art season was Dr. R's $15,400 for Wagner's score of *Das Rheingold*. The Doctor was Kennerley's best customer, but he did not boycott the American Art.

Henry E. Huntington died in May 1927. He had bought more great books and spent more money than any collector who ever lived—an estimated $15,000,000 in fifteen years. Among the entire collections bought by Huntington were the E. Dwight Church Americana ($1,200,000), the Beverly Chew early English literature ($500,000), the Britwell Court Americana ($350,000), the Duke of Devonshire Library ($1,000,000), the Pembroke Library ($100,000), the Grenville Kane Worthington MSS ($100,000), the 20,000-volume Frederick R. Halsey collection ($750,000), and the Bridgewater Library ($1,000,000). The Huntington Library and Art Gallery at San Marino, California, held an estimated 75,000 books, some 200 illuminated manuscripts, and more than 10,000 other manuscripts and documents. Huntington had spent another fortune on art; his most famous acquisition was Gainsborough's *The Blue Boy,* for which he paid $620,000 in 1921.

During 1927 Kennerley talked of his intention to open a London branch of the Anderson Galleries. He estimated that 90 percent of the art purchases abroad were by Americans, and he wanted to secure a piece of that action. At the same time he reiterated his desire to free himself from the responsibility for the day-to-day operation of an auction gallery.

Before he sailed for England in the summer of 1927, Kennerley informed John Farrar of *The Bookman* that he had retired as a publisher. "The two things that definitely drove me from publishing were the war, because I could not get interested in the publication of war books, and the rise in the price of book manufacture. I cannot bear to publish a book that is not rightly made, inside and out. That, as you well know, costs money these days." (The first part of this statement is not strictly true; Kennerley published sixteen war-related books between 1914 and 1919.) Farrar's article included a list of Kennerley's publishing achievements and credited him with starting "what might be called 'the new type of publishing.' " It is not clear what was meant by this phrase; but it probably referred to Kennerley's readiness to publish unknown authors and his commitment to poetry and drama. Yet Kennerley was not an innovative publisher. He published few avant-garde writers, and his books did not reflect the modern movements in literature. English imports were the backbone of his lists. Kennerley's main contribution to the literary scene was in launching young authors—who moved to other houses—and in introducing English writers to American readers. As Farrar observed, "His list speaks nobly for itself, and its ornaments grace the catalogues of half the publishers in America!"[82]

Kennerley was essentially a prewar publisher. More than 400 of his titles appeared before 1920 and less than 30 after 1920. The Twenties were a time of literary experimentation, but Kennerley was not involved in the new movements—as were Huebsch (launched in 1906), Knopf (1915), Boni & Liveright (1917), and Seltzer (1920). Kennerley was out of touch with the literary scene and had retired from the field while several of the major American publishing houses were being formed: Harcourt, Brace (1919), Simon & Schuster (1924), Viking (1925), and Random House (1927).

Lewis Mumford attempted to describe Kennerley's impact on literature in a 1930 article surveying the recent history of American publishing. "By 1910 the older publishing houses were barnacled in routine"; but Kennerley "started a new regime, a regime of personal publishing, which rested largely on the tastes and intuitions and interests of the publisher himself, and which sought to bring to the fore new writers, as well as continue safely with the old." Mumford hyperbolically claimed that "almost every promising young author before 1915 came under Mr. Kennerley's wing."

> The enterprise was a little unstable, to put its defects in the most kindly way possible; and the relations between publisher and author usually terminated in a one-sided but increasingly acrimonious correspondence; but no matter. The books themselves appeared, whether anyone made money on them or not. Literature does not necessarily flourish when the authors themselves are flush; what is necessary is that the writer should find an audience and break through the sacred egotism of adolescent solitude; and Mr. Kennerley provided this opportunity by bring-

ing back a spirit of fun and adventure and derring-do into the enterprise. His example was infectious.[83]

This generous tribute was a response to Kennerley's willingness to publish anything that interested him without much concern for its profitability. Indeed, he never had a best-seller.

CHAPTER SEVEN

Cortlandt F. Bishop—The Sale of the
Anderson Galleries—More Gwinnetts—
Jerome Kern—Margery Durant—
Departure from Anderson

THE AMERICAN ART ASSOCIATION had been acquired for $500,000 in 1923 by the very rich and very eccentric Cortlandt Field Bishop, M.A., LL.B., Ph.D. Bishop, who had inherited a New York City real estate fortune, was a bibliophile, pioneer motorist, and world traveler. He owned the *Paris Times* and had reportedly bought the Paris Ritz when there was a problem about his reservation; he also financed hotels in the Sahara. The vice presidents of the American Art, Hiram Parke and Otto Bernet, had expected that they would continue to operate the gallery, but Bishop was incapable of not interfering. He arranged disastrous sales of Italian and Spanish art and consequently found it necessary to pump money into the going concern he had bought. Bishop came to the conclusion that there was not enough prime material to support two major New York auction houses: one firm would be able to control the market.

In May 1927 Kennerley passed the word that he was willing to sell the Anderson Galleries, in which he had acquired most of the stock, repeating his complaint that the auction business required too much of his attention. Then the mating dance began. Kennerley left for

London, followed by Parke. They ignored each other in London; Kennerley wanted to deal directly with Bishop, and Parke wanted Kennerley to approach him. Kennerley then went to Paris, where Bishop was. Again Parke followed, but still no contact was made by either side. Finally Kennerley asked Parke for an appointment, after which a Kennerley-Bishop meeting was arranged for London. Kennerley's note thanking Parke for his help indicates a change in signals: "I hope that you will be present and that we may return to America together. I feel that together we can do marvels!"[1] Kennerley did not plan to retire from the auction scene, after all. He was anticipating a collaboration with Parke and American Art. Nonetheless, the bargaining session took place without Parke's participation. Kennerley asked $500,000 for the Anderson Galleries—which was capitalized at $350,000. All he was really selling was the Anderson Galleries' name and good will. The Park Avenue building was leased, and he had managed to have the lease transferred to himself. Bishop and Kennerley settled at $417,500, but Parke protested that the price was double what Kennerley would have taken. The terms were not made public when the sale was confirmed in January 1928.

Kennerley returned from England on the *Leviathan* with a hundred Augustus John paintings and announced a major show, which was held at the Anderson in January 1928. One of the paintings exhibited was Morley Kennerley's portrait, owned by his father, which Kennerley later sold to Tallulah Bankhead.

Having acquired the Anderson to eliminate competition, Bishop proceeded to operate both houses in competition—with Kennerley remaining at the head of the Anderson. This puzzling situation is accounted for by a private agreement between Kennerley and Bishop whereby Kennerley would buy back both American Art and the Anderson for $1,500,000. Kennerley intended to finance his purchase of the two galleries by marrying the daughter of William C. Durant, the president of General Motors. Both Margery Durant and Kennerley were married at the time, and the money from the Anderson sale was required to facilitate his divorce.

Margery Durant Campbell Daniel was forty in 1927; Kennerley was forty-nine. She was married to Robert W. Daniel, president of the Liberty Bank of New York. The newspapers described her as an art collector and patroness of artists; her relationship with Kennerley was supposed to have resulted from her purchases at the Anderson. Margery made good newspaper copy. She flew over Europe and Africa in her own plane—which she did not pilot—and survived crash landings. Moreover, there was a family curse in the background: at her first marriage, to Dr. W. R. Campbell, Margery was given the wedding ring worn by a bride who had died on her wedding night.[2]

While Kennerley and Margery were sorting out their matrimonial situations, he operated the Anderson as an employee though the catalogue covers continued to carry his name as PRESIDENT. After the nonmerger, Bishop dismissed Arthur Swann, the head of the American Art book department. It was believed that Bishop had acted at Kennerley's instigation. His long-standing enmity toward Swann was well known, and Swann had managed to compete with the Anderson in the book field. In October 1927 Kennerley informed Stieglitz: "Confidentially I am now directing the American Art Association from my little room. Swann has left and I have put our Kingsland in his place. The others come over here to see me. It will mean more responsibility but less work."[3]

Kennerley missed publishing. In 1927 he persuaded George H. Doran to sponsor a contest for poems inspired by Charles A. Lindbergh's transatlantic flight. There were more than 4,000 submissions by 3,000 poets; the best one hundred poems—selected by Christopher Morley, John Farrar, and Kennerley—were published in *The Spirit of St. Louis,* edited by Charles Vale. The judges awarded the $500 first prize to Nathalia Crane's "The Wings of Lead." The fourteen-year-old poet's effusion concludes:

> We hear the clinking tambourine of Miriam anew,
> We believe in every miracle since Lindbergh flew the blue,
> The wonder of the long draw when the bow-string is a thread—
> The beauty of courage that can raise the wings of lead.[4]

Publishers' Weekly greeted the opening of the 1927–1928 season by declaring that "the immediate future of the American book auction system rests squarely on the shoulders of Mitchell Kennerley," and credited him with developing the confidence of consignors and stabi-

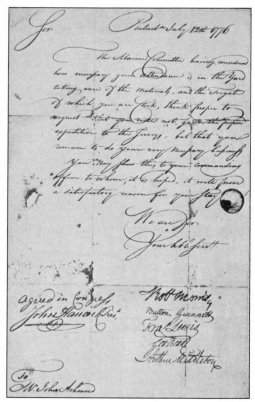

LEFT: *The $51,000 Gwinnett signature*

ABOVE: *Cortlandt F. Bishop*

BELOW: *Margery Durant in vintage Buick (GMI Alumni Foundation's Collection of Industrial History, Flint, Michigan)*

lizing the market. "The value of books the world over was due in no inconsiderable degree to Mr. Kennerley's success."[5] The new season would be another record-setter at the Anderson, starting with a string of brilliant November sales.

On the second, Jerome Kern sold 347 culls from his collection for $28,110;[6] the inclusion of Gray's *Elegy* ($4,900—the top price), a presentation copy of Dickens's *The Cricket on the Hearth* ($1,075), and one of the six known trial copies of Stevenson's *The Hanging Judge* ($1,250) presaged the quality of the legendary Kern sale to come in 1929. The next day the Charles F. Jenkins set of Signers brought $40,038.50;[7] the Gwinnett signature fetched a conservative $18,600 from Dr. R, but a volume with two Thomas Lynch signatures reached $7,500—the record for this Signer. On 25 November a sale of literary material brought $86,937.50 for 153 lots;[8] the $568 average was very high for a made-up sale—that is, a sale for several consignors. Dr. R went to $14,000 for one of the six known copies of Kipling's *The Smith Administration,* a paperbound work published in India—thereby setting the Kipling record as well as the record for a book by a living author. The Doctor also paid the record price of $6,000 for Kipling's *Echoes* with an unpublished poem written on the flyleaf. A Keats letter with four stanzas of "Song of Sorrow" brought $6,600; Gabriel Wells paid $6,100 for Blake's watercolor "Simeon Prophesying Over the Infant Jesus"; and the first copy of T. E. Lawrence's *The Seven Pillars of Wisdom* to be auctioned in America brought a surprisingly high $2,500. This sale included the manuscript of Wilde's play *The Duchess of Padua,* which Kennerley had obtained from George Arliss.[9] During a shipboard conversation with Kennerley the actor mentioned that his father, a printer, had retained the manuscript after producing a private edition for Wilde. A search was made at Kennerley's urging, and it was found in Arliss's country home. Sir Robert Abdy bought the 266 pages for $3,850, which the *New York Times* considered "paltry."[10] Three days later in November the Zachary Hollingsworth collection of American historical manuscripts reached the highest total of the season: $181,927 for 939 lots.[11] Hollingsworth's two sets of Signers brought $60,735 (a record) and $25,692.50. The better of the two Gwinnetts brought $19,200 from Dr. R, and Wells paid $5,200 for a Gwinnett signature cut from a document. Within a month three complete sets of Signers had been sold at the Anderson for a total of $125,650. During November 1927 there were seven book and manuscript sales at the Anderson as against two unimportant sales at the American Art.

In December came 217 lots of historical letters and documents from the collections of Schuyler Colfax and others,[12] which brought $41,223, far exceeding the estimates. One of the three transcripts of the Thirteenth Amendment—signed by Lincoln, Vice President Hannibal Hamlin, and Speaker of the House Colfax fetched $12,000 (a printed copy signed by Lincoln reached $270,000 in 1984); an 1859 Lincoln letter to Colfax about the Republican platform brought $3,050; and Washington's 1795 letter offering Patrick Henry the post of Secretary of State was worth $4,400. At the end of 1927 Dr. Rosenbach prophesied: "Following the financial center, the book market has gradually shifted to New York. In a few years it will be impossible to purchase the finest English books in London."[13]

S. N. Levy's collection of Elizabethan literature was sold in January 1928.[14] The market was soft after the Clawson highs; but still the 194 lots totaled $41,083. The top item was William Painter's *The Palace of Pleasure* (1556–1557)—a source for the Elizabethan dramatists—which brought $8,400 from Dr. R. In another January Anderson sale *Leaves of Grass* reached the record price of $1,800 from Dr. R.[15] Robert Louis Stevenson tapered off. The sale of Henry A. Colgate's Stevenson collection on 9 February brought $24,060.50 for 233 lots,[16] with an inscribed copy of *The Pentland Rising* reaching $2,850; 13 MS poems, including "Requiem" with an unpublished stanza, brought $3,100 as a lot.

The next evening 100 incunables from the collection of Dr. Otto Vollbehr totaled $26,450;[17] the top price was $2,000 for a woodcut book, *Schatzbehalter. Oder Schrein der wahren Reichthümer des Heils under der ewigen Seligkeit* (Nuremberg: Anton Koberger, 1491). At the conclusion of this sale nine volumes from the library of Prof. Paul Soubeiran De Pierres with manuscript *horae** and "the only perfect

---

* *Horae* or books of hours are manuscript or printed collections of prayers, often illuminated with miniatures.

copy in America" of Nicolaus De Lyra's *Postillae Super Bibliam* (c. 1472) brought a total of $2,616.[18] Dr. Vollbehr was back the next month with *Bibliotheca Americana Vetustissima,* fifteenth- and six-tenth-century European works relating to the discovery of the New World.[19] The 139 items totaled $28,438 with two printed Cortez letters about Mexico bringing the highest prices of $4,600 and $3,300.

In March 1928 Donald Friede sold his collection of modern first editions to finance the new publishing house of Covici-Friede.[20] These books were true moderns—there were no Stevensons or Kiplings—and the results demonstrated that the collecting fraternity was still cautious about contemporary writers. The values of early books were established by the tests of time and proven rarity; but collectors felt that it was impossible to determine which of the twentieth-century authors was a sound investment. A single lot of four F. Scott Fitzgeralds fetched $3; *Ulysses* was worth $50; but a signed *Renascence* reached $105. None of the catalogue descriptions mentioned the presence of dust jackets, for the cult of condition did not yet apply to contemporary books. Today the four Fitzgerald books in mint-condition jackets might bring the total $7,221.25 realized by Friede's 505 lots. By way of contrast, Dr. Rosenbach's April purchase of the *Alice in Wonderland* MS for $72,250 in London made headlines all over the world.

The E. V. Lucas sale in May[21] occasioned criticism of the consignor because it consisted of Sir Sidney Colvin's private correspondence in connection with his research on Keats and Stevenson, which had been given to Lucas by Colvin. The 376 lots—including letters from Stevenson, Hardy, Kipling, and Conrad—brought only $9,820.50. This catalogue was the final work of Arthur Hooley, who died in March 1928 at fifty-four. In many ways Kennerley's successes were linked to his versatile cousin, who had assisted him in three ventures—magazines, books, and auctioneering—handling details while Kennerley promoted. Kennerley characterized Hooley as "undeniably a genius" in his statement to the press: "Few men had the sympathetic insight and pure taste for what is abiding and distinguished in literature."[22] He later described Hooley's approach to cataloguing: "There was a Napoleon letter in the Arnold sale, which I gave him to decipher and identify. He kept it so long I had to beg him to give it me at once. After a few days he turned it in with the explanation that he had been obliged to consult 27 books in French before he could complete his description. Of course his work always paid, as items he catalogued always brought large prices."[23]

Another 1928 loss to the book world was the death of Herschel V. Jones, whose sales at the Anderson had totaled $692,149.15. Kennerley, who was an honorary pallbearer, said: "Mr. Jones was in spirit the great collector of his generation, the quickest I have ever known to appreciate the best in literature and art."[24]

The splendid 1927–1928 season ended sadly with the last four George D. Smith liquidation sales which totaled $55,519: books and autographs (359 lots, $26,163),[25] Americana (450 lots, $9,661),[26] autographs (281 lots, $4,525),[27] and books and prints (1,439 lots, $15,170).[28] Thus one of the two richest stocks of rare books and manuscripts (along with Rosenbach's) ever assembled in America was finally dispersed at an average of $22 per lot.

During 1927–1928 Kennerley again lured major art sales to the Anderson. Dr. John E. Stilwell had collected oriental art, porcelains, and fabrics; Gothic and Renaissance wood carvings and paintings; European porcelains, paintings, sculptures, furniture, and fabrics. The ads for the sale printed a congratulatory letter to Kennerley from John O'H. Cosgrave: "It is the most brilliant private show that has been made in New York in my time. . . . I'm delighted also that this show of big names and fine examples is so well buttressed with authorities. The Fifth Avenue Blackhanders are powerless for once."[29] The 720 Stilwell pieces that were sold in five sessions during December 1927 totaled $352,035.[30] A pair of Foo dogs brought $10,000; Jakob Van Oostsanen's *The Adoration of the Shepherds*, $10,250; two companion "Flower and Fruit" pieces by Jan Weenix, $10,000; Raphael's *The Mystic Marriage of St. Catherine*, $21,000; El Greco's *Portrait of the Master of the House of Mois of Aragon*, $19,000.

Among the greatest paintings sold at the Anderson were those collected by sugar tycoon Charles H. Senff. Kennerley took the sale away from American Art by convincing the heirs that the seventy-seven paintings would bring $1,500,000; but the total for the March 1928 auction was $580,375.[31] Two Frans Hals portraits brought $55,000 and $47,500; the Valesquez *Portrait of General Marchese Spinola*, $53,000; and Corot's *Woman Reading*, $31,000. Kennerley did not have the influence with art dealers than he had with bookmen.

The first season during which Kennerley operated the Anderson for

Bishop grossed $3,894,096. The forty sales of books and autographs brought $501,546.50; prints added $504,233.45; furniture and objects of art yielded a surprising $1,831,096; and paintings totaled $1,065,714. At American Art the total was $6,229,670, of which books, autographs, and prints contributed $756,212.50. Anderson was the bibliophiles' resort, but American Art piled up the money. Even so, Parke and Bernet complained to Bishop about Kennerley's unethical competition. It was particularly galling to them that Bishop interfered in the conduct of American Art while allowing Kennerley a free hand at the Anderson.

After the exertions of the 1927–1928 season Kennerley spent part of the summer in France with Augustus John, whom he had introduced to architect M. Hawley McLanahan; they were guests at the Château de Missery in Burgundy while John painted the McLanahans. Morley Kennerley joined his father there. On 24 August Kennerley reported to Stieglitz that he was just back from Reno: "I have had and am having a glorious fight all along the line and am winning out and the end is in sight—and will be worth the [struggle]. I am negotiating the purchase of both concerns . . . and shall probably buy if I can dispose of this lease which I think I can."[32] The purpose of his Nevada trip was to visit Margery, who was obtaining her divorce. Yet at the time Kennerley was negotiating for control of both American Art and the Anderson, he was telling friends of his plans to move permanently to England and resume publishing.

During 1928 Kennerley was involved in another arcane art transaction. On 16 April the *New York Times*[33] announced that six small paintings of calla lilies by Georgia O'Keeffe on exhibit at Anderson had been sold to an anonymous collector for $25,000.* The *Brooklyn Daily Eagle* subsequently described the group as consisting of two larger and four smaller paintings, claiming that the price was "so far as can be learned, the largest sum ever paid for so small a group of modern

---

* Herbert J. Seligmann's *Alfred Stieglitz Talking* (New York: Yale University Press, 1966) states that these paintings were "on private view for a few days" from 11 May 1928—almost a month after the *Times* article—and that the purchaser was an "American living in Paris" (pp. 133–35).

paintings by a present day American."[34] The buyer was never identified; but there is evidence indicating that Kennerley was the purchaser—acting for Margery. The announcement therefore appears to have been a fabrication intended to publicize O'Keeffe and raise her prices. In August 1928 Kennerley wrote Stieglitz: "I have received a wonderful letter about the Lilies which are in Reno. . . . The others are at the Sherry-Netherland. . . ."[35] Margery had some of the paintings in Nevada, and Kennerley had some of them in his apartment five months after the sale to the anonymous collector.

When Kennerley was broke in 1930, he asked Stieglitz for an extension on his debt to O'Keeffe, explaining that Margery had not paid him "for all my O'Keeffes. Had she done so I should have been obliged to deliver the pictures to her long ago."[36] On 3 February 1931 Kennerley informed Stieglitz: "All the pictures are here [in his Sherry-Netherland apartment]. I will send them one at a time. . . ."[37] A week later Kennerley asked Stieglitz to return two of the lily paintings because he had borrowed money on the contents of his apartment and needed to show the paintings to the lender.[38] The lilies were presumably returned to Stieglitz by Kennerley, but their location is now unknown.

What would be the fifty-one-year-old Kennerley's final season at the Anderson Galleries was punctuated by rumors of his impending resignation. Meanwhile he prepared to leave with a triumph. The sale of Jerome Kern's library in January 1929 was Kennerley's greatest auction; it remains the most glamorous literary sale held in America. The 1912 Hoe sale had more and better books, but the Kern sale marked the peak of bibliomaniacal fever before the Crash.

Kern had been collecting for some fifteen years and had invested half a million dollars of his song-writing royalties in books and manuscripts. Like Herschel Jones, he was a superb example of the collector for whom the pleasure of acquisition is greater than the gratification of ownership. Kern wanted the best and paid top prices. Yet it was not a great collection in terms of depth or scope, as was John Quinn's. Kern's early mentor was his former collaborator Harry B. Smith, who had assembled a notable "Sentimental Library" of association items. The Kern books were high spots—exceptional copies of famous books, often enriched by inscriptions. The strength was in English literature of the eighteenth and nineteenth centuries, with manuscripts. By 1928 Kern was finding his library a burden. His wife did not share his enthusiasm, and he was annoyed by the necessity of maintaining a staff of servants to guard the books while he was traveling. He refused to put his collection in a vault: if he couldn't have the pleasure of living with it, he would dispose of it. Moreover, Kern had the feeling that it was the right time to cash in. He also got out of Wall Street.

Preliminary discussions commenced in September 1928, as documented by Kennerley's letter to Kern:

> I am very much interested in what we talked about yesterday. I had dinner last night with Rosenbach and Beyer just to get out of them their ideas on the subject of a book sale. They were both enthusiastic. . . . After I got home I went through your list again, and allowing for books and manuscripts which you have purchased since it was made up, I do not think the results would fall short of the amount we mentioned.

Kennerley did not name the figure; but he advised him to buy a $75,000 *First Folio* to sweeten the pot—which Kern did not do. Kennerley's letter includes the information that he is leaving for Reno: "While I am away I will give the matter very careful consideration and by the time I return I shall know if I can do it. I think I can unless something unexpected turns up to call me away from New York for a long period."[39] Helen had not yet agreed to a divorce, and Kennerley's "something unexpected" probably refers to his divorce negotiations and marriage plans.

On 3 October 1928 the contract for the Kern sale was executed, stipulating an inclusive 10 percent commission with a two-year payment schedule.[40] The collection was insured for $650,000. An announcement was made by Kern and Kennerley on 17 October. Kern informed the press:

> As my collection has grown, books have not only fascinated me, they have enslaved me. As rare books became rarer, I battled for them, treasured them, and so became a collector. I never captured a prize, the prize always captured me.
>
> In spite of this, it would not have occurred to me to sell my library

Jerome Kern

Mitchell and Morley Kennerley,
Château Missery, 1928 (Courtesy
of Morley and Jean Kennerley)

if my friend, Mitchell Kennerley, had not suggested that within a short time he would give up the active management of the Anderson Galleries. Somehow I could not think of my books ever being sold by any one else, even after my death, and in a flash I saw an escape from my slavery.[41]

While the Kern catalogue was being compiled in some haste, there were other sales. In October Kennerley had the ironic satisfaction of selling the modern firsts and press books from the collection of Alfred A. Knopf, who had outdistanced him as publisher. It is impossible to determine which of the lots in the sale were actually Knopf's because it included "additions from other private libraries." As in the Friede sale during the preceding season, the true moderns did not fare well; the total for 303 lots was $6,090.50.[42] The star author was John Galsworthy, who in 1928 seemed a sure bet for classic status. *The Man of Property* (1906)—the first Forsyte novel—reached $390, three times what it had brought the previous year. *A Man of Devon* (1901) was worth $270. Yet *A Portrait of the Artist as a Young Man* and *Exiles* with a postcard from Joyce to Elkin Mathews brought only $37.50 for the lot.

Then came January 1929 and the Kern sale, rich in books collectors could respond to, by the authors A. Edward Newton had praised. Dealers who had been driving up prices were obliged to support the Kern sale—with or without bids in hand. The sale fed the Twenties appetite for records; even so, the results were surprising.

The two-volume catalogue was issued on 20 December, with 1,484 entries to be sold in ten sessions on 7–10 and 21–24 January 1929.[43] The foreword signed M.K. commented on the value of proven rarities:

Occasionally a book fifty years old or more may have been miraculously preserved in its original state so as to appear like new, and we have mentioned such cases in this catalogue, but the collector who confines himself to new copies of old books had better content himself with the manufactured "First Editions" of today, which like the theatre ticket of today he can buy for several times its original price before it is issued. Nearly every First Edition in Mr. Kern's library once sold for less than its published price and the fact that it will sell today for many times its published price is a case of the survival of the fittest and not just of the best-advertised.

The presale consensus among the trade was that the Kern sale might bring $1,000,000 with luck.

Kennerley publicized the sale with ads and press releases; and— more important to the outcome—he encouraged competition among the top dealers. Delayed payments were arranged for favored bidders; meetings were held with dealers to persuade them to go after certain items; and collectors who came to the presale exhibits were steered to dealers. Gabriel Wells, who chafed in his role as consistent underbidder to Dr. R, was urged to make the Kern sale a showdown. Kennerley insured Wells and Rosenbach for $250,000 each with Lloyd's of London during the Kern sessions. Nonetheless, there was concern about the paucity of bids placed with dealers by collectors. Owen D. Young, Carl Pforzheimer, and Richard Gimbel were represented by dealers, but much of the dealer bidding was for stock. Young, chairman of the boards of RCA and General Electric, had seen his RCA stock climb from 1½ to 420; he divided his bids among several dealers and bid on books personally, giving rise to the rumor that he inadvertently bid against himself on some items.

Before the sale Kennerley asked Kern what he would take for his library, and Kern replied that $650,000 or $700,000 would satisfy him. That figure was passed in the letter G of the catalogue. The opening session was held on Monday, 7 January, at 8:15 P.M. Kern's *Show Boat* was on Broadway, and the Dow-Jones average had closed that day at 297—up ninety-four points from January 1928 and 142 points from January 1927. The boys were in a mood to sing "Make Believe." Admission was by ticket only, and 600 crowded the gallery. Anthony Bade was in the rostrum.

At item 19 it became clear that the market was being tested when Dr. R bought *Sense and Sensibility* for $3,600 and went on to acquire four more Jane Austen books and a letter for $10,600. Then at #57A Dr. R went to $5,200 for a copy of Boswell's *Life of Samuel Johnson* with letters from both Boswell and Dr. Johnson laid in. The first item to break $10,000 was #84, Elizabeth Barrett Browning's first book, *The Battle of Marathon*, for which Dr. R went to a record $17,500 against Beyer. Kern had bought it for $1,650 in 1924. Thirty Robert Browning items totaled $34,085, with Beyer securing *Pauline*, Browning's first book, at $16,000. At #149 Dr. R paid the top price of the first session, $23,500, for the second edition of Robert Burns's *Poems, Chiefly in the Scottish Dialect*, enhanced by an inscription by Burns to John M'Murdo: ". . . to no man, whatever his station in life, or his power to serve me, have I ever paid a compliment at the expence of Truth." As was his custom, Rosenbach had bought a book that the newspapers would headline; but he was never able to sell it. The 154 items in the first session totaled $166,363, an astonishing average of $1,080. That night Kern, who had remained home, telegraphed Kennerley: MY GOD WHATS GOING ON.

There were two sessions the following day. In the afternoon fifty-seven Byron items totaled $96,301.50. Wells paid $20,000 for forty-nine pages of the *Don Juan* manuscript; but Dr. R stole the headlines again by outbidding Wells at $27,000 on the complete 142-page manuscript of *Marino Faliero* for Pforzheimer. Item 240 was the suppressed first edition of *Alice in Wonderland*,* which Rosenbach was compelled to buy because of his reputation as the man who had bought the *Alice* manuscript. He took it for stock at $10,000 and sold it to Young. The remaining excitement of the session was provided by the Conrad manuscripts and typescripts from the Quinn sale: *Youth* brought $2,800 ($2,000 at Quinn); "Because of the Dollars," $850 ($750); *Under Western Eyes*, $7,250 ($6,900); *Victory*, $4,000 ($850); "Preface to My Reminiscences," $600 ($700); "Admiralty Paper," $1,400 ($1,750); "One Day More," $1,200 ($1,800). The moderns were still regarded as speculative. The 174 items in the second session totaled $175,071.50.

There were great expectations for the evening session on 8 January because of the 113 Dickens items. But first Drake went to $11,500 for *Robinson Crusoe* (the same copy had reached $5,350 in the 1924 Chew sale). The Dickens total was $252,540, with Scheuer paying the record price of $28,000 for the "perfect" *Pickwick Papers* in parts that Kern had bought for $3,500. Other five-figure Dickens bids were Dr. R's

---

* The author was dissatisfied with the illustrations in the first edition and had it withdrawn.

$15,000 on behalf of Young for a twenty-eight-page Dickens notebook and $10,500 for *The Strange Gentleman* enhanced with a letter; Sessler's $15,000 for the ninety-page manuscript of "The Perils of Certain English Prisoners" by Dickens and Wilkie Collins; and Wells's $10,250 for an inscribed *Tale of Two Cities*. The third session totaled $273,952.50.

On Wednesday evening, 9 January, the fourth session set the record for Fielding's *Tom Jones*—the only known copy in original boards—which Dr. R bought for $29,000 and later sold to Young for cost plus 10 percent; Kern had paid $3,500. (This copy became the subject of a lawsuit after it had been acquired by Lord Rothschild and was discovered to have been sophisticated by the insertion of leaves.) It was mainly an eighteenth-century night, highlighted by thirty-nine Oliver Goldsmith items which realized $80,840. Bidding for himself, Young went to $27,000 for the thirty-four-page manuscript of Goldsmith's translation of "Vida's Scacchis, or Chess"—for which Kern had paid $33,000. (The authenticity of this manuscript was subsequently disputed, and it was returned to Anderson.) The total for this session was $176,400.

The fifth and final session of the first part of the Kern sale was held the following evening. The highest price so far was Beyer's $34,000 for the incomplete 160-page manuscript of Thomas Hardy's *A Pair of Blue Eyes*; it was also the highest price in America for a modern manuscript to date. Kern had reportedly paid $10,000. Beyer also went to $4,100 for the inscribed copy of *Jude the Obscure* which had fetched $47.50 at the 1914 James Carlton Young sale. One page of Dr. Johnson's manuscript for his *Dictionary*, for which Kern had paid $1,750, was the object of bidding between enemies Charles Sessler representing Gimbel and Rosenbach representing Young; Sessler was the victor at $11,000. The total for the fifth session was the lowest in the first half of the sale: $141,588.

At the close of the four days that were required for A–J the total for 748 items stood at $933,375. Eighteenth-century authors exceeded the estimates; but competition for the Elizabethans, which were not a Kern strength, was soft. The *New York Times* editorialized: "In time, no doubt, there will be a Book and Manuscript Exchange, where a seat may cost as much as it now costs on the Stock Exchange. The connection between the transactions of the institutions will then be clear, day by day."[44] As the Kern auction progressed, it became known as "the sale of a thousand editorials."

Between the first and second parts there was an 11-day hiatus for dealers to recoup and for collectors to recalculate their bids at the next five sessions. There were some complaints about the Kern "exaggerations"; but most bookmen were pleased. Dealers were busily repricing their stocks, and collectors were happily reappraising their collections. Everything else was booming, so why not books? Hadn't Rosenbach and other authorities been proclaiming for years that books were better investments than stocks? As the sixth session opened the participants were ready to determine how high the book market could go. Kern had already doubled his investment, and Kennerley smiled. Keats did well; acting for Young, Dr. R outbid Beyer at $17,000 for a copy of *Poetical Works* with the manuscript of "I Stood Tiptoe Upon a Little Hill," which had cost Kern $500. Charles Lamb was one of Newton's pets, and the thirty Lamb items totaled $96,155. Dr. R, who had built a reputation as a collector of children's books, went to $8,750 for Lamb's *Poetry for Children*, one of three or four copies known at the time; but he was never able to sell it. Sessler then outbid Rosenbach at $48,000 for the eighty-page manuscript of Lamb's contributions to William Hone's *Table Book*, which had cost Kern $3,000. Sessler was bidding for Barton Currie, author of a popular work about collecting, *Fishers of Books*. The sixth session closed at $221,490.

There were two sessions on 22 January. The afternoon session featured a four-page letter by Edgar Allan Poe quoting Elizabeth Barrett Browning's praise for "The Raven." Dr. R took it at $19,500, setting the record for an American literary letter; Kern had acquired it for $1,250. Thirty Alexander Pope items followed; acting for Young, Dr. R bid $29,000—the top price of the seventh session—on forty pages of the manuscript of *Essay on Man*. Wells, the underbidder, had sold it to Kern for $6,000. The session closed with seven Shakespeares. Only the *Third Folio* reached five figures, with Dr. R paying $15,500 for the Hoe copy. The total for the seventh session was $162,167.50.

The evening session on 22 January was the most remunerative because of the forty-one Shelley items, which totaled $124,265. The surprise glamour piece of the Kern sale was Shelley's revised copy of *Queen Mab*. Privately published by Shelley in 1813, the poem was a passionate early statement of his radical and anti-Christian views. The original publication was suppressed; only two copies were known in 1929. Kern's copy had been bought by Rosenbach at the 1920 Forman sale for $6,000 and resold to Kern for $9,500. (Forman had paid £6 in 1896.) The bidding opened at $10,000, and the competition was be-tween Wells and Dr. R until Wells took it at $68,000—regarded as a wildly inflated price. It was the second highest price to date for a book at an American auction, exceeded only by Rosenbach's 1926 bid of $106,000 for the Gutenberg Bible. Perhaps Wells, frustrated by his role as Rosenbach's underbidder, wanted to steal the headlines. Book-dealer David Randall later recounted that Kennerley "gently explained to me that the day of the sale was G. W.'s sixty-eighth birthday and that 'some of us conspired to help him celebrate it appropriately.' "[45] Randall enjoyed telling a good story; Wells could not have been driven to $68,000 unless he was determined to buy at any price. Headlines were his only reward. He couldn't dispose of *Queen Mab*, and it was sold for $8,000 after his death in 1951. In the March issue of *The Bookman* Robert Benchley published "Do I Hear Twenty Thousand?" an Elysian conversation among Shelley, Swift, Tennyson, Pope, and Poe—in which Shelley smugly makes sure that the others know about the Kern sale: "I really don't understand it, though, for *Queen Mab* was never one of my favorites."[46]

The rest of the eighth session was anticlimactic. Dr. R went to $12,500 for Young on Laurence Sterne's *Tristram Shandy* (about $10,000 more than it brings in the eighties). The Robert Louis Stevenson boom had peaked, but the forty-two items brought $41,390. Beyer paid the top Stevenson price of $8,500 against Dr. R for the dedication copy of *A Child's Garden of Verses* with Stevenson's letter explaining why he dedicated the book to his nanny; the Doctor had bought it for Kern in the 1924 Arnold sale for $2,000. This session totaled $227,605.

The ninth session, on the evening of 23 January, was a disappoint-ment because the seventy Algernon Charles Swinburne items failed to arouse strong competition. Only two items reached four figures: Young paid $1,100 for an early notebook and $2,400 for the 114-page manuscript of *Chastelard*. Tennyson did much better. Dr. R paid $4,500 ($6,900 in the Arnold sale) for one of the six copies of the privately printed "trial edition" of *The Lover's Tale*, $9,500 for the sixteen-page

SHELLEY'S OWN COPY OF "QUEEN MAB"
WITH HIS MANUSCRIPT REVISIONS

1077 SHELLEY (PERCY BYSSHE). [Queen Mab; A Philosophical Poem: With Notes.]   [London: Printed by P. B. Shelley, 1813]

8vo, original boards, uncut (shaken, rebacked, and back worn). In a sage green levant morocco silk-lined box, with snap.

FIRST EDITION, AND WITHOUT DOUBT THE MOST VALUABLE AND DESIRABLE SHELLEY VOLUME WHICH HAS EVER OCCURRED FOR SALE BY AUCTION. IT IS SHELLEY'S OWN COPY, PROFUSELY FILLED WITH HIS MANUSCRIPT NOTES from Canto VIII to the end of the Poem, which he terms the "Second Part."

This is the copy Shelley used for an abridged and amended text of the poem, which he entitled "The Daemon of the World", and which he printed in 1816 in the volume "Alastor and other Poems". It lacks the title and dedication leaves and, of course, the lower portion of the leaf (pp. 239-240) containing the imprint, which Shelley himself cut from the copies he distributed among his friends.

This book was once the property of H. Buxton Forman who used it for completing "The Daemon" in his edition of Shelley's Poetical Works, and is fully described there. It contains many deletions and very many alterations and additions all in Shelley's hand.

Until 1905 it was believed that this copy was the only one in existence, containing such alterations and additions, but in that year another copy came to light which proved to be a transcript from this copy made for the printer to follow, the first copy—this copy—evidently, being kept by Shelley.

In the case enclosing this book are letters which passed between H. Buxton Forman and Dr. Thomas J. Wise who acquired the second copy. These letters tell the story of the discovery and the acquisition of the copy now in the Ashley Library.

It is evident that Shelley used this copy for his first attempt at forming the text of "The Daemon", and that when he came to prepare the printer's "copy" he made the copy now in the Ashley Library.

When Mr. Forman was afforded the opportunity to collate and compare the two volumes, he dealt with the respective differences in a communication to "The Athenaeum" of October 14, 1905. Dr. Wise, describing his copy in his "A Shelley Library" (1924), makes this note: "In the main the changes made in both agree, but to a certain extent each carries revisions peculiar to itself." It is interesting to learn, from the correspondence which passed between Dr. Wise and Mr. Buxton Forman, that after the former had acquired the second copy of Shelley's book, he offered the latter one thousand pounds for his copy, and another Shelley book. Mr. Forman declined the offer.

68,000.00

Catalogue description of
"Queen Mab"; The Library of
Jerome Kern Part Two
(21–24 January 1929)

FACSIMILE OF PAGE OF "QUEEN MAB"
[NUMBER 1077]

manuscript of "Maud," and $8,000 for the twenty-three-page manu-
script of "The Coming of Arthur"—all for Young. The seventy-seven
Thackeray items were split between the ninth and tenth sessions; none
reached five figures, and the top bid was Scheuer's $8,500 for 155
manuscript pages of the lectures on George I, George II, and George
IV. The total for the ninth session was $106,827.50.

The final session on the evening of 24 January was the dullest. The
boys were tired. Whitman's *Leaves of Grass* brought a record $3,400;
Kern had paid $268. (Within three weeks other copies sold for $3,450
and $3,300.) Neither Wilde nor Wordsworth generated bidding bat-
tles. Six stanzas of *The Ballad of Reading Gaol* fetched $1,600, and
the 123-page manuscript of *A Woman of No Importance* realized only
$550. The top Wordsworth item was an inscribed copy of *Ode to The
Memory of Charles Lamb*, which Dr. R took at $2,500. The total for
the final session was the lowest and the only one below six figures:
$77,997.50.

The five sessions of the second part totaled $993,375; and the grand
total for the Kern sale was $1,729,462.50. The biggest spender was
Rosenbach whose successful bids came to $410,000; his purchases for
Young amounted to $198,210, and Young subsequently bought about
$175,000 worth of the Kern books from Dr. R's stock. Beyer and
Scheuer, regarded as book speculators, spent $230,000 and $215,000
respectively. Including the *Queen Mab* purchase, Wells spent only
$185,000. At that point the trade could calculate how many records
had been broken. The total was $202,593.50 less than the $1,932,056
for the 1911–1912 Hoe sale. But the Hoe sale required seventy-eight
sessions for ten times as many books. The Hoe sessions averaged
$24,456.20 whereas the Kern sessions averaged $172,946.25. The most
impressive figure was that Kern's 1,484 items averaged $1,165.41 com-
pared to $125.58 for the 14,588 Hoe lots. This record stands.

After the sale Jerome Kern made a vindicating statement to the
press:

> I never thought much about money value when buying books. I set out
> to collect a library of distinguished volumes of association and senti-
> mental interest. For many of the volumes it was said that I had paid
> excessive prices, even ridiculously high prices. I was always willing to

pay for what I wanted. Now it is said that the prices paid for these same volumes at the auction were high, but in a few years I believe that it will not seem so. In some cases when I was carried away by personal enthusiasm, I paid more for volumes than they realized at the sale. This was the case with some of the Swinburne, Rossetti, Thackeray and even Shakespeare volumes. Even dealers said that I had paid excessively high prices for some of my books, and I can recall times when ripples of laughter went round the auction rooms at prices that I paid that seemed too high. At the time I bought my books I had no idea of selling them.[47]

Kern is reported to have invested the bulk of the proceeds in what were regarded as safe bank stocks, which depreciated after October 1929. The day after the close of the auction he went out and bought a book, starting a small collection which was auctioned in 1941.

During the Thirties there were complaints that the Kern prices had been absurdly inflated by speculation fever. It is true that some of the dealer purchases for stock proved to be albatrosses; nonetheless, the Kern collection was studded with supreme rarities. In 1930 the *New York Times* rare book columnist commented: "Really, the more one goes into it, the more one perceives the justice of the Kern prices. If it is unlikely that this generation will see them reached on such a considerable scale again, it is because such copies will not come upon the market again in quantity. If Mr. Kern's books were not unique, with their annotations or other association interest, they were at least in the rarest and most desirable form imaginable. . . . "[48]

One of the persistent legends about the sale is that Kern never received all of his money because the dealers who had bought on credit were unable to meet their obligations after the Wall Street Crash. Kennerley denied this charge: "There was not a single bad debt in the entire sale. It is true that one or two reckless collectors—chiefly, intoxicated Barton Currie and conservative Owen D. Young—bought heavily on credit from the big dealers—Rosenbach and Wells—and when the crash came in October owed large amounts for Kern *and Other* books and settled by returning some books—(probably and rightly at reduced prices for was not First National Bank stock which was selling at $10,000 a share during the Kern sale then selling at $700. a share?)."[49] That is, although some dealers got stuck, Kern and the Anderson were paid.

After the Kern sale the *New York Times* resuscitated an unpublished interview with Kennerley in which he discoursed on the psychological explanations for collecting:

(a) A development in a more or less specialized form of the possessory instinct. (b) The basis is intellectual: there is a deliberate selection of a particular field which offers continuous interest, stimulates study and suggests possibilities of completeness. In many cases the intellectual need seeks satisfaction solely in some special field of study; but even here material objects enter importantly, as records, illustrations, and so on; and the definite collecting of material objects of a certain class is a connected issue. The suggestion of possible completeness implied in collecting in a specified field is not without ethical significance. The conception of the unity of self-completeness of the universe may present itself with varying degrees of clearness and fullness to different minds, but it can never be altogether absent; and the collector's desire for approximate completeness in his special section of systematized effort is in its way a partial recognition of the larger principle of total completeness. (c) Based on more or less clearly acknowledged desire for the well-known "pleasures of pursuit." (d) Due to the imitative tendency. A prevalent habit, or the custom of a personal acquaintance, is followed more or less consciously. Modifications and developments ensue. (e) Force of suggestion. This suggestion may come from other individuals, from environment, from events. (f) The need for a "hobby." (g) Desire for tangible "trophies" of prowess in some field of effort. (h) Combinations of some of these motives.[50]

When Kennerley was in funds he was generous with loans. In January 1929 he lent Richard Ellis $2,500 to save the Georgian Press. A series of pleading letters from R. A. Lindsay, author of *One Man* (1915) who was unable to provide for his nine children, elicited $1,000 from Kennerley in 1929.

An entire floor of the Anderson was given over to a retrospective exhibition of seventy-eight Gari Melchers paintings while the Kern sale was in progress. Kennerley and Melchers were close friends, and Kennerley claimed to have underwritten the publication of Henriette Lewis-Hind's *Gari Melchers, Painter* (New York: Rudge, 1928). Kennerley paid Melchers $12,000 for the portrait of Theodore Roosevelt which was exhibited as on loan from Margery Durant Daniel.[51] Melchers painted Kennerley's portrait in 1929, but the sittings were termi-

Gari Melchers. Portrait of Mitchell Kennerley,
1929. Oil on canvas 46" by 26⅝".
*(Belmont, The Gari Melchers Memorial
Gallery, Mary Washington College,
Fredericksburg, Va.)*

nated by Kennerley's departure for England on 12 April: I AM AFRAID
EVERYTHING ENDED BY COMPLETE BREAKDOWN STOP I AM LEAVING
TONIGHT ALONE AND SHALL ALWAYS BE GRATEFUL FOR THOSE HAPPY
HOURS IN THE MIDST OF GREAT UNCERTAINTY.[52] This telegram refers
to Kennerley's divorce negotiations, but it also marks his severance
from the Anderson Galleries.

Kennerley's final major art sale at the Anderson was staged in May
1929 after he had left the country. Two old masters owned by Carl
W. Hamilton—Fra Lippo Lippi's *Madonna and Child* and Piero della
Francesca's *Crucifixion*—were sold in the first American auction ever
broadcast.[53] Before the sale Anderson announced appraisals of $800,000
for the *Crucifixion* and $650,000 for the *Madonna*; the auction was
expected to bring well over a million dollars. Chapman asked for an
opening bid of $150,000 on the 14-inch by 16-inch *Crucifixion*; but
there were no offers at this figure, and the bidding started at $100,000.
The painting went to Sir Joseph Duveen at $375,000, an American
record which broke the 1926 American Art record of $350,000 for
Gainsborough's *The Harvest Waggon* and was $2,000 short of the world
auction record for Lawrence's *Pinkie*. The 32⅝-inch by 24¾-inch *Madonna and Child* opened at $100,000 and fell to cigarette manufacturer
Leon Schinasi at $125,000 after tame bidding. The ten-minute sale
generated years of bitterness and litigation. Parke and Bernet claimed
that Kennerley had obtained the Hamilton paintings by commission-
cutting and asserted that the results demonstrated that he did not
know how to run an art auction. In 1935 Hamilton sued Duveen for
$2,000,000, charging that Duveen had disparaged the paintings at the
time of the Anderson auction and advised clients to stay away. Curiously, Hamilton had purchased both paintings from Duveen for $135,000.
The case dragged on until 1938, when the judge urged an out-of-court
settlement.[54]

The 1928–1929 season generated the largest combined volume of
business in American auction history. There were twenty book sales
and fifty-one art sales at the Anderson. The sixty-five sales at American
Art totaled $4,302,397, of which the seventeen book sales contributed
$566,640—one-third of the Kern take.

PART IV

EXILE—RESTORATION—DEPOSAL, 1930–1938

CHAPTER EIGHT

London Interlude—Restoration at the
American Art Association-Anderson
Galleries—the Bishop Sale—
Another Departure

AFTER KENNERLEY'S DEPARTURE at the end of the 1928–1929 season, the two houses were merged as the American Art Association–Anderson Galleries (AAA-AG) at the American Art headquarters on Madison Avenue. Kennerley retained the lease on the Park Avenue building. He let it be known that he planned to return to publishing. In the spring of 1929, while Kennerley was still at the Anderson, he published two books—Arnold Genthe's photographs of *Isadora Duncan* and a limited edition of Archibald Henderson's *Is Bernard Shaw a Dramatist?*

The private agreement that Kennerley would purchase the American Art and the Anderson from Bishop depended on his forthcoming marriage to Margery, and Bishop grumbled about Kennerley's delaying tactics. The impediment to the marriage was removed when Helen Kennerley obtained a Paris divorce in 1929, having secured his promise to set up their two sons as publishers. This venture was Helen's idea, for neither son was particularly interested in publishing at the time.

On 3 May 1929 Margery Durant Campbell Daniel unexpectedly married John Hampton Cooper in Newark, New Jersey. The *New*

York Daily Mirror headlined a 16 July story by Arthur James Pegler: "Kennerley Jilted by Rich Patron." This tardy article described him as a "world famous connoisseur" who had been replaced in Margery's affections by "a younger and handsomer man." Cooper was identified as a New York broker. William C. Durant told the press:

> It is perfectly true that my daughter was formerly engaged to Mitchell Kennerley. All I can say is the lady apparently exercised a feminine prerogative and changed her mind.
>
> Kennerley is an intimate friend of mine and a charming fellow. It is true he consulted me after my daughter reached her decision not to marry him. I was unable to be of aid in that matter. I regard Mitchell Kennerley with affection. We have just spent some time in England. It was an agreeable experience.[1]

As is sometimes the case with men who live close to the edge, Kennerley was subject to bouts of depression between coups. Around 1929 he insisted to Christopher Morley and Bainbridge Colby (Secretary of State under Woodrow Wilson) that he had a "self-destroying impulse." Morley and Colby sat with Kennerley in his Anderson office "and took turns drinking him down (it wasn't easy) until he collapsed."[2] On a happier occasion he telephoned Morley to reread Shelley's "Ode to the West Wind"; the poem torn from a book was on his mantelpiece the next day. "I read it eleven times," Kennerley said.[3]

For about a year in 1929 and 1930 Kennerley lived in suites at the London Savoy and at the Cavendish where he formed a friendship with the proprietor Rosa Lewis, "the Duchess of Duke Street." Jo Davidson was also at the Savoy, executing busts of English authors on a commission Kennerley had arranged with George H. Doran. Kennerley was ostensibly organizing his sons' London publishing company. The letterhead was "Mitchell Kennerley—Publisher," with the names of his two sons and Dan Rider; but he did little more than recommend titles and buy books to give the Essex Street office a literary atmosphere. Twelve volumes were published in London under the Morley & Mitchell Kennerley, Jr., imprint—including two books by Rex Stout. One 1929 volume, *The Etchings and Lithographs of Arthur B. Davies*, appeared with a joint imprint—New York: Mitchell Kennerley; London: Morley & Mitchell Kennerley, Jr. In addition, Kennerley published two volumes under his solo imprint: *Moby-Dick* with Rosenbach's introduction (1929) and Bainbridge Colby's *The Close of Woodrow Wilson's Administration and the Final Years* (1930). When the London firm terminated in 1932 Mitchell, Jr., returned to America and later operated a New York bookshop. Morley remained in England, where he became a prominent figure in British publishing at Faber & Faber.

Despite their acrimonious break in 1914 Kennerley maintained his belief in D. H. Lawrence's stature. At the time of the suppression of *Lady Chatterley's Lover* in 1928, Kennerley printed Lawrence's *Sex Locked Out* as a Christmas keepsake. This article had appeared in the *London Dispatch* and was probably appropriated by Kennerley without Lawrence's knowledge. In July 1929 the Mandrake Press published *The Paintings of D. H. Lawrence* in London. When an exhibition of the paintings was closed by the London police, the publisher—Edward Goldston, from whom Kennerley had acquired the Gutenberg Bible—feared that the book would be confiscated and destroyed. Kennerley bought 150 of the 511-copy edition at five guineas each—half the published price—and put them in storage. A copy Kennerley later had mailed to him in America was held in customs. He threatened to fight the case, but the book was released without a trial in 1933.[4]

By the spring of 1930 Kennerley was back in New York at an apartment in the Sherry-Netherland Hotel and scrambling for money. The $417,000 he had received in 1927 from the sale of the Anderson Galleries was gone, and he owed Bishop $100,000. Where Kennerley's money went remains a mystery. There is no indication that he played the stock market. His friends concluded that he spent it on women. (As one long-time associate put it, "The fuckin' hoors got it all.") Kennerley's principal asset was the lease on the Anderson building; but his plans to convert it into a movie palace never materialized, and the rent was a drain on whatever resources he had.

There was renewed possibility of a union with Margery. Her father—the King of the Bulls—had been wiped out in the Crash, but she was still wealthy in her own right. On 26 March 1930 the *Mirror* again headlined the fractured romance: "Durant Heiress, Thrice Freed, Will Wed Mitchell Kennerley." Margery had divorced Cooper, now identified as a "playboy and ginger-ale salesman." The article disclosed that "it was reported that the former Mrs. Cooper will lose no time in accompanying Mitchell Kennerley, wealthy art connoisseur, to the altar."[5] Instead, in 1933 she married Lt. Commander Fitzhugh Green, a polar explorer who had been Lindbergh's collaborator for We. In 1947 the Greens were found guilty of receiving narcotics.

During 1930–1931 Kennerley juggled loans. He mortgaged the furnishings of his apartment and was dunned by the Sherry-Netherland for back rent. An obvious way for him to raise money was to sell the literary material he had accumulated. Although he had never been a major collector, many excellent things had come his way. He had anonymously auctioned his own material in the Anderson sales over the years, but valuable items remained. In April 1930 the merged AAA-AG auctioned an important group of George Bernard Shaw letters with other material as "The Property of a Private Consignor."[6] Most— if not all—of the 232 lots were Kennerley's. Many had obvious associations with him, such as the Millay and Newton items. The 162 Shaw lots consisted mainly of letters to Frank Harris, Frederick H. Evans, and Arnold Dolmetsch. The catalogue explained, not very helpfully, that the letters to Dolmetsch and Evans had been obtained from the recipients, and that the letters to Harris were "acquired from the bookseller to whom they were sold by Mr. Harris." Kennerley may have purchased all of the Shaw letters for resale. The top price of $2,200 was paid for an inscribed copy of Mrs. Warren's Profession with ten Shaw letters and his photographs of the original cast. The first issue of An Unsocial Socialist—one of three known copies—made $1,550. Kennerley's 1921 private edition of The Great Fight fetched $70; but Shaw's postcard reaction to this unauthorized publication was worth only $62.50: "Do you mean to say that M.K. pirated my Carpentier-Beckett article? It is like his cheek; but he did not go so far as to thrust his crime on my notice."[7] The ninety-five-page manuscript of Arnold Bennett's Anna of the Five Towns brought $1,300, and there was a run of books inscribed by Bennett. A Keats letter including stanzas of "To Sorrow" reached $1,900; it had sold at the Anderson in 1927 for $6,600. Puzzlingly, two books from the Kern sale were included. Richard Crashaw's Steps to the Temple which had been sold to a Mrs. Jones for $650 now brought $370; and Spenser's

Colin Clouts Come Home Again which Wells had bought for $2,300 was reacquired by him for $1,700. Millay's corrected page proofs for *Second April* went for $90. The sale totaled $34,353.50, of which the Shaw material contributed $24,066.50. The November 1930 auction of Christopher Morley properties at the Union Square Book Shop included 86 "Additions From the Library of a Friend," which appear to have been Kennerley's.

Kennerley's plans to resuscitate his publishing house never materialized. Only the Colby book appeared with his imprint in 1930 and none thereafter until 1937. The likeliest way for him to mount a comeback would have been in the auction field, where his contacts were excellent. But this road was closed to Kennerley because he had signed a document prohibiting his return to auctioneering. Bishop and the people at the AAA-AG were taking no chances. Nonetheless, in 1930 Kennerley was trying to enter the art business. In June he wrote Stieglitz from 489 Park Avenue requesting postponement of a payment due on notes to Georgia O'Keeffe for paintings he had acquired from her: "I am forming a new corporation—The Art World Galleries—to take over the lease here. Two men, not personally affected by the market, have promised to buy stock but they are busy and it will take time. Meanwhile this building has cost me $47,000. to carry, (including taxes), since October 1st."[8] Nothing further is known about The Art World Galleries. Presumably it was intended to be an exhibition gallery—not an auction house—in order to conform to Kennerley's agreement with Bishop.

After the 1930 AAA-AG auction of his material, Kennerley proceeded to dispose of his own Kennerley collection. In September he wrote to Fanny Borden, the Vassar College librarian:

> As you probably know, I was actively engaged in publishing from 1904 to 1917. During these years, I published the first books of Edna Millay, Joseph Hergesheimer, Nicholas Vachel Lindsay, John Neihardt, Walter Lippmann, and the early books of John Masefield, Edgar Saltus, D. H. Lawrence, Lord Dunsany, and innumerable other authors, now more or less well known. I never published a book that, at the time, I did not think a good book, nor did I ever publish a book at the author's expense.
>
> I suppose I published about 400 books, and I have copies of nearly

all of them. They represent an epoch in American publishing which will some day be written about. I have autograph letters from many of these authors, and a number of relating documents.

I should like to present this collection to Vassar College, with the understanding that they would be kept together as a unit rather than distributed under the authors' names. I do not want any fuss made about them, or any acknowledgment of the gift, but I do want to feel that they will be held together though they may be catalogued individ' ually under the names of the authors. Perhaps they do not deserve this apparent importance, but I have had several applications for a complete catalogue of the books I have published for use by students of publishing. For some time I have had the books packed in boxes, and could ship them at once, if the suggestion is an agreeable one. You could take your own time—as many years as you liked—before placing the books on your shelves.[9]

The generous gift constituted a research archive. In addition to copies of the books, there were contracts, readers' reports, correspondence with authors, and books inscribed to Kennerley. He later donated the Davidson busts of Emilie Grigsby, Diana Norman, Morley Kennerley, and himself. For the next decade he sent Vassar copies of books he had published as he picked them up in used-book shops.

Kennerley's reasons for choosing Vassar as the repository for his archive are not clear; but he was probably attracted by Vassar's col' lection of books and type designed by Frederic W. Goudy, to which he also presented his own Goudy collection. Morley Kennerley was given to understand that his father selected Vassar because Margery Durant's daughter went there. When Kennerley's gift became known, the wisecrack circulated that he had selected Vassar as the recipient of his bounty in order to set up a farm team for mistresses. His claim to Miss Borden that he wanted no "fuss" over his benefaction was sincere, for he did not attempt to publicize it. After he began shipping the material he self-deprecatingly declined a formal announcement: "I wanted to send these books to Vassar . . . because I believe they will give more pleasure and joy there than anywhere else in the world; and I do not want that freedom to enjoy to be hampered by any pre-thought of the source from which they came."[10] Nonetheless, ego was a mo' tivating factor. As his letter indicates, Kennerley was aware that his imprint represented "an epoch in American publishing that will some day be written about," and he wanted to preserve the evidence—as much of it as would bear scrutiny—for researchers. At this point of decline, the fifty-two-year-old Kennerley was no doubt occupied with thoughts of posterity. Broke and unemployed, he didn't know where his next career was coming from. He did not stake his reputation on Vassar, for he subsequently gave and sold a large collection of his correspondence to the New York Public Library and donated a small group of his books to the Clements Library at the University of Michigan. Along with books he sent scores of notes to Borden and to Randolph G. Adams, director of the Clements, commenting on the volumes or their authors. Although he was in an eclipse, Kennerley's name still had publicity value. When he read an advance copy of Pearl Buck's *The Good Earth* in 1931, he wrote a letter to the publisher declaring it to be "a work of genius. . . . It is a beautiful, poignant and tragic book. It is perfectly written. The words come as naturally as rain falls to the ground." The John Day Company printed a facsimile of his letter as a full-page ad in *Publishers' Weekly* with the headline: "A LETTER with 'the good smack of truth'—from a man who knows a good book, but rarely endorses one".[11]

When he had been operating the Anderson, Kennerley had done business with The Printing House of William Edwin Rudge, which enjoyed a high reputation for the meticulous press work at its Mt. Vernon, New York, plant. After Rudge died, Kennerley was appointed managing director in October 1931 at a salary of between eight and ten thousand dollars. In addition to contract printing, Rudge published its own expensive editions—such as *The Private Papers of James Boswell* in twenty-one volumes. With the Depression there was a reduction in the demand for fine printing, and the stock of expensive books did not move. The firm was losing money; Kennerley cut costs by canceling the time-consuming hand-labor procedures on which Rudge's reputation had been built. His policies created a morale problem; when Rudge's two sons complained, Kennerley fired them. After less than a year Kennerley was dismissed. On the day he was fired, the janitor found Kennerley tearing books in the Rudge library and drove him out of the room with a poker.[12]

After Kennerley left Rudge he did not have a steady job until 1937.

In June 1936 Christopher Morley announced in his *Saturday Review of Literature* column that Kennerley, "who knows the creative arts of printing and publishing as well as any man living," had joined the Davidson Printing Corporation on Forty-fifth Street.[13] It must have been a very brief tenure, for Kennerley never mentioned it. During this period he rented a series of offices in midtown Manhattan from which he brokered book collections, but his activities were not remunerative. He was dropped from the Grolier Club for nonpayment of dues in 1932. Morley Kennerley, who had married the daughter of Lady Marion and General Sir Hugh Simpson-Baikie in England, brought his bride Jean to New York in December 1932. When Kennerley delayed repaying a loan from his son, she collected it. Christopher Morley told Jean that she was the only woman in the world who terrified Kennerley.

Given his contacts and knowledge of books it was automatic for Kennerley to consider entering the rare-book trade. In 1933 he reported to Huebsch: " . . . I have detailed plans for a great International Bookshop in N.Y. Unfortunately the one man who would—and could—back it is in Europe for an indefinite stay on account of his wife's health. I believe it would pay from the beginning. I would not start without 100,000 cash capital."[14] Surprisingly, Kennerley never operated an antiquarian book shop, although he privately dealt in rare books. In 1932, for example, he tried to sell the Huntington Library "the only known copy of the first separate edition" of Clement Clarke Moore's *Visit from St. Nicholas* (New York: Onderdonk, 1848) for $250;* his offer was declined with the explanation that the Library would not be able to spend $250 on a single item for some years to come.[15] Henry E. Huntington was indeed dead. In 1933 Kennerley offered Huebsch, who had joined the Viking Press, 120 copies of *The Paintings of D. H. Lawrence* for $1,377.71—half his 1929 cost—from his London hoard. "I know this is a ridiculously low price, but these are ridiculous times and I am in great need of money."[16] Only 100

---

* Kennerley's claim for the priority of this publication is questionable. Broadsides of the poem were printed c. 1830 and c. 1842. His sixteen-page booklet would have represented the first separately bound edition.

copies were delivered, but the matter was settled amicably because Huebsch later made personal loans to Kennerley.

One of Kennerley's attempts to raise money involved an autobiography. In August 1933 he offered the project to Little, Brown for a $600 advance on signing with $600 on delivery and $600 on publication—saying that he "could finish it in two months."[17] The working title was "Now Is the Time: Forty Years of People and Books." He accepted the counteroffer of $600 on signing plus $600 more. The contract stipulated 1 March 1934 delivery. The letters from Little, Brown in March, April, and May 1934 requesting a delivery date were not answered; there is no surviving draft of the book, although he later told friends that he had deposited the manuscript at the New York Public Library.

Money, which had once been abundant, became scarce. Tycoons had sought Kennerley's guidance when they were all successful together; but failure is lonely. Doors that once welcomed Kennerley were now closed. His friendship with Dr. Rosenbach had terminated. A story made the rounds that Kennerley had taken a girl away from the Doctor's domineering brother and that Philip Rosenbach had decreed an end to the friendship. Another explanation is that Dr. Rosenbach—never a generous man—didn't need Kennerley now.

During this period he continued to send material and frequent friendly letters to Fanny Borden. In 1934 he asked her for a loan:

> I am writing this letter in a rather desperate mood, which I am sure you will understand and forgive.
>
> When I sold the Anderson Galleries I invested all my money in real estate, and thought I had a comfortable income for life. I was so sure of never having to go back to work that I agreed, in writing, never again to enter the auction business. Then the crash came, and I put all my surplus funds into paying taxes and interest on mortgages, until two years ago I had no money left, and my buildings were taken over by banks. Since then I have made many attempts to get back into business, but it has been impossible. I have had a perfectly splendid publishing idea, but none of my friends have been able - or willing - to supply the necessary capital. For several weeks there has been a decided upswing in the attitude of my friends and I am promised support in November. Meanwhile I am in urgent need of the money to keep going, and I am

writing to ask if you have any fund out of which you could advance me one thousand dollars. I would at once send you valuable books and autograph letters to cover this amount, and would eventually pay back the thousand dollars. These books etc I have always intended to send you, but have been keeping for company, until I had other interests to take their place.

If it would be possible for you to arrange this it would be a kindness I could never repay.[18]

Miss Borden, who was by no means well off, lent him a $1,000 Treasury Bond which he used as collateral for a loan. Kennerley sent her a list of his books and manuscripts to be held by her as security. There is no indication that the loan was repaid.

In 1934 the rare-book world was stunned by the revelation that the eminent bibliographer T. J. Wise had fabricated many rare nineteenth-century literary pamphlets. At this time 500 copies of a small book consisting of the introductions written by distinguished bookmen for the ten-volume catalogue of Wise's Ashley Library were published. Although the imprint read William H. Smith, Jr., at 9 E. 57th Street, Kennerley was the publisher. The address was that of an office Kennerley shared for a while with Walter Grant, who had been in charge of art exhibits at the Anderson. It is not known why Kennerley concealed himself behind the name of Smith, his former employee at Anderson. The unsigned foreword, written by Kennerley, indirectly explained why the introductions had been reprinted: "They contain matter of interest about the Ashley Library and its owner, and about the practice of bibliography which will interest a larger audience than the few fortunate possessors of the complete—and cumbersome—Catalogue."[19]

During 1936 Kennerley planned a new magazine to be called "Listening Post" and claimed to have arranged backing—which fell through. Nothing is known about the editorial rationale, although he attempted to resuscitate the project during the next decade. In 1937 Kennerley attempted another publishing comeback. He planned "an anthology of non-copyright poems, one for each day of the year, to be called 'The Lyric Year' "[20] and a one-volume edition of Goudy's *The Alphabet* and *The Elements of Lettering*. These books did not appear, but he published one book in June. *Mr. Pirate*, a novel set in a bookshop, was written by A. B. Shiffrin. Kennerley provided a blurb that he credited to Sam Goldwyn: "People are reading it who never read it before." *Mr. Pirate* received some warm reviews; Percy Hutchingson erroneously predicted in the *New York Times* that it "will become as much a minor classic as 'Goodbye Mr. Chips.' "[21] Kennerley distributed review copies generously, but it is almost impossible to market one title to the trade. Even so, the first printing of 1,449 copies sold out, and there was another printing in August.

Shiffrin was the proprietor of the Academy Bookshop. Once, when he was in the chips, Kennerley had walked into Shiffrin's shop with a thousand-dollar bill and demanded a thousand-dollar book. Shiffrin has described Kennerley in his prime as princely and arrogant, with a flickering smile and a faint aroma of whiskey. In the Thirties Shiffrin bought the remainder stock of Kennerley's publications and acquired the Lotus Club library through him.[22]

The ferris wheel that Kennerley had been riding for thirty years took another turn. The death of Cortlandt F. Bishop in 1935 put the AAA-AG under the control of his widow and Edith Nixon, their longtime companion and Bishop's putative mistress. The ladies felt that they were not receiving an adequate return on their investment. Hiram Parke and Otto Bernet continued to operate the gallery under a barrage of instructions from Miss Nixon who rejected their offer to buy the AAA-AG. She also declined to sell a controlling interest to R. Milton Mitchill, the discharged president of the AAA-AG. (He committed suicide in 1939; the similarity of the names *Mitchill* and *Mitchell* has caused considerable confusion in the accounts of the galleries.) Miss Nixon had come under the influence of Shirley Falcke, an Englishman with aristocratic connections who had been formerly employed by Bishop to acquire consignments for American Art and became Bishop's principal enemy in a crowded field. On Falcke's advice, in the fall of 1937 Miss Nixon and Mrs. Bishop consulted Kennerley about reorganizing the AAA-AG, and his ideas impressed them favorably. When Parke and Bernet learned that Kennerley was back in the picture, they informed the ladies through counsel that "Mr. Kennerley at the present time owes the American Art Association-Anderson Galleries, Incorporated, a sum in the neighborhood of $70,000; that a suit was brought against him for the recovery of the amount of the indebtedness and that Mr. Kennerley is at the present time in default of that suit, having interposed no defense thereto. . . . "[23] This letter was ignored. On 12 November 1937 Mitchell Kennerley became president of the AAA-AG. That day Parke and Bernet walked out with forty key employees and set up the Parke-Bernet Galleries. Kennerley issued a statement to the press:

> For some time the estate of Cortlandt F. Bishop, the majority stock interest of the Association, has felt the conduct of the business was not satisfactory in many respects. At the annual meeting of the stockholders of the corporation held on November 12th some of the executors of the estate nominated as directors the executors and certain other persons, including Mr. Mitchell Kennerley, president and manager of the Anderson Galleries, Inc., both prior and subsequent to the acquisition of that corporation by the late Cortlandt F. Bishop. The minority stockholders nominated as directors the executors of the estate, and, among others, Mr. Parke and Mr. Bernet.
>
> The meeting elected the directors nominated by the executors of the Bishop estate, and did not reelect either Mr. Parke or Mr. Bernet as directors of the corporation.
>
> At the directors' meeting immediately following the annual meeting, Mr. Kennerley was elected president of the corporation and Mr. Milton B. Logan was elected secretary and treasurer. No vice-president was elected.
>
> The staff of the Galleries is now complete and includes A. N. Bade and E. Harold Thompson as auctioneers and W. H. Smith, Jr., and F. Bianco in charge of the Book Department.[24]

Kennerley claimed that he offered to retain Parke as chairman of the board but had no place for Bernet or Arthur Swann.

At fifty-nine Kennerley was back on the throne after eight years of exile. Charles Heartman responded to Kennerley's restoration with a panegyric:

> Mitchell Kennerley, with for example, the Quinn sales catalogue to his credit, has also of course the magnificent Kern sale on his slate, an example of supreme showmanship, never before attained in the auction history of the world. While hailed at the time as the great achievement,

when the debacle came, this sale was blamed for all the ensuing troubles. It was during this period that I raised my voice—it was a lonely one— and proclaimed that the time would come when Kern prices would look like bargains. What Mr. Kennerley can, and will do, for the Book collecting Game, is of course a futile speculation. It will all depend on the large or small collections which come into the market. How they are handled, and what new buyers he will add to the list. An almost virgin field can be tapped. Perhaps we can leave it to Mr. Kennerley to spring some surprise.[25]

Kennerley's immediate priorities on taking over at 30 East Fifty-seventh Street were to assemble a staff and to salvage the 1937–1938 sales scheduled by the old regime. He put together a crew of sixty-nine, many of whom were former Anderson hands. Kennerley reported that Parke and Bernet "persuaded all the current consignors to send me notice of cancellation . . . but I was able to have all these cancellations cancelled and have not lost a single consign-ment. . . . I have brought with me my old following of private buyers, so that the business is no longer controlled by a combina-tion of insolvent dealers."[26] This last assertion can be challenged. His success at Anderson had largely depended on his close coopera-tion with book dealers.

Since between two and four months were required to produce a catalogue, it is impossible to identify the first 1937 AAA-AG sale that was entirely Kennerley's responsibility. But the first catalogue to bear the imprimatur MITCHELL KENNERLEY, PRESIDENT was the December sale of "The Renowned Collection of Dr. William C. Braislin,"[27] whose earlier collections had been sold at the Anderson in 1923 and 1927. This catalogue offered the best group of American literature to go on the block since the 1924 Wakeman sale. Braislin's 618 lots included rarities by William Cullen Bryant, Mark Twain, James Fen-imore Cooper, Bret Harte, Nathaniel Hawthorne, Washington Irving, Herman Melville, James Kirke Paulding, and William Gilmore Simms— as well as Hardy and Stevenson. Cooper's first novel, *Precaution*, brought $1,150; and his rarest novel, *The Spy*, made the top price of $1,350. The forty-three Irving items, "Believed to Be the Most Im-portant Ever Offered for Public Sale at One Time," featured *The Sketch Book of Geoffrey Crayon* in seven parts at $1,300. The first American edition of Melville's *Typee* in the original paper covers brought $450, but the London edition—which preceded it—fetched only $6.* Two of the great rarities of early American fiction went cheap: Susanna Rowson's *Charlotte* (1794) for $600 and Jeremy Belknap's *The Foresters* (1792) in the original paper wrappers for $200. The total of $22,998.50— an average price of $37.21—was a clear signal that Kennerley would not be able to reduplicate the bibliophilic ebullience of the twenties.

Other important book sales in the first months of the season were Joseph B. Shea's Americana with hundreds of Indian captivity narratives (674 lots, $30,105.50) and Literature (474 lots, $15,707).[28] The January 1938 sale of Alfred Meyer's autographs was regarded as an encouraging portent when 288 lots brought $26,841.[29] The star item was the Thirteenth Amendment to the constitution signed by Lincoln, the vice-president, the speaker, and most of the congressmen who voted for it. It made $3,300; but the copy sold at the Anderson in 1927 had brought $12,000. The next highest Meyer price was $3,000 for a three-page Washington letter written to his brother after the fall of Fort Mercer. The collections of Crosby Gaige and Franklin Joiner with additions brought only $11,007 for 393 lots[30]—with 140 Joseph Conrad letters to Richard Curle reaching the dismal price of $480. Kennerley unsuccessfully tried to secure the A. Edward Newton collection for auction.

Kennerley's main challenge was to mount an epic sale for Cortlandt Bishop's own library, for it is likely that his appointment to the presidency of the AAA-AG was largely the result of his having convinced Bishop's ladies that he could make the sale another Kern extravaganza. The material was present. Bishop had spent lavishly for forty years on illuminated manuscripts, books of hours, specimens of early printing, Bibles, and historical bindings. Moreover, he had supported the market during his seigneurship at the galleries, especially in the 1932 AAA-AG Marquess of Lothian sale. Even so, the abundance of Bishop treasures came as a surprise because most of his purchases had been

---

* Collectors were still under the influence of the "follow-the-flag" rule, which deemed that the first edition published in the author's native country was more desirable than an earlier edition published in another country.

made anonymously or secretly. The richest collection of its kind to go to the auction block since the Hoe sale, it lacked the breadth of Hoe's library; but the best items were in the stratosphere of rarity. Another rich Bishop library was stored in France for a future sale.

Because the two ladies insisted on an early AAA-AG sale, it was impossible to have the entire Bishop collection catalogued. The first two parts consisting of 1,840 items covering A–Q were auctioned in April 1938.[31] Kennerley described his strategy:

> . . . When I announced the sale of the Cortlandt F. Bishop Library, Part One, I was told that it would be a failure. I heard on all sides that there was reliable information—I should say misinformation—that the Estate would buy in all the leading lots. However, I went about my business of keeping my contract with the Estate to sell this Library, this year, and I sold it the way I thought it should be sold: in alphabetical order instead of picking out three-hundred "nuggets"—and I set out to advertise the value of the books and manuscripts in this great library. I succeeded to the point where it is my belief that not one percent of the books bought by the trade were bought for stock. On the other hand, our entire staff devoted themselves to the careful consideration of the visitors to the exhibition who were prospective purchasers through our valued friends, the booksellers, and we made them feel all the more at home because we would not, under any circumstances, have accepted bids from them. The only private bid we accepted was from the client of a bookseller who declined to take this particular bid because he knew that another of his best customers was bidding on this particular book through another bookseller.[32]

Dealer Edgar H. Wells commented on this letter: "God damn his soul for making us think that there is some good in him!"[33]

Part I, A–H, was sold in six sessions on 5–8 April. Kennerley's foreword to the first catalogue was a restrained discussion of the cataloguing process, acknowledging the contributions of the compilers. The lavish Bishop catalogues were what the trade had come to expect for a Kennerley sale: 610 well-printed pages with full descriptions and many facsimiles. Anthony Bade, the crier of the Kern sale, was in the rostrum. Again, Kennerley took out insurance on Dr. Rosenbach and Gabriel Wells.

The first session opened tamely with a surprising frequency of $2.50

raises. No item broke $1,000 until #109, *The Annals of Sporting and Fancy Gazette* (1822–1828), brought $3,500 for seventy-eight parts in original wrappers. The successful bidder was Maggs of London, and the presence of English dealers was regarded as a favorable sign. The five-figure mark was reached at #155, an illuminated manuscript for Saint Augustine's *De civitate Dei* (c. 1410), which Sessler took at $20,250. Bishop had paid $31,500 for it at the 1932 Lothian sale; however, the Lothian prices were regarded as flukes.* The first session (A'Beckett-Balzac) brought $46,745 for 183 items, but it included few of Bishop's treasures.

In the second session (Bandello-British) Dr. R took the Latin Bible printed by Fust & Schoeffer in 1462 for $12,000, a low figure for the first dated Bible and the first printed work divided into two volumes. It had brought $19,000 in the Lothian sale. Dr. R was bidding for Sears, Roebuck heir Lessing Rosenwald, who acquired some of the best Bishop books and manuscripts. The first English book to break $5,000 was a copy of *Songs of Innocence and of Experience* (1789–94), colored by Blake, which went to Sessler for $5,400.

The item that was regarded as the indicator for the rest of the sale was #285, "THE FAMOUS BLICKLING HOMILIES OF THE TENTH CENTURY A SUPREME ANGLO-SAXON MANUSCRIPT THE EARLIEST AND GREATEST

---

* The account of the Lothian sale in Edwin Wolf II and John Fleming's *Rosenbach* is:

> The story leaked out that in effect the sale had been rigged. Kennerley had made an arrangement with Beyer to protect the great pieces. Quite contrary to the ethics of auctions Beyer was given the opportunity of buying and making payment only after he had sold what he had bought. When Cortlandt Field Bishop, a collector himself, and the owner of the American Art-Anderson Galleries, discovered the arrangement a few years later, he dismissed Kennerley, who, financial and personal difficulties compounded, committed suicide. The Doctor never forgave Kennerley for his Lothian chicanery.[34]

This report requires correction. Kennerley had left the Anderson Galleries in 1929 and had no connection with the AAA-AG in 1932. (Milton Mitchill was at the AAA-AG during the Lothian sale.) Bankrolling Beyer at the Lothian sale was Bishop's own scheme. Although the friendship between Kennerley and Dr. R terminated, the Lothian sale was not the cause of their falling out.

ENGLISH LITERARY MONUMENT AVAILABLE EMBODYING THE ELEMENTS OF THE FUTURE GREATNESS OF ENGLISH POETIC PROSE." The 149 vellum leaves were the greatest Anglo-Saxon manuscript in private hands; no American library held a single leaf in Anglo-Saxon. It had been owned by the city of Lincoln for some 400 years, and the mayors and sheriffs had used the margins to record their elections until 1609. Dr. R took the *Blickling Homilies* at $38,000 for Pennsylvania oilman John Scheide. Bishop had paid $55,000 at the Lothian sale, but $38,000 was a strong price in 1938.* Maggs went to $8,750 for Boccaccio's *Le livre de Jehan bocasse de la lovenge et vertu des nobles et cleres dames* (1493) in the copy bound for Diane de Poitiers, "beautiful and accomplished mistress of King Henry II of France." The 173 items in the second session totaled $92,345.

The third session (Broadsides-Daniel) was the weakest in Part I, with 181 items totaling $30,332.50. The top bid was Dr. R's $3,400 for the Kilmarnock Burns that had made $2,100 in the 1918 Herschel V. Jones sale.

The fourth session opened with THE HOLFORD COPY OF THE FIRST ILLUSTRATED EDITION OF "THE DIVINE COMEDY" WITH THE FULL SERIES OF NINETEEN PLATES ATTRIBUTED TO SANDRO BOTTICELLI. Dr. R took it for Rosenwald at what was regarded as the bargain price of $13,500. The surprise of this session was the group of nine of Dickens's annotated reading copies, which totaled $29,875. Seven of these were acquired by Chicago dealer Walter M. Hill, who went to $7,700 for *The Chimes [and] Sikes and Nancy*. Bishop's books were not strong in English literature; except for Blake and Dickens, the books in this field generated little competition. The three volumes of *Robinson Crusoe* went for $775; Kern's set had brought $11,500. The fourth session added $64,305 for 182 lots.

The star of the fifth session (Entrien-Gombauld) was the fourteenth-century illuminated manuscript of Froissart's *Chronicles* on 363 vellum leaves, which Dr. R took at $14,000 for the Morgan Library; it had sold for $12,900 in 1922. The session's 180 books totaled $33,742.50.

---

* In 1985 two leaves of a seventh-century manuscript in Latin—the earliest extant MS written in Britain—made $105,600 at Sotheby's.

THE FAMOUS BLICKLING HOMILIES
OF THE TENTH CENTURY
A SUPREME ANGLO-SAXON MANUSCRIPT
THE EARLIEST AND GREATEST ENGLISH LITERARY
MONUMENT AVAILABLE EMBODYING THE ELEMENTS
OF THE FUTURE GREATNESS OF ENGLISH POETIC PROSE

285 BLICKLING HOMILIES, THE. NINETEEN HOMILIES IN ANGLO-SAXON, for various Sundays and Festivals, and on a few special subjects, including "The Annunciation", "The Assumption of the Virgin Mary", "The Birth of St. John the Baptist", and "The Lives of the Saints". *Manuscript on vellum, 149 leaves (8⅛ by 6 inches), apparently written by two scribes, one using a smaller and more angular hand. Prefixed are a Calendar (folia 1-6), in a fifteenth century hand, and five leaves (folia 7-11) of a fourteenth century breviary.* X Century

Folio, finely bound by CHARLES LEWIS in fawn morocco with a clasp. (Some leaves cropped or repaired in the corners and margins and some misplaced in binding.) TENTH CENTURY OR EARLIER, THE DATE 971 APPEARING ON PAGE 141.

THIS WONDERFUL MANUSCRIPT, THE BLICKLING HOMILIES, IS ONE OF THE MOST IMPORTANT EXAMPLES OF EARLY ANGLO-SAXON LITERATURE, representing the very foundation of English prose. The Homilies are apparently by different authors; one is dated with the year of delivery, 971. A number of the others seem to antedate it considerably. BLICKLING IS IN NORFOLK AND THESE HOMILIES CONSTITUTE THE FIRST ANGLO-SAXON PROSE THAT CAN BE DIRECTLY CONNECTED WITH EAST ANGLIA.

EVER SINCE THEY HAVE BEEN KNOWN, THE BLICKLING HOMILIES HAVE RECEIVED A PLACE OF HONOR IN EVERY HISTORY OF ENGLISH LITERATURE. No other Anglo-Saxon manuscript of any importance exists in private hands: No AMERICAN PUBLIC OR PRIVATE LIBRARY OWNS ONE SINGLE LEAF IN ANGLO-SAXON.

FURTHERMORE, THE PALEOGRAPHICAL VALUE OF THIS GREAT MANUSCRIPT IS AS IMPORTANT AS ITS LITERARY AND LINGUISTIC INTEREST. Specimens of English writing before the year 1000 are hardly to be found outside of the great English national repositories, and the year 971 is clearly to be read in the Eleventh Homily, "ON THE HALGAN THUNRES DEI" (ON HOLY THURSDAY), of this remarkable manuscript.

FOR SEVERAL HUNDRED YEARS, THIS HISTORIC TREASURE BELONGED TO THE CITY OF LINCOLN. From the thirteenth century to the year 1609 the margins of the manuscript were used by various mayors and sheriffs of Lincoln in lieu of the Bible to record their nomination or election. These historical records of the great English city, although of considerable local importance, escaped the attention of all British historians and have remained unnoticed and unpublished to this day.

THE STYLE OF THIS CORNERSTONE OF OUR LANGUAGE AND LITERATURE IS PERMEATED WITH THE SENTIMENT AND IMAGERY OF THE BIBLE. The First Homily on "The Annunciation" begins: "[Jesus came into the world in order that His divine] nature might be manifested, and that sin might be eradicated; and the doom of Eve's infelicity, which was denounced against her (that she should bring forth her children in pain and in sorrow) was reversed when Mary brought forth the Lord with rejoicing . . ." Further on Gabriel extols the Virgin and glorifies her in these words: "The redness of the rose glitters in thee, and the whiteness of the lily shines in thee"—imagery reminiscent of the grand style of Holy Scriptures.

IN ANOTHER HOMILY, HEAVEN IS PICTURED AS A PLACE WHERE THERE "IS YOUTH WITHOUT AGE; NOR IS THERE HUNGER NOR THIRST, NOR WIND NOR STORM NOR RUSH OF WATERS". The palm branch in the hand of the angel who announces to the Virgin her approaching death "is bright as the morning star" and the Lord appears to Andrew with a face "like that of a fair child". THROUGHOUT THE HOMILIES THERE ARE OTHER NUMEROUS COLORFUL AND POETICAL PASSAGES that illumine the early Christian spirit of the age.

IT IS BELIEVED THAT THESE HOMILIES WERE WRITTEN FOR THE QUEEN OF ENGLAND to be used by her as a Book of Meditations. That being the case, a beautiful religious and literary masterpiece was created which not only helped to crystallize the language of the period, but left to the English speaking world an immortal heritage emulating in beauty the King James Version of the Bible.

[DESCRIPTION CONTINUED ON PAGE 82]

80

Catalogue description of the Blickling Homilies;
The Cortlandt F. Bishop Library Part One (5–8 April 1938)

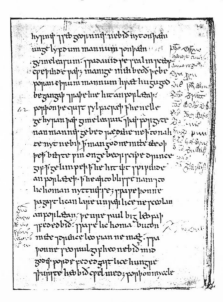

The closing session of Part I (Goncourt-Huysmans) included the top American literature item: Hawthorne's first book, *Fanshawe* (1828), at $1,900. The best items in this session were printed Books of Hours from the fifteenth and sixteenth centuries—seven of which were unique. Yet only one reached $5,000, the price Dr. R paid for *Horae, in laudem beatiss . . .* (1524–1525), the fourth known copy of the first issue of the earliest Book of Hours with illustrations and borders engraved by Geofroy Tory. The disappointing total for these fifty-two rarities was $34,985. The 193 items in the sixth session brought $58,462.50.

The total for the 1,091 items in Part I was $325,931.50—for a low average of $298.74. Rosenbach's tab was about $100,000. During the sale there was disagreement as to whether it was a triumph or a disaster. It was claimed that some of the best items would have reached five times their prices if they had been in the Kern sale. Quite possibly. But it was 1938, not 1929. Some of the old boys were dead; some had stopped collecting; and some were broke. The gauge of the 1938 sale was 1938 prices. By this measure the first part of the Bishop sale was a surprising success. The *New York Times Book Review* congratulated Kennerley for having restored confidence in the rare-book market:

> The book trade has lost something of its humility. There had been anxious days last month when the sober-minded were asking how it would be possible for the market to absorb the fabulous riches of the Cortlandt Field Bishop library. There was little cause for optimism then. The business outlook was not a happy one, industrial charts were curving downward perilously, and booksellers were finding collectors scarce and shy.
>
> All doubts were resolved three weeks ago in the six historic sessions when the books and manuscripts in the first part of the alphabet went under the hammer to the tune of $325,000. Whether the success of the occasion was due to the well-known managerial skill and showmanship of Mitchell Kennerley, to the widespread good-will the auction engendered, or to a general recognition of the inherent and enduring value of fine books, the sale did take on some of the aspect of a revival meeting. It served to revive the tenuous notion that good books would sell well anywhere. Competition from abroad, notably England and France, figured largely in the results, although the lion's share went to American dealers.
>
> It is undeniable that the sale gave a genuine impetus to book buying

and caused an increased respect for books as commodities. What is especially heartening is that the enthusiasm was not restricted but extended to all areas of the collecting field. Here was one auction where the rank and file gave an excellent account of themselves. Even the dubious group of modern French illustrated books, the Ashendenes and the Doves Press limited editions exceeded expectations. Of course there were some bargains along the way, as is inevitable in a sale of such length.[35]

A contradictory assessment of the Bishop sale is provided by Wesley Towner's *The Elegant Auctioneers*, which treats it as a catastrophe.[36] According to this undocumented account, Kennerley was frantic during the sale and his behavior was noticeably erratic. After the first session he berated Anthony Bade for incompetence and disloyalty. The next morning when Bade reported Rosenbach's enthusiasm, Kennerley was distraught and said he wanted to leave before the inevitable collapse of the AAA-AG. Again according to Towner, Kennerley disappeared for a week in April between the two Bishop sales. Towner also states that Bade closed the fourth session after the first item: the $13,500 Dante; but no such occurrence was reported in the press. Kennerley was no doubt disappointed at seeing many valuable books go cheaply; nevertheless, Towner's claim that he expected $300,000 per day seems absurd. Rosenbach and Wells were still stuck with some of their 1929 Kern purchases. Towner's account must be evaluated in light of the circumstance that Hiram Parke is a hero of *The Elegant Auctioneers*—and that Parke's foe Kennerley is perforce a villain. The real question is whether Bishop's books would have done better at Parke-Bernet in 1938. Not likely.

Between the two Bishop sales Kennerley and Karl Freund presented a radio talk on station WQXR. In his introductory statement Freund declared that the first sale "was a victory for idealism expressed in dollars and cents, a triumphant vindication of Mitchell Kennerley's dauntless belief in the book and art business. . . . the Cortlandt Bishop sale has acted like a tonic, an elixir of rejuvenation. It has even been suggested that the American Art Association-Anderson Galleries open a book department on the floor of the Stock Exchange to put life into a dull market—you have of course noticed that the market went up due to the brilliant Cortlandt Bishop sale." Kennerley responded with an anecdote:

> One of the most entertaining coincidences of my long life—I might as well admit it now because the story I am going to tell will betray it—occurred at this sale. I have always remembered an occasion in 1901 when I went to dinner in Boston with the late Herbert Copeland of the famous publishing house of Copeland & Day, and a young gentleman who was in his first or second year at Harvard. We dined at a Bohemian restaurant called Marliaves, frequented by Bliss Carman and Richard Hovey and Bertram Goodhue and the innumerable fledgling geniuses that lived in Boston at that time. I had in my pocket a copy of the little Mosher edition of Stevenson's "Virginibus Puerisque" which I gave to our young friend. That was thirty-seven years ago and I had never seen this young man again or heard from him until he came into my room at the conclusion of the Bishop sale and told me of the many books he had bought in it, including Blake's "Songs of Innocence", and he added, "I still have the copy of 'Virginibus Puerisque' you gave me."[37]

Part II of the Bishop Sale, I–Q, occupied four sessions on 25–27 April.[38] The opening session (Imbert-La Rochefoucauld) included sixty-eight volumes printed by William Morris's Kelmscott Press, which brought a strong total of $13,825. The top Kelmscott bid was Beyer's $6,100 for *The Works of Geoffrey Chaucer* (1896) on vellum. The star of this session was the illuminated manuscript of *Lancelot du Lac* on 382 vellum leaves dating from the thirteenth to fifteenth centuries. The gallery's presale estimate was $10,000 to $20,000, and Dr. R took it at $16,500 for the Morgan Library. The seventh session brought $53,010 for 184 items.

The eighth session (Las Cases-Marocchus) featured seven fifteenth- and sixteenth-century copies of *Le roman de la rose* by Guillaume de Lorris and Jean de Meun, a thirteenth-century French allegorical poem on courtly love. The total for these manuscripts and printed books was $17,310. The illuminated copy executed for King Francis I in the early sixteenth century and described as PROBABLY THE MOST PERFECTLY PRESERVED MANUSCRIPT OF "THE ROMANCE OF THE ROSE" IN EXISTENCE—which the gallery estimated would bring $6,000 to $10,000—went to dealer Richard Wormser for $9,500. He was bidding for Beatrice Berle, Bishop's disinherited daughter, who presented it to the Morgan in memory of her father. The richest items in this session were twenty-eight illuminated manuscript *horae* which totaled $61,455. Two broke five figures: Dr. R, acting for Rosenwald, acquired the 1524 Book of Hours "attributed to Geofroy Tory" for $18,000—topping the pre-sale estimate of $10,000 to $15,000; and Wells paid $14,250—well under the $25,000 to $35,000 estimate—for the Pembroke Book of Hours (c. 1440), which had reached $33,000 in the Hoe sale. The *horae* made the eighth session the most remunerative at $98,755 for 175 items.

The ninth and tenth sessions (Marryat-Nores; Norvin-Quinze) were dull, bringing $29,600 and $27,902. There were two four-figure Melville items: his annotated copy of the *Moby-Dick* source book, *Narrative of the Most Extraordinary Shipwreck of the Whale-Ship Essex*, brought $1,700,* and Melville's letter expounding *Moby-Dick* to Mrs. Hawthorne went for $1,500.

The total for the 749 items in Part II was $209,287.50—of which Dr. R contributed about $50,000—bringing the total for A–Q to $535,220.† Additional evidence correcting Towner's inflated claim for Kennerley's expectations is provided by a copy of the Part II catalogue marked with the gallery's presale estimates.[39] The high figure was $311,345, and the low figure was $197,335. Therefore the results topped the low estimate by about $12,000.

The $290.88 average for the 1,840 lots was modest compared to the levels of the twenties, and the collection almost certainly brought less than Bishop had paid for it. Nonetheless, half a million dollars was an impressive figure for a Depression sale. Although Rosenbach and Wells were the biggest buyers, the sales were not dominated by a few dealers. There were 108 buyers in Part I and ninety-four in Part II, indicating that Kennerley had attracted a cross-section of the trade. Moreover,

---

* In his radio talk with Freund, Kennerley mentioned that he had traced this book to Mrs. A. T. Osborne, Melville's granddaughter, and had learned that the manuscript of *Moby-Dick* was in existence. This manuscript has never been found.
† The remainder of Bishop's library was sold in November 1938 after Kennerley had left the AAA-AG; 578 items brought $81,377 (an average of $140.79). A fourth sale of leftovers in 1939 totaled $10,874.50 for 1,208 lots.

he estimated that only one percent of the books were bought for stock. Whatever his private feelings were, Kennerley claimed a victory:

> I believe that the reasons for the success of this sale were as follows: We got out a good catalogue containing original research work and we circulated it widely. I sent out about two hundred copies from my office to speculative prospects whose names I saw in the newspapers or re-membered because of something I chanced to think of or to hear of or to read.
>
> I believe that the radio talks of Mr. Freund and myself brought a lot of visitors. We put up a good show of the books and manuscripts, and instead of leaving visitors to the tender mercies of ignorant attendants, I had the men who had actually done the catalogue work showing the books and manuscripts they had worked on. In not a single instance did we solicit a bid. One lady spent several hours looking at the books for two days running and we did not know her name. A few days later she came in and said how pleased she was with the books she had bought through Rosenbach (amounting to at least $20,000). The dealers soon found out that we were not soliciting bids of their customers and that we were doing everything in our power to take care of their cus-tomers whether they came alone or accompanied by a bookseller.
>
> . . . .
>
> Finally, the sale was "unreserved", which was recognized after the conclusion of the second session when several high priced numbers were sold to announced buyers at prices less than Mr. Bishop paid in the "notorious" Lothian sale.[40]

During the Bishop sale Kennerley published what would prove to be the final volume to bear his imprint, Augusta Rathbone's aquatints of *French Riviera Villages* (with photographs by Juliet Thompson and text by Virginia Thompson). This expensively produced book sold for $10 and was limited to 1,000 copies.

There was another Bishop sale in May 1938 when his stamp col-lection was auctioned through Walter S. Scott at the AAA-AG for $19,547.[41] The final book sale of the 1937–1938 season on 6–9 June marked a Kennerley innovation.[42] Robert Dunning Dripps's collection of modern American, English, and Irish writers was described as the most extensive sold at auction since the John Quinn sale. Instead of grouping the less valuable books in lots, Kennerley catalogued the 3,070 items separately to attract new and less affluent bidders. The experiment was a failure; the total was $8,001, an average of $2.60. This catalogue was the last to bear Kennerley's name, and he took his farewell by printing Carman's "At the End of a Book" on the back cover. The final quatrain reads:

> Ah, trust the Vendor, wise and kind!
> He knows the outside and the in,
> And loves the very least of those
> He tosses in the dusty bin.

The season's record for an art sale was the $114,467 total in January 1938 for V. Everit Macy's 584 pieces of Near Eastern pottery, miniatures, brocades, and velvets;[43] the top price was $9,500 for a fourteenth-century Persian miniature drawing of the bier of Iskander. Kennerley boasted to Randolph Adams that the Macy sale "restored the prestige of the auction business. We sold to standing room only—literally—and the audience was the most distinguished I have known for years. . . . All the buyers want is to have their confidence restored in clean handling of sales."[44] A certain historical symmetry was achieved in April when a collection of J. M. W. Turner drawings was sold for $5,410; they were the property of John Anderson, Jr., founder of the Anderson Galleries.[45]

During the course of the 1937–1938 season the AAA-AG held twenty book sales and fifty-six art auctions. Sales totaled $2,020,974.25, of which books and manuscripts contributed $846,635.25 ($535,219 from the Bishop sessions). Parke-Bernet held thirteen book sales and forty-three art sales—a remarkable achievement for a newly organized house—of which books and manuscripts accounted for $192,294.50.

By most standards Kennerley's restoration at the AAA-AG was remarkably successful; yet he was forced out at the end of the season. Charles Heartman's daughter, Dolley, who was employed at the galleries, reports that Kennerley was under pressure from those trying to oust him. He conscripted her for dictation of letters he didn't want his secretary to see. "He'd take the letters and copies himself, sign, and most of the time would seem to keep and mail himself. . . . I have a dim recollection that he sometimes asked for my note book back."[46]

The secretary-treasurer of the AAA-AG was Milton Logan, formerly Bishop's private secretary. He knew very little about books or art, and Kennerley held him in contempt. In the summer of 1938 Logan's offer of $185,000 for the gallery was accepted by the ladies.[47] The down-payment was $10,000. That Kennerley was not privy to these negotiations is documented by his August 1938 letter explaining to his fourteen-year-old son Richard that he would not be able to visit him at summer camp: ". . . last Friday, quite suddenly and unexpectedly to me, a group of speculators bought the galleries, and will run it themselves."[48] Kennerley made no public statement on his deposal.

Kennerley's departure was lamented in the book-trade press. The *New York Times Book Review* declared:

> That he will be missed there can be no question, particularly in the light of his brilliant record at the American Art Anderson Galleries last season. Nothing in recent auction history has been more dramatic than the phenomenon of Mr. Kennerley, whose entrance and exit both caused no little flurry among the collecting audience. In the brief interval during which he flashed across the scene he gave an excellent demonstration of his creative ability. Not only did he put on a good show, but he stimulated a renewed enthusiasm for books among those who had begun to falter and he won new converts to the cause.[49]

Life in Letters. American Autograph Journal, published by Guido Bruno, was even warmer in its tribute:

> Mr. Kennerley is a genius born to head an important literary auction house, such a one as he created twice, the last time only a few months ago, when he caused phenix to rise out of his ashes. He is an unequalled show man with a thorough knowledge of the entire field, inclusive all manner of men and women he has to deal with. He is scholarly inclined with the soul of an artist and poet. He keeps tap almost hourly on everything that is going on everywhere in all branches of Life and Letters. He knows how to attract to himself experts in the various branches of collector's materials, and does not hesitate to draw upon their services whenever the occasion arises, allowing them full credit for their erudition and their work. But above all and everything he has "hunches" to do the right thing at the right time. His first autograph sale last year was the ALFRED C. MAYER SALE. It followed the most

deplorable debacle of an important collection. There was the atmosphere of an expensive funeral at the opening of the sale, but it proved the first sale in years that brought prices something near the actual value of the material. For the first time in years a magnificent Lincoln letter sold for $1000.00, a Washington letter fetched $3000.00. The letters were of great historical importance, they were rare prizes, BUT equally fine material had brought quite different prices during the past few years (Remember the Terry sales etc). All other items brought in proportion equally good prices. Then came the BISHOP SALE. No other person living could have managed an important sale under more difficult auspices at this particular time with such MAGNIFICENT SURPRISING, almost UNBE-LIEVEABLE results. Collectors once more began to show interest. The material was not absorbed by dealers exclusively. New hopes arose everywhere. And now! There is little else left but the memory of a miraculous though short season and of the "coming and going" of Mr. Kennerley.[50]

PART V

FALLEN ENTERPRISES, 1939–1950

CHAPTER NINE

The Sixty-Fifth Street Bookshop—
The Berg Collection—Another Bishop Sale—
Joan Coons—Fallen Enterprises—An Old Man
with No Money and Nothing to Do

AT SIXTY KENNERLEY was broke and unemployed. He operated out of several offices after leaving the AAA-AG. (In the 1938–39 volume of *Who's Who in America* his address is listed as 255 Varick Street, but it is not known what he was engaged in there.) During 1938 and 1939 he lived on West Seventy-seventh Street with Diana and Richard. Kennerley was concerned about providing for the boy; in an undated letter to Christopher Morley he stated: "Had it not been for Richard I should have used my Iron Ration [committed suicide] long ago."[1]

In 1939 Kennerley printed *An Invitation to Join The Book-Collector's Club of America*. The four-page prospectus included the following expectations:

THE Book-Collector's Club of America will be conducted on a non-profit basis under the Membership Corporation laws of New York State.

THE Club is being founded by Mitchell Kennerley, and a group of friends, who will be responsible for its management for one year, after which an undetermined number of members will be invited to become directors and to share in the management.

THERE will be two classes of members: Life-and-family members who will pay one hundred dollars and Annual members who will pay ten dollars a year. Membership is open to both men and women.

. . . .

THE services have been secured of several bibliographers and booklovers of experience and eminence, who may be consulted by members, either at the Club or by mail, free of charge.

A BULLETIN with Club news and contributions of interest to members will be issued at frequent intervals. Frank and authentic reports of auction and bookseller catalogues, both American and foreign, will be printed. During the season auction catalogues will be immediately reviewed and special Bulletins mailed to members. The names of members will be printed in the Bulletin.

. . . .

TEMPORARY Club rooms have been rented at 15 East 53rd Street, between Fifth and Madison Avenues. As soon as a sufficient number of members have joined, a Club house will be rented in the neighborhood.

THERE will be frequent exhibitions of books and manuscripts, and as far as possible all material in exhibitions will be open for examination and comparison.

AS one of the aims of the Club will be to encourage collecting, it is hoped that it may be possible to set aside a room where member book-sellers and collectors may meet to discuss the business of buying and selling, without interfering with the general activities of the Club.

A LIBRARY of reference and other books of interest and value to collectors will be formed as quickly as possible. All periodicals, American and foreign, of interest to collectors will be available, as well as all auction and bookseller's catalogues, including priced auction catalogues immediately after the sales.[2]

Three hundred life memberships and 5,000 annual memberships ($80,000) were required. In addition to providing a meeting place, the club would hold book auctions. The prospects for success were slim. The book-collector's clubs that have flourished in America have always been private organizations for the affluent; much of the satisfaction in belonging to such a club derives from its exclusivity. The venture was abandoned before any real attempt was made to enlist members. Kennerley explained to Randolph Adams in June: "I have not gone ahead with my proposed book club as I have three things in mind and have not determined which to push. A lot depends on daily meetings with the two auction galleries which will be concluded within a few days."[3]

Milton Logan, the new president of the AAA-AG, had obtained backing from insurance broker John T. Geery, who sold his interest in the Brooklyn Dodgers to raise capital. When Geery discovered that his investment was a money pit, he insured Logan for $150,000 and planned his murder in 1940. But Logan proved hard to kill, and Geery committed suicide.[4] Logan was convicted on nine counts of grand larceny, and Parke-Bernet acquired the bankrupt AAA-AG for $12,500. While this melodrama was unfolding, Kennerley briefed Adams on his plans in September 1939: "Next week I hope to be free of my old agreement not to go into the auction business and shall make every effort to open a book auction house. I have had numerous appeals to do so but until the AAA folded my hands were tied. It will not require much space or a large staff, or large capital. It was the art end of the business that required all these things and ate up all the profits of the book sales."[5] Kennerley never returned to the auction business.

The wish to repeat past victories is a familiar response of the defeated. In 1939 Kennerley asked Christopher Morley's help in persuading the *Saturday Review of Literature* to sponsor a poetry competition for the New York World's Fair: "I should like to do another Lyric Year."[6] This project, too, was stillborn. Kennerley's principal activity at this time was brokering book collections—acting as a middleman for a commission or finder's fee. The most important collections he was involved with were the libraries of W. T. H. Howe and Owen D. Young. Howe, president of the American Book Company, had spent an estimated two million dollars during forty years of acquiring 16,000 English and American books and manuscripts—including an "unsurpassed" collection of New England authors. His material would have made for an epic auction; but the heirs did not want to chance the uncertain auction situation. The en bloc sale was handled by Chicago dealer Walter M. Hill, who appraised the library at $600,000 for tax purposes. Early in 1940 Dr. Albert A. Berg donated to the New York Public Library the 3,000 books he had collected with his late brother Dr. Henry W. Berg. They were wealthy bachelors, and Dr. Albert Berg was advised that the Howe books would make a proper memorial to his brother. Kennerley managed the difficult negotiations among the Howe heirs, Hill, the New York Public Library, and Dr. Berg.[7] The deal was made for $450,000, with Kennerley receiving a fee from Hill's commission.

Young, who had been the largest buyer of Kern's books, collected mainly eighteenth and nineteenthcentury English literature. After the stock market crash he had pledged his library as collateral against his debts. Late in 1940 Kennerley approached him: "I believe that I could sell your library, and to a buyer entirely unknown to the book world as a book buyer."[8] Young replied that he was interested in selling en bloc or selling a half interest on the understanding that the purchaser would join him in donating the entire collection to an institution.[9] Kennerley was unable to make the sale to his unidentified candidate, but he opened negotiations with Dr. Berg. In April 1941 Young, dealing directly with the New York Public Library, sold a halfinterest in his 15,000 books and manuscripts to Dr. Berg for $375,000.[10] Among the Young treasures were 2,500 Fanny Burney letters and manuscripts; the *Oliver Twist* manuscript; the four Shakespeare *Folios* and the 1640 *Poems*; Poe's *Tamerlane*; the manuscript of Byron's *Don Juan*; and the manuscripts of *Tom Sawyer*, *A Connecticut Yankee in King Arthur's Court*, and *More Tramps Abroad*. Kennerley received a $5,000 finder's fee from Young—considerably less than the 10 percent commission he had hoped to earn. The New York Public Library was to select the books it wanted to retain, and Young granted Kennerley "the exclusive right to sell such remainder, which ought to be pretty large, at the usual commission, which I understand is 10%."[11] Presumably the Library kept all the books, for there is no record of Kennerley's efforts to sell the surplussage. In accepting this arrangement Kennerley insisted that his name be left out of the announcement. Despite his refusal to claim credit, Kennerley was in some part responsible for the stature of the Berg Collection as one of America's major rarebook research repositories. The Howe and Young acquisitions upgraded the Berg from an interesting small collection to a great library, adding some 31,000 books and manuscripts in less than eighteen months.

With the backing of friends Kennerley opened the SixtyFifth Street Bookshop at 866 Lexington Avenue in December 1940. Among the rejected names for the business were Kitty Foyle's Bookshop (in honor of Christopher Morley's heroine) and the Nine O'Clock Bookshop (because it was open from 9 A.M. to 9 P.M.). The business was incorporated with $10,000 in preferred stock and $20,000 in common stock—with subscribers to preferred stock receiving an equal amount of common stock. It is not known how much of the stock was sold. James Rosenberg tried to make his $300 investment a gift, but Kennerley firmly declined the offer.[12] The shop's letterhead—set in Kennerley type—stated *Many new Books and a few old Books & Rental Library*. There was a small stock of collector's books, and Kennerley tried to specialize in poetry; but the main business was supplying current books to neighborhood customers. The sixty-three-year-old man who had auctioned the Gutenberg Bible for $106,000 claimed to be happy selling dollar items and renting books at 10 cents per day. He wrote his friends that he had always wanted his own bookshop (it was actually his fourth shop) and reported that trade was brisk. One day a stranger who made a purchase engaged the proprietor in conversation about the Anderson Galleries and asked what had become of Mitchell Kennerley. "He's dead," Kennerley told him. Kennerley lived above the shop and continued to broker collections. He was unable to get a piece of the action for the A. Edward Newton library, which sold at Parke-Bernet in 1941 for $376,560.

One of his poetry customers was Dorothy Gordon, a Yale faculty wife, and Kennerley developed a close friendship with the Gordons. They met infrequently; but he wrote her almost daily, enclosing clippings or recommending books. In December 1941 he wrote: "It is nice, when you are out of the running, to be reminded by someone you are fond of, of when you were in the running . . . I look back on the Forum, and the old Galleries, and such like, as of another world, which of course they were."[13] Mrs. Gordon found Kennerley the best raconteur she had ever known, but she learned that some questions about his career were deflected. "Of course I have led a wicked life but always from the temptation to be good!" he remarked.[14] Kennerley's letters sometimes quoted his favorite verse passages, one of which, from William Watson's "The Tomb of Burns," seems like a self-assessment:

> *All bright and glorious at the start*
> *'Twas his ignobly to depart,*
> *Slain by his own too affluent heart,*

> *Too generous blood;*
> *A voyager that lost Life's chart*
> *In midmost flood.*[15]

He encouraged her writing, and in 1948 she published "To M.K." in *The Saturday Review of Literature* under the pseudonym of Dorothy Webster. The 23-line poem closed:

> *In sunlight or at dusk, the*
> *   heart is free*
> *And unashamed to weep at beauty's*
> *   end,*
> *Or drought or death. Love makes*
> *   deep music here,*
> *And immortality surrounds my friend.*[16]

Yet in attempting to describe Kennerley after his death, Mrs. Gordon wrote that "he had so many facets that I have the impression of knowing nothing about him."[17]

Even though trade publishing was closed to him, Kennerley retained a pleasure in typography. In 1941 he produced two pamphlets related to the war. Richard Le Gallienne's 1903 poem "The Cry of the Little Peoples" was printed for Eva Le Gallienne by Richard Ellis and sold for the benefit of The Eagle Club of London and The British War Relief Society. Kennerley's name did not appear on the pamphlet, which had the information that "Copies may be obtained, price Fifty Cents, from Sixty-Fifth Street Bookshop, Inc." Kennerley also distributed 500 copies of *". . . and the not-known end,"* a short story by bookseller Colton Storm, about the destruction of America. This pamphlet designed by Ellis bore the imprint of the Sixty-Fifth Street bookshop.

In June of 1942 the sixty-four-year-old Kennerley met Joan Coons, an aspiring writer in her twenties who had been sent to him by a friend who thought Kennerley would be interested in her unpublished novel, "Without Passport." After Kennerley read it, he wrote her: "The book is very uneven but I am told that is true of 'Hamlet.' There are passages of extraordinary sympathy and comprehension, and the book as a whole has a very definite meaning. I believe that readers of today would be grateful for its message of youth and faith."[18] He recorded his response to her in a letter to Christopher Morley: "When she came in the shop I thought it was Edna Millay as she came to see me at 29th Street 30 years ago. She is the most fascinating mind and body I have ever known. Her novel is incredible. Her poems lack Edna's craftsmanship but surpass her work in insights and achievement. I do want her to know you before . . . I do not know what. When may we come and take you and Wini to lunch? She is wierdly shy and strangely strong."[19] In August he wrote Mrs. Gordon: "I saw a lot of people today: the most extraordinary girl-writer I have ever met, and Arnold Genthe—(who took her photograph)—and Christopher Morley. All of which makes me want to live forever instead of being already dead."[20]

Joan Coons was from Chatham, New York. She had received a doctorate in pharmacy and pharmacology from Columbia University in 1939 when she was twenty-three, but her ambitions were literary. She wrote scripts for the radio shows *Crime Doctor* and *Perfect Crime*. Her poem "Faith," which Kennerley predicted "might well become the Negro national anthem," was probably printed at his expense. He also privately published Coons's short story, *The Christmas Gift: A Memory of Stalingrad*, as a pamphlet in 1943.

Kennerley and Joan became constant companions; his daughter-in-law Jean—Morley's wife—has commented that he was "absolutely bewitched" by her. He introduced Joan to his friends and took her to meet Stieglitz, who "began talking about me—how I had come to his rescue years ago and that he owed all his later, happy years to me . . . and Stieglitz drew me to him and kissed my hands which appalled and astonished and humbled me as I have never been before."[21] Kennerley used his contacts to secure publication of her novel. "Joan is very low today," he wrote Richard Ellis. "I hope you and Esther will be able to write her about 'Without Passport'. I have no fear about your liking it. It is extraordinary what she has put in it. You would swear that she was an experienced woman of the world, but it is all mental, not practical. She is adorable but a problem."[22] Kennerley planned to publish *Without Passport: An Everyday Novel* himself under the Stirling Bliss imprint; but he persuaded the John Day Company to publish it in 1943 after Pearl Buck put in a good word. The novel—

Owen D. Young

ABOVE: Mitchell Kennerley with granddaughter Diana outside Sixty-Fifth
Street Bookshop, c. 1941. Photo
by Richard Ellis (Ellis Collection,
Samuel Paley Library, Temple University)

LEFT: The Sixty-Fifth Street Bookshop
(Collection of American Literature,
the Beinecke Rare Book and
Manuscript Library, Yale University)

which was dedicated to Kennerley—traces the lives of two musically gifted youths. The boy wins the scholarship that they compete for and becomes a successful violinist but is unhappy. The girl abandons her career to marry a farmer and is ultimately rewarded by her son's genius. *Without Passport* was not widely reviewed, but it went into a second printing and sold 4,000 copies—a respectable performance for a first novel. An English edition appeared as *Passport to Destiny*. Joan Coons did not publish another book.

The Sixty-Fifth Street Bookshop failed at the end of 1942, and Kennerley sold it. He blamed the mail-order book clubs and corrupt contemporary taste. People weren't reading the books he wanted to sell. During the forties Kennerley attempted to promote backing for several blue-sky publishing projects. In January 1943 he approached Richard Walsh, head of John Day, in connection with a magazine to be called "Listening"—an attempt to salvage his plans for "Listening Post."

> I should like to talk with you about a publishing idea, which I believe to be the most profitable and important since The Reader's Digest was started. It has nothing to do with books. I have it all planned and could put it into operation immediately. I could do all the editorial work. I want someone to undertake the business and promotion management. I have approached no one on the subject so far. It is a project that I believe would immediately make money and grow to power and influence exceeding that of Time, Life, Fortune—and The Reader's Digest! It would take an uninterrupted twenty minutes, or less, to place the entire plan before you.[23]

Nothing resulted.

Later in the year he offered to organize a book club for Montgomery Ward:

> I have watched with interest the beginnings and growth of the different book clubs. It would seem that any book club would have to be very similar to one already established. I have, however, conceived an idea that has in it all the elements of popular appeal of The Book-of-the-Month Club and of Sears People's Book Club. It has an additional element that it is unique, surprising, and saleable.

I have told this idea to *no one*. I could supervise and guarantee the management of the special feature I propose to introduce, leaving all manufacture, distribution, and promotion to you.[24]

In 1945 Kennerley wrote Daniel Longwell of *Life* requesting an interview for Joan, "whose mind has been working on a plan for a magazine to leap ahead of 'The Ladies' Home Journal' and such-like magazines. She has a wonderful title FAMILY which she will present to you if you will give her a job."[25]

Kennerley dropped out of sight after the demise of his bookshop, and rumors circulated that he was clerking in a department store. His address was a post office box. He lived for a while at the Belmont Plaza Hotel and then moved to the Shelton Hotel at Lexington Avenue and Forty-eighth Street—twelve blocks from the old Anderson Galleries. These were modest establishments but by no means flophouses.

The man who had once had so many irons in so many fires now had nothing to do. He spent a good deal of time browsing in the used book shops along lower Fourth Avenue and on Fifty-ninth Street, buying 10-cent books that were sent to Vassar and the Clements Library. In 1945 he arranged for columnist George Matthew Adams to donate a Millay collection to the University of Michigan. Kennerley was in the habit of tearing pages from a book that interested him— appalling behavior for a bookman, which he defended by claiming that he was "releasing its values."[26] These pages were often mailed to friends with notes. He informed Fanny Borden that he was assembling a collection of the title pages from the volumes he had published, intending to make a book of his comments on them.[27]

If he found a sleeper while book scouting, he would sell it to a better shop. One of the dealers who occasionally bought from him was Frances Steloff of the Gotham Book Mart. In 1945 she lost her lease and was preparing to close after twenty-three years at 51 West Forty-seventh Street. When Kennerley learned about her problem, he contacted someone he knew at Columbia University, which owned 41 West Forty-seventh, and arranged for Miss Steloff to acquire the building on extremely easy terms. She was reluctant to undertake the commitment, and Kennerley enlisted Christopher Morley to persuade her.[28] The Gotham Book Mart still operates at 41 West Forty-seventh Street; the shop cat is named Mitchell.

Kennerley regularly dropped in at David Kirshenbaum's Carnegie Bookshop on Fifty-seventh Street.[29] Kirshenbaum appreciated Kennerley's help in the old auction days and made him welcome. Kennerley and Irving Halpern, the cataloguer, engaged in long book talks.[30] Kirshenbaum lent Kennerley money and arranged for him to receive a commission on the sale of Guido Bruno's American Autograph Shop; Kennerley had tried to buy the stock but was unable to raise the $50,000 required. On one of Kennerley's birthdays Kirshenbaum gave a lunch for him, at which Kennerley insisted on eating a whole coconut cream pie. He was a drinker, but Kirshenbaum never saw him drunk. Some of his drinking was done in Third Avenue saloons where the whiskey was 15¢ a shot. At the Carnegie Bookshop Kennerley met Charles Feinberg, the preeminent Whitman collector, who was interested in his connection with Horace Traubel. Feinberg was impressed by his fund of book lore but noticed his shabbiness. When cars were hard to obtain after the war, Kennerley asked Feinberg to buy a new Ford for him in Detroit; Kennerley took delivery on the car but never paid for it.[31]

Kennerley liked to have a mid-morning eye-opener in the Ritz Men's Bar at Madison Avenue and Forty-sixth Street, from which he would often repair to the nearby Chiswick Bookshop operated by Herman Cohen. Since the shop specialized in fine printing and books about books, Kennerley enjoyed handling the books and talking about them. During one visit he asked Cohen to read aloud a newspaper article about a troupe of English actors celebrating Christmas in New York: "Aren't the English wonderful!" he remarked.[32]

Book-trade hands who had lost track of Kennerley were surprised when his article "My Ten-Cent Shelf" appeared in the March 1945 *American Mercury*. It is an expression of a booklover's pleasure in scouting the bargain bins—not for profit, but for the gratification of discovery and rediscovery. The tailor's term *hand* for the feel of cloth applies perfectly to Kennerley's response to books: "And here let me say that you do not know how friendly a second-hand copy of a book can be until you have carried it home and wiped off the dust from the cover and from the top edge and from the endpapers and maybe also from the inside pages, and have fondled it back to renewed life and service."[33] The volumes listed among his finds had little monetary value, but each stimulated him as a well-made book or as an unusual bit of literature: W. Compton Leith, *Sirenica*; Alfred Ollivant, *Redcoat Captain*; Lord Houghton, *Stray Verses*; Ralph Adams Cram, *Excalibur*; Leo Tolstoy, *Sevastopol* (for William Dean Howell's introduction); *Pensées from the Journal Intime of Henri-Frédéric Amiel*; Ralph Waldo Emerson, *Compensation* (The Roycroft Press edition); Jessie B. Rittenhouse, *The Lover's Rubaiyat*; the 1907 Duffield edition of *The Declaration of Independence*; *Recollections of Oscar Wilde* by Ernest La Jeunesse, André Gide, and Franz Blei; *Witty, Wise and Wicked Maxims*; Temple Scott, *The Friendship of Books*; and four inexpensive series —Cassell's National Library, the Camelot Library, The Canterbury Poets, and the Unit Books. He cited with approval the epigraph in *The Friendship of Books*: "Without books God is silent." Forgoing the sentimentality or pretentiousness that sometimes renders bibliophilic writings precious, Kennerley's appreciation and affection come through as sincere. Randolph Adams was so pleased with "My Ten-Cent Shelf" that he reprinted it as a pamphlet for the Clements Library.

Between abortive promotions Kennerley occupied himself with correspondence and unremunerative bibliographical activities. His letters document his retentive book memory. In 1946 he sent Christopher Morley—who was editing a new edition of *Bartlett's Familiar Quotations*—a list of analogues for Winston Churchill's "blood, toil, tears and sweat":

John Donne in his "Anatomie of the World" wrote: "Mollifie it with thy teares, or sweat, or blood."
Byron in his "The Age of Bronze", published in 1823, wrote:
"Year after year they voted cent, per cent.
Blood, sweat and tear-wrung millions. Why? for rent!"
In a note on poetry in the collected edition of the Poems of Lord Alfred Douglas he wrote:
"It is forged slowly and patiently, link by link, with sweat and blood and tears."
In 1931 Churchill published a book "The Unknown War: The Eastern Front", dedicated to "Our faithful Allies the Russian Imperial Armies". On the first page he states, in reference to the old Czaristic Russian armies, "their sweat, their tears, their blood bedewed the endless plain".
In the latest Columbia Pleasures of Publishing which unfortunately I sent away without copying there is another reference to "Blood, Sweat and Tears". I believe it was in a book by Samuel Butler.[34]

When the English literature collection of Frank Hogan was auctioned at Parke-Bernet in April 1946 Kennerley approached David
Randall, head of the Scribner rare-book department, with the propo-
sition that Randall act as his agent in buying all the important
Elizabethan books up to $500,000—explaining that because of his
longstanding feud with Parke and Bernet he didn't want to bid himself.
Kennerley revealed that his principal was Barbara Hutton, a close
friend of his daughter-in-law Jean Kennerley. Randall agreed to act
for him, but shortly before the Hogan sale Kennerley canceled the deal.
Barbara Hutton had decided to divorce Cary Grant and leave the
country; she was no longer interested in rare books.[35]

One more rich collection remained from the Bishop accumulation.
Shirley Falcke had married Edith Nixon and acquired control of Bishop's Paris library. The long-delayed sale was held in December 1948
at the Kende Galleries,[36] of which Falcke had become president. (In
1939 Kennerley had informed Fanny Borden that he was "directing
the cataloguing of the great French library of Cortlandt Bishop which
has just arrived from Paris.")[37] Kennerley was brought in by Falcke
to oversee the sale.* He hired two young experts, Lucien Goldschmidt
and John S. Kebabian, to compile the catalogue while he promoted
interest in the books. Kebabian found the seventy-year-old Kennerley
"courteous, patient and quiet (subdued, even) in all dealings with him
about the catalogue. He was obviously in poor shape, seedy in appearance, bullied by Falcke, and low in spirits. Falcke (an obnoxious
little stinker) at one point summoned Kennerley, L. G., and myself
into his presence . . . announced that the preparations for the sale were
going poorly, that he had been cheated by every auctioneer with whom
he had dealt (except Kende), and made vague and noisy threats about
what would happen to us if the sale was not a success."[39]

Like the 1938 Bishop sales at the AAA-AG, the 1948 sale has been
variously regarded as a flop and a success. Before the auction Seymour

---

* According to *The Elegant Auctioneers*, Falcke tried to hire Bade to cry the Bishop
books by offering him the inducement of working with Kennerley; but Kennerley
declined Falcke's job offer: "I only take presidencies, and not even those . . . now."[38]
This account is clearly in error because Kennerley did direct the preparation of the
catalogue.

de Ricci appraised the 322 books at a million dollars. The total was $306,000 (a strong average of $950.31), which Kennerley called "an incredible sum in these times."[40] His assessment is endorsed by Kebabian: ". . . there was vigorous competition, and, considering the level of prices then, the return was excellent."[41] The star book was a 1501 *Aesop* at $24,000; other five-figure items were the *Oeuvres de Molière* with original Boucher drawings and Molière's signature ($20,250—Bishop reportedly had paid $50,000 for it), a fifteenth-century woodcut book ($14,000), Tasso's *La Gerusalemme Liberata* ($23,500), and Catherine de Medici's copy of *La Cyropedie de Xenophon* ($16,250). Some of the best books were bought by European dealers. After terminating his employment at Kende, Kennerley wrote Irving Halpern, "I feel as if I had escaped from prison!"[42]

The seventy-one-year-old Kennerley's final attempt at a comeback was launched in the fall of 1949 when he printed a prospectus for the "Distaff Who's Who."

Announcing
DISTAFF
WHO'S WHO
Authentic Biographies of Women
in American Life

It is proposed in the initial volume of DISTAFF WHO'S WHO to list authentic biographies of American women who are distinguishing themselves by their contributions to the world of today. It is no longer a man's world. Women have made their mark in all phases of modern life; have found places for themselves in all branches of human endeavor. These places will never be relinquished.

Modern inventions have not only brought the world about us closer, but have brought it right into the home. No longer can one say, "Woman's place is in the home", and mean, "Woman's interests should concern only her immediate family"; for today the home has become the hub of every great change or movement and of innovations of thought. It is the power of women which can yet rule the world.

.   .   .   .

Joan Coons (Princeton
University Library)

Mitchell Kennerley on
seventy-first birthday. Photo
by Richard Ellis (Ellis Collection,
Samuel Paley Library,
Temple University)

Once awakened to the full power of their strength, women will advance at an even more rapid pace in directing the course of the world. The future is theirs. DISTAFF WHO'S WHO will keep you informed of exactly what is being done and of who is doing it. It is a book indispensable to individuals, schools, libraries, business firms, and organizations; a source book of American Woman's accomplishments in our world today.

New York:
DISTAFF WHO'S WHO
No. 4 East 43rd Street[43]

This announcement did not bear Kennerley's name. He attempted to form a corporation capitalized at $50,000, of which $10,000 was required for the first volume. The project had considerable promise—as the subsequent success of *Who's Who in American Women* demonstrates. Kirshenbaum acceded to Kennerley's desperate pleadings by putting up $2,000. But there weren't enough investors, and the venture was abandoned.

Christopher Morley kept in touch with Kennerley but was reluctant to spend time with him: ". . . I cd see he was really mentally ill, and I admit he rather frightened me. . . . I knew his possessive enthusiasms & frankly I feared to start a new entente which I couldn't possibly keep up. . . . with M. K. it had to be all or nothing." Kennerley told him, "When I go down I'll take some of my friends with me."[44] At this time Kennerley often saw his former wife, who was known as Mrs. Morley Kennerley. Helen retained her belief in his genius. She was still wealthy, thanks to her trust funds, and helped him with loans.

Kennerley had developed a friendship with Mrs. Vernon Wright, a wealthy Minnesota widow, who was fascinated by his literary conversation and impressed by his plans. She promised him a $50,000 legacy but died in January 1950 without making provision for it. He was unable to accept this disappointment and insisted that the inheritance was forthcoming.

Kennerley wrote Mrs. Gordon on 17 February 1950 calling her attention to a talk Alfred Knopf was giving at Yale and asked her to mention him to Knopf. "I haven't done a thing worth while for God knows how long. May never again!"[45] On the weekend of 18–19

February Kennerley visited the Falckes and Mrs. Bishop at Lenox, Massachusetts, in an attempt to raise money.[46] According to Towner, on the 21st he phoned Shirley Falcke to report a $50,000 inheritance and asked for $500 to claim it. Falcke advised him that a bank would be willing to lend money on the security of the will.[47]

On the 22nd Joan Coons received a note from Kennerley asking her to call him at the Shelton, instructing her to come to the hotel if he couldn't be reached by phone. She went to room 1828 twice in the afternoon and got no response to her knock. Later a maid tried to use a pass key, but the door was double locked. She reported it to the management who found Mitchell Kennerley hanging from a belt over the bathtub at 4:10 P.M. Mitchell Kennerley, Jr., and lawyer Amos Basel were notified. Basel later wrote to Morley Kennerley in London: "There were suicide notes all over the place, one to Richard, one to the editor of the New York *Post*, a note to call me, clippings and quotations about the quiet and peace of death. There was one evidently long note which I never saw, nor did Mitchell. . . . I had the impression that it was a rather weird note and that is why the police walked off with it."[48] The letter to the *Post* was not printed; the *New York Daily News* mentioned two notes—"one indicating that he felt unable to cope with advancing age, and the other asking that his body be cremated."[49] Basel's main concern was to prevent the tabloid reporters from learning about Joan Coons's involvement with Kennerley.

The death certificate listed Kennerley's occupation as publisher and provided the information that he had been divorced from an unidentified wife in Mexico in 1936. Other documents identified Mrs. Diana Kennerley as his widow. The Surrogate's Court valued Kennerley's estate at $50.

Mitchell Kennerley's funeral was at the Frank E. Campbell Chapel on Madison Avenue. The mourners included a cluster of no-longer-young women. Christopher Morley and B. W. Huebsch delivered eulogies. Morley—who privately described the suicide as a mercy killing—recalled him as a wild, brilliant, poetic figure who "was a law unto himself, and legislation of that kind is usually uncomfortable to the constituency." In concluding his remarks, Morley took from his pocket a copy of *Modern Love*—the first book published with the Mitchell Kennerley imprint in 1906—observing that some of the poems had been printed without permission. "If he liked something he made it his." From this volume Morley read William Ernest Henley's "Crosses and Troubles."

> *Crosses and troubles a-many have proved me.*
> *One or two women (God bless them!) have loved me.*
> *I have worked and dreamed, and I've talked at will,*
> *Of art and drink I have had my fill.*
> *I've comforted here, and I've succoured there;*
> *I've faced my foes, and I've backed my friends.*
> *I've blundered, and sometimes made amends.*
> *I have prayed for light, and I've known despair.*
> *Now I look before, as I look behind,*
> *Come storm, come shine, whatever befall,*
> *With a grateful heart and a constant mind,*
> *For the end, I know, is the best of all.*

Morley closed by citing the colophon in *Modern Love*—"It will not be reprinted"—adding: "Nor will Mitchell. He was unique."[50]

Biography has no obligation to solve its subjects. All such solutions run the risk of distortion. The trauma or Rosebud approach to a life is a convenient simplification. Wounds only cripple unless they are incurred by those with uncommon sensitivity, talent, and intelligence—which are unaccountable.

What is there to explain Mitchell Kennerley who achieved so much and squandered his achievements? Fame was not the spur, although he relished the perquisites of celebrity. Money obviously motivated him because it allowed him to play the game; but the game itself provided his rewards. Kennerley never consolidated his success because he was compelled to test fortune by taking risks, especially risks that involved manipulating others.

Depending on their timing and luck, such figures may be remembered as titans or as admonitory examples; they may be forgotten. If Kennerley had died in 1929 there would have been occasion for wonder and perhaps lamentation. Instead, he lived out a long denouement until he took his quietus. Yet all was not wasted. Mitchell Kennerley left a bookman's legacy.

APPENDIX I

The Kern Sale:
Items Sold for $5,000 or More, 1929

57A. Boswell, James. *The Life of Samuel Johnson* (1791). First edition with ALSs of Boswell and Johnson laid in. Rebound. $5,200. Rosenbach.

 84. Browning, Elizabeth Barrett. *The Battle of Marathon* (1820). First edition of her first book; presentation copy with ALS from Robert Browning laid in. Rebound. $17,500. Rosenbach.

101. Browning, Robert. *Pauline* (1833). First edition of his first book; original boards. One of eleven known copies. The W. H. Arnold copy. $16,000. Beyer.

137. Burney, Frances. *Evelina* (1778). First edition. Original calf. $5,800. Rosenbach.

141. Burns, Robert. *Poems Chiefly in the Scottish Dialect* (Kilmarnock, 1786). First edition. With eight lines of MS verse inserted. Rebound. $6,750. Grasberger.

149. Burns. *Poems, Chiefly in the Scottish Dialect* (1793). With full-page inscription to John M'Murdo. Rebound. The W. K. Bixby copy. $23,500. Rosenbach.

183. Lord Byron. *Childe Harold's Pilgrimage, Cantos I–II* (1812) Inscribed copy linking Byron to Anna Milbanke. Rebound. $5,100. Wells.

187. Byron. *Waltz* (1813). Pamphlet in original state. $8,250. Wells.

205. Byron. *Don Juan.* MS of Cantos XIV–XV, 49 pages. $20,000. Wells.

206. Byron. "The Dream." MS, 14 pages. With printed text. "Apparently" Byron's copy. $8,000. Beyer.

207. Bryon. *Marino Faliero.* MS, 142 pages. Fair copy. With two ALSs to John Murray. $27,000. Rosenbach.

240. Carroll, Lewis. *Alice's Adventures in Wonderland* (1865). Suppressed first edition. Rebound. $10,000. Rosenbach.

288. Conrad, Joseph. *Under Western Eyes.* MS, 1,351 pages. $7,250. Brick Row.

309. Cruikshank, George. Sixteen drawings for William Combe's *Life of Napoleon.* $5,000. Hill.

346. DeFoe, Daniel. *The Life and Strange Surprizing Adventures of Robinson Crusoe* (1719). First edition. With *The Farther Adventures of Robinson Crusoe* (1719) and *Serious Reflections during the Life and Surprizing Adventures of Robinson Crusoe* (1720). Rebound. The Beverly Chew copies. $11,500. Drake.

364. Dickens, Charles. *The Posthumous Papers of the Pickwick Club* (1836–1837). Twenty parts in nineteen, with all points. Original wrappers. The R. T. Jupp copy, perfected. $28,000. Scheuer.

367. Dickens. Original wash drawing by Hablot K. Browne for the frontispiece of *Pickwick.* From the Sir Stuart Samuel collection. $6,500. Beyer.

369. Dickens. Original wash drawing by Robert Seymour for *Pickwick.* From the Sir Stuart Samuel collection. $6,200. Gimbel.

370. Dickens. Original wash drawing by Hablot K. Browne for *Pickwick.* Annotated by Dickens. From the Sir Stuart Samuel collection. $7,500. Gimbel.

371. Dickens. Original wash drawing by Hablot K. Browne for *Pickwick.* Annotated by Dickens. From the Sir Stuart Samuel collection. $5,000. Beyer.

382. Dickens. *The Strange Gentleman* (1837). With ALS laid in. Rebound. $10,500. Rosenbach.

388. Dickens. *Oliver Twist*. MS, 3 pages. $8,500. Drake.

394. Dickens. *Barnaby Rudge* (1841). First edition; inscribed to Walter Savage Landor. Rebound. $5,500. Beyer.

412. Dickens. *The Cricket on the Hearth* (1846). First issue; inscribed to George Cruikshank. Original cloth. $5,000. Rosenbach.

417. Dickens. *The Haunted Man and the Ghost's Bargain* (1848). Second issue; inscribed to William Harrison Ainsworth. Original cloth. $6,750. Hill.

423. Dickens. *A Child's History of England* (1853–1854). First editions of volumes 2 & 3; three volumes inscribed. Original cloth. $6,250. Drake.

433. Dickens. *A Tale of Two Cities* (1859). First issue; inscribed to Dr. Elliotson. With Thackeray letter to Elliotson laid in. Rebound. $10,250. Wells.

434. Dickens. *A Curious Dance Round a Curious Tree* (1860). First issue. With ten pages of MS. Rebound. $9,000. Drake.

448. Dickens. Book of Memoranda, 28 pages. $15,000. Rosenbach.

470. Dickens & Wilkie Collins. "The Perils of Certain English Prisoners and their Treasures in Women, Children, Silver, and Jewels." MS, 101 pages. With ALS from Dickens to Collins. $15,000. Sessler.

511. Fielding, Henry. *The History of Tom Jones* (1749). First issue, six volumes in original boards. $29,000. Rosenbach. *See* text.

520. Fielding. "Of Outlawry in Criminal Causes." MS, 18 pages. $6,700. Rosenbach.

522. Fitzgerald, Edward. *Rubaiyat of Omar Khayyam* (1859). First edition. Original wrappers. $8,000. Drake.

569. Goldsmith, Oliver. *The Traveller* (1764). One of two known copies "ante-dating the regular first edition." Rebound. From the Sir Stuart Samuel collection. $5,500. Rosenbach.

573. Goldsmith. *The Vicar of Wakefield* (1766). First issue. Possibly a presentation copy. Original calf. The Robert Hoe copy. $6,600. Brick Row.

588. Goldsmith. *She Stoops to Conquer* (1773). First issue. Original wrappers. $8,000. Rosenbach.

592. Goldsmith. *The Haunch of Venison* (1776). Original wrappers. $5,500.

596. Goldsmith. Translation of "Vida's Scacchis, or Chess." MS, 34 pages. $27,000. Young. *See* text.

601. Gray, Thomas. *An Elegy Wrote in a Country Church Yard* (1751). First edition. Contemporary boards, bound up with six other pieces. $12,000. Sessler.

619. Hardy, Thomas. *A Pair of Blue Eyes.* MS, 160 pages. Incomplete. $34,000. Beyer. *See* text.

717. Johnson, Samuel. *Dictionary of the English Language.* MS, 1 page. Definition of "Versification." $11,000. Sessler. *See* text.

741. Johnson. ALS to Mrs. Thrale about Gray's *Elegy,* 3 pages. $5,500. Sessler.

752. Keats, John. "Isabella; Or, the Pot of Basil." MS, 4 pages. Stanzas 30–31, 33–40. $7,500. Beyer.

753. Keats. *Lamia, Isabella, The Eve of St. Agnes and Other Poems* (1820). With MS of stanzas 60 and 63 of "Isabella." First edition. Original boards. $7,000. Sessler.

754. Keats. *Poetical Works* (1854). With 22-line MS of "I stood tiptoe upon a little hill." Rebound. $17,000. Rosenbach.

764. Kipling, Rudyard. *Under the Deodars* (1888). Inscribed. Original wrappers. First edition. $5,000. Brick Row.

772. Kipling. *Life's Handicap* (1891). First edition. Inscribed, with verse written in by Kipling. Original cloth. $6,250. Bissell.

800. Lamb, Charles. *Tales from Shakespeare* (1807). First edition. With ALS laid in. Original boards. $5,700. Beyer.

802. Lamb. *Poetry for Children* (1809). First edition. Original boards. "The rarest of all Lamb's books." $8,750. Rosenbach. *See* text.

811. Lamb. *Album Verses* (1830). First edition. Inscribed. Rebound. $5,900. Sessler.

814. Lamb. MS for Lamb's contributions to William Hone's *Table Book,* 80 pages. With ALS laid in. The W. K. Bixby copy. $48,000. Sessler.

816. Lamb. ALS to S. T. Coleridge, 4 pages. $5,100. Rosenbach.

836. Leech, John. 22 water colors to illustrate A'Beckett's *Comic History of England* and *Comic History of Rome*. $7,300. Scheuer.

856. Lovelace, Sir Richard. *Lucasta* (1649). First edition. Rebound. The Huth copy. $5,800. Drake.

893. Milton, John. *Poems of Mr. John Milton* (1645). First collected edition. Original calf. The John L. Clawson copy. $6,750. Scheuer.

933. Poe, Edgar Allan. ALS, 4 pages. Quotes E. B. Browning's opinion of *"The Raven."* $19,500. Rosenbach. *See* text.

940. Pope, Alexander. *The Works of Mr. Alexander Pope* (1717). First collected edition. Annotated by Pope. The Richard Heber copy. $5,500. Wells.

950. Pope. *Essay on Man.* MS of first three books, 40 pages. $29,000. Rosenbach. *See* text.

1019. Rowlandson, Thomas. The Three Tours of Dr. Syntax: *In Search of the Picturesque; In Search of Consolation; In Search of a Wife* (1812, 1820, 1821). With original drawings. Volumes 1 & 3 in original boards. $5,300. Brick Row.

1043. Scott, Sir Walter. *Tales of a Grandfather.* MS, 156 pages. $6,000. Rosenbach.

1050. Shakespeare, William. *Poems* (1640). First edition. Rebound. $8,500. Wells.

1051. Shakespeare. *The Second Folio* (1632). Rebound. $5,750. Brick Row.

1052. Shakespeare. *The Third Folio* (1663). First issue. With seven additional plays formerly attributed to Shakespeare. Rebound. $8,000. Brick Row.

1053. Shakespeare. *The Third Folio* (1664). Second issue. With seven additional plays. Rebound. The Robert Hoe copy. $15,500. Rosenbach.

1077. Shelley, Percy Bysshe. *Queen Mab.* First edition. Annotated by Shelley. Original boards. The H. Buxton Forman copy. $68,000. Wells. *See* text.

1084. Shelley. *Laon and Cythna* (1818). First edition. With ALS laid in. Original boards. $5,500. Beyer.

1091. Shelley. *Adonais* (1821). First edition. Rebound with original wrappers. The Maurice Baring copy. $6,000. Wells.

1124. Smollett, Tobias. *The Expedition of Humphrey Clinker* (1771). First issue. Original boards. $6,200. Scheuer.

1134. Sterne, Laurence. *The Life and Opinions of Tristram Shandy, Gentleman* (1760–1767). First editions. Nine volumes in original boards and calf. $12,500. Rosenbach.

1152. Stevenson, Robert Louis. ALS to W. E. Henley about *Treasure Island*, 4 pages. $5,250. Rosenbach.

1154–1155. Stevenson. *A Child's Garden of Verses* (1885). First edition. Dedication copy. With ALS to his mother in which Stevenson explains why he dedicated the book to his nanny. $8,500. Beyer. *See* text.

1185. Surtees [Robert Smith]. *Mr. Sponge's Sporting Tour; Handley Cross; "Ask Mamma"; "Plain or Ringlets?"; Mr. Facey Romford's Hounds* (1853–1865). Original parts. $5,000. Scheuer.

1191. Swift, Jonathan. *Travels into several Remote Nations of the World. . . . By Lemuel Gulliver* (1726). First issue. Original calf. $17,000. Scheuer.

1296. Tennyson, Alfred, Lord. "Maud." MS, 16 pages. Incomplete. $9,500. Rosenbach.

1312. Tennyson. "The Coming of Arthur." MS, 23 pages. The A. H. Japp copy. $8,000. Rosenbach.

1342. Thackeray, William Makepeace. *Vanity Fair* (1847–1848). The original 20 parts in 19. $7,750. Beyer.

1366. Thackeray. Lectures on George I, George II, and George IV. MSS, 155 pages. $8,500. Scheuer.

APPENDIX 2

The Bishop Sale:
Items Sold for $5,000 or More, 1938

155. Saint Augustine. *De civitate Dei* (c. 1410). Illuminated vellum MS, 173 leaves. The Lothian copy. $20,250. Sessler.

246. *Biblia Latina* (Mainz: Fust & Schoeffer, 1462). The first dated edition of the Bible and the first printed work formally divided into two volumes. The Lothian copy. $12,000. Rosenbach.

279. Blake, William. *Songs Of Innocence and Of Experience* (1789–1794). Illuminated by Blake. $5,400. Sessler.

285. *The Blickling Homilies* (tenth century). Manuscript on 149 vellum leaves. The Lothian copy. $38,000. Rosenbach.

289. Boccaccio, Giovanni. *Le livre de Jehan bocasse de la louenge et vertu des nobles et cleres dames* (1493). The first edition in French, bound for Diane De Poitiers. The only known privately owned copy. $8,750. Maggs.

537. Dante Alighieri. *La Divina Commedia* (1481). The first illustrated edition, with plates attributed to Sandro Botticelli. The Holford copy. $13,500. Rosenbach.

563. Dickens, Charles. *A Christmas Carol* (1849). Annotated "Reading Copy." $5,000. Hill.

569. Dickens. *The Chimes: A Reading . . . Sikes and Nancy: A Reading from Oliver Twist.* Annotated "Reading Copy." $7,700. Hill.

830. Froissart, Jehan. *Chronicles, 1326 to 1385.* Manuscript, 363 vellum leaves. $14,000. Rosenbach.

1064. *Horae, in laudem beatiss. . . . .* (Paris: Simon de Colines, 1524–1525). The earliest printed Book of Hours with illustrations and borders engraved by Geofroy Tory. $5,000. Rosenbach.

1192. Kelmscott Press. *The Works of Geoffrey Chaucer* (1896). One of thirteen copies printed in vellum. $6,100. Beyer.

1264. *Lancelot du Lac* (thirteenth-fifteenth centuries). Illuminated manuscript on 382 vellum leaves. $16,500. Rosenbach.

1365. Lorris, Guillame De and Jean De Meun. *Le Roman de la Rose* (sixteenth century). Illuminated manuscript on 206 vellum leaves. $9,500. Wormser.

1414. *Horae beatae virginis secundum usum Angliae, cum calendario* (c. 1440). Illuminated manuscript, 195 vellum leaves. The Pembroke Book of Hours. The Hoe copy. $14,250. Wells.

1432. *Horae Beatae Mariae Virginis secundum usum Romanae Ecclesiae* (sixteenth century). Illuminated manuscript Book of Hours, 116 vellum leaves. $18,000. Rosenbach.

APPENDIX 3

Checklist of Mitchell Kennerley Publications: 1906–1938

This list omits keepsakes and books of other publishers distributed by Kennerley. Only the first Kennerley printings are noted. If a book was dated on its title page, that date is provided here; but if a book was not dated on its title page, an inferred year is provided in brackets. However, a book may have actually appeared in the year before or the year after the title-page date. Asterisks identify books not seen by the compiler.

Abercrombie, Lascelles. *Speculative Dialogues*. 1913.
———. *Thomas Hardy A Critical Study*. 1912. Critical Biographies Series.
Adams, Francis. *Songs of the Army of the Night and The Mass of Christ*. New and revised edition. 1910.
Akins, Zoë. *Interpretations A Book of First Poems*. 1912.
———. *Papa An Amorality in Three Acts*. 1913. Modern Drama Series.
Andrews, Edward. *Napoleon and America*. . . . 1909.
Andreyev, Leonid. *Savva, The Life of Man: Two Plays*, trans. with introduction by Thomas Seltzer. 1914. Modern Drama Series.
Anon. *Altogether Jane by herself*. 1914.

Anon. *Elbow Lane by the author of "Altogether Jane."* 1915.

Anon. *English Nature Poems.* [1907]. Little Classics Series.†

Anon. *The Laws of American Divorce by a Lawyer.* 1912.

Anon. *Love Letters of St. John.* 1917.

Anon. *Modern Love An Anthology.* 1906.

Anon. *Thysia An Elegy.* 1910.

Apuleius. *The Golden Asse,* trans. William Adlington with introduction by Thomas Seccombe. 1913.

Arms, Mary W. *Italian Vignettes.* 1909.

Atkin, G. Murray. *Flowers of the Wind.* 1919.

Bacon, Josephine Daskam. *The Twilight of the Gods.* 1915.

Bailey, John C. *The Claims of French Poetry Nine Studies in the Great French Poets.* 1909.

[Barker, Elsa.] *Last Letters from the Living Dead Man written down by Elsa Barker.* 1919.

———. *Letters from a Living Dead Man written down by Elsa Barker.* 1914.

———. *Songs of a Vagrom Angel written down by Elsa Barker.* 1916.

———. *War Letters from the Living Dead Man written down by Elsa Barker.* 1915.

Barker, Granville [Harley Granville-Barker]. *The Madras House A Comedy in Four Acts.* 1914.

———. *Three Plays by Granville Barker: The Marrying of Ann Leete, The Vosey Inheritance, Waste.* [1911].

———. *See Arthur Schnitzler.*

Barnesby, Norman. *Medical Chaos and Crime.* 1910.

———. *The Mother and the Child.* 1913.

Barton, Frank Townsend. *Terriers, Their Points and Management.* 1908.

Barzini, Luigi. *Pekin to Paris An Account of Prince Borghese's Journey Across Two Continents in a Motor-Car,* trans. L. P. De Castelvecchio; introduction by Prince Borghese. 1908.

Bates, W. O. *Jacob Leisler A Play of Old New York.* 1913.

Beale, Truxtun. *See Herbert Spencer.*

Beall, Dorothy Landers. *The Bridge and Other Poems.* 1913.

———. *Poems.* 1910.

Becque, Henry. *The Vultures, The Woman of Paris, The Merry-Go-Round: Three Plays,* trans. with introduction by Freeman Tilden. 1913. Modern Drama Series.

Bellamy, Francis, ed. *Effective Magazine Advertising 508 Essays About 111 Advertisements.* [1909].

---

† (The "Little Classics" series was also advertised as the "Little Omar Classics.")

Benson, Arthur Christopher. *Memoirs of Arthur Hamilton, B. A. of Trinity College, Cambridge Extracted from his letters and diaries with reminiscences of his conversation by his friend Christopher Carr of the same college.* 1907.

Bergstrom, Hjalmar. *Karen Borneman, Lynggaard & Co.: Two Plays,* trans. with introduction by Edwin Björkman. 1913. Modern Drama Series.

Berle, A. A. *The World Significance of a Jewish State.* 1918.

Berle, Lina Wright. *George Eliot and Thomas Hardy: A Contrast.* 1917.

Bigelow, John. *World Peace How War Cannot Be Abolished How it May Be Abolished.* 1916.

Björkman, Edwin. *Gleams A Fragmentary Interpretation of Man and his World.* 1912.

————. *Is There Anything New Under the Sun?* 1911.

————. *Voices of To-Morrow: Critical Studies of the New Spirit in Literature.* 1913.

Bland, Hubert. *The Happy Moralist.* [1907].

————. *Letters to a Daughter.* [1907].

Bojer, Johan. *The Power of a Lie,* trans. Jessie Muir with introduction by Hall Caine. [1909].

————. *Treacherous Ground,* trans. Jessie Muir. 1912.

Boole, Mary Everest. *The Forging of Passion into Power.* 1911.

Braby, Maud Churton. *Modern Marriage and How to Bear It.* 1909?*

Branford, Victor. *Interpretations and Forecasts: A Study of Survivals and Tendencies in Contemporary Society.* 1914.

Brennan, George H. *Anna Malleen.* 1911.

Bronson-Howard, George. *The Red Light of Mars Or A Day in the Life of the Devil A Philosophical Comedy.* 1913. Modern Drama Series.

Brooks, Van Wyck. *John Addington Symonds A Biographical Study.* 1914.

————. *The Wine of the Puritans A Study of Present-Day America.* 1909.

————. *The World of H. G. Wells.* 1915.

Brown, John Calvin. *Every American's Business The Tariff and the Coming Trade War.* 1916.

Brown, Kenneth. *Sirocco.* [1906].

Butler, Samuel. *The Fair Haven A Work in Defence of the Miraculous Element in our Lord's Ministry upon Earth . . . ,* ed. R. A. Streatfeild. 1914.

————. *The Humour of Homer and Other Essays,* ed. R. A. Streatfeild. 1914.

————. *The Note-Books of Samuel Butler,* ed. Henry Festing Jones. 1914.

Bynner, Witter. *The Little King.* 1914.

————. *The New World.* 1915.

————. *Tiger.* 1913.

———— & Arthur Davison Ficke. *Spectra A Book of Poetic Experiments* (as by Anne Knish and Emanuel Morgan). 1916.

————. *See* Euripedes.

Caffin, Caroline. *Vaudeville*, illus. Marius de Zayas. 1914.

Calderon, George & St. John Hankin. *Thompson A Comedy in Three Acts.* 1913.

Campbell, F. W. Groves. *Apollonius of Tyana A Study of his Life and Times*, introduction by Ernest Oldmeadow. [1909].

Carman, Bliss. *The Rough Rider and Other Poems*. 1909.

———— & Mary Perry King. *Daughters of Dawn A Lyrical Pageant or Series of Historic Scenes for Presentation with Music and Dancing.* 1913.

———— & Mary Perry King. *Earth Deities and Other Rhythmic Masques.* 1914.

Carpenter, Edward. *The Drama of Love and Death A Study of Human Evolution and Transfiguration.* 1912.

————. *The Intermediate Sex A Study of Some Transitional Types of Men and Women.* 1912.

————. *Intermediate Types Among Primitive Folk A Study in Social Evolution.* 1914.

————, ed. *Iolaus An Anthology of Friendship.* 1917.

————. *Love's Coming of Age A Series of Papers on the Relations of the Sexes.* 1911.

————. *Towards Democracy Complete in Four Parts.* 1912. Reprinted with introduction by Charles Vale, 1922.

Carrel, Frederic. *John Johns, A Portrait.* [1908].

————. *The Methods of Mr. Ames.* [1908].

Carter, Huntly. *The New Spirit in Drama & Art.* 1913.

————. *The Theatre of Max Reinhardt.* 1914.

Chambers, Julius. *News Hunting on Three Continents.* 1921.

————. *On a Margin A Novel.* [1908].

Cheney, Sheldon. *The New Movement in the Theatre.* 1914.

————. *The Open-Air Theatre.* 1918.

Clay, John Cecil & Oliver Herford. *Happy Days.* [1917].

Clayton, Joseph. *Leaders of the People Studies in Democratic History.* 1911.

Clifford, Mrs. W. K. *Plays: Hamilton's Second Marriage, Thomas and the Princess, The Modern Way.* 1910.

Coburn, Alvin Langdon. *Men of Mark.* London: Duckworth; New York: Mitchell Kennerley, 1913.

Colby, Bainbridge. *The Close of Woodrow Wilson's Administration and the Final Years.* 1930.

Cook, Frederick A. *My Attainment of the Pole. . . .* 1912.

Copping, Arthur E. *Gotty in Furrin' Parts.* [1909].

————. *Gotty and the Guv'nor . . .* , illus. Will Owen. [1908].

Cory, Vivian. *See* Victoria Cross.

Cory, Winifred. *See* Winifred Graham.

Cowan, Sada. *The State Forbids A Play in One Act.* 1915.

Cox, Marian. *Spiritual Curiosities.* 1911.

———. *Ventures in Worlds.* 1915.

[Cranston, Ruth]. *Ashes of Incense A Novel by the Author of Mastering Flame.* 1912.

———. *Mastering Flame A Novel.* 1912.

Cronau, Rudolf. *Our Wasteful Nation The Story of American Prodigality and the Abuse of Our National Resources.* [1908].

Cross, Victoria [Vivian Cory]. *Anna Lombard.* [1907].

———. *The Eternal Fires.* [1910].

———. *Five Nights.* [1908].

———. *A Girl of the Klondike.* [   ].

———. *Life of My Heart.* [   ].*

———. *Life's Shop Window.* [1907].

———. *Paula; A Sketch from Life.* [   ]. (Walter Scott edition with Mitchell Kennerley label on title page.)

———. *The Religion of Evelyn Hastings.* [1908].

———. *Six Chapters of a Man's Life.* [1908].

———. *Six Women.* [1906].

———. *To-morrow?* [   ]. (Walter Scott edition with Mitchell Kennerley label on title page.)

———. *The Woman Who Didn't.* [   ].

Davidson, John. *Fleet Street and Other Poems.* New York: Mitchell Kennerley; London: Grant Richards. 1909.

Davies, Arthur B. *The Etchings & Lithographs of Arthur B. Davies,* ed. Frederic Newlin Price. New York: Mitchell Kennerley; London: Morley & Mitchell Kennerley, Jr., 1929.

Dickens, Charles. *The Wisdom of Dickens,* ed. Temple Scott. [1911].

Donnay, Maurice. *Lovers: The Free Woman: They: Three Plays,* trans. with introduction by Barrett H. Clark, 1915. Modern Drama Series.

Dostoieffsky, Fedor. *Crime and Punishment: A Realistic Novel 1911.*

Drinkwater, John. *William Morris A Critical Study.* 1912. Critical Biographies Series.

Dunsany, Edward J. M. D. P., Lord. *Fifty-One Tales.* 1915.

———. *Five Plays: The Gods of the Mountain, The Golden Doom, King Argimenes and the Unknown Warrior, The Glittering Gate, The Lost Silk Hat.* 1914. Modern Drama Series.

Earle, Ferdinand, ed. *The Lyric Year One Hundred Poems.* 1912.

———. *Sonnets.* London: Elkin Mathews; New York: Mitchell Kennerley, 1910.

Eastman, Max. *Child of the Amazons And Other Poems*. 1913.

———. *Understanding Germany The Only Way to End War and Other Essays*. 1916.

Echegaray y Elizaguirre, Jose. *See* Charles Frederic Nirdlinger.

Ehrmann, Max. *The Wife of Marobius A Play*. 1911.

Ellis, Edith. *Mary Jane's Pa A Play in Three Acts*. 1914. Modern Drama Series.

Ellis, Mrs. Havelock [Edith M. Ellis]. *Love-Acre An Idyl in Two Worlds*, 1914.

———. *Three Modern Seers James Hinton—Nietzsche—Edward Carpenter*. 1910.

Euripides. *Iphigenia in Tauris*, trans. Witter Bynner. 1915.

Everyman A Morality Play, ed. Montrose J. Moses. [1908].

Falls, Cyril. *Rudyard Kipling A Critical Study*. 1915.

Ferguson, Charles. *The Great News*. 1915.

———. *The Religion of Democracy*, revised edition. 1911.

———. *The University Militant*. 1911.

Ficke, Arthur Davison. *An April Elegy*. 1917.

———. *The Breaking of Bonds A Drama of the Social Unrest*. 1915.

———. *The Man on the Hilltop And Other Poems*. 1915.

———. *Mr. Faust*. 1913. Modern Drama Series.

———. *Sonnets of a Portrait-Painter*. 1914.

———. *Sonnets of a Portrait-Painter and Other Sonnets*. 1922.

———. *See* Witter Bynner.

Figgis, Darrell. *Broken Arcs*. 1912.

———. *Shakespeare A Study*. 1912.

Finger, Charles J. *In Lawless Lands*. 1924.

Fish, Horace. *The Great Way A Story of the Joyful the Sorrowful the Glorious*. 1921.

———. *The Saint's Theatre A Novel*. New York: B. W. Huebsch & Mitchell Kennerley, 1924.

———. *Terassa of Spain*. 1923.

———. *The Wrists on the Door A Short Story*. New York: B. W. Huebsch & Mitchell Kennerley, 1924. Possibly distributed gratis.

Fitch, Clyde. *A Wave of Life A Novel*. [1909].

Fitzgerald, Edward, trans. *The Rubaiyat of Omar Khayyam*. [1907]. Little Classics.

Ford, Sewell. *Cherub Devine: A Novel*. [1909].

———. *Honk, Honk!! Shorty McCabe at the Wheel*, illustrated by F. Vaux Wilson. 1909.

———. *Just Horses*. 1910.

———. *Shorty McCabe*. [1906].

———. *Side-stepping with Shorty*, illustrated by Francis Vaux Wilson. [1908].

Fornaro, Carlo de. *Carranza and Mexico.* 1915.

———. *A Modern Purgatory.* 1917.

Frank, Florence Kiper. *The Jew to Jesus and Other Poems.* 1915.

Freeman, A. Martin. *Thomas Love Peacock A Critical Study.* 1911. Critical Biographies Series.

Furness, Edith Ellis. *See* Ellis, Edith.

Gambier Parry, Major Ernest. *"Murphy" A Message to Dog-Lovers.* 1912.

Gardner, Robert. *In the Heart of Democracy.* 1910.

Garrison, Theodosia. *The Earth Cry and Other Poems.* 1910.

———. *The Joy o' Life and Other Poems.* 1909.

Genthe, Arnold. *The Book of the Dance.* [1916].

———. *Isadora Duncan Twenty-Four Studies,* foreword by Max Eastman. 1929.

———. *Old Chinatown A Book of Pictures,* text by Will Irwin. 1913.

Giacosa, Giuseppe. *The Stronger: Like Falling Leaves: Sacred Ground: Three Plays,* trans. with introduction by Edith & Allan Updegraff. 1913. Modern Drama Series.

Goldmark, Pauline & Mary Hopkins. *The Gypsy Trail An Anthology for Campers.* 1914.

Goodman, Daniel Carson. *Hagar Revelly.* 1913.

———. *Unclothed A Novel.* 1912.

Goodnow, Elizabeth. *The Market for Souls.* 1910.

Goudy, Frederic W. *The Alphabet.* 1918.

———. *Elements of Lettering.* 1922.

Gould, Gerald. *My Lady's Book.* 1914.

———. *Poems.* 1912.

Gracie, Archibald. *The Truth About the Titanic.* 1913.

Graham, Winifred [Winifred Cory]. *Can a Man Be True?* 1915. Railroad Novels.

———. *The Enemy of Woman.* 1914.

———. *Mary.* 1910.

Grantham, F. *Life, Ideals and Death.* 1913. Enlarged edition: *The Book of Life and Death.* 1914.*

Gribble, Francis. *The Court of Christina of Sweden and the Later Adventures of the Queen in Exile.* 1913.

Hammerton, J. A. *George Meredith in Anecdote and Criticism.* New York: Mitchell Kennerley; London: Grant Richards, 1909.

Hammond, Josephine. *Everywoman's Road A Morality of Woman, Creator—Worker—Waster—Joy-Giver and Keeper of the Flame.* [1911].

Hankin, St. John. *Dramatic Works,* introduction by John Drinkwater, 3 v., 1912.

———. *See* George Calderon.

Harré, T. Everett. *The Eternal Maiden A Novel.* [1913].

Harris, Frank. *The Bomb.* 1909.

——. *Contemporary Portraits.* 1915.

——. *Great Days, a Novel.* 1914.

——. *The Man Shakespeare and his Tragic Life-Story.* 1909.

——. *Montes the Matador and Other Stories.* 1910.

——. *Unpath'd Waters.* [1913].

——. *The Women of Shakespeare.* 1912.

Harvey, Alexander. *The Toe and Other Tales.* 1913.

Haywood, John Campbell. *The Silver Cleek.* [1908].

Hazeltine, Horace. *The City of Encounters.* [1908].

Henderson, Archibald. *Interpreters of Life and the Modern Spirit.* 1911.

——. *Is Bernard Shaw a Dramatist? A Scientific, but imaginary Symposium in the neo-Socratic Manner.* . . . 1929.

Henham, Ernest George. *See* John Trevena.

Herford, Oliver. *See* John Cecil Clay.

——. *See* Ferenc Molnar.

Hergesheimer, Joseph. *The Lay Anthony A Romance.* 1914.

——. *Mountain Blood A Novel.* 1915.

Herrick, Robert. *Love Poems.* [1907]. Little Classics.

Herron, George D. *Germanism and the American Crusade.* 1918.

——. *The Greater War.* 1919.

——. *The Menace of Peace.* 1917.

——. *Woodrow Wilson and the World's Peace.* 1917.

Hichens, Robert. *The Green Carnation.* [1908].

Hind, C. Lewis. *"What's Freedom?" A Commentary on "Freedom" A Play by E. Lyal Swete and C. Lewis Hind.* 1918.

Hinton, James. *The Mystery of Pain A Book for the Sorrowful.* [1914].

Holley, Horace. *Bahaism The Modern Social Religion.* New York: Mitchell Kennerley; London: Sidgwick & Jackson. 1913.

——. *Creation Post-Impressionist Poems.* 1915.

——. *Divinations and Creation.* 1916.

——. *Read-Aloud Plays.* 1916.

Hooley, Arthur. *See* Charles Vale.

Hopkins, Mary. *See* Pauline Goldmark.

Housman, A. E. *A Shropshire Lad.* [1907]. Little Classics. Illustrated by William Hyde. [1908].

How, Louis. *See The Life of Lazarillo de Tormes.* . . .

Howe, P. P. *Dramatic Portraits.* 1913.

——. *J. M. Synge A Critical Study.* 1912. Critical Biographies Series.

——. *The Repertory Theatre A Record & a Criticism.* 1911.

Hudson, W. H. *Adventures Among Birds*. 1915.

[Hutchings, Emily Grant.] *Jap Herron A Novel Written from the Ouija Board*. 1917.

Hutchinson, A. S. M. *Once Aboard the Lugger—The History of George and his Mary*. [1909].

Ibsen, Henrik. *Peer Gynt: A Dramatic Poem*, trans. with introduction by R. Ellis Roberts. 1913. Modern Drama Series.

Ireland, Alleyne. *Joseph Pulitzer Reminiscences of a Secretary*. 1914.

Irwin, Will. *See* Arnold Genthe.

Jackson, Holbrook. *All Manner of Folk Interpretations and Studies*. 1912.

———. *The Eighteen Nineties A Review of Art and Ideas at the Close of the Nineteenth Century*. 1914.

———. *Platitudes in the Making Precepts and Advices for Gentlefolk*. London: D. J. Rider; New York: Mitchell Kennerley, 1911.

———. *Romance and Reality Essays and Studies*. 1912.

———. *Rudyard Kipling*. 1911.

Jap Herron. *See* Emily Grant Hutchings.

Jarintzov, N. *The Russians and their Language*. . . , preface by Nevill Forbes. 1916.

Johnson, Lionel. *Post Liminium: Essays and Critical Papers*, ed. Thomas Whittemore, 1912.

Johnson, William Samuel. *Nothing Else Matters A Novel*. 1914.

———. *Prayer for Peace and Other Poems*. 1915.

Kebbel, T. E. *Lord Beaconsfield and Other Tory Memories*. 1907.

Kehler, James Howard. *An Open Letter to the Nation with Regard to a Peace Plan*. 1915.

Keller, Elizabeth Leavitt. *Walt Whitman in Mickle Street*. 1921.

Kelly, Russell A. *Kelly of the Foreign Legion*. . . . 1917.

Kemp, Harry. *The Cry of Youth*. 1914.

———. *Judas*. 1913.

King, Mary Perry. *See* Bliss Carman.

Knish, Anne. *See* Witter Bynner.

Kremer, Ida. *The Struggle for a Royal Child Anna Monica Pia, Duchess of Saxony* . . . [1908].

Ladd, Frederic P. *One Fair Daughter A Story*. [1909].

———. *The Woman Pays*. [1908].

Lawrence, D. H. *Love Poems and Others*. 1913.

———. *Sons and Lovers*. 1913.

———. *The Trespasser*. 1912.

———. *The Widowing of Mrs. Holroyd A Drama in Three Acts*. 1914. Modern Drama Series.

Lawton, Frederick. *François-Auguste Rodin*. 1908.

Lee, Gerald Stanley. *The Air-Line to Liberty A Prospectus for All Nations*. 1918.

———. *Inspired Millionaires: A Forecast*. 3rd edition. 1911.

Lee, Vernon [Violet Paget]. *Sister Benvenuta and the Christ Child An Eighteenth-Century Legend*. [1907]. Little Classics.

Le Gallienne, Richard. *October Vagabonds*. 1910.

———. *Omar Repentant*. [1908].

———. *Orestes A Tragedy*. 1910.

Legouis, Emile. *Defense de la Poésie Française à l'usage des lecteurs Anglais*. 1912.

Level, Maurice. *The Grip of Fear*. 1911. Popular Fiction Series.

Leverson, Ada. *Tenterhooks*. 1912.

The Life of Lazarillo de Tormes and his Fortunes and Adversities . . ., trans. Louis How; introduction and note by Charles Philip Wagner. 1917.

Lindsay, Nicholas Vachel. *Adventures While Preaching the Gospel of Beauty*. 1914.

———. *General William Booth Enters into Heaven and Other Poems*. 1913.

Lippmann, Walter. *Drift and Mastery An Attempt to Diagnose the Current Unrest*. 1914.

———. *A Preface to Politics*. 1913.

Lloyd, John. *The Captain's Wife*. [1908].

Lowndes, Mrs. Belloc. *Studies in Wives*. [1910].

———. *The Uttermost Farthing*. [1909].

———. *When No Man Pursueth*. 1911.

Lowrie, Donald. *My Life in Prison*. 1912.

———. *My Life Out of Prison*. 1915.

McArthur, Peter. *The Prodigal and Other Poems*. 1907

McCabe, Joseph. *George Bernard Shaw A Critical Study*. 1914.

McComas, Ina Violet. *See* H. B. Somerville.

MacFall, Haldane. *The Splendid Wayfaring*. 1911.*

MacGill, Patrick. *Songs of the Dead End*. 1914.

Machar, J. S. *Magdalen*, trans. Leo Wiener, 1916. Slavic Translations Series.

Machen, Arthur. *Hieroglyphics A Note Upon Ecstasy in Literature*. 1913.

MacKaye, Percy. *The Civic Theatre in Relation to the Redemption of Leisure A Book of Suggestions*. 1912.

McKenzie, J. Hewat. *Spirit Intercourse Its Theory and Practice*. 1917.

Magoun, Jeanne Bartholow. *The Light*. 1911.

Manners, J. Hartley. *Hate with a Will to Victory*. 1918.

Mariett, Paul. *The Poems of Paul Mariett*. 1913.

Masefield, John. *Multitude and Solitude*. 1911.

————. *The Tragedy of Nan and Other Plays.* 1910.

Mason, Stuart. *A Bibliography of the Poems of Oscar Wilde.* 1908.

Maude, Joan. *Behind the Night-Light: The By-World of a Child of Three, described by Joan Maude and Faithfully Recorded by Nancy Price.* 1912.

Maunder, Edward Walter. *The Astronomy of the Bible An Elementary Commentary on the Astronomical References of Holy Scripture.* [1908].

Mauzens, Frederic. *The Living Strong-Box.* 1911.*

Melville, Herman. *Moby Dick or The Whale,* introduction by A. S. W. Rosenbach. 1929.

Meredith, George. *Modern Love,* introduction by Richard Le Gallienne. 1909.

Merrick, Leonard. *The Actor-Manager.* 1912.

————. *Conrad in Quest of his Youth An Extravagance of Temperament.* 1911.

————. *The Man Who Understood Women.* 1911.

————. *One Man's View.* 1913.

————. *The Position of Peggy.* 1911.

————. *This Stage of Fools.* 1913.

————. *"When Love Flies Out o' the Window."* 1914.

————. *Whispers About Women.* 1912.

Michell, Sir Lewis. *The Life and Times of the Right Honourable Cecil John Rhodes 1853–1902,* 2 vols. 1910.

Middleton, Richard. *The Day Before Yesterday.* 1913.

————. *The Ghost Ship and Other Stories,* introduction by Arthur Machen. 1913.

————. *Monologues.* 1914.

————. *Poems and Songs,* introduction by Henry Savage. 1913.

————. *Poems and Songs Second Series,* preface by Henry Savage. 1913.

Millay, Edna St. Vincent. *Aria da Capo A Play in One Act.* 1921.

————. *Renascence And Other Poems.* 1917.

————. *Second April.* 1921.

Modern Germany in Relation to the Great War By Various German Writers, trans. W. W. Whitelock. 1916.

Molnar, Ferenc. *The Devil,* adapted by Oliver Herford. [1908].

Monahan, Michael. *Adventures in Life and Letters.* 1912.

————. *An Attic Dreamer.* 1922.

————. *At the Sign of the Van Being the Log of the Papyrus with Other Escapades in Life and Letters.* 1914.

————. *Heinrich Heine.* 1911.

————. *Nova Hibernia Irish Poets and Dramatists of Today and Yesterday.* 1914.

Morgan, Emanuel. *See* Witter Bynner.

Moses, Montrose J. *Children's Books and Reading.* [1907].

———. *Henrik Ibsen The Man and his Plays.* [1908].
Muddock, J. E. Preston. *Pages from an Adventurous Life by "Dick Donovan."* 1907.
Müller, Johannes. *Hindrances of Life,* trans. F. F. Strecker. 1909.
Neihardt, John G. *A Bundle of Myrrh.* 1911.
———. *The Dawn-Builder.* 1911.
———. *Life's Lure.* 1914.
———. *Man-Song.* 1909.
———. *The Stranger at the Gate.* 1912.
Newte, Horace W. C. *The Lonely Lovers A Love-Story.* [1910].
———. *Sparrows The Story of an Unprotected Girl.* [1909].
Nirdlinger, Charles Frederic. *Four Short Plays: Look After Louise, an Everyday Tragedy; Big Kate, a Diplomatic Tragedy; The Real People, a Sawdust Tragedy; Aren't They Wonders? A Holiday Tragedy.* 1916.
———. *Just Off the Avenue A Play in Three Acts.* 1917.
———. *The World and his Wife . . . After the Verse of Jose Echegaray's El Gran Galeoto.* [1908].
Noguchi, Yone. *From the Eastern Sea.* New York: Mitchell Kennerley; Kamakura: Valley Press, 1910.
———. *Lafcadio Hearn in Japan . . . with Mrs. Lafcadio Hearn's Reminiscences,* 2nd edition. New York: Mitchell Kennerley; London: Elkin Mathews; Yokahama: Kelly & Walsh, 1911.
———. *The Pilgrimage.* New York: Mitchell Kennerley; London: Elkin Mathews, 1912.
O'Brien, Howard Vincent. *New Men for Old.* 1914.
O'Donovan, Gerald. *Father Ralph.* 1914.
———. *Waiting.* 1915.
Ostrander, Isabel. *The Primal Law.* 1915.
Paget, Violet. *See* Vernon Lee.
Palmer, John Leslie. *The Censor and the Theatres.* 1913.
Parsons, Albert Ross. *The Road Map of the Stars . . . a Pocket Folding Chart of the Heavens. . . .* [1911].
Peer, Frank Sherman. *The Hunting Field with Horse and Hound in America, the British Isles and France.* 1910.
Phythian, J. E. *Burne-Jones.* [1909].
———. *Turner.* [1911].
Pratz, Claire de. *Elizabeth Davenay.* 1910?
Price, Frederic Newlin. *See* Arthur B. Davies.
Price, Nancy. *See* Joan Maude.
Putnam, Nina Wilcox. *Orthodoxy.* 1914.
Ransome, Arthur. *Edgar Allan Poe A Critical Study.* 1910. Critical Biographies Series.

————. *Oscar Wilde A Critical Study.* 1912. Critical Biographies Series.

Rathbone, Augusta. *French Riviera Villages*; acquatints by Augusta Rathbone, photographs by Juliet Thompson, text by Virginia Thompson. 1938.

Reed, Margery Verner. *Futurist Stories.* 1919.

Reynolds, Minnie J. *The Crayon Clue.* 1915.

Rice, Muriel. *Poems.* 1910.

Richardson, Frank. *2835 Mayfair A Novel.* [1907].

————. *Love: And All About It.* 1908.

————. *The Other Man's Wife.* [1908].

Rose, Heloise Durant. *Dante A Dramatic Poem.* 1910.

Rosenbach, A. S. W. *An Introduction to Herman Melville's Moby-Dick.* . . . 1924. Privately printed for Kennerley.

————. *The Unpublishable Memoirs.* 1917.

Rosenberg, James N. *The New Magna Carta.* 1918.

————. *Punchinello A Ballet.* 1923.

————. *The Return to Mutton.* 1916.

Rossetti, Dante Gabriel. *Early Poems.* [1907]. Little Classics.

Rozant, Ina. *Life's Understudies A Novel.* [1909].

Rutter, Frank. *James McNeill Whistler An Estimate & A Biography.* [1911].

————. *Dante Gabriel Rossetti Painter & Man of Letters.* [1908].

Saben, Mowry. *The Spirit of Life a Book of Essays.* 1914.

Saleeby, C. W. *Health, Strength and Happiness A Book of Practical Advice.* New York: Mitchell Kennerley; London; Grant Richards, 1908.

————. *Woman and Womanhood A Search for Principles.* 1911.

Saltus, Edgar. *Daughters of the Rich.* [1909].

————. *Historia Amoris A History of Love Ancient and Modern.* 1906.

————. *Imperial Purple.* 1906.

————. *The Lords of the Ghostland A History of the Ideal.* 1907.

————. *Mary Magdalen A Chronicle.* 1906.

————. *The Pomps of Satan.* 1906.

Sampter, Jessie E. *The Seekers,* introduction by Josiah Royce. 1910.

Savay, N. L. *The Science of Foreign Trade.* 1916.*

Scarfoglio, Antonio. *Round the World in a Motor-Car,* trans. J. Parker Heyes. New York: Mitchell Kennerley; London: Grant Richards, 1909.

Schnitzler, Arthur. *Anatol: A Sequence of Dialogues . . . Paraphrased for the English Stage by Granville Barker.* 1911.

————. *The Lonely Way: Intermezzo: Countess Mizzie Three Plays,* trans. with introduction by Edwin Björkman. 1915. Modern Drama Series.

Schoonmaker, Edwin Davies. *The Americans.* 1913.

Scott, Temple. *Frank Harris: The Man of To-day and To-morrow.* [1914]. Probably distributed gratis.

————. *The Pleasure of Reading.* 1909.

————. *The Pleasure of Reading the Bible.* 1909.

————. *See* Charles Dickens.

Sedgwick, S. N. *The Last Persecution.* London: Grant Richards; New York: Mitchell Kennerley, 1909.

Selborne, John. *The Thousand Secrets.* 1915. Railroad Novels.

Selincourt, Basil de. *Walt Whitman A Critical Study.* 1914. Critical Biographies Series.

Sherard, Robert H. *The Life of Oscar Wilde.* . . . 1906.

Shiffrin, A. B. *Mr. Pirate.* 1937.

Shipman, Louis Evan. *The True Adventures of a Play.* 1914.

Shorter, Dora Sigerson. *Sixteen Dead Men and Other Poems of Easter Week.* 1919.

Simonds, Frank H. *The Great War The First Phase.* . . . 1914.

————. *The Great War The Second Phase.* . . . 1915.

Simpson, Joseph. *Three Living Lions.* [1909].*

Sinclair, Upton. *The Fasting Cure.* 1911.

————. *Love's Pilgrimage A Novel.* [1911].

————. *Plays of Protest: The Naturewoman, The Machine, The Second-Story Man, Prince Hagen.* 1912.

[Smidovich, V. V.] *In the War: Memoirs of V. Veresaev,* trans. Leo Wiener. 1917. Slavic Translations Series.

Smith, Alexander. *Dreamthorp A Books of Essays Written in the Country.* 1907.

Somerville, H. B. [Ina Violet McComas]. *Ashes of Vengeance. A Romance of Old France.* 1914.*

The Song of Songs. 1907. Little Classics.*

Sotheran, Charles. *Horace Greeley and Other Pioneers of American Socialism.* 1915.

Spencer, Anna Garlin. *Woman's Share in Social Culture.* 1913.

Spencer, Herbert. *The Man Versus the State A Collection of Essays,* ed. Truxtun Beale, with Critical and Interpretative Comments by William Howard Taft, Charles W. Eliot. . . . 1916.

Stanley, Marion Cummings, ed. *The House of Birth.* 1915.*

Steele, Robert [R. A. Lindsay]. *One Man: A Novel.* 1915.

Stout, Charles Taber. *The Eighteenth Amendment and the Part Played by Organized Medicine.* 1921.

Strange, Michael. *Miscellaneous Poems.* 1916.

Street, G. S. *People and Questions.* 1910.

Street, Julian. *The Need of Change.* 1910.*

Stringer, Arthur. *Irish Poems.* 1911.

Swinburne, Algernon Charles. *Anactoria and Other Lyrical Poems.* 1906.

Swinnerton, Frank. *George Gissing A Critical Study.* 1912. Critical Biographies Series.

———. *R. L. Stevenson A Critical Study.* 1915.

Tabb, John Bannister. *Later Poems.* 1910.

Tchekhof, Anton. *Two Plays . . . The Seagull, The Cherry Orchard,* trans. with introduction by George Calderon. 1912.

Tennyson, Alfred Lord. *In Memoriam.* 1907.* Little Classics.

Thomas, Edward. *Algernon Charles Swinburne A Critical Study.* 1912. Critical Biographies Series.

———. *Walter Pater A Critical Study.* 1913. Critical Biographies Series.

Thompson, Juliet. *See Augusta Rathbone.*

Thompson, Vance. *French Portraits Being Appreciations of the Writers of Young France.* 1913.

———. *Verse . . . The Night Watchman and Other Poems.* 1915.

Thompson, Virginia. *See Augusta Rathbone.*

Thurston, E. Temple. *The Garden of Resurrection Being the Love Story of an Ugly Man.* 1911.

———. *The Greatest Wish in the World.* [1910].

———. *Sally Bishop A Romance.* [1910].

Titterton, W. R. *Me as a Model,* illustrated by Edmund Blampied. 1914.

Towne, Charles Hanson. *Beyond the Stars And Other Poems.* 1913.

———. *Manhattan.* 1909.

———. *The Quiet Singer And Other Poems.* 1914.

———. *Youth And Other Poems.* 1911.

Traubel, Horace. *With Walt Whitman in Camden* (March 28–July 14, 1888). 1915. (Reprint of 1906 Small, Maynard.)

———. *With Walt Whitman in Camden* (July 16, 1888—October 31, 1888). 1915. (Reprint of 1908 Appleton.)

———. *With Walt Whitman in Camden* (November 1, 1888—January 20, 1889). 1914.

Trevena, John [Ernest George Henham]. *Bracken A Novel.* 1911.

———. *Granite A Novel.* 1914.

———. *Matrimony.* 1915.

———. *Sleeping Waters A Novel.* 1914.

———. *Wintering Hay A Novel.* 1914.

Tyler, Royall. *Spain A Study of her Life and Arts.* New York; Mitchell Kennerley; London: Grant Richards, 1909.

Underwood, Edna Worthley. *The Garden of Desire Love Sonnets to a Spanish Monk.* 1913.

Underwood, John Curtis. *Literature and Insurgency Ten Studies in Racial Evolution . . .* 1914.

————. *Processionals.* 1915.

Upward, Allen. *Lord Alistair's Rebellion.* 1910.

————. *The New Word An Open Letter addressed to the Swedish Academy in Stockholm on the meaning of the word Idealist.* 1910.

Vale, Charles [Arthur Hooley]. *John Ward, M.D.* 1913.

————. ed. *Forum Stories.* 1914.

Van Eeden, Frederik. *The Bride of Dreams,* trans. Mellie von Auw. 1913.

————. *The Quest,* trans. Laura Ward Cole. 1911.

Viereck, George Sylvester. *Songs of Armageddon And Other Poems.* 1916.

Voute, Emile. *The Passport.* 1915.

Wagstaff, Blanche Shoemaker. *Atys A Grecian Idyl and Other Poems.* 1909.

————. *The Book of Love.* 1917.

Wales, Hubert. *The Old Allegiance.* [1908].

Wayne, Charles. *See* Horace Hazeltine.

Wells. H. G. *The Door in the Wall and Other Stories,* with photos by Alvin Langdon Coburn. 1911.

Wentworth-James, Gertie De S. *The Price.* 1911.

Westlake, Albert. *Baby's Teeth to the Twelfth Year.* 1912.

Weyl, Maurice. *The Choice.* 1919.

————. *The Happy Woman.* 1920.

White, Mary Blount. *Letters from Harry and Helen Written Down by Mary Blount White.* 1917.

White, W. Holt. *The Man Who Dreamed Right.* 1911. Railroad Novels.

Whitman, Walt. *Complete Prose Works.* 1914. "Library Edition" and "Popular Edition."

————. *Complete Leaves of Grass.* 1914. "India Paper Edition," "Library Edition," and two "Popular Editions."

Whitty, Michael J. *A Simple Study in Theosophy.* 1917.

Wilde, Oscar. *The Portrait of Mr. W. H. . . .* [1921].

Wilson, Rufus R., ed. *The Golden Year.* 1917.*

Wilson, Wood Levette. *The End of Dreams.* [1911].

Wing, J. Thurber, Jr. *Taliput Leaves in the Path of the Sunrise.* 1921.

Woods, Alice. *The Thicket A Novel.* 1913.

Wrench, G. T. *The Mastery of Life.* [1911].

Young, Filson. *The Lover's Hours.* 1907.* (Copies destroyed by fire.)

Zayas, Marius de. *See* Carolyn Caffin.

SOURCES AND
ACKNOWLEDGMENTS

Since many of Mitchell Kennerley's activities did not bear scrutiny, he preserved only the documents that he wanted to share with posterity. Although much of the personal record is irretrievable, there is ample evidence for reconstructing Kennerley's achievements as publisher and auction impresario. Regrettably, the archives of the Anderson Galleries have not survived.

The best account of the American auction business is Wesley Towner's *The Elegant Auctioneers* (New York: Hill & Wang, 1970), which focuses on the American Art Association and Parke-Bernet galleries. I am obligated to this book; but since it is undocumented, I have performed my own research. I have also had access to Laurence Gomme's unpublished biographical sketch of Mitchell Kennerley. (This short work was commissioned by Kennerley's former wife after his death, but Morley and Mitchell Kennerley, Jr., decided against publication.) Drafts of my book were vetted by two of the best bookmen I know, Charles Mann and William Cagle. This study of a publisher received support from two distinguished publishers, William Jovanovich and Julian Muller.

Judith Baughman improved this book in hundreds of ways. My research assistants—Daniel Henson, Matt Brook, Anne Little, and Mark Dolan—brought back the answers. I am grateful to Dr. George Geckle, chairman of the University of South Carolina English Department, and Dr. Robert Oakman for providing research aid.

Daniel Boice, Jan Squire, Dana Rabon, and Susan Bradley of the Thomas Cooper Library, University of South Carolina, performed prodigious interlibrary loan services on my behalf.

It is difficult to single out individuals for special acknowledgment, but the following were extraordinarily helpful: William Cagle (Lilly Library, Indiana University), Nancy S. MacKechnie (Vassar College Library), Charles Mann (Penn State University Library), Dr. Michael Rhodes (Westfield College, University of London), Anastasio Teodoro (New York Public Library), and Thomas M. Whitehead (Samuel Paley Library, Temple University).

Readers of my previous biographies will be prepared to find a great deal of evidence imbedded in the text of this one. Here I have provided a concentration of details to establish the record of Kennerley's manifold activities. The following people and institutions helped me to find the facts: Dr. Lucile F. Aly (University of Oregon), Nicholas Barker (British Library), Kathryn L. Beam (University of Michigan Library), Wendy Belsky (Harper & Row), Edmund Berkeley, Jr. (Alderman Library, University of Virginia), Dr. Beatrice B. Berle, Elise Bernier-Feeley (Forbes Library), Dr. D. M. R. Bentley (University of Western Ontario), Carol Bickler (Stanford University Library), John Bidwell (Clark Library, University of California at Los Angeles), William F. Boni (Readex Microprint Corp.), Thomas Boss, Michael Bott (University of Reading Library), Christopher Bready, Mrs. James Brennan, Dr. Lisa Brower (Vassar College Library), Andreas Brown, Josephine Bruccoli, Mary Bruccoli, Helen S. Butz (University of Michigan Library), Herbert Cahoon (Pierpont Morgan Library), Joseph Caldwell, Nicholas Callaway, Josephine Young Case, C. E. Frazer Clark, Douglas Clark, Herman Cohen, J. Michael Courtney, Joan Crane (Alderman Library, University of Virginia), Kenneth Craven (Harry Ransom Humanities Research Center), Anthony M. Cucchiara (Bryant Library), Elena S. Danielson (Hoover Institute, Stanford University), Dr. John Dann (Clements Library, University of Michigan), Richard Dougherty (University of Michigan Library), Ellen Dunlap (Rosenbach Museum & Library), Maggie Donovan DuPriest, Viscountess Mary Eccles, J. M. Edelstein (National Gallery of Art), Dr. William Emerson (Franklin Delano Roosevelt Library), Dr. Charles E. Feinberg, Barbara A. Filipac (Brown University Library), Quentin Fiore, Mary Flagg (University of New Brunswick Library), John F. Fleming, Dr. Ian Fletcher (University of Arizona), Stephen W. Foster, Valerie Franco (Huntington Library), Dr. W. E. Fredeman (University of British Columbia), Francis J. Gagliardi (Central Connecticut State University Library), Donald Gallup, Elmer Gertz, Paul Gitlin, William J. Glick, Millicent Godfrey, Lucien Goldschmidt, Walter Goldwater, Douglas Gordon, Mrs. Leo Greenebaum, H. Pearson Gundy, Gladys Haddad (Lake Erie College), Dr. George Haimbaugh (University of South Carolina School of Law), Irving Halpern, J. C. Harriman, Diana Haskell (Newberry Library), Cathy Henderson (Harry Ransom Humanities Research Center), Dr. James Hepburn (Bates College), Mrs. Peter S. Hitchcock, Marion

Caming Hoeflich, Kathleen Humphreys, James H. Hutson (Library of Congress), H. Montgomery Hyde, Dr. Herbert H. Johnson (Rochester Institute of Technology), Waring Jones, John S. Kebabian, John M. Kelly (University of Southern Mississippi Library), David Mitchell Kennerley, Mary Kennerley, Michael Kennerley, Mrs. Mitchell Kennerley, Jr., Mrs. Richard Kennerley, David Kirshenbaum, Dr. Joe W. Kraus (University of Illinois Libraries), Clinton Krauss, Hyman Kritzer, Daniel Leab, Dr. Felice F. Lewis, Sue Davidson Lowe, Dr. Maxwell Luria, Clarke W. McCants, Jr., Dr. Marcus McCorison (American Antiquarian Society), Garnett McCoy (Archives of American Art), Mrs. Dolley Madison McKinney, Jerald Maddox (Library of Congress), Alexandra Mason (University of Kansas Library), Stephen Massey, Dr. William J. Matheson (Library of Congress), Mary Maynard (Chatham Public Library), Peter Michel (Missouri Historical Society), Betty Kern Miller, Mrs. Harry T. Moore, Dr. Ruth Mortimer (Smith College Library), Timothy D. Murray (Washington University Library, St. Louis), Dorothy Norman, Jeri Nunn (Oral History Collection, Columbia University), Helen McK. Oakley, David Pankow (Rochester Institute of Technology), Stephen Parks (Beinecke Library, Yale University), Dr. Max Putzel, Nora J. Quinlan (University of Colorado at Boulder Library), Toby Quitslund, Dr. B. L. Reid (Mt. Holyoke College), Richard S. Reid (Belmont, the Gari Melchers Memorial Gallery), Irving F. Rigby, Martha Riley (St. Louis Public Library), Randy Roberts (University of Missouri Library), Anthony Rota, Carol A. Rudisell (Stanford University Library), Frederick G. Rudge, William Runge (Alderman Library, University of Virginia), Virginia Rust (Huntington Library), Dr. Nicholas Salerno (Arizona State University), Richard P. Scharchburg (General Motors Institute Alumni Foundation Historical Collection), David E. Schoonover (Beinecke Library, Yale University), Dr. Horst Schroeder (Technische Universität Braunschweig), Elaine Seaton (Bryant Library), A. B. Shiffrin, Bruce N. Shyer, Jr., Hobart O. Skofield, Timothy d'Arch Smith, Colin Smythe, Shirley C. Spragge (Queen's University Library), Frances Steloff, John Stinson (New York Public Library), Roger Stoddard (Houghton Library, Harvard University), W. A. Swanberg, Dr. Lola Szladits (Berg Collection, New York Public Library), Sen. Strom Thurmond, Sara Timby (Stanford University Library), V. Tyrrell (City Central Library, Stoke-on-Trent), Peter Van-Wingen (Library of Congress), Carol Venaleck, Peter Viereck (Mt. Holyoke College), Richard J. Walsh, Jr., Keith Walter, Dr. Stanley Weintraub (Penn State University), Dr. Bernard A. Weisberger, Dr. Neda Westlake (University of Pennsylvania Library), Dr. William White (Oakland University), Alden Whitman, R. Wilbur, Dr. Patricia Willis (Rosenbach Museum & Library), Ian Willison (British Library), Galen R. Wilson (Clements Library, University of Michigan, David Wooters (George Eastman House).

NOTES

INTRODUCTION

1. Laurence Gomme memoir. Samuel Paley Library, Temple University, and Bruccoli Collection.
2. Christopher Morley to Morley Kennerley, 22 February [1950]. Courtesy of Morley and Jean Kennerley.

CHAPTER ONE

1. "Kennerley, Expert On Art, Found Dead," *New York Times* (23 February 1950), 28.
2. *Sketches for Autobiography*, ed. James Hepburn (London: Allen & Unwin, 1979), p. 38.
3. MK to Dorothy Gordon, 19 June 1942. Harry Ransom Humanities Research Center, University of Texas at Austin.
4. "Publishing Then and Now," TS. Courtesy, Vassar College Library. *See also* J. Lewis May, *John Lane and the Nineties* (London: John Lane The Bodley Head, 1936) and James G. Nelson, *The Early Nineties: A View From the Bodley Head* (Cambridge: Harvard University Press, 1971).
5. MK to Grant Richards, 4 September 1945. Harry Ransom Humanities Research Center, University of Texas at Austin.
6. Hutton to Laurence Gomme, 19 December 1956. Bruccoli Collection.
7. *Along the Trail* (Boston: Small, Maynard, 1898), p. 92.

8. H. Pearson Gundy, "Kennerley on Carman," *Canadian Poetry*, #14 (Spring–Summer 1984), 69–74.
9. This copy is at the Vassar College Library. Kennerley also produced a keepsake of the poem.
10. "Kennerley on Carman," 69–74.
11. *Poems by Bliss Carman* (Boston: Page, 1915), p. 197.
12. *Reedy's Mirror*, 29 (5 August 1920), 607. *See* Max Putzel, *The Man in the Mirror: William Marion Reedy and his Magazine* (Cambridge: Harvard University Press, 1963).
13. Christopher Morley, *John Mistletoe* (Garden City: Doubleday, Doran, 1931), p. 320.
14. "Recollections of Thomas Bird Mosher" (5 September 1923).
15. MK to Mosher, 21 April 1897. By permission of the Houghton Library, Harvard University.
16. MK to Mosher, n.d. By permission of the Houghton Library, Harvard University.
17. MK to Mosher, 17 May 1897, 4 June 1897, 6 June 1897. By permission of the Houghton Library, Harvard University.
18. Alfred A. Knopf, "Notes of a luncheon April 14th, 1964 with T. M. Cleland and Laurence Gomme (28 May 1964)." Courtesy of Alfred A. Knopf. Hereafter cited as Knopf Notes.
19. W. D. Orcutt to Lane. John Lane Papers, University of London. The Lane Papers were auctioned at Sotheby's, London, 18 December 1985.
20. John Lane Papers, University of London.
21. John Lane Papers, University of London.
22. 14 December 1920. John Lane Papers, University of London.
23. In 1946 Kennerley wrote a memo on his association with *The Smart Set* in a copy of Burton Rascoe's *Smart Set History* (New York: Reynal & Hitchcock, 1934). This volume is in the University of Michigan Library.
24. Knopf Notes.
25. *Cleveland Plain Dealer* (15 December 1901), part 3, p. 2.

CHAPTER TWO

1. MK to Joe W. Kraus, n.d. Courtesy of Joe W. Kraus.
2. *The Reader*, 1 (November 1902), 99.
3. "Death Calls J. H. Morley," *Cleveland Plain Dealer* (22 June 1903), 1. Last will and testament of Jesse H. Morley, 25 February 1903, Cuyahoga County Probate Court.
4. Dr. H. S. Fuller Library; and other property. Merwin, 26 February 1907, item 140.

5. 1908. Courtesy of Mary Kennerley.
6. *Publishers' Weekly* ad, 69 (12 May 1906), 1386.
7. *Publishers' Weekly* ad, 69 (16 June 1906), 1690.
8. Christopher Morley, "The Bowling Green," *New York Post* (undated clipping).
9. Courtesy, Vassar College Library.
10. MK memo on Saltus. Rare Books and Manuscripts Division, The New York Public Library, Astor, Lenox and Tilden Foundations.
11. *Publishers' Weekly*, 71 (11 May 1907), 1509.
12. "Muck and Mysticism," 19 (26 May 1910), 16–17.
13. The Archives of Grant Richards, 1897–1948. Microfilm. Cambridge: Chadwyck-Healy.
14. *Publishers' Weekly*, 72 (5 October 1907), 1026.
15. Laurence Gomme, "My First Fifty Years in New York," *Antiquarian Bookman*, 22 (10 November 1958), 1587–1590; "The Little Book-Shop Around the Corner," *The Colophon*, 2 (Autumn 1937), 573–93.
16. A draft of Rider's unfinished autobiography, "Adventures with Frank Harris," is in the University of Reading Library.
17. Courtesy, Vassar College Library.
18. *Scenes and Portraits* (New York: Dutton, 1954), p. 159.
19. Gomme memoir.
20. MK to Randolph G. Adams, 30 April 1944. Clements Library, The University of Michigan.
21. MK to R. H. Hathaway, 18 October 1919. University of New Brunswick Library.
22. Courtesy, Vassar College Library.
23. MK to Dorothy Gordon, n.d. Harry Ransom Humanities Research Center, University of Texas at Austin.
24. Frank Harris to MK, 19 July 1909. Courtesy, Vassar College Library.
25. MK to Frank Harris, 20 August 1909. Harry Ransom Humanities Research Center, University of Texas at Austin.
26. American Literary Authors Collection, The Department of Rare Books and Special Collections, The University of Michigan Library.
27. Frank Harris to MK, 20 February 1909. Courtesy, Vassar College Library.
28. Memo. Bruccoli Collection.
29. Kennerley ad, *New York Times Review of Books* (15 December 1912), 773.
30. Lilly Library, Indiana University.
31. *Publishers' Weekly*, 82 (7 December 1912), 2013.
32. 26 October 1909. *Frank Harris to Arnold Bennett Fifty-Eight Letters 1908–*

1910 (Merion Station, Pa.: Privately printed by the American Autograph Shop, 1936), p. 27.

33. *Publishers' Weekly* ad, 82 (14 December 1912), 2153.
34. Harry Ransom Humanities Research Center, University of Texas at Austin.
35. Courtesy, Vassar College Library.
36. Albert Boni Papers, Readex Microprint Corporation.
37. *Ibid.*
38. Courtesy, Vassar College Library.
39. *Papyrus*, Third Series, 1 (November 1910), 21.
40. *Forum* ad, unlocated.
41. Courtesy, Vassar College Library.
42. *New York Times Review of Books* (26 May 1912), 313–14.
43. Quoted from *The North American Review* in Kennerley's *New York Times Review of Books* ad (24 March 1912), 162.
44. 11 March 1910. Courtesy, Vassar College Library.
45. Courtesy, Vassar College Library.
46. 28 March 1910. The American Authors Collection (M122), Department of Special Collections, The Stanford University Libraries.
47. *The Autobiography of Upton Sinclair* (New York: Harcourt, Brace & World, 1962), p. 176.
48. "Kennerley Type: The Circumstances which Brought about its Conception," *Monotype* (Special Kennerley Issue), #70 (May 1924), 5–7.
49. "An Englishman's Comment on Kennerley Type," *A Note on Letter-Design & The Village Types* (December 1915).
50. 26 April 1912. The Archives of Grant Richards.

CHAPTER THREE

1. "Emilie Busbey Grigsby Dead: American Hostess in England," *New York Times* (14 February 1964), 29; "Miss Emilie Grigsby," *London Times* (12 February 1964), 15.
2. "Grigsby Sale Books Are Under Question"; "Never Gave Books to Miss Grigsby"; "More Flyleaf Writing"—January 1912 clippings in *New York World-Telegram* morgue, University of South Carolina.
3. "Novels Bad, Half Bad and Very Bad," *The Smart Set*, 38 (November 1912), 156.
4. Christopher Morley, *Ex Libris Carissimis* (Philadelphia: University of Pennsylvania Press, 1932), pp. 86–88. "Earle's Affinity Hides Her Identity," *New York Times* (4 September 1907), p. 1; "Earle Makes Plea to Be Understood," *New York Times* (7 September 1907), 1; "Husband Beat

Her, Says Mrs. Earle," *New York Times* (14 September 1907), 1; "Earle Put in Jail, Beat His Affinity," *New York Times* (26 August 1908), 1; "Earle Boastful at Kidnapping Trial," *New York Times* (7 March 1914), 3; "F. P. Earle Guilty; Escapes With Fine," *New York Times* (8 March 1914), 1.

5. *Publishers' Weekly*, 82 (14 December 1912), 2153.
6. "The Lyric Year," *Forum*, 49 (January 1913), 91–106.
7. 18 April 1912. *Letters of Edna St. Vincent Millay*, ed. Allan Ross Macdougall (New York: Harper, 1952), pp. 39–40.
8. Courtesy, Vassar College Library.
9. 18 July 1913. Henry W. and Albert A. Berg Collection, The New York Public Library, Astor, Lenox and Tilden Foundations.
10. *New York Times Review of Books* (28 September 1913), 504.
11. *New York Times Review of Books* (22 February 1914), 85.
12. 7 April 1913. Rare Books and Manuscripts Division, The New York Public Library, Astor, Lenox and Tilden Foundations.
13. 5 October 1913. *The Letters of D. H. Lawrence*, ed. George J. Zytaruk and James T. Boulton (Cambridge: Cambridge University Press, 1981), Vol. II, pp. 80–81.
14. 18 September 1914. *Ibid.*, Vol. II, pp. 216–17.
15. Bynner, *Journey with Genius* (New York: Day, 1951), p. 300.
16. *New York Times* (27 December 1914), VIII, 3.
17. 2 July 1913. Courtesy of The Huntington Library, San Marino, Cal.
18. MK to Vachel Lindsay, 5 April 1913. Alderman Library, University of Virginia.
19. Eleanor Ruggles, *The West-Going Heart* (New York: Norton, 1959), pp. 206–207.
20. Christopher Morley to Morley Kennerley, 22 February [1950]. Courtesy of Morley and Jean Kennerley.
21. Vachel Lindsay to his family, 19 July 1914. *Letters of Vachel Lindsay*, ed. Marc Chenetier (New York: Burt Franklin, 1979), pp. 100–103.
22. MK to Vachel Lindsay, 23 September 1914. Alderman Library, University of Virginia.
23. Memo on MK's funeral. Courtesy of Morley and Jean Kennerley.
24. Christopher Morley to Morley Kennerley, 22 February [1950]. Courtesy of Morley and Jean Kennerley.
25. Courtesy, Vassar College Library.
26. MK to Randolph G. Adams, 9 July 1943. Clements Library, University of Michigan.
27. Max Eastman, *Enjoyment of Living* (New York: Harper, 1948), pp. 384, 397, 541–42.

28. Quoted from *The Outlook* in Kennerley's ad for *Drift and Mastery*, *New York Times Review of Books* (22 November 1914), 512.

29. Lippman to Brooks, 20 September 1916. Special Collections, Van Pelt Library, University of Pennsylvania.

30. P. 169.

31. Kennerley ad, *New York Times Review of Books* (25 May 1913), 318.

32. 84 (23 August 1913), 529.

33. "Arrest Kennerley on Comstock Writ," *New York Times* (24 September 1913), 6.

34. *Ibid.*

35. " 'Hagar' Foe To Vice Says Book's Author," unidentified clipping.

36. 22 (3 October 1913), 3.

37. United States v. Kennerley (District Court, S. D. New York. December 1, 1913). 209 *Federal Reporter*, pp. 119–21. "Court Is Liberal In Sex Discussion," *New York Times* (3 December 1913), 11.

38. "$50 For Selling Novel," *New York Times* (30 December 1913), 4.

39. "Judge Bars Experts on 'Hagar Revelly,' " *New York Times* (6 February 1914), 6.

40. "Writers Turn Out For Book Trial," *New York Times* (7 February 1914), 9.

41. "Acquit Kennerley in Sex Novel Case," *New York Times* (10 February 1914), 4.

42. *Ibid.*

43. " 'Hagar Revelly' Not Immoral, Says Jury," *Publishers' Weekly*, 85 (14 February 1914), 515–16.

44. Huebsch to MK, 1 October and 9 October 1913. Manuscript Division, Library of Congress.

45. "The Kennerley Case," *Publishers' Weekly*, 85 (14 February 1914), 521.

46. "Author Goodman Sues Publisher for $20,575," unidentified clipping.

47. MK to Quinn. Rare Books and Manuscripts Division, The New York Public Library, Astor, Lenox and Tilden Foundations.

48. MJB interview with Alfred A. Knopf, 16 August 1983. Hereafter cited as Knopf Interview.

49. Knopf Interview.

50. *The Elegant Auctioneers* (New York: Hill & Wang, 1970), p. 299.

51. *Publishers' Weekly*, 85 (5 December 1914), 1886.

52. Invoice. Pierpont Morgan Library.

53. Knopf Interview.

54. Alfred A. Knopf transcription. Oral History Program, Columbia University.

55. *Ibid.*

56. Knopf Interview.
57. Alfred A. Knopf transcription.
58. 18 March 1914. University of Pennsylvania Library.
59. 25 March 1914. *The Letters of Theodore Dreiser A Selection*, ed. Robert H. Elias (Philadelphia: University of Pennsylvania Press, 1959), Vol. I, p. 164.
60. 27 March 1914. *Letters of H. L. Mencken*, ed. Guy J. Forgue (New York: Knopf, 1973), p. 44.
61. 19 May 1914. John Lane Papers, University of London.
62. Carman to MK, 19 July 1914. *Letters of Bliss Carman*, ed. H. Pearson Gundy (Kingston & Montreal: McGill-Queen's University Press, 1981), p. 213.
63. 5 May 1914. Harry Ransom Humanities Research Center, University of Texas at Austin.
64. Courtesy, Vassar College Library.
65. "Mush for the Multitude," *The Smart Set*, 44 (December 1914), 307–308.
66. *Forum* ad, unlocated.
67. 10 September 1915. Charles E. Feinberg Whitman Collection, Library of Congress.
68. "Preface," *Forum Stories*.
69. "Here Are Novels!" *The Smart Set*, 46 (June 1915), 290–93.
70. "Portrait of an Immortal Soul," *Prejudices First Series* (New York: Knopf, 1919), 224–35.
71. *Ibid.*
72. Warburg Institute, London.
73. Pound to Quinn, n.d. Rare Books and Manuscripts Division, The New York Public Library, Astor, Lenox and Tilden Foundations.
74. Knopf Interview.
75. 21 May 1915. Copy. Harry Ransom Humanities Research Center, University of Texas at Austin.
76. A. Davidson to Alfred A. Knopf, 3 July 1917. Harry Ransom Humanities Research Center, University of Texas at Austin.

CHAPTER FOUR

1. *The Literary Collector*, 1 (1 November 1900), [49].
2. *Beautiful Bindings Rare And Fine Books Autograph Letters Valuable Manuscripts Being Duplicates and Selections from the Famous Libraries of Mr. Henry E. Huntington of New York and Mr. William K. Bixby of St. Louis With an Important Consignment of Rare Books on Early English*

Literature from the Estate of Mr. E. Dwight Church Formerly of Brooklyn To Be Sold March 29, 30, and 31, 1916.

3. John Edgar Burton Library. Part I: Lincolniana, 25 October 1915. Part III: miscellaneous books (#1172), 8 November 1915. Part IV: miscellaneous books (#1174), 17 November 1915. Part V: Civil War material (#1190), 12 January 1916. Part VI: Lincolniana and Civil War material (#1206), 6 March 1916.

4. John Boyd Thacher. Part VI: English autographs, F–M, 3 November 1915. Part VII: English autographs, N–Z, 10 January 1916.

5. Edwin W. Coggeshall Library. Part I: Dickens and Thackeray, 25 April 1916. Part II: Dickens and Thackeray letters and Thackeray manuscripts, 15 May 1916.

6. *John Mistletoe*, pp. 305–306.

7. 21 March 1916. The Archives of Grant Richards.

8. William Jay Smith, *The Spectra Hoax*. Middletown, Conn.: Wesleyan University Press, 1961.

9. "The Spectric School of Poetry," *The Forum*, 55 (June 1916), 675–78.

10. "The Spectric Poets," *The New Republic*, 9 (18 November 1916), 13.

11. "The Forum Exhibition," *The Forum*, 55 (April 1916), 457–71.

12. *The Forum Exhibition of Modern American Painters, March Thirteenth to March Twenty-Fifth 1916.* New York: Anderson Galleries, 1916.

13. 7 September 1924. Rare Books and Manuscripts Division, The New York Public Library, Astor, Lenox and Tilden Foundations.

14. 14 March 1916. Painesville, Ohio, Public Library.

15. Interview with MJB, April 1984.

16. To Christopher Morley, 15 March [1950]. Courtesy of Morley and Jean Kennerley.

17. James Carleton Young Library. Part I: inscribed books, nineteenth century (#1247), 15 November 1916. Part II: inscribed books, nineteenth century (#1258), 11 December 1916. Part III: inscribed books, nineteenth century (#1276), 14 February 1917. Part IV: inscribed books, nineteenth century (#1285), 12 March 1917. Part V: uninscribed books, nineteenth century, 11 April 1917.

18. Part I, item 933.

19. Part I, item 431.

20. H. V. Jones Library (#1250), 20 November 1916.

21. Frederic R. Halsey. Part I: Americana, naval prints, and New York views, 1 November 1916. Part II: sporting prints, 23 November 1916. Part III: French engravings of the eighteenth century, 11 December 1916. Part IV: eighteenth-century stipple engravings, 8 January 1917. Part V: English mezzotints, 5 February 1917. Part VI: nineteenth-century prints, 26 Feb-

ruary 1917. Part VII: old masters, 14 March 1917. Part VIII: Napoleon and French Revolution, 29 March 1917. Part IX: eighteenth-century French prints, 24 April 1917.

22. Henry E. Huntington Duplicates and Selections. French books (#1251), 21 & 22 November 1916.

23. *Selections and Duplicates, Part III From Mr. H. E. Huntington's Library Extraordinary Collection of Americana Comprising the Principal Part of the Famous Christie-Miller Collection . . .* (#1269), 24 & 25 January 1917.

24. *Rare and Fine Books Autograph Letters Valuable Manuscripts Being Duplicates and Selections from the Famous Libraries of Mr. Henry E. Huntington of New York and Mr. William K. Bixby of St. Louis . . .* (#1280), 26–28 February & 1 March 1917.

25. 2 January 1917. By permission of The Houghton Library, Harvard University.

26. 6 March 1917. Rare Books and Manuscripts Division, The New York Public Library, Astor, Lenox and Tilden Foundations.

27. Mary Desti, *The Untold Story* (New York: Liveright, 1929), p. 68.

28. "The Real Estate Field," *New York Times* (10 January 1917), 22.

29. To Christopher Morley, n.d. Harry Ransom Humanities Research Center, University of Texas at Austin.

30. Courtesy, Vassar College Library.

31. Quoted on dust jacket for *Second April.*

32. *New York Times Book Review* (9 December 1917), 546.

33. To Mrs. Cora B. Millay and Norma Millay, 22 September 1917. *Letters of Edna St. Vincent Millay,* pp. 73–75.

34. Christmas Day. Courtesy, Vassar College Library.

35. Unlocated clipping.

36. *New York Times Book Review* ad (11 December 1921), 19.

37. 29 October 1920. *Letters of Edna St. Vincent Millay,* pp. 102–104.

38. MK memo. American Literary Authors Collection, The Department of Rare Books and Special Collections, The University of Michigan Library.

39. *Publishers' Weekly,* 100 (9 July 1921), 102.

40. *Letters of Edna St. Vincent Millay,* p. 160.

41. Pp. 43–44.

42. To MK, 26 June 1916. Rare Books and Manuscripts Division, The New York Public Library, Astor, Lenox and Tilden Foundations.

43. "My Acquaintance with Jap Herron." Rare Books and Manuscripts Division, The New York Public Library, Astor, Lenox and Tilden Foundations.

44. "Latest Works of Fiction," *New York Times Book Review* (9 September 1917), 836.

45. "Spiritualism in Lawsuit," *New York Times* (28 July 1918), III, 3.
46. *Ibid.*
47. Henry W. and Albert A. Berg Collection, The New York Public Library, Astor, Lenox and Tilden Foundations.
48. 22 September 1917. Bruccoli Collection.
49. Carman to Irving Way, 16 October 1917. *Letters of Bliss Carman*, p. 250.
50. Gomme memoir.

CHAPTER FIVE

1. MK to Stieglitz, 22 May 1917. Collection of American Literature, Beinecke Rare Book and Manuscript Library, Yale University.
2. Pp. 323–326.
3. To Morley Kennerley, 22 February [1950]. Courtesy of Morley and Jean Kennerley.
4. 92 (6 October 1917), 1134.
5. *Catalogue Of Early and Modern English Literature Part IV of the Consignment of Selections and Duplicates from the Library of Mr. Henry E. Huntington of New York A Notable Collection Containing Many Books of the Greatest Rarity . . .* (#1308), 10 December 1917.
6. Henry E. Huntington. Americana (#1309), 11 December 1917.
7. Henry E. Huntington. Early and Modern English Literature (#1333), 4–6 February 1918.
8. Henry E. Huntington. Duplicates and selections. Part VIII: English literature (#1351), 24 April 1918.
9. Winston H. Hagen Library (#1352), 13–16 May 1918.
10. 31 May 1918. Grolier Club.
11. 20 January 1918. Courtesy, Vassar College Library.
12. 93 (2 February 1918), 320.
13. Henry E. Huntington. Duplicates and selections. Part IX: English literature (#1365), 6 November 1918.
14. Henry E. Huntington. Americana. Part X: Americana (#1406), 6 March 1919.
15. James Carleton Young. Inscribed books and manuscripts. Part I: (#1390), 15 January 1919. Part II: (#1398), 3 February 1919.
16. Herschel V. Jones Library. Part I: A–H (#1375), 2–3 December 1918. Part II: H–P (#1394), 29–30 January 1919. Part III: P–Z (#1405), 4–5 March 1919.
17. Edwin Wolfe II and John F. Fleming, *Rosenbach* (Cleveland & New York: World, 1960), p. 122.

18. Frederic R. Halsey, Henry S. Van Duzer, and others. Books and manu-scripts (#1401), 17 February 1919.
19. John W. R. Crawford Library (#1402), 24 February 1919.
20. *New York Times Book Review* (7 September 1919), 447.
21. MK to Huntington, 24 May 1921. Courtesy of The Huntington Library, San Marino, Cal.
22. Charles F. Heartman, *Twenty-Five Years in the Auction Business And What Now?* Privately printed, 1938.
23. Henry E. Huntington. Duplicates and selections. Part XI: English liter-ature (#1460), 28–29 January 1920. Part XII: *Early French Literature Mostly French Drama [From The Bridgewater Library] Early English Lit-erature and Americana* . . . (#1477), 11–12 March 1920.
24. Henry F. De Puy Library. Part I: A–E (#1440), 17–18 November 1919. Part II: F–N (#1458), 26–27 January 1920. Part III: N–Z (#1490), 19–20 April 1920.
25. Roland R. Conklin, Mrs. Mary E. Plummer, Henry H. Peck, and others. Books and manuscripts (#1462), 9 February 1920.
26. [William A. White]. Rarities in English literature and in other languages and Americana (#1464), 6 February 1920.
27. [Alfred T. White]. Seventy American historical nuggets (#1465), 6 Feb-ruary 1920.
28. H. Buxton Forman Library. Part I (#1480), 15–17 March 1920. Part II (#1493), 26–28 April 1920. Part III (#1516), 4–7 October 1920.
29. Charles F. Heartman, *George D. Smith. G. D. S. 1870–1920* (Beauvoir, Miss.: Book Farm, 1945), p. 18.
30. *Keats · Wilde · Morley · Rosenbach* (Philadelphia: Rosenbach Foundation, 1978). MK memo, 29 April 1940: "This reproduction was made from the original manuscript, which is now in the library of Mr. Frank Hogan." Rare Books and Manuscripts Division, The New York Public Library, Astor, Lenox and Tilden Foundations.
31. Walter T. Wallace Library. American Art Association, 22 March 1920.
32. John F. Fleming to MJB, 17 August 1983.
33. *The Oscar Wilde Collection of John B. Stetson, Jr.* . . . (#1484), 23 April 1920.
34. *Californiana* (#1468), 19 February 1920. *California And The Far West*, Part II (#1494), 29 April 1920.
35. *American Pioneer Life . . . Assembled During Twenty Years by Dr. Frank P. O'Brien* (#1500), 10 May 1920.
36. C. E. Graham to Huntington, 12 April 1923; MK to Huntington, 21 May 1923; Huntington to Graham, 21 May 1923; MK to Huntington, 21 May 1923; Graham to MK, 22 May 1923; MK to Huntington, 23 May 1923;

Huntington to Graham, 25 May 1923; MK to Huntington, 9 June 1923; MK to Graham, 11 June 1923; Graham to MK, 12 June 1923. Courtesy of The Huntington Library, San Marino, Cal.

37. *Purchases in London and Paris of the Late George D. Smith*, Part I (#1504), 24–25 May 1920.

38. "Two Rodins Bring $14,975 At Auction," *New York Times* (7 February 1920), 6.

39. *Ninety-Six Original Drawings By Auguste Renoir* . . . (#1489), 16 April 1920.

40. "Renoir Drawings Doubted," *New York Times* (14 April 1920), 8; "Brisk Bidding for Renoir Sketches," *New York Times* (17 April 1920), 16.

41. Mignon to MK, 26 May 1920. Rare Books and Manuscripts Division, The New York Public Library, Astor, Lenox and Tilden Foundations. Edwin L. James, "French Artist Says He Painted Pictures Recently Sold Here as Renoir's Works," *New York Times* (2 June 1920), 1.

42. "Mignon Claims Pictures Sold as Renoir's," *New York Herald Tribune* (3 June 1920), 9.

43. "A Neighborhood Bookshop," *Publishers' Weekly*, 98 (30 October 1920), 1323. MK to Gomme, 15 September 1920 and 11 March 1922. Bruccoli Collection.

44. "The Auction Season of 1920–1921: The Rare Book Experts Prophesy," *Publishers' Weekly*, 98 (2 October 1920), 995.

45. George D. Smith. Purchases and stock. Part II (#1527), 11 November 1920. Part III (#1550), 20 January 1921. Part IV (#1561), 23 February 1921. Part V: Autographs, manuscripts, and broadsides (#1565), 14 March 1921. Part VI: Selections from the library of the Newdigate family (Arbury Hall, Warwickshire) and other purchases (#1580), 28 April 1921. Part VII: Americana from the Arbury Library (#1585), 16 May 1921.

46. *George D. Smith*, pp. 29–30.

47. Edwin W. Coggeshall. Association books (#1525), 4 November 1920.

48. Herman Le Roy Edgar Library. Part I (#1534), 22–23 November 1920. Part II (#1552), 24–25 January 1921.

49. John L. Clawson. Later English literature (#1537), 29 November 1920.

50. Dr. Frank P. O'Brien. Part II: Books, tracts, broadsides, manuscripts, letters, documents (#1543), 13 December 1920.

51. William Loring Andrews. Maps, prints, books, and other Americana (#1571), 18 April 1921.

52. "Oscar Wilde's Lost Manuscript Found," *New York Times* (17 June 1921), 13; "Wilde Manuscript Unsolved Mystery," *New York Times* (19 June 1921), 6.

53. Courtesy, Vassar College Library.

54. "W. H. a Boy Actor, Wilde's Theory," *New York Evening Post* (20 June 1921), 7.
55. MK to Martin Secker, 9 February 1940. Donald and Mary Hyde Collection. H. Montgomery Hyde, "The Portrait of Mr. W. H.," *Times Literary Supplement* (5 December 1958), 705.
56. Horst Schroeder, *Oscar Wilde, The Portrait of Mr. W. H.—Its Composition, Publication and Reception.* Braunschweig: Technische Universität Carolo-Wilhelmina zu Braunschweig Seminar Für Anglistik und Amerikanistic, 1984; also Schroeder, *Annotations to Oscar Wilde, The Portrait of Mr. W. H.* Braunschweig: Privately printed, 1986.
57. Proof for "Horace Fish and 'The Great Way.'" New York Public Library. *See also The Wrists on the Door* (New York: B. W. Huebsch & Mitchell Kennerley, 1924), pp. 1–2.
58. 8 July 1940. Rare Books and Manuscripts Division, The New York Public Library, Astor, Lenox and Tilden Foundations.
59. *The Wrists on the Door*, p. 35.
60. *Ibid.*, p. 1.
61. Rare Books and Manuscripts Division, The New York Public Library, Astor, Lenox and Tilden Foundations.
62. n.d. Collection of American Literature, Beinecke Rare Book and Manuscript Library, Yale University.
63. *Publishers' Weekly*, 101 (20 May, 3 June, 10 June 1922), 1482, 1647, 1708.
64. 10 January 1921. Collection of American Literature, Beinecke Rare Book and Manuscript Library, Yale University.
65. 1921: Stieglitz photos. 1923: Stieglitz photos; O'Keeffe paintings. 1924: Stieglitz photos; O'Keeffe paintings. 1925: Seven Americans—Marin, O'Keeffe, Demuth, Dove, Hartley, Strand, Stieglitz—paintings and photos.
66. James N. Rosenberg and Marsden Hartley (#1586), 17 May 1921.
67. *The Artist's Derby* (23 February 1922).
68. 7 February 1924. Collection of American Literature, Beinecke Rare Book and Manuscript Library, Yale University.
69. The artists exhibited were John Marin, Arthur G. Dove, Georgia O'Keeffe, Charles Demuth, Gaston Lachaise, Oscar Bluemner, Peggy Bacon, Francis Picabia, Marsden Hartley, and Paul Strand.
70. *The Intimate Gallery . . . announces its Sixteenth Exhibition—Feb. 4 to March 16, 1929* FORTY NEW PAINTINGS BY GEORGIA O'KEEFFE. New York Public Library.
71. 9 September 1923. Rare Books and Manuscripts Division, The New York Public Library, Astor, Lenox and Tilden Foundations.

72. n.d. Collection of American Literature, Beinecke Rare Book and Manuscript Library, Yale University.
73. "Rockefeller Buys $1,100,000 Tapestry," *New York Times* (27 February 1923), 1; "$377,000 Tax Saved When Rockefeller Bought Tapestries," *New York Times* (2 March 1923), 1.
74. Frederick Corder and others. American Art Association. 26 January 1922.
75. Dr. R. T. Jupp. Dickens collection (#1629), 1 February 1922.
76. Henry Sayre Van Duzer. Thackerary library (#1629), 6 February 1922.
77. William G. Wilkins. Dickens collection (#1630), 13 February 1922.
78. *The West Its History & Romance Rare, Curious And Important Books, Pamphlets, Broadsides And Maps Relating To The Western States From The Ohio To The Pacific Including The Original Manuscripts of Sutter's Fort 1846–1847* (#1604), 28–29 November 1921.
79. *The Library of Dr. Frank P. O'Brien [Part III] The West And The Wilderness Including Many Of The Great Overland Narratives Rare and Important Maps Rare Prints and Views The Original MS. Surveys of Washington's Dismal Swamp Lands, 1763 and Swagerty's Foundation MS. Survey of Tennessee, 1795* (#1642), 27–28 March 1922.
80. *Publishers' Weekly*, 102 (11 November 1922), 1816.
81. To whom it may concern (copy), 7 July 1922. Courtesy of The Huntington Library, San Marino, Cal.
82. Theodore N. Vail Library (#1658), 2 May 1922.
83. Henry Cady Sturges Library. Part I: American literature (#1682), 20 November 1922. Part II: English literature (#1690), 11 December 1922. Part III: Americana (#1701), 15 January 1923.
84. Dr. Thomas A. Emmet, James S. Hardy, Mrs. Julie Le Gallienne, S. H. Taylor (#1691), 4 December 1922.
85. (#1686), 27–29 November 1922.
86. (#1698), 8–10 January 1923.
87. (#1699), 23 January 1923.
88. Archives of American Art.

CHAPTER SIX

1. *The Library of John Quinn.* Part I: A–C (#1768), 12–14 November 1923. Part II: D–H (#1783), 10–12 December 1923. Part III: I–M (#1794), 14–16 January 1924. Part IV: M–S (#1806), 11–13 February 1924. Part V: S–Z (#1820), 17–20 March 1924. See B. L. Reid, *The Man from New York: John Quinn and his Friends* (New York: Oxford University Press, 1968).
2. Unlocated clipping.

3. Part I, pp. 123–24.
4. Part I, p. 164.
5. Part III, pp. 485–86.
6. To Frederick A. Chapman, 14 November 1923. Rare Books and Manuscripts Division, The New York Public Library, Astor, Lenox and Tilden Foundations.
7. To Nelson Doubleday, 14 November 1923. Rare Books and Manuscripts Division, The New York Public Library, Astor, Lenox and Tilden Foundations.
8. To MK, 14 November 1923. Rare Books and Manuscripts Division, The New York Public Library, Astor, Lenox and Tilden Foundations.
9. G. Jean-Aubry, *Joseph Conrad: Life and Letters* (Garden City, N.Y.: Doubleday, Doran, 1927), II, p. 324.
10. Noel Riley Fitch, *Sylvia Beach and the Lost Generation* (New York: Norton, 1984), p. 121.
11. 28 February 1924. Rare Books and Manuscripts Division, The New York Public Library, Astor, Lenox and Tilden Foundations.
12. James Joyce to Harriet Weaver, 8 February 1924. *Letters of James Joyce*, ed. Stuart Gilbert (New York: Viking, 1957), I, pp. 210–11.
13. MK to John Quinn, 14 February 1924. Rare Books and Manuscripts Division, The New York Public Library, Astor, Lenox and Tilden Foundations. MK to A. S. W. Rosenbach, 4 March 1924. Rosenbach Museum and Library.
14. Richard Ellmann, *James Joyce* (New York: Oxford University Press, 1959), p. 570.
15. 15 May 1924. Rare Books and Manuscripts Division, The New York Public Library, Astor, Lenox and Tilden Foundations.
16. 1 October 1924. Courtesy of The Huntington Library, San Marino, Cal.
17. MK to Dr. William S. Thomas, 7 February 1924. Rare Books and Manuscripts Division, The New York Public Library, Astor, Lenox and Tilden Foundations.
18. Stephen H. Wakeman. Nineteenth-century American literature. American Art Association, 28 April 1924.
19. Mrs. Phoebe A. D. Boyle Library (#1772), 19 November 1923.
20. *Western Americana An Extraordinary Collection Dealing With The Local History And March Of Events In The Regions Lying Within The Ohio And Mississippi Valleys And Westward To The Pacific Ocean Embracing Pioneer Narratives, Frontier Exploration Indian Wars, Historical Annals, Memoirs of Early Settlement, Personal Relations Of The Empire Builders, Etc. Etc.* (#1781), 3–5 December 1923.
21. *The Magnificent Furnishings, Paintings And Objects Of Art Removed*

From The Residences Rockwood Hall, Tarrytown And 689 Fifth Avenue (#1777), 19 November 1923.

22. William W. Nolen Collection. Part I: Early American and Anglo-American furniture and objects of art (#1766), 29 October 1923. Part II: Washingtoniana, early American silver, American furniture, pewter (#1793), 7 January 1924. Part III: (#1813), 6 March 1924. Part IV: Currier & Ives prints (#1814), 4 March 1924.

23. Karl Freund. Furniture and objets d'art (#1809), 20 February 1924.

24. *Furniture & Objets D'Art From The Apartment Hotel Netherland, New York Of Karl Freund And the Remaining Objects From Mr. Freund's Exhibitions Of Interiors During The Last Two Years With Paintings & Objects Of Art From Sion House, Twickenham, England* [Part Two] *Early American Furniture From The Estate Of The Late Henry F. De Puy Easton, Maryland* . . . (#1941), 25–28 March 1925.

25. John J. Klaber, "On a Certain Bust of Washington," *Art and Archeology*, 7 (March-April 1918), 145–47; "Find Blackened Stone Is Washington's Bust, Carved by David and Lost in Fire in 1851," *New York Times* (19 August 1924), 1; *New York Herald Tribune* (21 August 1924), 7.

26. Rare Books and Manuscripts Division, The New York Public Library, Astor, Lenox and Tilden Foundations.

27. MK to Huntington, 7 August 1924; Huntington to MK, 8 August 1924. Courtesy of The Huntington Library, San Marino, Cal.

28. *Catalogue Of The William Harris Arnold Collection of Manuscripts, Books & Autograph Letters* . . . (#1873), 10–11 November 1924.

29. *The Library Of The Late Beverly Chew* [Part One] *English Literature Before 1800 Manuscript Horae Printed Horae* . . . (#1890), 8–9 December 1924.

30. *The Library Of The Late Beverly Chew* [Part Two] *English Literature After 1800 Presentation Copies Bibliography* (#1905), 5–7 January 1925.

31. Franklin D. Roosevelt and John Brenton Copp. Americana (#1901), 9 January 1925.

32. Franklin D. Roosevelt and others. Naval and marine prints and paintings (#1902), 9 January 1925.

33. Henry E. Huntington. Duplicates. English literature early and modern (#1884), 2 December 1924.

34. Henry E. Huntington. Duplicates. Americana (#1904), 12 January 1925.

35. Arthur Davison Ficke. Japanese print collection (#1915), 29 January 1925. Jade dragons, etc. (#1917), 29 January 1925.

36. Alfred E. Hippisley. Chinese porcelains (#1916), 30 January 1925.

37. *Publishers' Weekly*, 108 (28 June 1925), 249.

38. "A Woman's Bust by Jo Davidson," *International Studio*, 80 (March 1925), 499.

39. *Publishers' Weekly*, 108 (28 November 1925), 1779.

40. *The Autograph Collection Formed By The Late Col. James H. Manning . . . Part One American Autographs Comprising A Complete Collection Of The Signers Of The Declaration Of Independence A Complete Collection Of The Presidents Of The United States Letters And Documents From Noted Participants In The French and Indian War, American Revolution, War Of 1812, Mexican And Civil Wars, And Famous American Statesmen And Patriots* (#2026), 19–20 January 1925. *Part Two American, English & Continental Autographs Literary & Historical Including Royalty & The World War* (#2029), 1–3 February 1926.

41. Item 423.

42. (#2030), 8–9 February 1926.

43. *English Literature From the Library of Mr. R. B. Adam . . .* (#2032), 15–16 February 1926.

44. *The Gutenberg Bible The First Printed Book The Melk Copy . . .* (#2033), 15 February 1926.

45. Wire. MK to Huntington, 12 February 1926. Courtesy of The Huntington Library, San Marino, Cal.

46. Oliver Henry Perkins Library (#2047), 23–24 March 1926.

47. *The Fine Historical Library of Dr. George C. F. Williams . . . Part One A Most Comprehensive Collection of Books, Pamphlets And Broadsides Relating To The American Revolution Part Two Autographs, Manuscripts And Documents Relating To The Same Period Including a Complete Collection Of Autographs Of The Signers Of The Declaration of Independence* (#2075), 17–18 May 1926.

48. John L. Clawson. Part I: Alabaster-Massinger (#2077), 20–21 May 1926. Part II: May-Zouch (#2078), 24–25 May 1926.

49. 19 May 1925. Clark Library, University of California at Los Angeles.

50. 8 July 1926. Rare Books and Manuscripts Division, The New York Public Library, Astor, Lenox and Tilden Foundations.

51. Frederick M. Hopkins, "The World of Rare Books," *The Saturday Review of Literature*, 2 (12 June 1926), 863.

52. Rare Books and Manuscripts Division, The New York Public Library, Astor, Lenox, and Tilden Foundations.

53. "Transfer of Leverhulme Art to New York Will Cost $100,000 and Take Two Months," *New York Times* (26 September 1925), 6.

54. "Explains Disposal of Leverhulme Art," *New York Times* (30 September 1925), 13.

55. 19 October 1925. Collection of American Literature, Beinecke Rare Book and Manuscript Library, Yale University.
56. *The Art Collections Of The Late Viscount Leverhulme.* Part I (#2031), 9–13 February 1926. Part II (#2035), 17–19 February 1926. Part III (#2036), 20 February 1926. Part IV (#2037), 22–23 February 1926. Part V (#2038), 24–27 February 1926. Parts VI–VII (#2039), 2–4 March 1926.
57. "Leverhulme Art Brings High Prices," *New York Times* (10 February 1926), 15.
58. *New York Times* (11 February 1926), 7 (12 February 1926), 13 (13 February 1926), 16.
59. Harry Glemby Library (#2099), 15 November 1926.
60. Theodore Sedgwick. American autographs (#2100), 26 November 1926.
61. *New York Times* (27 November 1926), 17.
62. *The John Lane Collection Of Original Drawings By Aubrey Beardsley* (#2104), 22 November 1926.
63. A. Edward Newton (#2108), 29 November 1926.
64. Newton to Tinker, 2 December 1926, 8 January [1927]. Collection of American Literature, Beinecke Rare Book and Manuscript Library, Yale University.
65. *Autograph Manuscripts Of Lafcadio Hearn, Theodore Roosevelt, Henry James, Joseph Conrad Magnificent & Unique Nelson Collection Incunabula & Illuminated Manuscripts . . .* (#2110),16 December 1926.
66. *The American & English Autograph Collection of Mr. A. C. Goodyear* (#2130), 1–2 February 1927.
67. "Talking of Old Books," *Saturday Evening Post,* 199 (22 January 1927), 100.
68. Mrs. Wade Roberts, Mr. & Mrs. Earl J. Knittle, and other consignors (#2146), 16 March 1927.
69. "Gwinnett Letter Stored in Old Barn," *New York Times* (25 February 1927), 2; "Gwinnett Letter Is Sold For $51,000," *New York Times* (17 March 1927), 9.
70. *The Important American Library Formed By Dr. William C. Braislin . . . Books, Broadsides Maps, Pamphlets Relating To The Early Voyages To America The History Of The West Rare Indian Captivities Overland Narratives Tales of Pioneers, ETC.* Part I (#2149), 21–22 March 1927. Part II (#2156), 4–6 April 1927.
71. 9 September 1926. Collection of American Literature, Beinecke Rare Book and Manuscript Library, Yale University.
72. Nathan Samuel Kaplan Art Collections (#2109), 30 November 1926.
73. Frank Lloyd Wright. Japanese prints (#2120), 6 January 1927.

74. "Backs Mrs. Wright's Claim," *New York Times* (18 February 1927), 44; "Retain Auction Proceeds," *New York Times* (20 February 1927), 6.
75. Tom G. Cannon. English porcelains (#2123), 11–14 January 1927.
76. H. Kevorkian. Near and Far Eastern art (#2121), 7 January 1927.
77. "Art From Britain Will Be Sold Here," *New York Times* (18 September 1926), 5.
78. 8 July 1940. Rare Books and Manuscripts Division, The New York Public Library, Astor, Lenox and Tilden Foundations.
79. 31 August 1926. Rare Books and Manuscripts Division, The New York Public Library, Astor, Lenox and Tilden Foundations.
80. Marquess of Reading. English furniture and art objects (#2125, 15 January 1927. MK to Lord Reading, 27 January 1927. Rare Books and Manuscripts Division, The New York Public Library, Astor, Lenox, and Tilden Foundations.
81. Archduke Leopold Salvator, Marquess of Reading, Lord Grimthorpe, and other consignors (#2128), 20 January 1927.
82. "Anonymously—John Farrar," *The Bookman*, 70 (September 1927), 67–68.
83. "Publishing Old and New," *The New Republic*, 64 (1 October 1930), 176–78.

CHAPTER SEVEN

1. This account is drawn from *The Elegant Auctioneers*, pp. 429–431.
2. "Jinx Can't Bar Romance, She Declares," *New York Journal* (26 March 1930).
3. 12 October 1927. Collection of American Literature, Beinecke Rare Book and Manuscript Library, Yale University.
4. *The Spirit of St. Louis*, ed. Charles Vale (New York: Doran, 1927), pp. 65–70.
5. Frederick M. Hopkins, "Prospects for the Auction Season Now Beginning," *Publishers' Weekly*, 112 (19 November 1927), 1897–1898.
6. *Books & Autographs From The Library of Jerome Kern* (#2184), 2 November 1927.
7. Charles Francis Jenkins. American historical autographs (#2186), 3 November 1927.
8. *A Few Choice Books & Manuscripts Chiefly From Private English Collections* (#2198), 25 November 1927.
9. "Long Lost Wilde MS. Is Found By Arliss," *New York Times* (8 November 1927), 24.
10. *New York Times Book Review* (4 December 1927), 40.

11. Zachary Taylor Hollingsworth. American historical autographs (#2201), 28 November 1927.
12. Schuyler Colfax, Mrs. Elmer J. Sherman, and others. Historical autograph letters and documents (#2205), 8 December 1927.
13. *Publishers' Weekly*, 112 (24 December 1927), 2249.
14. *Elizabethan & Later Literature Part One Of The Library Of S. N. Levy* (#2217), 10 January 1928.
15. John Canfield Tomlinson Library (#2219), 17 January 1928.
16. Henry A. Colgate. Stevenson library (#2229), 8 February 1928.
17. *One Hundred Incunabula Duplicates From The Collection of Dr. Otto H. F. Vollbehr* (#2230), 9 February 1928.
18. Prof. Paul Soubeiran De Pierres. Manuscript horae (#2233), 9 February 1928.
19. *Bibliotheca Americana Vetustissima The Collection of Dr. Otto F. Vollbehr* (#2262), 24 April 1928.
20. Donald S. Friede. Modern first editions (#2244), 12–13 March 1928.
21. *Letters To The Colvins Mainly About Stevenson & Keats Sold By Order Of E. V. Lucas, Esq. . . .* (#2267), 7 May 1928.
22. "Charles Vale Dies of Pneumonia At 54," *New York Times* (26 March 1928), 21.
23. MK to Randolph G. Adams, 20 August 1946. Clements Library, University of Michigan.
24. *Publishers' Weekly*, 113 (2 June 1928), 2290–2291.
25. *Books & Autographs Sold By Order Of The George D. Smith Book Company, Inc. In Liquidation. Part I* (#2273), 16 May 1928.
26. *Americana. Part II* (#2274), 17 May 1928.
27. *Autographs. Part III* (#2275), 18 May 1928.
28. *Books & Prints. Part IV* (#2276), 21–23 May 1928.
29. *New York Times* (30 November 1927), 16.
30. *The Important Art Collection Of Dr. John E. Stilwell. . . . ,* 1 December 1927.
31. Charles H. Senff. Paintings, 28 March 1928. Books (#2248), 28 March 1928.
32. Collection of American Literature, Beinecke Rare Book and Manuscript Library, Yale University.
33. "Artist Who Paints for Love Gets $25,000 for 6 Panels," 23.
34. Lillian Sabine, "Record Price for Living Artist," *Brooklyn Daily Eagle Sunday Magazine Section* (27 May 1928), 11. See also Vladimir Berman, "She Painted the Lily and Got $25,000 and Fame for Doing It!" *New York Evening Graphic Magazine Section* (12 May 1928), 3. Documen-

tation provided by Nicholas Callaway, who called my attention to this episode.

35. 6 September 1928. Collection of American Literature, Beinecke Rare Book and Manuscript Library, Yale University.
36. 25 June 1930. Collection of American Literature, Beinecke Rare Book and Manuscript Library, Yale University.
37. Collection of American Literature, Beinecke Rare Book and Manuscript Library, Yale University.
38. 10 February 1931. Kennerley's accounting of his payments due O'Keeffe is dated 19 June 1931. Collection of American Literature, Beinecke Rare Book and Manuscript Library, Yale University.
39. 6 September 1928. Rare Books and Manuscripts Division, The New York Public Library, Astor, Lenox and Tilden Foundations.
40. Rare Books and Manuscripts Division, The New York Public Library, Astor, Lenox and Tilden Foundations.
41. "Noted Kern Library Will Be Auctioned," *New York Times* (18 October 1928), 19.
42. *Modern First Editions & Private Press Books Selections From The Library of Alfred A. Knopf New York City With Additions From Other Private Libraries* (#2281), 23 October 1928.
43. *The Library of Jerome Kern New York City.* Part I: A–J (#2307), 7–10 January 1929. Part II: J–Z (#2311), 21–24 January 1929.
44. "Bulls and Books," *New York Times* (10 January 1929), 28.
45. David A. Randall, *Dukedom Large Enough* (New York: Random House, 1969), 12.
46. 69 (March 1929), 14–17.
47. Frederick M. Hopkins, "Old and Rare Books," *Publishers' Weekly*, 115 (9 February 1929), 678.
48. "Notes on Rare Books," *New York Times Book Review* (25 May 1930), 25.
49. MK to Dorothy Gordon, n.d. Harry Ransom Humanities Research Center, University of Texas at Austin.
50. "Notes on Rare Books," *New York Times Book Review* (7 April 1929), 17.
51. *Paintings and Drawings by Gari Melchers.* New York: The Anderson Galleries, 1929. MK to Adams, 1 August 1945. Clements Library, University of Michigan.
52. Belmont, the Gari Melchers Memorial, Fredericksburg, Virginia.
53. Carl W. Hamilton. *Two Masterpieces of Renaissance Painting* (#2346), 8 May 1929.
54. "Duveen Is Named in $2,000,000 Suit," *New York Times* (9 June 1936),

25; "$2,000,000 Art Suit Will Open Monday," *New York Times* (18 March 1938), 21; "Settlement Urged in $2,000,000 Art Suit," *New York Times* (19 April 1938), 22; "$2,000,000 Suit Ends Against Lord Duveen," *New York Times* (22 September 1938), 25.

CHAPTER EIGHT

1. *New York Daily Mirror* (16 July 1929), 3, 6.
2. Christopher Morley to Morley Kennerley, 22 February [1950]. Courtesy of Morley and Jean Kennerley.
3. *John Mistletoe*, p. 411.
4. MK to Huebsch, 7 December 1933. Library of Congress.
5. *New York Daily Mirror* (26 March 1930), 3, 23.
6. *Autograph Letters of Bernard Shaw To Frank Harris, Frederick H. Evans Arnold Dolmetsch & Others First Editions & Presentation Copies Of Bernard Shaw The Original Manuscript Of Arnold Bennett's "Anna Of The Five Towns" First Editions & Presentation Copies Of Arnold Bennett Letters Of John Keats Etc. Etc. The Property Of A Private Consignor* (#3845), 24 April 1930.
7. Item 194.
8. 25 June 1930. Collection of American Literature, Beinecke Rare Book and Manuscript Library, Yale University.
9. 18 September 1930. Courtesy, Vassar College Library.
10. 5 November 1930. Courtesy, Vassar College Library.
11. *Publishers' Weekly*, 119 (28 February 1931), 1031.
12. Fred Rudge to MJB, 2 March 1985. Irving Rigby to MJB, 12 March 1985.
13. P. E. G. Quercus, "Trade Winds," *Saturday Review of Literature*, 14 (6 June 1936), 22.
14. 17 March [1933]. Huebsch Papers, Library of Congress.
15. MK to Leslie Bliss, 8 December 1932; Bliss to MK, 12 December 1932. Courtesy of The Huntington Library, San Marino, Cal.
16. 7 December 1933. Library of Congress.
17. MK to Alfred R. McIntyre, 18 August 1933; McIntyre to MK, 21 August 1933; MK wire to McIntyre, 22 August 1933; Little, Brown to MK, 14 April 1934 and 31 May 1934. Little, Brown & Co. Archives.
18. 18 September 1934. Courtesy, Vassar College Library.
19. *Introductions by Richard Curle, Augustine Birrell, Edmund Gosse, John Drinkwater, E. V. Lucas, A. Edward Newton, R. W. Chapman, David Nichol Smith, Alfred W. Pollard, J. C. Squire to the Catalogue of The Ashley Library [1922–1930] Collected by Thomas James Wise*. New York: William H. Smith, Jr., 1934.

20. MK to Christopher Morley, 18 June 1937. Harry Ransom Humanities Research Center, University of Texas at Austin.
21. *New York Times Book Review* (11 July 1937), 7.
22. A. B. Shiffrin to MJB, 24 July 1983.
23. *The Elegant Auctioneers*, p. 523.
24. *Publishers' Weekly*, 132 (20 November 1937), 2024–2025.
25. Galley proof. Courtesy of Dolley Madison McKinney.
26. MK to William Roberts, 26 November 1937. Rare Books and Manuscripts Division, The New York Public Library, Astor, Lenox and Tilden Foundations.
27. *First Editions Of American And English Authors Mostly In Original Bindings The Renowned Collection of Dr. William C. Braislin Brooklyn, N. Y.* (#4354), 7–8 December 1937.
28. Joseph B. Shea Library. Part I: Americana, 1–2 December 1937. Part II: English and American Literature (#4359), 5–6 January 1938.
29. Alfred C. Meyer. Historical and literary autographs, 12–13 January 1938.
30. *Important Manuscripts From The Library of Crosby Gaige . . . The Library Of The Rev. Franklin Joiner, D. D. . . . & Other Valuable Properties . . .* (#4381), 22–23 March 1938.
31. *The Cortlandt F. Bishop Library Part One [A–H] . . .* (#4385), 5–8 April 1938.
32. To Geoffrey Gomme, n.d. Bruccoli Collection.
33. To Laurence Gomme, 15 April 1938. Bruccoli Collection.
34. *Rosenbach*, p. 367.
35. Philip Brooks, "Notes on Rare Books," *New York Times Book Review* (24 April 1938), 23.
36. *The Elegant Auctioneers*, pp. 528–32.
37. *Announcing The Exhibition And Sale of Part Two [I–Q] Of The Cortlandt F. Bishop Library A Radio Talk Over Station WQXR April 12, 1938 Between Carl Freund International Art Expert And Mitchell Kennerley President Of The American Art Association Anderson Galleries, Inc.*
38. *The Cortlandt F. Bishop Library Part Two [I–Q] . . .* (#4391), 25–27 April 1938.
39. Courtesy of Dolley Madison McKinney.
40. To Charles F. Heartman, 5 May 1938. Rare Books and Manuscripts Division, The New York Public Library, Astor, Lenox and Tilden Foundations.
41. "$1,300 Paid for U. S. Revenue Stamp of 1871; Opening of Bishop Sale Brings $14,223," *New York Times* (10 May 1938), 23; "Stamps Sold for $19,547," *New York Times* (11 May 1938), 15.

42. *The Modern Library of Robert Dunning Dripps* . . . (#4402), 6–9 June 1938.
43. V. Everit Macy. Persian and Eastern art (#4360), 6 January 1938.
44. 10 January 1938. Clements Library, University of Michigan.
45. J. M. W. Turner drawings. American Art Association-Anderson Galleries (#4387), 13 April 1938.
46. To MJB, 18 August 1985.
47. "Art Auction House Sold to Syndicate," *New York Times* (6 August 1938), 14.
48. 10 August 1938. Courtesy of Michael Kennerley.
49. Philip Brooks, "Notes on Rare Books," *New York Times Book Review* (9 October 1938), 27.
50. *Life in Letters: American Autograph Journal*, 1 (October 1938), 36.

CHAPTER NINE

1. Harry Ransom Humanities Research Center, University of Texas at Austin.
2. Courtesy, Vassar College Library.
3. 8 June 1939. Clements Library, University of Michigan.
4. Hugh Peterson, "Gallery of Eccentrics," *Crime Detective*, 2 (June 1940), 16–21, 110–12.
5. 11 September 1939. Clements Library, University of Michigan.
6. n.d. Harry Ransom Humanities Research Center, University of Texas at Austin.
7. New York Public Library archives. MK to Fanny Borden, 21 September 1940. Courtesy, Vassar College Library. MK to F. W. Goudy, n.d. Library of Congress.
8. 28 December 1940. Courtesy of Josephine Young Case.
9. 21 January 1941. Courtesy of Josephine Young Case.
10. Memo to MK, 21 March 1941. Courtesy of Josephine Young Case. *See also* "Young Collection of Rare Volumes Is Gift to Library," *New York Times* (5 May 1941), 1; Philip Brooks, "Notes on Rare Books," *New York Times Book Review* (22 June 1941), 20.
11. 21 March 1941. Courtesy of Josephine Young Case. *See* Lola L. Szladits, *Owen D. Young Book Collector* (New York: New York Public Library, 1974).
12. Rosenberg to MK, 13 December 1940; MK to Rosenberg, 14 December 1940. Archives of American Art.
13. 16 December 1941. Harry Ransom Humanities Research Center, University of Texas at Austin.

14. n.d. Harry Ransom Humanities Research Center, University of Texas at Austin.
15. n.d. Harry Ransom Humanities Research Center, University of Texas at Austin.
16. *Saturday Review of Literature*, 31 (14 August 1948), 40.
17. Undated memo. Harry Ransom Humanities Research Center, University of Texas at Austin.
18. 2 June 1942. John Day Papers, Princeton University Library.
19. n.d. Harry Ransom Humanities Research Center, University of Texas at Austin.
20. 3 August 1942. Harry Ransom Humanities Research Center, University of Texas at Austin.
21. MK to Dorothy Gordon, n.d. Harry Ranson Humanities Research Center, University of Texas at Austin.
22. n.d. (November 1942). Samuel Paley Library, Temple University.
23. 28 January 1943. John Day Papers, Princeton University Library.
24. To W. A. Richardson, 17 September 1943. Huebsch Papers, Library of Congress.
25. 20 March 1945. Columbia University Library.
26. MK to Dorothy Gordon, 19 June 1942. Harry Ransom Humanities Research Center, University of Texas at Austin.
27. 15 January 1949. Courtesy, Vassar College Library.
28. W. G. Rogers, *Wise Men Fish Here* (New York: Harcourt, Brace & World, 1965), pp. 176–77. MJB interview with Frances Steloff, 28 May 1984.
29. MJB interviews with David Kirshenbaum, 4 November and 29 December 1983.
30. MJB telephone conversations with Irving Halpern, 1983–1984.
31. MJB telephone conversations with Charles E. Feinberg, 1983–1985; interview, 19 October 1984.
32. MJB telephone conversations with Herman Cohen, 1983–1984.
33. Vol. 60, 361–66. Separately reprinted by the Clements Library, University of Michigan.
34. 2 February 1946. Harry Ransom Humanities Research Center, University of Texas at Austin.
35. *Dukedom Large Enough*, pp. 312–13.
36. *The Magnificent French Library Formed by the late Courtlandt F. Bishop The Property of Mr and Mrs Shirley Falcke . . . ,* 7–8 December 1948.
37. 14 January 1939. Courtesy, Vassar College Library.
38. P. 534.
39. To MJB, 19 November 1984.

40. MK to Fanny Borden, 22 December 1948. Courtesy, Vassar College Library.
41. To MJB, 19 November 1984.
42. n.d. Courtesy of Irving Halpern.
43. Courtesy, Vassar College Library.
44. To Morley Kennerley, 22 February [1950]. Courtesy of Morley and Jean Kennerley.
45. Harry Ransom Humanities Research Center, University of Texas at Austin.
46. Douglas Gordon, "Cortlandt Field Bishop and the Death Struggles of the American-Anderson Galleries," *The Book Collector*, XXXIV (Winter 1985), 452–60.
47. *The Elegant Auctioneers*, p. 535.
48. 15 March 1950. Courtesy of Morley and Jean Kennerley.
49. "Ex-Publisher Found Hanged, Leaves Notes" (23 February 1950), 37.
50. Memo on MK's funeral. Courtesy of Morley and Jean Kennerley.

SELECTED BIBLIOGRAPHY

Alfred A. Knopf Portrait of a Publisher 1915–1965, 2 vols. New York: Typophiles, 1965.

Alvin Langdon Coburn Photographer An Autobiography, ed. Helmut & Alison Gernshemim. New York & Washington: Praeger, 1966.

The Archives of Grant Richards, 1897–1948. Microfilm. Cambridge: Chadwyck-Healey.

Arnold Genthe A Pictorialist and Society. New York: International Center of Photography, 1984.

Berle, Beatrice Bishop. *A Life in Two Worlds*. New York: Walker, 1983.

Blanck, Jacob. Kennerley obituary. *Antiquarian Bookman*, 5 (4 March 1950), 775.

"A Brief Account of the Life and Works of William Edwin Rudge." *PM*, 3 (February 1937), 1–34.

Briggs, Mitchell Pirie. *George D. Herron and the European Settlement*. Stanford: Stanford University Press; London: Humphrey Milford Oxford University Press, 1932.

Brooks, Van Wyck. *Scenes and Portraits*. New York: Dutton, 1954.

Bruccoli, Matthew J. "Mitchell Kennerley, Entrepreneur of Books." *AB Bookman's Weekly*, 73 (19 March 1984), 2079–2080, 2082, 2084, 2086, 2088.

Bruno, Guido. *Adventures in American Bookshops, Antique Stores and Auction Rooms*. Detroit: Douglas Book Shop, 1922.

Cannon, Carl L. *American Book Collectors and Collecting*. New York: Wilson, 1941.

Cappon, James. *Bliss Carman.* Toronto: Ryerson, 1930.

Carlton, W. N. C. *Notes on the Bridgwater House Library.* New York: Privately printed, 1918.

Carman, Bliss. *Letters of Bliss Carman,* ed. H. Pearson Gundy. Kingston & Montreal: McGill-Queen's University Press, 1981.

Case, Everett N. & Josephine Y. Case. *Owen D. Young and American Enterprise: A Biography.* Boston: Godine, 1982.

A Catalogue of Mitchell Kennerley's Publications (June, 1914).

Catalogue of Publications Mitchell Kennerley Publisher. . . . 1914.

"Charles Vale Dies of Pneumonia at 54." *New York Times* (26 March 1928), 21.

A Classified Brief Order List of Mitchell Kennerley's Books. August 1911.

Coons, Joan. *Without Passport.* New York: Day, 1943.

Currie, Barton. *Fishers of Books.* Boston: Little, Brown, 1931.

Davidson, Jo. *Between Sittings.* New York: Dial, 1951.

Desti, Mary. *The Untold Story The Life of Isadora Duncan 1921–1927.* New York: Liveright, 1929.

Drabble, Margaret. *Arnold Bennett.* London: Weidenfeld & Nicolson, 1974.

Dreiser, Theodore. *The Letters of Theodore Dreiser,* ed. Robert H. Elias. Vol. 1. Philadelphia: University of Pennsylvania Press, 1959.

Dreiss, Joseph G. *Gari Melchers His Works in the Belmont Collection.* Charlottesville: University Press of Virginia, 1984.

"Durant Heiress, Thrice Freed, Will Wed Mitchell Kennerley." *New York Daily Mirror* (26 March 1930), 3, 23.

Eastman, Max. *Enjoyment of Living.* New York & London: Harper, 1948.

Ellman, Richard. *James Joyce.* New York: Oxford University Press, 1959.

Ewen, David. *The World of Jerome Kern.* New York: Holt, 1960.

Farrar, John. "Anonymously—John Farrar." *The Bookman,* 70 (September 1927), 67–68.

The First Quarter Century of the Pierpont Morgan Library A Retrospective Exhibition in Honor of Belle Da Costa Greene. New York: Pierpont Morgan Library, 1949.

The Forum Exhibition of Modern American Painters, March Thirteenth to March Twenty-Fifth, 1916. New York: Anderson Galleries, 1916.

Gale, Edward D. *Herschel V. Jones.* Privately printed, 1928.

Genthe, Arnold. *. . . As I Remember.* New York: Reynal & Hitchcock, 1936.

Glick, William J. *William Edwin Rudge.* New York: Typophiles, 1984.

Gomme, Laurence. "The Little Book-Shop Around the Corner." *The Colophon,* 2 (Autumn 1937), 573–93.

Gomme. "My First Fifty Years in New York." *Antiquarian Bookman,* 22 (10 November 1958), 1587–1590.

Gomme. "A Neighborhood Bookshop." *Publishers' Weekly*, 98 (30 October 1920), 1323.

Gordon, Douglas. "Cortlandt Field Bishop and the Death Struggles of the American-Anderson Galleries." *The Book Collector*, XXXIV (Winter 1985, 452–60.

Goudy, Frederic W. *Goudy's Type Designs His Story and Specimens.* New York: Typophiles Chap Books XIII & XIV, 1946; New Rochelle: Myriade Press, 1978.

Gould, Jean. *The Poet and her Book A Biography of Edna St. Vincent Millay.* New York: Dodd, Mead, 1969.

Grolier 75 A Biographical Retrospective. . . . New York: Grolier Club, 1959.

Gundy, H. Pearson. "Kennerley on Carman." *Canadian Poetry,* #14 (Spring-Summer 1984), 69–74.

Hackett, E. Byrne. "Ave Atque Vale—M.K." *Antiquarian Bookman,* 5 (11 March 1950), 842.

Harris, Frank. *Frank Harris to Arnold Bennett Fifty-Eight Letters 1908–1910.* Merion Station, Pa.: American Autograph Shop, 1936. Introduction by Mitchell Kennerley.

Heartman, Charles. *George D. Smith. G. D. S. 1870–1920.* Beauvoir, Miss: Book Farm, 1945.

Heartman. *Twenty-Five Years in the Auction Business And What Now?* Privately printed, 1938.

Ingran, Alison. *Index to the Archives of Grant Richards 1897–1948.* Cambridge: Chadwyck-Healey; Teaneck, N.J.: Somerset House, 1981.

Jean-Aubrey, G. *Joseph Conrad: Life and Letters.* Garden City, N.Y.: Doubleday, Doran, 1927.

Joyce, James. *Letters of James Joyce,* ed. Stuart Gilbert, Vol. 1. New York: Viking, 1957.

Keats · Wilde · Morley · Rosenbach. Philadelphia: Rosenbach Foundation, 1978.

Kennerley, Mitchell. "An Appreciation." *Publishers' Weekly,* 98 (30 October 1920), 1324.

Kennerley. "The Day of the Published Play." *New York Times* (27 December 1914), VIII, 3.

Kennerley. "The First Edition of Millay's Poems." *Publishers' Weekly,* 95 (7 June 1919), 1587.

Kennerley. "The Free Lance." *Reedy's Mirror* (5 August 1920).

Kennerley. Foreword. *Introductions by Richard Curle, Augustine Birrell, Edmund Gosse, John Drinkwater, E. V. Lucas, A. Edward Newton, R. W. Chapman, David Nichol Smith, Alfred W. Pollard, J. C. Squire to the*

Catalogue of the Ashley Library [1922–1930] Collected by Thomas James Wise. New York: William H. Smith, Jr., 1934.

Kennerley. "Honesty in Printing." *News-Letter of the AIGA* (December 1932), 3–4.

Kennerley interview. "Notes on Rare Books." *New York Times Book Review* (7 April 1929), 17.

Kennerley. "Kennerley Type: The Circumstances Which Brought about its Conception." *Monotype,* #70 (May 1924), 5–7. "Special Kennerley Issue."

Kennerley. "Leonard Merrick." *New York Times Review of Books* (26 May 1912), 313–14.

Kennerley. Letter on John Trevena. *New York Times Review of Books* (21 March 1915), 104.

Kennerley. Letter to Charles Heartman (23 July 1934). *The American Book Collector,* 5 (August–September 1934), 242–43.

Kennerley. "Metropolitan Memo." *The Village Press by Three Friends.* Marlborough, N.Y.: 1938.

Kennerley. *Modern Love.* Gouverneur, N.Y.: Privately printed, 1899.

Kennerley. "My Ten Cent Shelf." *The American Mercury,* 60 (March 1944), 361–66. Reprinted by the Clements Library, University of Michigan, 1944.

Kennerley. "The New Reading." *New York Times Review of Books* (16 April 1911), 235.

Kennerley. "Recollections of Thomas Bird Mosher." *New York Evening Telegram* (5 September 1923).

Kennerley. " 'The Sign of the Four,' " in Christopher Morley, "The Bowling Green." *Saturday Review of Literature,* 10 (7 April 1934), 609.

Kennerley. Statement. "Public Taste Away from Fiction this Season." *New York Times Review of Books* (6 April 1913), 185.

Kennerley. Tribute. *In Memoriam Elbert and Alice Hubbard.* (East Aurora, N.Y.: The Roycrofters, 1915), p. 328.

Kennerley. "Uncle Sam Has a Book." *Saturday Review of Literature,* 22 (1 June 1940), 9.

Kennerley. "A Wandering Poem." *The Mirror* (5 October 1905), 22.

Knopf, Alfred A. *Some Recollections.* New York: Typophiles, 1949.

Lancour, Harold. *American Art Auction Catalogues 1785–1942 A Union List.* New York: New York Public Library, 1944.

Lawrence, D. H. *The Letters of D. H. Lawrence,* ed. George J. Zytaruk and James T. Boulton, Vol. 2. Cambridge: Cambridge University Press, 1981.

Lawrence. *Sex Locked Out.* Privately printed by Mitchell Kennerley, 1928.

Le Gallienne, Richard. *The Romantic '90s.* London & New York: Putnam, 1926.

Lehmann-Haupt, Helmut. *The Book in America.* Second edition. New York: Bowker, 1952.

The Letters of John Quinn to William Butler Yeats, ed. Alan Himber. Ann Arbor: UMI Research Press, 1983.

Lewis, Felice Flanery. *Literature, Obscenity, and Law.* Carbondale & Edwardsville: Southern Illinois University Press, 1976.

Lindsay, Vachel. *Letters of Vachel Lindsay,* ed. Marc Chenetier. New York: Burt Franklin, 1979.

Lisle, Laurie. *Portrait of an Artist A Biography of Georgia O'Keeffe.* New York: Seaview, 1980.

A List of Books Published by Mitchell Kennerley from April First, 1914 to April First, 1915.

A List of Books to Be Issued During the Autumn of 1917 by Mitchell Kennerley.

Lowe, Sue Davidson. *Stieglitz.* New York: Farrar, Straus & Giroux, 1983.

McKay, George L. *American Book Auction Catalogues 1713–1934 A Union List.* New York: New York Public Library, 1937; Detroit: Gale Research Company, 1967.

Madison, Charles A. *Book Publishing in America.* New York, Toronto & London: McGraw-Hill, 1966.

May, J. Lewis. *John Lane and the Nineties.* London: John Lane The Bodley Head, 1936.

Mencken, H. L. "Here Are Novels!" *The Smart Set,* 46 (June 1915), 290–93.

Mencken. *Letters of H. L. Mencken,* ed. Guy J. Forgue. New York: Knopf, 1973.

Mencken. *Prejudices First Series.* New York: Knopf, 1919.

Millay, Edna St. Vincent. *Letters of Edna St. Vincent Millay,* ed. Allan Ross Macdougall. New York: Harper, 1952.

Millay. *Renascence.* New York: Anderson Galleries, 1924. Printed by Frederic W. Goudy.

Miller, Muriel. *Bliss Carman A Portrait.* Toronto: Ryerson, 1935.

Mitchell Kennerley . . . New Books Fall of 1914.

Mitchell Kennerley New Books Spring of 1914.

Mitchell Kennerley's New List. 1924.

Moore, Harry T. *Priest of Love: A Life of D. H. Lawrence.* New York: Farrar, Straus & Giroux, 1974.

Morley, Christopher. *Ex Libris Carissimis.* Philadelphia: University of Pennsylvania Press, 1932.

Morley. *In an Auction Room.* Privately printed by Mitchell Kennerley, 1927.

Morley. *John Mistletoe.* Garden City, N.Y.: Doubleday, Doran, 1931.

"Mrs. Daniel Weds John H. Cooper." *New York Times* (5 May 1929), II, 6.

Mumford, Lewis. "Publishing Old and New." *The New Republic,* 64 (1 October 1930), 176–78.

Nelson, James G. *The Early Nineties: A View From the Bodley Head.* Cambridge: Harvard University Press, 1971.

Nelson, Raymond. *Van Wyck Brooks A Writer's Life.* New York: Dutton, 1981.

Newton, A. Edward. *The Amenities of Book Collecting and Kindred Affections.* Boston: Atlantic Monthly Press, 1918.

Newton. *A Magnificent Farce And Other Diversions of A Book-Collector.* Boston: Atlantic Monthly Press, 1921.

Norman, Dorothy. *Alfred Stieglitz.* New York: Random House, 1973.

Oakley, Helen McK. *The Hours for Lunch The Life and Times of Christopher Morley.* New York: Watermill, 1976.

Pater, Walter. *Walter Pater's Conclusion to his Book The Renaissance.* New York: Privately printed, 1910.

Patterson, Betsy. "Dead Bride's Wedding Ring a Jinx to Motor Heiress, Thrice Divorced." *New York Graphic* (12 April 1930).

Pegler, Arthur James. "Kennerley Jilted By Rich Patron." *New York Daily Mirror* (16 July 1929), 3, 6.

Pennell, Elizabeth Robins. *The Life and Letters of Joseph Pennell.* Boston: Little, Brown, 1929.

Pennell, Joseph. *The Adventures of an Illustrator Mostly in Following His Authors in America & Europe.* Boston: Little, Brown, 1925.

Peterson, Hugh. "Gallery of Eccentrics." *Crime Detective,* 2 (June 1940), 16–21, 110–12.

Pomeroy, Elizabeth. *The Huntington.* London: Scala/Wilson, 1983.

Pullar, Philippa. *Frank Harris.* London: Hamish Hamilton, 1975.

Putzel, Max. *The Man in the Mirror: William Marion Reedy and his Magazine.* Cambridge: Harvard University Press, 1963.

Randall, David A. *Dukedom Large Enough.* New York: Random House, 1969.

Ransom, Will; Park, Charles E.; Kennerley, Mitchell. *Intimate Recollections of the Village Press.* Marlborough, N.Y.: 1938.

Reid, B. L. *The Man from New York: John Quinn and his Friends.* New York: Oxford University Press, 1968.

Rogers, W. G. *Wise Men Fish Here.* New York: Harcourt, Brace & World, 1965.

Rosenbach, A. S. W. *A Book Hunter's Holiday: Adventures with Books and Manuscripts.* Boston & New York: Houghton Mifflin, 1936.

Rosenbach. *Books and Bidders: The Adventures of a Bibliophile.* Boston: Little, Brown, 1927.

Rosenberg, James N. *A Painter's Self-Portrait.* New York: Crown, 1958.

Rowe, Robert R. "Mann of Town Topics." *American Mercury*, 8 (July 1926), 271–280.

Ruggles, Eleanor. *The West-Going Heart: A Life of Vachel Lindsay*. New York: Norton, 1959.

Schroeder, Horst. *Annotations to Oscar Wilde, The Portrait of Mr. W. H.* Braunschweig: Privately printed, 1986.

Schroeder. *Oscar Wilde, The Portrait of Mr. W. H.—Its Composition, Publication and Reception*. Braunschweig: Technische Universität Carolo-Wilhelmina zu Braunschweig Seminar Für Anglistik und Amerikanistic, 1984.

Scott, Temple. *Frank Harris The Man of To-Day and To-Morrow*. [New York: Mitchell Kennerley, 1914].

Sinclair, Upton. *The Autobiography of Upton Sinclair*. New York: Harcourt, Brace & World, 1962.

Smith, William Jay. *The Spectra Hoax*. Middletown, Conn: Wesleyan University Press, 1961.

The Spirit of St. Louis One Hundred Poems, ed. Charles Vale. New York: Doran, 1927.

Steel, Ronald. *Walter Lippmann and the American Century*. Boston: Little, Brown, 1980.

Strouse, Norman H. *An Exhibition of Books from the Press of Thomas Bird Mosher*. Philadelphia: Free Library of Philadelphia, 1967.

Swanberg, W. A. *Dreiser*. New York: Scribners, 1965.

Szladits, Lola L. *Owen D. Young Book Collector*. New York: New York Public Library, 1974.

Tanselle, G. Thomas. "Ficke's *Sonnets of a Portrait-Painter*: Textual Problems in a Modern Poet." *Yale University Library Gazette*, 36 (1961), 33–39.

Tanselle. "Lindsay's *General William Booth*: A Bibliographical and Textual Note." *Publications of the Bibliographical Society of America*, 55 (1961), 371–380.

Tanselle. "*The Lyric Year*: A Bibliographical Study." *Publications of the Bibliographical Society of America*, 56 (1962), 454–471.

Tanselle. "Millay's *Renascence* and *Second April*: A Bibliographical Study." *The Library*, 19 (1964), 175–186.

Tanselle. "The Mitchell Kennerley Imprint." *The Book Collector*, 13 (Summer 1964), 185–193.

Tebbel, John. *A History of Book Publishing in the United States: Volume II The Expansion of an Industry 1865–1919*. New York & London: Bowker, 1975; *Volume III The Golden Age Between Two Wars 1920–1940*. New York & London: Bowker, 1978.

Tobin, A. I., and Elmer Gertz. *Frank Harris A Study in Black and White*. New York: Haskell House, 1970.

Towner, Wesley. *The Elegant Auctioneers*. New York: Hill & Wang, 1970.

The Village Press A Retrospective 1903–1933. New York: American Institute of Graphic Arts, 1933.

A Village Press Collection Is Given to Vassar. Poughkeepsie: Vassar College, 1932.

Weisberger, Bernard A. *The Dream Maker William C. Durant Founder of General Motors*. Boston & Toronto: Little, Brown, 1979.

Whittington-Egan, Richard. *The Quest of the Golden Boy The Life and Letters of Richard Le Gallienne*. London: Unicorn, 1960.

Wolf, Edwin II and John F. Fleming. *Rosenbach*. Cleveland & New York: World, 1960.

INDEX

The following abbreviations are
used in the index:
AAA American Art Association
AAA-AG American Art
Association–Anderson
Galleries
AG Anderson Galleries

Abdy, Robert, 194
Adam, R. B., 165, 171
Adam library sale (AG), 171–72
Adams, George Matthew, 254
Adams, Randolph G., 223, 240, 246,
256
*Adventures While Preaching the
Gospel of Beauty* (Lindsay),
66
Air-Line to Liberty, The (Lee), 125
Alphabet, The (Goudy), 125
Amazing Emperor Heliogabalus, The
(Hay), 30n.
American Art Association (AAA),
57, 90–91, 186–87

Anderson Galleries, merger with,
190–91, 217, 247
Kennerley as director, 192
*See also specific sales marked
AAA*
American Art Association–
Anderson Galleries (AAA-
AG), 217, 247. *See also
specific sales marked AAA-
AG; subheading under
Kennerley, Mitchell*
Americana sales (AAA-AG), 230
Americana sales (AG), 105, 136,
140–41, 148, 167, 184
Anderson, John, Jr., 91
Anderson Galleries (AG)
advertising by, 118n.
American Art, merger with,
190–91, 217, 247
appraisal services, 118
Arion building offices, 117–18,
129
catalogues of, 98–99
dealer orientation, 100